# CONVERGING DIVERGENCES

CONVERGING DIVERGENCES

# CONVERGING DIVERGENCES

## WORLDWIDE CHANGES
## IN EMPLOYMENT SYSTEMS

**Harry C. Katz and Owen Darbishire**

ILR Press, an imprint of
Cornell University Press    ITHACA AND LONDON

Cornell Studies in Industrial and Labor Relations No. 32

Copyright © 2000 by Cornell University

First published 2000 by ILR Press/Cornell University Press

Printed in the United States of America

Library of Congress Cataloging-in-Publication Data

Katz, Harry Charles, 1951–
    Converging divergences : worldwide changes in employment systems /
Harry C. Katz and Owen Darbishire.
        p.  cm.
    Includes index.
    ISBN 0-8014-3674-5 (cloth)
    1. Comparative industrial relations.   2. Collective bargaining.
3. Wages.   I. Darbishire, Owen (Owen Richard), 1964–   .
II. Title.
HD6971.K3675  1999
331—dc21                                                99-16950

Cloth printing      10 9 8 7 6 5 4 3 2 1

# Preface

This book had its origins in a research project that initially was focused on analyzing the increasing decentralization within collective-bargaining structures. In the early 1990s, we had heard reports from various countries of a shift downward in the locus of collective bargaining, often from the national or the sectoral level to the enterprise or plant level. Although familiar with this trend in the United States, we were fascinated by claims that a similar decentralization was beginning to spread in a wide range of countries and industries. We initiated this research in an effort to document the extent of decentralization in collective bargaining and to identify the causes and consequences.

During the fieldwork that followed we began to observe striking similarities in the employment systems of the seven countries we studied, and this led us to broaden our analysis to include the nature and causes of these changes. As our fieldwork proceeded, we came to the view that while there was growing variation within the employment systems of these countries there also was much that was similar both in variation and the processes through which it was spreading. Examination of this employment system variation ("divergences") and the commonalities across countries ("convergences") thus became the focal point of our research.

Another factor shaping our research was the growing evidence of increased income inequality. Again, although this evidence had appeared in the 1980s in the United States, by the early 1990s there were similar reports coming from a variety of countries, including western European nations, where there had been a long tradition of purposeful moderation of income inequality through governmental and private policies. This led us to an institutional perspective that clarifies how the increasing variation in employment systems is contributing to income inequality and inequality in other employment conditions and practices.

In this book we report on specific changes in bargaining structures, pay procedures, and a host of other employment outcomes and the processes that either constitute or influence employment conditions. To gather this evidence, we greatly benefited from the kind assistance and insights provided by many managers, trade unionists, and academics in the seven countries. We cannot list them all by name because the list would be so long, but they all should know that we are grateful for their help. We also want to thank Rick Locke and Russell Lansbury for the stimulation they provided through their feedback on preliminary drafts of this book and Fran Benson of Cornell University Press for her steady advice and encouragement. Candace Akins provided enormous help getting the manuscript ready for publication.

This research also has benefited greatly from the generous financial assistance provided by the German Marshall Fund, the Alfred P. Sloan Foundation, and the National Center for the Workplace. In several ways, the ILR School, Cornell University, and Oxford University have made it possible for us to engage in this research. And last but by no means least, we thank our families and loved ones for their support and patience.

# CONVERGING DIVERGENCES

CONVERGING DIVERGENCES

# Table of Contents

# 1

# Introduction: The Links between Increased Inequality and Union Decline

Two of the most significant socioeconomic events of our time are growing income inequality and the decline of unions. In the early 1980s in the United States, alarming reports started to surface claiming that income distribution was becoming more unequal: as the rich got richer, the poor were becoming poorer, and the middle class was shrinking, if not disappearing (Kuttner 1983). By the late 1980s, serious academic research had documented that these fears were justified, and later research showed that a similar increasing polarization of income distribution has been underway in nearly all advanced industrial economies (Levy 1987; Harrison and Bluestone 1988; Freeman and Katz 1995).

Union decline has been just as apparent and ubiquitous. Again, events in the United States led the way as concession bargaining spread throughout the economy in the 1980s and union membership underwent an accelerated decline, in part due to the unions' inability to organize workers in the expanding high-technology and service sectors. In the 1990s, it became clear that union decline was more than temporary and that union power, if not membership, was undergoing similar declines in many countries, including Sweden and Germany, where unions had heretofore been so strong.

This book shows how the growth of income inequality in advanced industrial economies is linked to the declines in union membership and power. To uncover the relationship between income inequality and union decline requires examination of the increasing variation in employment systems. We therefore describe how changes in the distribution of employment practices within the United States and six other countries have been lead-

1

ing to not only income inequality but also to wider variation in employment practices, such as the nature of employment security and work organization across firms. In this way, our analysis takes a broader and more institutional focus than that of most contemporary economic analyses of income inequality.

We examine the increasing diversity of employment systems in Australia, Britain, Germany, Italy, Japan, Sweden, the United Kingdom, and the United States, with a special focus on the automobile and telecommunications industries. We selected these countries because they are economically important, and because they entered the 1980s with very different levels of union strength, with different trends in union growth, and with major differences in how employment relations are structured. For example, union membership declines have been extremely large in the United States, and large in Britain and Japan as well. In contrast, union membership has declined less severely in Australia and Italy and even less in Germany and Sweden. By looking at countries with different stating points in their employment systems, we can analyze the role that history and past practices play as influences on emerging trends.

The systems of employment relations, governing such matters as the rights of workers, unions, and managers; the nature of work practices; and the structure and mechanisms of union representation, also have historically differed substantially across these seven countries. Japan is noteworthy because of its enterprise union structure and work practices that include worker involvement in quality circles, seniority-based pay systems, and lifetime employment. Germany is distinguished by its system of codetermination, sectoral collective bargaining, and the heavy role played by works councils in personnel matters. Australia, like Germany, has had relatively strong and secure unions, yet its employment relations system possesses a distinctive role for government-run industrial tribunals and a national wage award system—an unusually centralized system. Sweden, like Australia, traditionally has had very centralized wage determination, although it was provided through the negotiation of a key collective bargaining agreement between an encompassing employers' federation and labor unions. Italy is distinguished by multiple levels of collective bargaining and periodic episodes of strong national incomes policies mixed with occasional labor or employer offensives. In contrast, the United States and Britain have a common attribute of relatively "voluntarist" employment relations, with significant differences in the level of union membership and the structure of union representation.

If common trends are apparent in countries seemingly so dissimilar, then the probability is great that these trends are more general. Furthermore, each country has interesting, distinctive qualities. The presence of a traditional enterprise union structure in Japan, for example, allows examination of whether trends apparent in initially centralized systems are also occurring in the Japanese system, which entered the 1980s with an already very decentralized employment relations system.

The automobile and telecommunications industries receive special attention in this book because of their importance to industrialized economies, derived in part from the fact that they employ a sizable fraction of the workforce. In the United States, for example, the auto industry directly employs roughly 1 percent of the workforce, and another 1 percent of the workforce is employed in related industries (auto suppliers or industries involved in auto repair, road maintenance, and the like). Although in the 1980s some analysts were claiming that deindustrialization and a world car strategy would greatly reduce domestic employment in the automobile industries in advanced economies, by the late 1990s the share of auto-related employment actually had not declined much from 1980 levels in either the United States or most other industrialized countries. The telecommunications industry likewise is a major employer, in most countries representing from 1 to 2 percent of total employment, with substantial indirect employment effects (Katz 1997).

The two industries we analyze are also noteworthy because of the indirect effects they exert as pattern setters in employment relations. Throughout the post–World War II period, the automobile industry has been viewed by many as the core industry within industrialized economies. In employment relations, auto negotiations often have set the pattern in wage determination and provided much innovation in the development of fringe benefits concerning insurance, vacations, pensions, and training (Katz 1985).

In recent years, it has become fashionable to view the telecommunications industry as the new bellwether industry because it provides the backbone of the information highway. Given the heavy role that fiber-optic cable is playing as the mechanism for transmitting Internet and other electronic messages, the heavy influence of telecommunication services and equipment is assured.

Our research includes analysis of the variation appearing in work practices, including work rules, work organization, and pay procedures at the firm level. There are little systematic data measuring the nature of that variation, let alone data that allow assessment of how those practices have changed over time.[2] Given that large firms dominate in the auto industry, especially in the auto assembly sector, and in the telecommunications industry, especially in the telecommunications services sector, through field research we are able to describe the variation in work practices in those industries and assess trends in those practices. It is the smaller number of firms and plants that allows this assessment in those two key industries, providing another reason to focus on them. Nevertheless, because of the manual nature of automobile work and the service and white-collar nature of telecommunications-related employment, there are marked differences in the history and continuing evolution of employment relations in these two industries. These differences make it valuable to compare and contrast trends.

At the same time, that both industries are heavily unionized and that much of their employment is in large firms distinguishes these industries from others in advanced economies. These distinguishing characteristics should be kept in mind when these two industries are compared to others.

### SOURCES OF INCOME AND EMPLOYMENT VARIATION

The intensity and source of the economic pressures that have been inducing changes in employment systems vary much across the seven countries we analyze. For example, countries differ in the extent to which they are open to international competition and the extent to which international competition emerged as a new source of economic pressure. The pace and nature of privatization and deregulation also differs much across countries.

Economic pressures vary as well across industries. In all the countries, the auto industry has been pressured by intensified international competition and the increasing globalization of production, while in the telecommunications industry, deregulation and privatization have been the pervasive pressures leading to changes in employment relations.

A key finding in our research, however, is that there is a common set of outcomes even in the face of this wide variation in economic pressures. Thus, whatever the source of economic pressures, variation in the processes and outcomes of employment relations have increased in all seven countries.

One important aspect of the change in employment systems in industrialized countries in recent years has been the decline of union strength and membership. This has led to increased variation in the employment conditions employees experience through the lower wages paid in the nonunion sector as compared to the union sector, and the differences that appear in union versus nonunion work practices, including differences in how employee complaints are resolved.

Yet, *within* both the union and nonunion sectors, the extent of variation in wages, work practices, and other employment conditions also has increased. This variation is particularly pronounced in workplaces that are adopting contingent (such as profit sharing) or individualized pay procedures. Variation also is growing in work organization and related work practices in part because only some union or nonunion plants use team concepts of work organization.

An important factor contributing to variation in employment practices within the union sector has been the expansion of work and union-participation processes at some unionized work sites, whereas conflictual labor-management relations prevail at other unionized sites. In the process, the middle ground of traditional labor-management relations that had included a bounded amount of conflict is becoming less common.

Although increased variation in employment relations is more obvious in the union sector, variation has also been spreading in nonunion firms, with some firms investing heavily in a human-resource management approach that emphasizes extensive individualized communication and pay practices, whereas other nonunion firms make use of low-wage and informal work practices. Meanwhile, in many countries, Japanese investments or efforts to imitate Japanese employment practices in domestically owned firms has spread Japanese-oriented work practices, thereby adding another source of variation in employment conditions. Although the United States represents an extreme case of employment system variation, having experienced heavy doses of both concessionary and participatory collective bargaining and rapid growth in nonunion and Japanese employment systems, similar variations in employment relations have appeared in other countries.

### PREVIOUS DEBATES AND EVIDENCE

The causes and consequences of increased variation in employment systems have been the source of much debate and confusion. Economists have drawn attention to a widening in income distribution within nearly all industrialized countries in recent years, yet more limited attention has been paid to the role of increased variation in firm-level employment relations as a source of that income variation.[3] Furthermore, the focus by economists on income distribution has ignored the extensive variation in other employment outcomes.

Employment relations have received attention from those analysts who explain recent developments as an era of declining union influence brought about by intensified international competition and managerial resistance to unions. To others, recent developments represent a "Japanization" of the world economy, entailing a shift to more enterprise (and hence more decentralized) employment relations. Other analysts see this era as one involving a breakdown of distinct national systems of employment relations and the growing influence of strategic choices made by managers and labor at the plant level. In addition, given the relatively large U.S. employment growth, especially relative to European countries, and the early and heavy application of managerial re-engineering initiatives, other analysts claim that the United States has become a best-practice model that is being emulated around the world.

### Debates about Industrial Adjustment

Union membership and bargaining power have declined sizably since the early 1980s in most countries. Although these declines do not explain the breadth of the variation in employment systems within and across countries, these declines have played an important role in promoting variation. While there is no simple measure of union bargaining power, various indicators suggest that union power also has been declining even in countries such as Germany, where union membership has not declined. The most obvious sign of union bargaining-power decline appears in the concessions that unions have accepted in collective bargaining in recent years. Concession bargaining first appeared in the early 1980s in a number of industries and countries and typically included either pay cuts or pay increases that were below historical standards. Concession bargaining also has been manifest in changes made to work organization (i.e., fewer job classifications or a weakening of seniority rights) that also reverse the gains that unions had achieved in previous bargaining. Although the form and depth of concessions have varied substantially within and across countries, it is clear that union membership declines, actual or threatened declines in employment, plant closings, and other factors have weakened union power, as is evident in the limited gains achieved by unions in strike actions, even in countries where union membership has to date held up.

The declines in union membership and bargaining concessions have led many observers to see this era as one involving a fundamental decline in union strength and an increase in the discretion and authority of management and market forces. Leo Troy (1990), for example, claims that union decline is a permanent and inevitable result of increased international competition and globalization. Unable to maintain strong multinational organizations, unions have not been able to (and according to Troy, will never be able to) expand their jurisdiction commensurate with the widening jurisdiction of the marketplace, and thus the decline in union power is said to be irreversible. John Purcell (1995) also makes a gloomy forecast for unions, although he sees the central challenge arising from managerial strategies that replace or at least deflect demand for unionism, through the elaboration of communication strategies and the individualization of personnel practices.

*The Convergence Debate*

The decline in the strength of unions raises the specter of a new convergence to a world of employment relations where management gains unilateral authority either through advanced personnel practices and heightened sensitivity to the needs of the workforce, or through the exercise of brute market power. In our view, although the growing internationalization of markets has helped spur nonunion competition and contributed to the elaboration of low-wage employment strategies, and managerial initiatives have led to the development of sophisticated and often individualized employment strategies, analysts have exaggerated the role played by this trend and ignored the more substantial variation that is simultaneously appearing *within* and *across* employment systems. Before developing this argument, we examine other convergence predictions.

A less gloomy vision of the future is provided by those analysts who see employment relations converging toward Japanese-style practices. Even in the face of the weaknesses in the Japanese economic system revealed by that economy's recent prolonged downturn, there are those who see much virtue in Japanese manufacturing practices. The claim here is that Japanese employment-relations practices are linked to Japanese manufacturing (and organizational) practices, which together produce superior economic performance, at least in the manufacturing sector, through their heightened attention to quality and flexibility, and their relatively low cost. Favorable performance outcomes are said to derive from continuous improvement efforts, low inventories, and other features of the Japanese production system that are facilitated by Japanese employment practices (Womack, Jones, and Roos 1990; MacDuffie 1995a). The net effect of this Japanization of employment relations is alleged to be a movement toward more enterprise-oriented employment relations, including very decentralized bargaining structures, team-oriented work practices, and lifetime employment (at least for a core of the workforce). Interestingly, among those who see a Japanization of employment relations occurring, there are some, such as Dore (1992), who are attracted to the increased organizational-orientation in Japanese practices and others, such as Parker and Slaughter (1988) and Babson (1995b), who claim these practices increase employee stress and union subservience.

Given the strong employment growth experienced in the United States, especially when compared to the high unemployment rates that have characterized the labor markets in most European countries since the late

1980s, other observers have claimed that a new international convergence toward U.S.-style flexible labor markets (and deregulated product markets) is underway (Krugman 1996). A related claim in this line of argumentation is that a key competitive advantage has emerged in the United States through the early and heavy re-engineering of managerial practices that has helped create an American model of lean management (Hammer and Champy 1993). Though these claims are expressed in very different terms, it is interesting to note the common assertion of American superiority found in this new school of thought and in the earlier convergence notions of Kerr, Dunlop, Harbison, and Myers (1964).

Kerr et al. claimed that industrialization would lead to a common "structuring" of the workforce across and within countries, a process that appeared to have a relatively strong role for unions. Although it is not obvious exactly what these analysts expected industrial relations systems to converge toward, we read Kerr et al. as expecting unionism to expand to much higher levels of representation and influence. (Unions represented one third of the U.S. workforce in the early 1950s, when they were conducting their research.) Kerr et al. wrote as if they expected industrialization to proceed relatively smoothly across the globe and, in the process, transform industrial-relations systems so that they would become similar to the collective-bargaining system that appeared to be maturing in core American industries in the mid-1950s.

Influential comparative social scientists earlier had rebutted the Kerr et al. convergence thesis by developing sophisticated analyses of the particularities of the industrial relations systems of various countries. The thrust of scholars such as Cole (1971), Streeck (1984), and Dore (1973) (and much of the comparative industrial relations literature that followed in the footsteps of these researchers) was that there was wide and persistent variation in industrial relations across countries in part due to the influence of nationally specific institutional factors (e.g., laws). With persistent national differences in employment relations as the backdrop, much comparative research was carried out in the 1980s examining the degree of commonality in the adjustment strategies being pursued in particular industries across countries, such as in autos (see Streeck and Katz [1984]). Although our analysis leads us to highlight the many similarities that now appear in the variation emerging in employment relations across countries, we draw from prior comparative research the imperative to examine the role that existing institutions play in shaping the changes affecting employment systems.

Drawing from research on employment relations in Italy, Richard Locke (1992) notes the wide variation appearing within employment relations in the 1980s. In the face of this variation, and the forecast that this variation would increase in the future, Locke sees no evidence of cross-country convergence to any common pattern. He also questions the relevance of notions of distinct national systems of employment relations in the face of the widening variation in employment relations occurring within countries.

We extend Locke's claims by examining in detail the nature and extent of the variation that is appearing in employment systems (outcomes and processes) in the seven countries.[4] We too are impressed by the decline of unions, but this decline does not describe the broad path of adjustment occurring in employment systems. Perhaps most important, in many firms a team-based approach has been extended in recent years, involving an expansion of union and employee involvement in business decisions and a broadening of the bargaining agenda into areas that strengthen union and employee influence. The spread of a team-based approach in some firms belies the claim that union decline is a uniform phenomena.

As this book will show, there are many commonalities in the way that variation in employment systems emerges. Union weakness is often associated with increased variation in employment relations because although unions are not being eliminated across the seven countries, nonunion firms are growing in the auto, telecommunications, and other industries. One of our research tasks is describing the differences that appear in the wages and work practices in nonunion firms and contrasting those outcomes to the outcomes that characterize the union sector. A key part of our argument, however, is that there is widening variation *within* the union and nonunion sectors. Our research has some similarity with the work of MacDuffie (1995b), but whereas MacDuffie focuses on the variation in manufacturing and work organization practices, our analysis focuses on work practices and employment-relations systems.[5]

We rely on survey evidence and secondary sources to describe the variation spreading across union and nonunion sectors.[6] We also examine broad trends to see if the key adjustment strategies and issues identified in the auto and telecommunication industries generalize to other industries.

### The Four Key Growing Patterns of Work Practices

In our view, similarity in employment system changes in part derives from four common patterns of work practices evident in the seven countries. The core elements of the patterns are outlined in Figure 1.1. Our analysis utilizes the notion that employment practices cluster within firms, which cre-

*Tayloran.*

*Switch to?*

**Figure 1.1.** Growing Patterns of Workplace Practices

| Low Wage | HRM | Japanese-Oriented | Joint Team-Based |
|---|---|---|---|
| Managerial discretion with informal procedures | Corporate culture and extensive communication | Standardized procedures | Joint decision making |
| Hierarchical work relations | Directed teams | Problem-solving teams | Semi-autonomous work groups |
| Low wages with piece rates | Above-average wages with contingent pay | High pay linked to seniority and performance appraisals | High pay with pay-for-knowledge |
| High turnover | Individualized career development | Employment stabilization | Career development |
| Strong anti-union animus | Union substitution | Enterprise unionism | Union and employee involvement |

ates discrete patterns of employment practices across firms. The clustering of employment practices arises from their being reinforced by and linked to one another. In this analysis, we make use of concepts developed in Kochan, Katz, and McKersie (1994), Katz and Kochan (1992), Arthur (1992), and Purcell and Ahlstrand (1994).

*TAYLOR .VS. HRM*

Column 1 of Figure 1.1 describes a low-wage employment pattern characterized by work practices that afford management substantial discretion and power. Work practices in this pattern are informally applied, and this pattern typically operates on a nonunion basis.

The human resource management (HRM) employment pattern (column 2 in Figure 1.1) focuses on individualized rewards and career development. The HRM approach, for example, includes teams that are more centrally directed by management when compared to the large role supervisors play in team-related and other work practices found in the Japanese-oriented pattern. However, like the Japanese-oriented system, the HRM approach attempts to sustain a strong, managerially driven corporate culture through extensive corporate communication, although the communication channels differ from the supervisory-based channels found in the Japanese-oriented workplaces.

In the United States, the HRM pattern has developed primarily in nonunion firms and is closely linked to efforts by those firms to stay nonunion. As described in later chapters, it is interesting to note that although this HRM pattern is spreading in other countries, there it is often being adopted as a complement and not an alternative to collective-bargaining procedures.

Column 3 of Figure 1.1 describes a Japanese-oriented workplace pattern. We distinguish this pattern from a more joint team-based approach (column 4 of Figure 1.1) in part based on the extent to which workers are granted autonomy to decide how and when they carry out their job tasks. In the Japanese-oriented employment pattern, jobs are highly standardized, and although workers may have input into this standardization process, once job tasks are standardized, there is little, if any, room for worker or team discretion, as is found in the joint team-based pattern. Furthermore, in the Japanese-oriented workplace, supervisors have very strong roles, whereas in the joint team-based system, workers take on many of the responsibilities previously carried out by supervisors and the number of supervisors is relatively low.

There is much variation in how these workplace patterns are actually implemented in each country in addition to the cross-country differences noted above. Important factors are the roles workers are asked to play and the roles any unions choose to play. In some joint team-based systems, for example, unions and workers participate extensively in business decisions. An extreme example of this pattern is the GM Saturn Corporation, where UAW representatives serve as co-managers and are engaged in numerous managerial decisions, including the selection of parts suppliers and the development of corporate business plans. But there are also less extreme illustrations of the joint team-based approach in the auto, telecommunications, and other industries (some are described in subsequent chapters) where unionists influence managerial decisions through their involvement in plant-level business committees or through worker representation on corporate boards.

There is variation in the practices followed by Japanese-owned firms that is analogous to the variation found elsewhere in the seven countries. All firms that are owned by a Japanese parent company have not adopted a Japanese-oriented workplace pattern. Some Japanese-owned plants in the United States, for example, follow a low-wage pattern of employment relations, including informal personnel policies, high job turnover, and low wages. Similar examples can be found in the United Kingdom and Australia (Milkman 1991).

Whatever workplace initiative they adopt, we do observe an important and growing influence of Japanese practices in the six other countries through either direct Japanese investments or the imitation of Japanese practices in domestically-owned firms. Our conclusion is that Japanization has contributed to the complexity of the variation that is appearing; however, we see no indication that employment relations are converging toward a Japanese-style pattern.

### The Role of Institutions

The effects of and outcomes produced by the various employment patterns depend very much on the basic employment relations institutions in each country and also upon the extent and nature of the representation afforded to workers and unions. For example, the extent to which semi-autonomous work groups lead to enhanced worker involvement in decision making differs in the United States and Germany because the latter already includes an extensive amount of worker involvement mandated through national codetermination laws. This difference illustrates how institutions affect the consequences of workplace practices.

Institutions also influence the extent to which variation in employment systems appears within a given country. Thus, it is just as important in our analysis to describe why Germany and Japan have experienced less extreme variation in employment systems in comparison with the English-speaking countries as it is to note the similarities that appear across the seven countries in this study.

To fully understand the nature and consequences of employment system variation, one must also understand the variation that prevailed in employment systems as each country entered the critical 1980s. In the United States, for example, a wide diversity of employment systems had developed over the post–World War II period within and between the union and nonunion sectors. Union and nonunion firms differed substantially in the wages provided to workers (with unionized firms paying wages that were, on average 10–20 percent higher) and in work rules (with work practices in the union sector regulated by negotiated seniority rules). In the nonunion sector in the United States, research has documented the existence of a rule-bound bureaucratic pattern that lacked the flexibility and individualized nature of the work practices that now appear in the HRM approach (Katz and Kochan 1992). A low-wage pattern of employment relations also has long prevailed in many secondary labor-market sectors in the United States. In Germany, in contrast, there has long been much less extreme variation in employment relations, given the presence of national codetermination laws and procedures that extend the terms of regional negotiated collective bargaining agreements to firms, whether or not they are unionized. In Australia, the wage tribunal system has helped ensure employment system standardization.

Although the traditional employment patterns differ much across countries and serve as a template upon which the four patterns have diffused, the spread of the employment patterns described in Figure 1.1 has led to declines in the role played by the traditional patterns in each country. One of our key research tasks was to identify the extent to which traditional employment patterns have been replaced by those described in Figure 1.1.

We use the word *converging* in the title of this book to reflect the many commonalities in the employment systems of the seven countries and in the processes through which these commonalities have developed. At the same time, readers are warned that our view of convergence is very different from the views of Kerr et al.

We do claim that a convergent trend across countries involves the expansion of a common set of employment patterns. But even though these patterns are a helpful analytic tool, as this book describes, there is substantial variation among countries in the meaning of various work practices depending on the institutional context and history. We also observe substantial diversity even within firms (or plants) that are following a particular pattern of work practices. This diversity arises in part from the decentralization that has occurred within managerial and corporate structures, which has shifted decision-making authority regarding employment relations to the shop floor.

Thus, for example, where team systems of work are utilized, there is much variation in the specific job duties assigned to the team leader or to team members. As team members directly take on more problem-solving tasks, they often develop particular solutions to workplace problems, which further spurs variety in work practices. Such variety is one reason why team systems are attractive as a mechanism to lower costs and improve quality and productivity. The increase in shop-floor variation in work practices is itself a common tendency across industries and countries.

Identifying the variation in employment systems is important because this variation affects the work life of employees. We find, for example, that the seven countries in our sample differ markedly in the extent to which wages vary across employees within particular firms and across firms in any given industry. Within-firm earnings variation has been increasing, for example, through mechanisms that make employee pay contingent on firm or employee performance. While the use of contingent pay has increased across the seven countries in our sample, as our data show, there is wide variation in the use of contingent pay in the auto, telecommunications, and other industries.

Although much harder to measure, the quality of employees' working lives is also influenced by the distribution of non-pay related work practices.

It makes a difference to employees, for example, whether teams are used in their firm or whether unions in their firm have a participatory relationship with management.

Fitting with the institutional perspective adopted in this book, we are also interested in understanding the consequences of the changes noted in our research for the roles and structure of unions and management. Thus, we analyze such things as how the growing variation in pay and other working conditions is producing strategic and internal dilemmas for the labor movement. And similarly for management, we seek to understand how wider variety in employment relations relates to reorganizations in the roles played by production (or operations) managers as well as industrial relations and human-resource managers.

### CHANGES IN THE ROLE AND STRUCTURES OF MANAGEMENT AND UNIONS

As this book shows, the growth in variation in employment conditions within firms is often linked to a decentralization occurring within businesses, a decentralization that is frequently associated with the rise in the importance of business units or profit centers within organizations. In telecommunications, for example, we observe a tendency for firms to oscillate between centralized and decentralized organizational forms, as these firms search for a structure that fits well with the more deregulated and uncertain economic environments. Understanding the nature of the decentralization occurring within managerial hierarchies, and the consequences of the changing organizational structures on the roles of managers, thus is one of our key sub-themes.

Another key subtheme in this volume is understanding how unions are being challenged by the variation appearing within and across countries. Unions generally do not like variation in employment relations. A key strategy of unions has been to raise wages and improve employment conditions through improvements won in particular firms or plants where they have bargaining power, and then the unions spread those advantages through bargaining leverage, legislation, and other institutional pressures. Once standardization in wages or other employment conditions was achieved, unions historically spent much of their effort in preserving that standardization. Variation thus came to be viewed by unionists as a bad thing, as it was expected to inevitably lead to a downward spiral in working conditions. At the same time, in recent years the pressure to accept concessions, or else suffer even more painful employment declines, has led unions often to go along with changes that differentiate one plant or firm from another.

Unions are now commonly put into situations where they have to decide whether to accept a deviation from standard terms in order to maintain employment.

Union acceptance and mediation of variation has challenged unions' roles and raised questions about the fundamental purpose of unionism. If unions can no longer preserve wage standards and in the process find themselves debating when and by how much employment conditions should be allowed to vary among workers, firms, or industries, do unions any longer have a unique role to play in employment relations? In other words, has the role of unions merged with that of management, as unions become one more factor that, in the end, must adjust to the wants of the market?

Our view is that unions can, and in many places already do, play a critical role guiding and shaping the variation in employment systems. But, to play this role, unions have to rethink their basic purpose and their internal structures. We conclude that unions can play a key part in coordinating the more decentralized bargaining structure that is emerging in unionized employment systems. In the process, unions will have to radically change their strategies by emphasizing the promotion of workplace change, education, training, and the career development of their membership. Furthermore, to carry out these new roles, unions will have to decentralize their organizational structures. The latter goes against not only the traditions within many unions, but it also flies in the face of the merger wave occurring within many labor movements in recent years. We return to a more detailed examination of the issues that increased employment-system variation raises for both unions and management in our concluding chapter.

## PLAN OF THE BOOK

The core of this book is analysis of the seven countries' employment practices. Our analysis of the two key industries, auto and telecommunications, relies on primary evidence, such as the wage scales reported in collective-bargaining agreements and other information provided in corporate and government documents. We also draw from interviews conducted with managers, unionists, and workers in these industries.

The analysis of developments in other industries relies more heavily on secondary sources, including the important work-practice surveys conducted in some of the countries. These surveys provide a valuable insight into, for example, work-practice evolution in Australia and Britain, insights enhanced by the longitudinal nature of those surveys. We also draw on survey evidence and case-study analysis carried out by other researchers in each of the seven countries to assess the nature and extent of employment-system variation.

The country chapters compare and contrast the union and nonunion sectors. Recognition of the role that institutional factors have played in limiting the growth of nonunion firms in Germany, Italy, and Sweden, and the opposite role played by such factors in the United States and Britain, is one of the contributions of this volume.

Because our field research in Japan, Italy, and Sweden was more limited as compared to the other four countries, we have less information to report regarding employment system variation. Nevertheless, these three countries add to our analysis because of the variation that has longed prevailed in the traditional employment practices in each of those countries and the recent increases in employment system variation produced by growth in the four key patterns in these three countries.

The earliest and widest variation in employment practices appears in the United States, and that is why we analyze that country first. Developments in the United States also reveal the role that institutional factors play in shaping the nature, causes, and consequences of employment system variation. In the United States, existing institutions allow management to press their demands for further employment system change, even in the face of an already wide variation in employment practices. Nevertheless, similar types of variation are appearing in the other six countries, as this book will show.

NOTES

1.  Detailed recent union membership statistics for other countries show that many countries have seen moderate declines in recent years; a few other countries have seen very large declines; and only in a very few other countries is union membership as stable as it is in Germany (Blanchflower and Freeman 1992).
2.  An exception to this is the extensive data provided in the workplace industrial relations surveys covering Australia and the United Kingdom, referred to in subsequent chapters.
3.  The literature on income distribution bifurcation is surveyed well in Levy and Murname (1992).
4.  Note that Locke (1995: 174–88) calls for the very sort of analysis provided in this book—a comparative examination of the distribution of subnational employment systems.
5.  Although his focus differs somewhat from ours, MacDuffie (1995b) also finds evidence of international convergence in practices in the auto industry.
6.  In part, we are pursuing the research agenda recommended by Osterman (1988).

# 2

# United States

Fitting with the relatively strong role that market forces have played in American economy history, the United States has long been noted for a high degree of diversity in the conditions that employees work under. As large corporations expanded in the twentieth century, observers noted the structured and bureaucratic nature of the "internal" labor markets within those firms, including well-defined job progressions and formal pay and fringe benefit policies (Doeringer and Piore 1971; Jacoby 1985). Jobs found in the union sector, even in such sectors as construction, which faced substantial cyclical economic volatility, led the way in developing structured and high-wage employment practices. Yet, the United States also retained more unstructured employment practices, often in smaller or rural firms, and where compensation was both lower and administered in a more informal manner. Furthermore, job progressions, dispute resolution procedures, and other employment practices were also relatively informal and of lower quality in these "secondary sector" firms, especially when compared to the work practices found in large private- or public-sector employers.

This chapter shows that even though the United States entered the 1980s with a relatively high degree of variation in employment practices, recent economic pressures have spurred a substantial increase in the amount and nature of that variation. Some of the increased variation has been spurred by a decline in unionization and the differences between the union and nonunion sectors. Most strikingly, even within the union and nonunion sectors, variation has been increasing through the spread of a diverse array of employment patterns.[1] The auto and telecommunications industries provide dramatic illustrations of these trends, which are reviewed in this chapter. First, however, we examine related trends in the general U.S. economy. Our research includes analysis of work practices (including pay procedures and work rules) as well as consideration of how the processes and structure of labor-management interactions have been altered.

The most alarming aspect of the growing variation in U.S. employment conditions is the sharp rise in income inequality. We trace both the basic trends in the income distribution and the relationship between income trends and changes in employment patterns at the end of the chapter.

## General Trends in U.S. Employment Relations

Variation in employment relations in the United States has increased in recent years with the spread of the four employment patterns described in Chapter 1 (see Figure 1.1). A key factor has been a substantial decline in the level of unionization and growth in various types of nonunion employment. The level of unionization in the general U.S. economy never approached the higher levels found in many other countries. As a result of the lower level of unionization and the limited influence of other constraints on managerial behavior, the United States generally always has had a relatively large low-wage employment sector. Despite a sizable low-wage sector, however, other nonunion firms chose to pay more, often as part of employment strategies that followed one of the employment patterns described later in this chapter: the bureaucratic, human resource management, or Japanese-oriented patterns.

The overall downward trend in unionization in the United States increased the variation in employment conditions, because unionization brought a high degree of standardization in employment conditions through the very existence of collective bargaining agreements and the "job-control" focus within American unionism.[2] Job-control unionism has put a high premium on contractual rules and strong pattern bargaining linking contractual settlements within and between industries (Katz 1985: 38–46). In contrast, a common feature of nonunion employment systems has been procedures that relate pay and other employment terms to individual traits. The resulting "individualization" of the employment relationship in nonunion settings has led to much higher variation across individuals, companies, and industries as compared to union employment systems.

*Nonunion Growth*

The level of unionization had grown substantially during World War II in the United States owing to the advantages unions gained from the National

Labor Relations Act, the organization of workers in the mass-production industries (in industrial unions), and the support unionism received from the
War Labor Board. By the late 1940s, one third of the workforce were union
members, and from that point on, the percentage of employees in the U.S.
labor force represented by a union declined sharply. Unions met with limited success organizing the service and high-technology industries and also
gained few members among the ranks of white-collar employees in the private sector.[3] Increasingly, in the post–World War II period, management
took advantage of the opportunities provided in the nation's labor laws and
the weak enforcement of those laws to carry out aggressive campaigns
against unions during any representation elections, and prior to the start of
any such campaign, managers developed personnel policies that deflected
employee interest in unionization (Lawler 1990; Kochan, Katz, and McKersie 1994).

After observing how managers in industries where unions had never been
strong successfully opposed unions, managers in industries with relatively
high levels of unionization began to successfully implement union-
avoidance techniques. In the early 1970s, unions suffered even absolute
membership declines in traditional union strongholds. Previously, union
membership had grown as employment increased in existing bargaining
units, while the share of the organized workforce fell as union efforts failed
in the growing service and high technology sectors of the economy. From the
early 1970s on, nonunion employment grew rapidly through the expansion
of nonunion subsidiaries, subcontracting, outsourcing, the opening of
greenfield plants on a nonunion basis, and union decertification. In the construction industry, for example, large, traditionally union contractors developed a "double-breasted" strategy, that is, the operation of separate union
and nonunion divisions (Kochan, Katz, and McKersie 1994). In a typical
double-breasted construction firm, commercial business is performed by
unionized employees while residential construction projects are carried out
by unorganized employees of the firm. Although nonunion growth occurred
in the general U.S. economy earlier than it did in the auto and telecommunications industries, the managerial strategies used to avoid unions in the
general economy were similar to the developments in these two industries.

In industries where unions were never dominant, the expansion of
nonunion employment per se did not create an entirely new type of employment system, because these industries always had large differences in
the employment conditions in union and nonunion firms. But union decline did lead to greater variation in employment conditions in those industries: nonunion firms put greater emphasis on personnel procedures
that linked rewards to individual traits, and these procedures contrasted

sharply with the standardized employment conditions of unionized settings. Furthermore, such industries as steel and rubber, and sizable sectors within other industries, such as over-the-road trucking and underground coal mining, like the auto and telecommunications industries, were once completely or nearly completely unionized and then experienced substantial non-union growth (Kochan, Katz, and McKersie 1994). In these once heavily unionized industries, one critical way the expansion of nonunion employment increased employment system variation was through the creation of an alternative to the previously dominant union norm.

The share of employment that is unionized has varied much across industries, but there was much commonality in the differences between union and nonunion employment conditions. The union sector has been distinguished by its heavy reliance on collective-bargaining rules to settle disputes; define jobs; and regulate workers layoffs, promotions, and other aspects of worker job mobility and career development. A key aspect of the union employment system is reliance on the grievance procedure, typically with binding outside arbitration, to settle disputes that arise during the daily implementation and administration of a collective bargaining agreement. Although some nonunion firms, and particularly those following a human resource management workplace employment system, have developed open-door or ombudsmen procedures to resolve employee complaints, even these procedures lack the worker voice and independence found in collectively bargained grievance procedures (Lewin and Peterson 1988). Furthermore, although the nonunion sector makes heavier use of seniority than managers espouse, the union sector is distinguished by the heavy role played by seniority and the formal manner in which personnel rules are applied (Abraham and Medoff 1985).

There also have been persistent differences in the level of compensation provided in union and nonunion workplaces. The relative wage of union workers has been, on average, 15 to 20 percent higher than the wages earned by nonunion workers, after controlling for the influence of worker education, experience, and other factors. Research shows that wage differentials vary much by occupation and demographic group (e.g., blacks experience a large union wage effect); union versus nonunion fringe-benefit differentials are even larger than wage differentials; and earnings differentials vary over time, particularly as a function of the business cycle (Freeman and Medoff 1984: 43–60). In the 1970s, the union relative wage effect increased, then declined in the 1980s, and stabilized in the 1990s (Katz and Kochan 1992: 261).

While the union and nonunion sectors differ along a number of key human-resource dimensions, it is interesting to note that the union and nonunion sectors do not clearly differ in the extent to which they have engaged in work restructuring in recent years. Team forms of work organization and other new work practices spread from the 1980s on in both the union and nonunion sectors. Paul Osterman (1994: 177), for example, finds that in 1992, 40.5 percent of establishments used team systems for 50 percent or more of their "core" employees.[4] Osterman's (1994: 180) survey also reveals that union establishments use team and related work practices with the same frequency as nonunion establishments.[5]

These data do not assess whether work restructuring is more successful in the union versus the nonunion sector. Some case study evidence suggests that unions can assist in the implementation of worker involvement and team work organization by providing greater voice to actors on the shop floor and by maintaining consistency in the application of new work methods. However, evidence on this score is mixed and limited (Kochan, Katz, and McKersie 1994).

While it is valuable to assess the differences *between* the union and nonunion sectors, a sizable amount of variation in employment relations now appears as a consequence of differences in employment practices *within* both sectors.

## Nonunion Employment Systems in the United States

In broad terms, nonunion industrial relations systems exhibit four basic patterns.[6] The common element across the patterns is that management policy is influenced by management's desire to stay nonunion. At the same time, management policy also is guided by the firm's desire to pursue objectives such as productivity and product quality goals that may have very little to do with union status. Note that the patterns described below are only ideal types; some firms contain elements of one or more of these employment patterns.

### The Low-Wage Pattern

In the low-wage pattern of employment relations, in addition to paying relatively low wages (and fringe benefits), personnel policies tend to be informally administered, and their administration gives substantial discretion to operating managers. Low-wage firms, for example, usually offer no formal leave and sickness policies, and supervisors in these firms grant paid leaves on a case-by-case basis. Supervisors and other managers in low-wage firms similarly exercise a high degree of discretion over discipline and pay policies. The employment conditions of employees in these firms also typically vary relatively widely across work groups, plants, and firms.

Employment in low-wage firms is often on a temporary, part-time, or defined (contract) basis. In light of the limited commitment to employment continuity made by low-wage firms, the limited promotional opportunities, and the absence of seniority-based pay, labor turnover tends to be high in low-wage firms due to both high quit and discharge rates.

The low-wage employment pattern is common among small retail stores, such as grocery stores and gas stations, and in small manufacturing plants; it is relatively common in rural locations. Managers in firms following this pattern like the discretion they gain through informal policies. Often, these firms are family owned or operated, with family members personally directing personnel policies. Family owners dislike losing control over decisions, and they particularly fear the reduction of control that would occur if unions represented employees. Hence, union avoidance is often a prime policy objective in firms following the low-wage pattern. Research shows that Japanese-owned firms that operate small manufacturing plants often follow this pattern rather than the Japanese-oriented pattern we describe later (Milkman 1991).

In the absence of any longitudinal governmental or comparable surveys regarding personnel (or workplace industrial relations) practices in the United States, it is difficult to determine whether the low-wage employment pattern has been growing in recent years. Data we discuss later in this chapter show that sizable declines have occurred in worker real earnings over the past twenty years, suggesting that the low-wage pattern has been growing, as do measures showing growth in various forms of "contingent labor" (Cappelli et al. 1997).

### The Bureaucratic Pattern

Larger firms have long found the high turnover and informality common to low wage firms too unsettling and costly. This has led large firms to seek greater stability and uniformity in personnel practices through the more formal and rule-based approach found in a bureaucratic employment pattern. These firms have also come to realize that the diversity in personnel practices resulting from informality can spur unionization if some employees believe other employees elsewhere in the firm are benefiting from more favorable policies. Furthermore, firms that follow a bureaucratic pattern are willing to pay better in order to recruit more able and more stable employees, and these firms generally have the resources to do so.

The bureaucratic pattern is characterized by highly formalized procedures, such as clear (and typically written) policies regarding pay, leaves, promotion, and discipline. Firms following the bureaucratic pattern generally also make use of highly detailed job classifications and use job evaluation schemes to determine pay levels and job duties. Examples of firms that conform to this pattern include most of the large, nonunion corporations that expanded in the early post–World War II period. In addition, for its white-collar nonunion employees, firms such as AT&T and General Motors have followed the bureaucratic employment pattern, whereas their unionized employees were covered by the New Deal employment pattern described below.

### The Human Resource Management Pattern

As an outgrowth of efforts to increase flexibility and cost competitiveness while maintaining their nonunion status, various firms began to adopt a new pattern of personnel policies in the 1970s—the human resource management (HRM) pattern.[7] Like the bureaucratic pattern, this pattern relies on formal policies, but the nature of the policies differs from those traditionally found in nonunion firms. The HRM pattern typically includes skill- (or knowledge-) based pay, and elaborate communication and complaint procedures. Team forms of work organization are also common in HRM-oriented firms. The activities of the teams and the selection of team leaders tends to be directly controlled by management. Employees are not regularly involved in joint forums, where the structure or guidelines for team operation are set, and thus team systems in HRM firms lack the joint nature and independence of the joint team-based employment pattern (described below).

In the 1960s and 1970s, employment stabilization was a common and core feature of the HRM employment system. Leading HRM firms such as IBM, Kodak, and Polaroid went to great lengths in this period through the use of employment buffers and personnel planning to avoid involuntary layoffs, even during economic downturns. But in the late 1980s, the employment security offered by these firms succumbed to corporate restructuring and downsizing. Employees have borne the burden of corporate restructuring, and even the remaining employees have been experiencing abrupt shifts across jobs and locations. Employees are being forced to assume the burden of developing and planning their careers. In effect, firms facing greater risk and uncertainty in the economic environment are passing a larger share of that risk and uncertainty on to their employees (Cappelli 1997). The HRM firms have been distinguished from other nonunion employers in the late 1980s and 1990s not by their employment security but rather by the extent to which they subsidize their employees' investments in skill development or job transfers (with the latter often including severance benefits) (Cappelli et al. 1997: 66–88).

Like the firms following the other nonunion patterns, the HRM firms vigilantly try to avoid unionization. Where they differ from other nonunion firms is in the extent to which they consider union-avoidance questions in such decisions as plant location and long-term personnel planning. Union-avoidance issues also influence how these firms design other personnel policies, for example, communication policies. The HRM firms also are noteworthy for the extensive measures they take in trying to induce employees to identify their interests with the long-term interests of the firm. Those measures include publishing company newsletters, paying all employees on a salary basis, and nurturing strong corporate cultures.

Among the best-known mature companies that continue to apply many of these practices successfully are Hewlett-Packard, Proctor and Gamble, Eastman Kodak, and Motorola. Marriott Hotels is an example of a company that has used these strategies successfully in more competitive environments and with a lesser-skilled workforce.[8] Even some construction contractors and a few coal mines have embarked on this approach in recent years.

### Japanese-oriented Employment Relations Pattern

A Japanese-oriented personnel system has emerged in nonunion firms owned by Japanese parent companies and is similar to the work practices of Japanese auto-assembly transplants. This work system, described in column 3 of Figure 1.1, is characterized by standardized jobs, problem-based teams, strong supervisors, and a hybridization of work practices common to firms in Japan. Spurred by expanding Japanese direct investment in the United States in the 1980s, these practices spread in the manufacturing sector, including among Japanese-owned steel minimills (Ichniowski, Shaw, and Prennushi 1997). By the late 1980s, some American-owned firms were imitating these practices, although in some cases, the actual work practices in the latter firms were a confused mixture of HRM and Japanese-oriented personnel practices.[9]

Several factors influence which of the three patterns are followed by nonunion firms. Management values and strategies play an important role. For instance, many HRM firms had strong founding executives who helped initiate strong corporate cultures.[10] Business strategy also makes a difference. The HRM pattern seems to allow for more flexible and adaptable work organization through the use of team systems and skill-based pay (Kochan, McKersie, and Chalykoff 1986). These characteristics are particularly attractive to firms with rapidly changing technologies and markets. Thus, it is no surprise that many firms in high-technology industries follow the HRM pattern.

Steel minimills illustrate how business strategy is linked to personnel practices. Among nonunion minimills, those producing a wide variety of products ("market" mills) and those concentrating on high-quality products tend to follow the HRM pattern, whereas those pursuing a low-cost and high-volume product strategy tend to follow a variant of the bureaucratic pattern (Arthur 1992).

## Union Patterns of Industrial Relations in the United States

In firms where at least some of the employees are unionized, industrial relations policies also follow distinct employment patterns. There currently are three dominant union patterns in the United States: the traditional or "New Deal" pattern, the conflict pattern, and the joint team-based pattern.

### The Traditional ("New Deal") Pattern

The form of collective bargaining in the United States that has dominated since World War II is characterized by highly detailed and formal contracts. This New Deal pattern includes grievance arbitration, seniority-based layoff procedures, numerous and detailed job classifications, and pay systems that rely heavily on formulaic rules and pattern bargaining.

The advantages to this pattern are that it is very good at stabilizing labor relations. Some of that stability derives from the formal channels (such as the grievance procedure) through which problems can be addressed. These procedures are attractive to employees because they provide due process; they are attractive to employers because adherence to the procedures ensures that production will not be interrupted by labor disputes during the term of a labor contract.

Until the shift to teams and greater worker and union participation in decision making, labor-management relations in the auto industry followed this traditional pattern, as did relations in other heavily unionized industries such as steel, trucking, coal mining, aerospace, and airlines. Although prolonged conflicts arose occasionally, such as the 1959 steel strike, the traditional pattern was quite successful in moderating the intensity of labor-management conflict. Furthermore, though neither labor nor management were ever completely satisfied by the outputs of this system, and the two sides respectively often complained of the need to attain higher wages and profits, in most unionized firms both sides remained firmly committed to operating within the traditional system. This truce started to come apart in the 1970s, when management began to more aggressively pursue nonunion options. Then, in the 1980s, experimentation with the joint team-based approach accelerated in the face of economic pressures, and both labor and management became increasingly unsatisfied by the outputs of the traditional collective-bargaining approach. The traditional pattern then increasingly was replaced either by a conflict or a joint team-based pattern.

*Conflict Pattern*

Under the conflict pattern, labor and management are engaged in a serious struggle over their basic rights. As a result, the conflict pattern typically involves prolonged strikes. In some cases, employees in such a relationship resort to sabotage or absenteeism to express their anger against employers. Conflict imposes high costs on the firm through lost output or low productivity and on employees in the form of lost earnings. Because of the high costs to both parties of engaging in intense conflict, the conflict pattern tends to be unstable.

The recent labor dispute involving the Caterpillar Corporation and the UAW illustrates the conflict pattern. The dispute started in November 1991, when the company insisted on concessions in medical-care benefits and an overall wage package that was less generous than settlements that had been negotiated at other agricultural implement companies, such as John Deere. At the time, the UAW and Caterpillar did not appear to be far apart in their negotiations, and this dispute had the appearance of the sort of disagreement that arises periodically between labor and management within the New Deal pattern of employment relations. The dispute escalated into a more severe conflict, however, and, in our terms, shifted into a conflict pattern of employment relations when the company began to hire what it declared would be permanent replacements for workers who remained on strike in the spring of 1992 (Rose 1995: A4). Although workers then returned to work in response to fears that they would be permanently replaced, an acrimonious series of strikes and job actions followed. A second strike, started in June 1994, was ended in December 1995, when the UAW promoted a return to work even though a negotiated contract had not been reached (Bureau of National Affairs 1995b: D5).

Earlier, a conflict pattern also had emerged at Eastern Airlines. A strike started in 1989 by the International Association of Machinists (IAM) quickly received the support of Eastern's unionized pilots and flight attendants. Although the pilots and flight attendants later voted to end their walkouts, disagreement between the machinists union and the airline persisted, in part as a result of the union's animosity toward Frank Lorenzo, the forceful owner of the airline. This conflict eventually ended with the bankruptcy of the airline in 1991 (Katz and Kochan 1992: 128–29).

In the past, a conflict pattern was often spurred by disputes concerning union representation, arising amid a union-organizing campaign or a management-led campaign to decertify an existing union. The Caterpillar and Eastern strikes were ominous for the American labor movement precisely because the parties had shifted to a conflict pattern from a New Deal pattern of employment relations, absent a direct dispute over union representation.

*Joint Team-Based Employment Pattern*

Pressured by the need to improve productivity, product quality, and production flexibility, in recent years both firms and unions have been experimenting with a joint team-based approach characterized by contingent compensation systems (linking firm or work-group pay to economic performance), team forms of work organization, employment security programs, and more direct participation by workers and unions in business decision making. Although the nature and depth of team-based work practices varies much across firms (which makes it especially difficult to measure the diffusion of these practices), the case study and survey evidence cited above finds sizable diffusion of the work practices associated with this pattern.

The joint team-based pattern tries to create mechanisms through which workers can directly solve production and personnel problems. Quality circles or team meetings are used to facilitate discussions between supervisors and workers and among workers in different work areas. In firms using this approach, workers become involved in business decisions, such as scrap disposal or new technology implementation. Not all organizations that set out to create greater participation by employees, however, end up with more employee participation. The reasons for these failures include supervisor or employee resistance to change (Applebaum and Batt 1994: 146–60).

Examples of the joint team-based approach are found in a wide range of industries, including steel, electrical products, and paper (Walton, Cutcher-Gershenfeld, and McKersie 1994; Applebaum and Batt 1994; Kochan, Katz, and McKersie 1994). There are many similarities in the joint team approach used in the auto industry, telecommunications, and other American industries, and variation in the specific details of how the approach is implemented.

## DECENTRALIZATION OF COLLECTIVE-BARGAINING STRUCTURES IN THE UNION SECTOR

A key related change in employment relations in unionized settings in the United States is the decentralization of collective bargaining. As is noted in subsequent chapters, however, similar trends have been occurring in many other countries in recent years.[11]

In the early 1980s, the structure of bargaining affecting unionized employees in the United States was a mixture of multiemployer, firm-wide, and plant-level bargaining. From the early 1980s on, the structure of collective bargaining in the United States began to decentralize as formally centralized structures broke down; the locus of bargaining shifted to the plant level within structures that maintained both company and plant levels; and pattern bargaining weakened.[12]

Multiemployer bargaining in the United States in some cases ended, for example, the basic steel agreement was eliminated in 1986. In some other industries, the number of firms and unionized employees covered by a multifirm agreement declined as companies withdrew from master agreements, for example, in the trucking industry (eroding the influence of the Master Freight Agreement negotiated by the Teamsters and an employers' association that had set employment terms for intercity truck drivers), and in the underground coal-mining sector (eroding the influence of a master agreement negotiated between the United Mineworkers and the Bituminous Coal Operators Association) (Kochan, Katz, and McKersie 1986: 128–30; Katz and Kochan 1992: 195–97).

There are also widespread reports of a shift to plant-level collective-bargaining agreements and away from company-wide agreements. In many cases, such as the tire and airline industries, this shift has involved the negotiation of local pay or work-rule concessions. Often these negotiations involved whipsawing by management, with local unions and workers being threatened with the prospect of a plant closing if adequate concessions were not granted (Cappelli 1985; Kochan, Katz, and McKersie 1994: 117–27). In some cases, concessions on work rules have been accompanied by new arrangements that provide extensive participation by workers and local union officers in decisions that had formerly been made solely by management (Kochan, Katz, and McKersie 1994: 146–205). With increasing frequency, work-rule bargaining has come to involve the decision whether to implement a joint team-based approach or center on disputes arising from implementation of that type of employment system.

Even where company-level collective bargaining has continued, greater diversity in collective-bargaining outcomes have appeared across companies. This diversity has replaced the strong pattern bargaining that informally had served to centralize bargaining structures to the multiemployer level, through either formal collective bargaining agreements or informally through pattern bargaining.[13] In the case of the aerospace and agricultural implements industries, over the post–World II period until the mid-1980s, company-level pattern bargaining had included the same COLA (cost of living adjustment) clause and 3 percent annual improvement factor wage increases found in the Big Three auto agreements. Erickson (1992, 1996) documents the weakening of pattern bargaining and the emergence of significant intercompany variation in the aerospace industry and agricultural implements industries in the 1980s and 1990s.

The introduction of profit sharing or stock ownership is one of the ways variation in pay is emerging in major collective bargaining agreements. By 1990, 36 percent of workers in large bargaining units were covered by a profit-sharing plan (Katz and Keefe 1992: A-5). The specific form of the profit-sharing plan varies much across firms and industries, and notably the payouts provided in these plans vary along with the financial performance of the respective companies. The use of lump-sum wage increases also grew in the early 1980s as a replacement for the traditional base-pay increases. Lump sums appeared first in aerospace and became a sizable item. (Machinists at Boeing, for example, received sizable lump-sum payments in their 1992–1995 and 1995–1998 contracts [Erickson 1996].) Lump sums became a partly contingent element of labor contracts as their size varied over time and across firms in part as a reflection of the financial performance of firms.

Simultaneously, the level of variation in fringe benefits has been growing and often increasing more than the variation in base wages, although there is no simple metric to compare compensation items, given the complexities in calculating the costs of various fringe benefits. Cross-firm variation increased in many unionized industries in medical care coverage and employment security contract provisions.

The greater variation may have appeared in fringe benefits as compared to base wages because it was more difficult for workers to make comparisons in the value of fringe benefits across labor contracts that gave union negotiators more room to adjust such benefits to economic pressures. Variation in fringe benefits as well as wages contributed to a weakening of interindustry as well as intraindustry pattern bargaining (Budd 1992).

Even wider variation appeared in work practices across firms and industries in light of the uneven spread of work reorganization. Some plants adopted team systems of work while others did not, and wide differences appear in the form and role of any work teams. Osterman (1994: 177), for example, finds that 36 percent of firms use none of a long list of innovative work practices. Applebaum and Batt (1994) provide a rich description of the diversity of work-practice changes and an insightful analysis of the sluggishness and variation in the diffusion of new work practices.[14]

The American research literature has numerous accounts of bargaining at the plant and work-group level involving team systems, pay for knowledge, and other contingent compensation mechanisms, and changes in work-time arrangements (Kochan, Katz, and McKersie, 1994: 146–205; Cutcher-Gershenfeld 1991; Arthur 1992).[15] There are also reports of more direct communication between managers and workers in many parts of the union sector in the United States (Eaton and Voos 1992; Kochan, Katz, and McKersie 1994: 132–34).

While the changes in employment relations observed in the auto and telecommunications industries bear many similarities to those elsewhere in the U.S. economy, certain characteristics of these two industries produce differences in outcomes and the processes through which those outcomes were determined. For example, the auto and telecommunications industries have much higher levels of unionization and are dominated by very large firms. As a consequence of the former, the variation appearing in these industries is more limited than that of the broader U.S. economy, although similar in form. In our analysis of how unionism and other factors are influencing employment practices, we find it useful to look separately at key segments of each industry—in autos, at the assembly and parts sectors, and in the telecommunications industry, at the services and equipment sectors.

## EMPLOYMENT RELATIONS VARIATION IN THE U.S. AUTO (ASSEMBLY AND PARTS) INDUSTRY

Analysis of employment relations in the U.S. auto industry requires separate consideration of the assembly and independent parts sector, for the timing and extent of nonunion growth differs in the two sectors. The independent parts sector excludes the assembly and parts operations within the Big Three automobile companies [General Motors (GM), Ford, and Chrysler] and the auto parts production carried out within other companies that include assembly operations (the Japanese and German "transplant" firms).

In recent years, there has been sizable growth in production levels in Japanese auto transplants (i.e., auto plant complexes that include assembly plants and are owned by Japanese companies) and also growth in German-owned auto transplants. The Japanese and German transplants have made a significant contribution to the growing variation in employment relations in the U.S. auto industry because the transplants operate on a nonunion basis. Furthermore, as is described in more detail below, work practices in the Japanese transplant plants follow a Japanese-oriented pattern and have served as a model for firms in many other industries.[16] The programmatic details of work-practice implementation and operation differ significantly

across the transplants, contributing another important element to the growing variation in employment relations in the U.S. auto industry.

*The Auto Assembly Sector*

*The Nonunion Transplant Challenge to the Big Three.* A chief source of employment variation in auto assembly plants in the United States has been the
growth of nonunion plants. Before the advent of Japanese-owned transplants, the auto assembly sector had been one of the key completely unionized sectors in the United States. The assembly plants of the Big Three auto
companies had been organized in the late 1930s and 1940s by the United
Automobile, Aerospace, and Agricultural Implement Workers (UAW). Collective bargaining in the Big Three then led to substantial growth in the
wages and fringe benefits received by auto workers and established
the UAW as one of the most pivotal unions in the country. The influence of
the UAW spread even wider as UAW bargaining with the Big Three emerged
as the source of much innovation in American employment relations. These
innovations include company-paid health and life insurance, formulaic
wage increases in multiyear contracts, supplementary unemployment benefits, and "thirty and out" pensions. These gains then spread to the auto
parts sector, and eventually to other American industries (union and
nonunion).

The union status of the assembly plants in the Big Three was first challenged in the 1970s through GM's southern strategy, which entailed the
opening of nonunion plants in the South. However, by the early 1980s,
nonunion GM assembly plants in the South were organized, in large part
through the automatic ("accretion") procedures the UAW won from GM after the union threatened to withdraw from the joint programs that were simultaneously spreading in GM's unionized plants and also threatened job
actions at GM's other plants if the issue of union recognition was not settled
(Katz 1985: 90).

Of more lasting importance was the "operating team" concept that GM
first utilized in its nonunion southern strategy. This proved to be an important testing ground for concepts GM later applied in other plants. The operating team system includes few job classifications and a lessening in the
role played by seniority, and contrasts sharply with traditional work practices
of the union sector.

The more recent growth of nonunion Japanese and German auto transplants has proved to be particularly troubling for the UAW and a significant
source of variation in employment relations in the auto industry. As can be
seen from Table 2.1, the transplants now provide a significant percentage of

**Table 2.1.** Production Levels at Automobile Assembly Transplants in the United States

| Company | Location | Production Began | 1989 Production | 1997 Production | Unionized |
|---|---|---|---|---|---|
| Honda | Marysville, Ohio | 1982 | [a]363,274 | [a]648,268 | No |
| Nissan | Smyrna, Tenn. | 1983 | 238,641 | 398,308 | No |
| New United Motor Manufacturing (Toyota and General Motors) | Fremont, Ca. | 1984 | 192,471 | 350,180 | Yes |
| Mazda (with Ford) | Flat Rock, Mich. | 1987 | 216,501 | [b]90,528 | Yes |
| Diamond-Star (Mitsubishi and Chrysler) | Normal, Ill. | 1988 | 90,741 | 189,086 | Yes |
| Toyota | Georgetown, Ky. | 1988 | 151,099 | 378,135 | No |
| Subaru-Isuzu | Lafayette, Ind. | 1989 | 11,160 | 102,180 | No |
| Honda | East Liberty, Ohio | 1989 | [a] | [a] | No |
| BMW | Spartansburgh, S.C. | 1994 | — | 46,891 | No |

*Sources:* Motor Vehicle Manufacturers Association and *Automotive News* (Detroit: Crain Communications), various issues. Christopher J. Singleton, "Auto Industry Jobs in the 1980's: A Decade of Transition," *Monthly Labor Review* 115, no. 2 (February 1992): 18–27. The 1997 figures include cars and trucks and are from an unpublished table compiled by General Motors.
[a] The Honda Marysville production level includes Honda East Liberty.
[b] Mazda production was as high as 246,991 in 1994 while at Subaru-Isuzu it was 389,048 in 1995. Production was slowed at both plants in recent years due to excess inventories.
*Note:* Mercedes Benz has a nonunion plant in Alabama that recently started regular production.

total U.S. auto assembly production. Only the transplants co-owned by an American company have been unionized.[17] The UAW conducted an unsuccessful organizing drive in the Nissan plant, receiving only 30.5 percent of the vote in a National Labor Relations Board (NLRB) representation election in 1989 and since has only been able to muster informal organizing efforts in the other transplants.

*Earnings Variation across Nonunion Assembly Plants.* Wage levels at the transplants vary between 80 to 90 percent of those at American-owned auto plants. For example, in January 1994, the hourly wage rate for assemblers at the Nissan and Honda transplants were, respectively, $15.08 and $15.65 (but $18.03 at General Motors). In March 1996, the hourly wage rate for assemblers at the BMW auto assembly plant in Spartansburg, South Carolina, was $17.00 (and $18.74 at General Motors).[18]

The small difference in the hourly wage rate at the Nissan and Honda transplants cited above illustrates wage rates have not varied significantly across the transplants. In the transplants, a variety of performance-based pay schemes supplements worker hourly earnings. These supplements generally range on the order of 5 to 20 percent of total worker pay, although the form of the performance pay varies across the plants. Toyota's Georgetown assembly plant, for example, has two bonus systems that supplement hourly earnings. One bonus has been tied to plant performance and has produced flat-rate bonus payments that varied between 8 to 12 percent of workers' total hourly earnings between 1987 and 1994 (Adler 1995: 27; Mishina 1995: 16).[19] Since 1990 at the Georgetown plant, there has also been a "discretionary bonus" paid annually at the discretion of the president of the company, ranging from $600 per worker in 1991 to $2,300 in 1997 (Bureau of National Affairs 1997: B-1).

At Honda's transplant operations, meanwhile, workers receive semi-annual bonuses that are based in part on the degree to which quality goals for the model year are being achieved (MacDuffie 1997: 490). The bonus at Honda in 1997 was $4,300 per employee (Bureau of National Affairs 1997: B-1).

With regard to fringe benefits, differences are more substantial between the compensation package provided to hourly workers in the Big Three plants and the benefits provided in the transplants. The transplants, for example, tend to provide significantly more modest medical insurance and pension plans, whereas the latter often include an individual retirement account or defined contribution plan rather than the more elaborate defined benefit programs found in the Big Three. Howes (1993: 46–50) and Ghilarducci (1991: Table 3, p. 10) find, for example, that pension costs per worker-hour in 1987 were $2.63 and $.95, respectively, at Ford and GM and much lower—$.50 and $.43, respectively—at the Honda and Toyota transplants.[20]

*Work Practices at the Japanese Transplants.* All the Japanese transplants use the Japanese-oriented workplace approach described in Figure 1.1, including standardized jobs and problem-solving teams. Given that team systems have spread unevenly throughout the Big Three assembly plants (as is discussed below), the Japanese transplants use teams more extensively than the average Big Three plant and are distinguished by a Japanese-oriented version of team systems. In Japanese transplants, worker autonomy is relatively limited, because team systems are oriented toward the identification and resolution of specific production problems. Furthermore, supervisors in the Japanese transplants tend to exert a strong role, one that is more similar to the duties of supervisors in auto plants in Japan than it is to the facilitator role of supervisors in American-owned assembly plants with team systems (using what we have referred to as a joint team-based approach). In addition, Japanese transplants have standardized job assignments, and although workers may participate in the development or refinement of these assignments, work tasks are set in detail by management and are not, as is common in Big Three teams, subject to frequent informal modification by team members. Team leaders in nonunion Japanese transplants are selected by management, rather than through the involvement of team members.

The nonunion Japanese transplants lack the formal grievance procedures of unionized American-owned auto plants to settle worker complaints and worker-supervisor disputes. In the transplants, supervisors are more active in settling disputes, often through informal channels (Graham 1995: 108). At some Japanese transplants, more formal procedures have been established to address worker complaints about discharges. At Honda, for example, a joint (worker and management) peer committee reviews disciplinary discharges and has reversed a high percentage of them (Katz and MacDuffie 1994: 214).

Five of the six nonunion Japanese transplants also maintain committees of worker representatives (appointed by management) that provide a form of worker representation (Pil and MacDuffie 1998: 7). Although these committees provide avenues for communication between workers and management, they clearly lack the independence and authority found in the grievance procedure and negotiated committee structures in the unionized auto plants.

### Variation within the Unionized Auto Assembly Sector

The extent of variation in wages and work practices is even larger in the unionized auto-assembly plants. Understanding how variation in earnings and work practices has grown in the unionized Big Three auto assembly plants requires an awareness of the collective-bargaining structure. In the basic structure that has prevailed at the Big Three auto companies since World War II, compensation is set by national company-specific and multiyear (from 1955 on, they were three-year) agreements. Some work rules, such as overtime administration, employee transfer rights, and seniority guidelines, are also set in the national contracts. Local unions, in turn, negotiate plant-level agreements that supplement the national agreements. These local agreements define work rules, such as the form of the seniority ladder, job characteristics, job bidding and transfer rights, health and safety standards, production standards, and an array of other rules that guide shop-floor production. The local agreements do not regulate either wages or fringe benefits, which are set in the national contracts. Some indirect influences on wage determination do occur at the plant level, in the definition and modification of job classifications provided through the local agreements. Local bargaining over work rules allows for local preferences, and in the face of the extreme economic pressures that confronted many plants from the 1980s on, local bargaining became increasingly important and volatile.[21]

*Earnings Determination in the Unionized Assembly Plants*

Formulaic mechanisms have been utilized to set wage levels in collective bargaining agreements at the Big Three (Katz 1985: 14–16). The mechanisms traditionally included in the company-wide collective bargaining agreements were an annual improvement factor (AIF) that, after the mid-1960s, amounted to 3 percent per year, and a COLA escalator that often provided full or close to full cost-of-living protection. The importance of these formulaic mechanisms was that they provided continuity in wage determination across time and also across the assembly companies at any given time. Continuity across the industry was ensured by intercompany pattern following and by the fact that in the plants covered by the company-wide agreements, the national contract wage was not modified in local bargaining.

Along with increases in real hourly earnings, in the post–World War Two period until the 1980s, auto workers received steady improvements in their fringe benefit package, and as noted above, these fringe benefit advances spread to auto supplier firms as well as to other industries. Over the postwar period, fringe benefits grew as a share of total worker compensation.

Intercompany variation first appeared in the hourly wages paid by the Big Three in 1980 when Chrysler, under threat of bankruptcy, negotiated pay concessions with the UAW that included the initial deferment and eventual cancellation of COLA and AIF payments.[22] Pay concessions followed in the 1982–1984 UAW contracts negotiated ahead of schedule at GM and Ford. Concessions in the contracts negotiated at Chrysler, Ford, and GM in 1982, 1984 and 1987 included the substitution of lump-sum pay increases for the traditional AIF base-pay increases (although profit sharing was provided as a partial substitute for the base-pay increases). These contracts included some relatively small differences in the timing of pay increases between Chrysler and the other two companies, in part as a result of the UAW's successful efforts to get Chrysler to repay workers for the sacrifices they made in the 1980 contract.

The 1990–1993 contracts provided identical pay increases across the Big Three (as did the subsequent 1993–1996 and 1996–1999 contracts), which signaled a return to strict pattern bargaining in contractual base-pay increases and lump-sum wage payments. Hourly base-pay rates were standardized even earlier across the Big Three, and the short life of hourly pay differentials suggests how seriously the UAW pursued hourly base-pay standardization. Right before the start of concession bargaining at Chrysler, as of the third quarter of 1979, hourly base-pay rates had been identical at the Big Three, at \$8.67 (for assemblers). By the third quarter of 1983, the relatively large concessions at Chrysler had produced hourly base-pay rates at

**Table 2.2.** Big Three Average Worker Profit Sharing, 1983–1997

| Year | Ford | GM | Chrysler |
|------|------|------|------|
| 1983 | $ 402 | $ 605 | $ 0 |
| 1984 | 1,993 | 515 | 0 |
| 1985 | 1,262 | 329 | 0 |
| 1986 | 2,177 | 0 | 0[a] |
| 1987 | 3,762 | 0 | 0[a] |
| 1988 | 2,874 | 242 | 725 |
| 1989 | 1,025 | 50 | 0 |
| 1990 | 0 | 0 | 0 |
| 1991 | 0 | 0 | 0 |
| 1992 | 0 | 0 | 425 |
| 1993 | 1,350 | 0 | 4,300 |
| 1994 | 4,000 | 550 | 8,000 |
| 1995 | 1,700 | 800 | 3,200 |
| 1996 | 1,800 | 300 | 7,900 |
| 1997 | 4,400 | 6,100 | 750 |
| 1998 | 200 | 4,600 | 7,400 |
| TOTAL | $ 32,845 | $ 4,341 | $ 36,550 |

*Source:* Unpublished table prepared by the UAW Research Department, February 8, 1995 and news reports in the *Daily Labor Report,* various years.
[a] Chrysler workers received a $500 contractual payment not tied to profits.

GM, Ford, and Chrysler, respectively, of $11.85, $11.86, and $9.85. In the first quarter of 1985, special adjustments provided in the 1985 Chrysler-UAW contract raised the Chrysler hourly base-pay rate back up to the rate being provided at that point at GM and Ford ($13.36).[23]

While the UAW fought hard to reinstate strict pattern following in base-pay rates and contractual increases, much dissension was created among the workforce over the introduction of profit sharing in the early 1980s, which had laid the groundwork for significant variation in worker earnings across the Big Three. The payouts of the profit-sharing plans, adopted in the Big Three from 1983 on, have varied substantially, in large part due to differences in the financial performance of the companies (see Table 2.2).[24] The profit-sharing payouts between 1983 and 1998 at GM, Ford, and Chrysler, respectively, totaled $4,341, $32,845, and $36,550 (as noted in Table 2.2). The annual payouts in the profit-sharing plans have been quite large in some years. For example, in 1998 at GM, Ford, and Chrysler, the respective profit-sharing payouts were $200, $6,100, and $7,400 per worker.

Earnings also have varied because of the uneven adoption of pay-for-knowledge schemes across auto plants and variations in pay-for-knowledge plans. In some plants, workers receive $1.25 more per hour than other workers as a result of their progression to the top of a pay-for-knowledge scale (attained through a worker's mastery of all the jobs in their respective work area or performance as an hourly team coordinator).

Unions often allow more substantial variation in fringe benefits than they allow in base-pay increases, presumably because variations in fringe benefits are more difficult to calculate and thus are somewhat less susceptible to comparisons made by the rank and file (Erickson 1996; Mitchell 1980: 188–89). The UAW followed this style in its bargaining with the Big Three in that substantial variation was accepted by the UAW in profit-sharing payouts and in the use and form of pay-for-knowledge plans at the same time that the UAW was working hard (and successfully) to eliminate variation in base-pay increases across the Big Three.

### Work-Rule Variation in Unionized Auto Assembly Plants

Even greater variation now appears in the work practices of unionized auto assembly plants, largely because work rules and work organization have been modified in different ways and at a varied pace across plants. The threat of increased employment loss due to either increased foreign sourcing of vehicles, plant closings due to excess capacity, or the outsourcing of certain operations all created pressures to lower costs and improve product quality. Ultimately, the pressure for increased interplant work-rule divergence came from the same source as the pressure for intercompany pay variation—the fear that even greater losses in employment would result if previous policies were maintained. Companies often used investment decisions as explicit leverage for these changes, in a strategy unions saw as whipsawing, or forcing plants to compete against one another through concessions.

Some of these work-rule changes involved increases in the "effort bargain" through a tightening of production standards. Other changes include efforts to lower production costs by increasing the flexibility with which labor is deployed. Common examples of the latter include classification consolidation; limits imposed on job-bidding rights; the use of work teams to promote multiskilling through job rotation; and a pushing down of certain responsibilities, such as quality inspection, to production workers on the shop floor.

At plants threatened with imminent closing, the work rules were typically changed in a disorganized and ad hoc manner. Excess capacity allowed management to directly pit assembly plants against one another in work-rule concession bargaining. This happened frequently from the late 1980s to the early 1990s in GM (and commonly in parts plants across the Big Three, as described later in this chapter). Although the particular work-rule changes made in any assembly plant at any particular moment varied widely, the trend across the Big Three companies over the past fifteen years has been to gradually shift from a traditional system of work organization to the joint team-based approach (outlined in column 4 of Figure 1.1).

The traditional work system in assembly plants involved numerous job classifications, a very heavy and highly structured role for seniority rights in job assignments (transfers, promotions, shift preferences, etc.), and a clear separation in the responsibilities of workers and managerial employees. The joint team-based approach, in contrast, provides greater and broader responsibilities to the blue-collar workforce, in many instances involving workers in production and, in some cases, even in basic business decisions. Typically, the work team is led by an hourly team coordinator. As teams have spread, the number of supervisors has been reduced and the role of the remaining supervisors shifted to a coaching and facilitating role (although discipline did remain a key function of supervision).

The pace at which this approach is spreading in the Big Three has varied. General Motors experimented most extensively with the approach by initially using nonunion "southern strategy" plants as a testing ground for the concept. Then, in the early 1980s, GM started implementing the approach in its northern assembly plants, first in new facilities such as the Lake Orion and Hamtramack plants; later in the decade, GM management often made a team approach a necessary precondition for the survival of redundant facilities. Ford and Chrysler were even more gradual in their implementation of the joint team-based approach in part because neither was building new assembly plants in the 1980s and 1990s and thus did not have the opportunity to experiment in greenfield sites, and in part because the GM experience of introducing teams in existing ("brownfield") plants did not always work out well.[25]

Yet, by the early 1990s, even at Ford and Chrysler assembly plants, the approach was more widespread. Both Ford and Chrysler management began pushing what they referred to as "modern operating agreements" (MOAs), which included teams and weakened seniority rights.[26]

At the same time, not all Big Three assembly plants adopted team systems. For example, at GM, the Linden, Doraville, and Wilmington assembly plants were not using teams as of early 1998.[27] In a 1994 survey of Big Three assembly plants, Pil and MacDuffie (1996: 437) found that 46 percent of the employees worked in teams.

Substantial variation also appears in how teams and other features of this approach are actually being implemented. In team plants, for example, there is wide variety in the procedures for selecting team leaders and in the role that hourly team members exert in the selection process. Some team plants use strict seniority rights to determine who serves as the hourly team coordinator; other plants allow team members to directly elect their coordinator.[28] In still other assembly plants, a joint labor-management selection committee screens

and interviews candidates for the coordinator position in a jointly designed assessment procedure.[29] And certain plants (such as GM's Shreveport truck assembly plant) allow the teams to chose their team leader, and as a result, the selection procedure varies by work group across the plant. The procedures used to select team leaders is not an incidental matter: selection procedure has been a key issue in disputes (some of which have entailed work stoppages) at the Ford-Dearborn and other Big Three assembly plants.[30]

Plants also vary widely in the specific duties performed by team members and leaders. In some plants, team members have the authority to directly contact and visit parts vendors to resolve production problems. Or hourly workers are put on scrap and quality-control task forces, freeing them from assembly-line responsibilities and giving them the time to carry out new duties.[31] Pay for knowledge has been adopted along with teams in some plants to encourage workers to learn more jobs in their work area and, in the process, become more capable of understanding the linkages between jobs in and across work teams. The presence and form of pay for knowledge varies across plants and, as noted earlier, is a source of earnings variation across plants, in contrast to the traditional work system that served to dampen such variation. Thus, assembly plants of the Big Three differ in terms of whether they use the traditional or a joint team-based work system, and there is much variation across plants in terms of the way that teams are introduced.

Team systems have increased the variation in work organization and work practices across auto plants through their operation as well as the structure of team administration. In team meetings, workers directly address production problems as they arise and, in the process, provide input into plant operations in order to settle the problems or avoid them in the first place. This process produces variety in plant operations as workers in a team adopt work modes to suit their preferences or respond to a particular problem that may differ from the modes of workers in other teams (or workers who reside in a plant that does not use teams).

Along with the variation produced by team systems, there is wide variation across assembly plants in the role that workers play in business decisions. The team work organization is part of a deepening worker involvement in business decisions. Yet, in many other ways not directly linked to teams per se, the role of workers and union officials in plant operations also varies widely. In broad terms, there is a blurring of the roles that workers and managers exercise in the plants, for example, when workers serve on a task force to solve a specific production problem, or when workers become part of in-sourcing, quality, scrap, and the many other types of joint committees that are now typically a key part of each plant's administrative structure. In some Big Three assembly plants, union officers meet regularly with plant managers as busi-

ness issues or crises arise; in a few cases, this participation extends to involvement in the preparation of a plant's long-term business plans.

The broader involvement of workers and union officers in plant affairs has been spurred by a decentralization within the ranks of management. As the negotiation of work-practice change has intensified at the plant level and in the face of wide plant-level (and within-plant) variations resulting from these negotiations, the influence of plant-level industrial relations or employee relations managers in unionized settings has increased relative to their corporate counterparts. In addition, the involvement of operating managers (such as production managers or production superintendents) in employee relations matters has increased in part through the reduced role that the formal grievance procedure is playing in conflict resolution and the increasing role of informal discussions between operating managers and workers (and union officers). Some of these discussions arise out of the natural operation of teams, whereas others occur through the broader roles workers are playing in problem-solving forums or through the activities of the various joint committees operating on the shop floor.

In some plants, a formal "area" management structure is spurring the decentralization of industrial relations down to the shop floor. Typically, three or four key operational areas are designated, and reporting lines are adjusted to fit these areas rather than the traditional plant hierarchy. In the traditional management structure, labor-relations staff report upward to the plant industrial relations (or personnel) director, not to an operating manager. In an area management structure, in contrast, the employee relations support staff report directly to an area operating manager and report in a matrix manner to an employee relations (or industrial relations) director. Area management represents a business-unit style of operation at the plant level and is intended to bring to the work area an awareness of and responsiveness to cost and profit pressures. This concept, used in plants such as Chrysler's Jefferson Avenue assembly plant, is leading to a reorganization of the employee relations function within management as well as a broader involvement of workers and union officers in plant operations.

The purpose of area management is to have the operations leaders of the work area take on more direct responsibility for employee relations and also have the employee relations staff learn about and respond more directly to area business needs. In the process, the staff function of industrial relations is being shifted downward inside the plant and is also being diffused to operating managers, who traditionally did not get directly involved in employee relations matters.

With this shift to area management and other more informal changes, management faces such human resource issues as how to reshape reporting and training lines accordingly. For instance, the career development of in-

dustrial relations staff (and that of operating managers) has to be reshaped to accommodate the requirement that industrial relations staff interact more extensively with operating managers and less often with higher-level staff within their functional area.

The most extensive decentralization of employment relations in a Big Three assembly plant (and perhaps the most extensive anywhere) has occurred at the Saturn Corporation. Notably, this decentralization has led to extensive involvement by workers and union representatives in business issues at Saturn.[32] The organizational structure of Saturn includes committees with worker or union representation (Rubenstein, Bennett, and Kochan 1993). At the shop-floor level, there are work units made up of between six to fifteen workers and a single production-worker classification. Work units participate as a problem-solving group and make decisions concerning job assignments, job rotation, overtime, and recruitment. Workers perform a variety of job tasks in their work area and also perform some of the planning and control tasks traditionally carried out by supervisors. At the top level of Saturn is a strategic advisory committee that engages in long-run business planning and includes the president of the UAW local.

One of the most novel aspects of shop-floor industrial relations at Saturn derives from the lack of a local seniority agreement in the UAW contract governing the Saturn complex. Thus, there is no formal role for seniority in matters such as job assignments, job bidding, overtime, and shift assignments. Most of these decisions are made informally by the work units (i.e., by workers themselves). Perhaps most revolutionary is the presence of union and management "partners" who co-manage decisions within the Saturn complex. Although the union does not have a formal place on the GM board of directors, which makes the ultimate decisions concerning Saturn's investments, products, and pricing, the strong role played by union partners at Saturn gives the union a level of involvement in decision making that is unparalleled in contemporary American industrial relations. This is not to say that Saturn has been free of labor-management conflict. In the summer of 1998, uncertain about the future of Saturn and upset with GM management's behavior, workers at Saturn voted to authorize a strike, although the parties eventually were able to settle their differences without striking and renewed their commitments to Saturn's joint decision-making structure (Bureau of National Affairs 1998a). Then, in February 1999 the long-standing head of the local union at Saturn, Michael Bennett, and his supporters were defeated by a slate favoring a more traditional approach to labor relations.

Even in the face of its uncertain future, Saturn continues to provide an extreme example of the work practices employed in the joint team-based approach. Compared to Saturn, most auto plants (and plants in other industries as well) have less dramatically meshed worker and manager roles.

At the same time, the existence of Saturn, and the fact that other plants have in their own ways restructured work and labor and management roles along related lines, adds to the rich variety across joint team-based plants.

Technology, managers' efforts to preserve their own role and control, and other factors still constrain the options available to workers and unions. Nevertheless, the spread of teams and other forms of participatory work reorganization are significantly increasing the variation in work practices, particularly where teams and the like are being linked to a decentralization within management structures.

## BOUNDARIES OF THE "INTERNAL" AND "INDEPENDENT" AUTO PARTS SECTOR

Variation in employment relations has increased in the auto-parts sector in a manner generally similar to developments in the assembly sector. At the same time, there are differences in these two sectors due in part to the timing and intensity of nonunion employment growth. The "internal" parts operations of GM, Ford, and Chrysler are the largest producers in the auto parts industry, accounting for approximately 60 percent of shipments in motor vehicle parts and accessories. The internal parts plants follow the same bargaining structure as the assembly plants, and nearly all are covered by the master company agreements negotiated between the Big Three and the UAW.[33] Since they are covered by company-wide collective bargaining agreements, wage rates and fringe benefits at the internal parts plants are identical to those at Big Three assembly plants.

In recent years, Big Three company negotiators have frequently complained about the competitive pressures confronting the internal parts plants and have sought to create separate lower-tier pay rates for the internal parts operations. The UAW has successfully resisted these demands, but the union has been less successful in constraining the outsourcing of parts production and the negotiation of work-rule concessions. In line with the Big Three–UAW bargaining structure, there are separate local (often plant) agreements at the internal parts operations, and from the early 1980s on, there were major concessions negotiated in work practices at the internal parts plants.

Now that some of these plants use teams, substantial variation has appeared in work practices. The form of the teams and other methods of worker and union involvement in decision making also vary enormously across these plants. The major changes in work practices are due to the enormous bargaining leverage management gained in the supplier sector owing to outsourcing opportunities; alternative suppliers, moreover, are often nonunion, with compensation that is significantly below that in internal parts plants.

### Declining Unionization of Independent Auto Suppliers

Because the growth of nonunion competition has become so significant in the auto parts industry, it is worth examining how this growth has occurred. The "independent" parts companies, that is, companies producing auto parts but not assembling those parts into final vehicles, were heavily although never completely organized, and this lagged behind the unionization of the Big Three.[34] The percentage of the supplier plants with a majority of workers covered by a collective bargaining agreement rose from 50–55 percent in 1940 to 95 percent in 1957, and unionization then produced a substantial rise in the earnings of organized workers. Mean earnings in the supplier firms relative to earnings in assembly firms rose from 87.5 percent to 95.3 percent from 1940 to 1957 (Katz 1987).

Union coverage in the independent parts plants fell substantially from the mid-1970s on, as is illustrated by Table 2.3. The fall in unionization was a major cause of the decline in the earnings of workers in the independent parts firms relative to the earnings of workers in auto assembly plants (see

**Table 2.3.** Unionized Workforce in the U.S. Auto Parts Industry (in %)

| Estimates for Independent Parts Establishments in BLS Industry Wage Surveys | | | |
|---|---|---|---|
| 1963 | 1974 | 1983 | 1989 |
| 82 | 80–84 | 58 | 56 |

| Estimates Using UAW Membership and SIC Employment Figures for Non-Big Three Parts Plants | | | | |
|---|---|---|---|---|
| 1976–1978 | 1979–1981 | 1982–1984 | 1985–1987 | 1988–1990 |
| 60 | 56 | 40 | 27 | 23 |

| CPS Estimates for Auto Parts Excluding Big 3 | | | | | | |
|---|---|---|---|---|---|---|
| 1983 | 1984 | 1985 | 1986 | 1987 | 1988 | 1989 |
| 20 | 26 | 20 | 21 | 15 | 21 | 18 |

*Source:* "The North American Auto Industry at the Onset of Continental Free Trade Negotiations," Economic Discussion Paper 38, U.S. Department of Labor, Bureau of International Affairs, July 1991, Table 22.

**Table 2.4.** Worker Earnings in the U.S. Auto Parts Industry Relative to Auto Assembly Plant Earnings

| | Average Hourly Earnings in Independent Parts Suppliers as a Percentage of Earnings in Auto Assembly Firms | | | | |
|---|---|---|---|---|---|
| | 1957 | 1963 | 1974 | 1983 | 1989 |
| | 95 | 89 | 78 | 68 | N.A. |

| | Relative Hourly Earnings by Size of Establishment | | | | |
|---|---|---|---|---|---|
| | 1957 | 1963 | 1974 | 1983 | 1989 |
| 50–499 workers | 86 | 77 | 67 | 62 | 56 |
| 500 or more workers | N.A. | 97 | 85 | 75 | 66 |
| 1000 or more workers | 99 | 101 | 94 | N.A. | N.A. |

*Source:* Figures are from BLS industry wage surveys, reported in "The North American Auto Industry at the Onset of Continental Free Trade Negotiations," Economic Discussion Paper 38, U.S. Department of Labor, Bureau of International Affairs, July 1991, Table 24.

Table 2.4). Relative earnings declines occurred earlier and have been much greater in small firms. These earnings declines are probably linked to the particularly large unionization declines in small auto supplier firms. Many of the small parts firms pursued an employment relations strategy that entailed either low-wage or bureaucratic nonunion employment practices (described more fully later in this chapter).

The push for concessions at the independent parts firms from the early 1980s on was exacerbated by all the same pressures that were impinging on the auto assemblers; these firms also lacked the financial resources of the assemblers and faced more low-wage domestic nonunion competition. Even in the light of common pressures, substantial diversity emerged in the employment relations strategies pursued by independent parts firms, a diversity influenced by business and union strategies and the degree to which new investments, or the lack thereof, gave management an interest in work reorganization or bargaining leverage.

### Earnings Variation across Independent Parts Firms

Negotiation outcomes at the Budd and Dana Corporations illustrate how the independent suppliers pulled away from the Big Three–UAW pattern and the cross-company variations created by this process. The UAW has been the dominant union at these companies since the later 1940s, although a growing fraction of these companies' plants operate on a nonunion basis.[35] In their unionized plants over the post–World War II period, Budd and Dana followed the pattern-setting agreements at GM and Ford through the 1979 negotiations. Then in 1982, both supplier firms negotiated concessionary agreements with the UAW, and some of these concessions went beyond those negotiated at GM and Ford in the spring of 1982. For example, at Dana, COLA increases scheduled after March 1982 were eliminated (and had been only deferred at GM and Ford). The 1982 Dana contract also did not include the new guaranteed income stream benefits negotiated at GM and Ford.

From 1983 to 1985, the contracts negotiated at Budd and Dana included deeper concessions than the agreements negotiated at the Big Three and also differed from one another in the timing and manner of these concessions. The 1982 concessionary contract at Dana was of shorter duration than the 1982 GM and Ford agreements, which enabled Dana in 1983 to negotiate an agreement that differed from the assemblers' pattern. Even though by 1983, employment at Dana had recovered to previous levels, the company was able to negotiate a contract that included unique features and overall was less favorable than the agreements negotiated at Chrysler in 1983, and at GM and Ford in 1984. A Dana official stated that the firm had "drifted away from the automotive-type market" and that it is "probably more appropriate that we strike out on our own" (Bureau of National Affairs 1983).

At Budd, employment continued to decline after 1983. In response to this economic pressure, Budd contracts with the UAW in 1985 included additional concessions and did not follow the 1984 pattern-setting agreements at GM and Ford. The 1985 Budd-UAW contract eliminated three quarters of COLA increases, had lower pension increases and no improvement in supplementary unemployment benefit funds, and did not include the training and job bank programs initiated at GM and Ford.

In 1987 and then again in 1991, Budd further differentiated itself from the Big Three by negotiating a four-year agreement with lump-sum and base-pay increases that were 1–2 percent per year lower than the terms of the Big Three contracts. In addition, the 1987–1991 and 1991–1995 contracts at Budd included concessions on retiree benefits that lowered these benefits below those of the Big Three. Profit sharing never has been included in either the Budd or Dana contracts—another important way in which these contracts differed from the Big Three settlements.

Recent UAW labor contracts at Budd and Dana differ from one another and from the UAW's contracts with the Big Three. In October 1995, the UAW and Budd negotiated a new five-year contract (in contrast to the continuing three-year agreements negotiated at the Big Three). The Budd agreement provides an initial 3 percent base-wage increase (and a $500 signing bonus); 2 percent lump-sum payments in the second and third years of the contract; and 3 percent lump-sum payments in the fourth and fifth year of the contract (Bureau of National Affairs 1995a: D-12).

In contrast, the Dana Corporation and the UAW in January 1996 negotiated a new three-year labor contract (Bureau of National Affairs 1996a: D-11). This agreement provides a 3 percent lump-sum payment as a signing bonus; a lump-sum payment of 2.5 percent in the second year; and a base pay increase of 2 percent in the third year of the contract. The Budd and Dana contracts also differed in terms of fringe benefits and noncompensation matters.

Thus, the trend from the late 1980s on was for independent auto supplier companies to gain deeper pay concessions than those being negotiated at the Big Three companies. In addition, important differences appeared across the independent suppliers in the pay and fringe-benefit concessions they each gained.

### Work-Practice Variation in the Independent Parts Plants

Corporate strategy and the extent to which new (often nonunion) investments gave management an interest in work reorganization and bargaining leverage influenced work practices within independent auto parts companies in a manner similar to developments in the assembly sector. As a result, auto-supplier firms now have sizable cross-company and cross-plant variations in work practices and union-management relationships (where union representation persists).

The Magna Corporation, for example, aggressively opened a number of small nonunion plants in the 1980s, and these plants had work practices that fit the human resource management pattern (including team systems) (Walton, Cutcher-Gershenfeld, and McKersie 1994: 121). TRW used acquisitions and investments (and disinvestment) to gradually transform itself over the post–World War II period from a company with significant union representation to the current low level of union representation in its auto parts plants. In its nonunion plants, TRW uses team systems (and frequently pay-for-knowledge plans) along with other practices that fit the human resource management pattern. TRW's approach is noteworthy in the high degree of independence it grants to plant managers regarding work-practice implementation. This decentralized approach to employment relations at TRW helps isolate existing union operations from the growing nonunion operations in the company. At the company's union plants generally a traditional (arms-length) employment pattern has been maintained (Walton, Cutcher-Gershenfeld, and McKersie 1994: 133–34; Verma and Kochan 1985: 89–117).

A different corporate strategy toward work practices has appeared in the Budd Corporation's unionized auto parts plants that have been incrementally modifying their traditional work practices. These incremental modifications involve on-line and off-line quality circles and increased direct communication between management (particularly supervisors) and workers. Notably, this incrementalist approach is a less radical restructuring of work organization or worker roles. Yet, at the same time, Budd has been experimenting more aggressively with union avoidance in a greenfield nonunion plant in Kentucky that has a human resource management-type employment pattern. Adding to this diversity within Budd is the movement toward a joint team-based employment pattern at the company's Phoenix plant (a movement begun in the late 1980s) (Walton, Cutcher-Gershenfeld, and McKersie 1994: 151).

Within the auto parts sector, as in the assembly sector, the spread of joint team-based or HRM approaches varies across and within companies. Generally, management has found it easier to gain concessions in parts plants where employment has been declining or where they could make credible threats of further employment declines. Another similarity with developments in the assembly sector arises from the greater use of these workplace initiatives in new greenfield parts plants and a tendency for more incremental modification of labor relations in older brownfield parts sites.[36]

## UNION PROBLEMS WITH EARNINGS AND WORK-RULE VARIATION

For the UAW, the decentralization of collective bargaining and the associated elevation in the importance of local bargaining in the assembly and parts sectors makes it difficult to develop a unified national strategy with respect to work practices. The potential for whipsawing is particularly distressing for the union when plant closings are threatened. For example, when GM's December 1992 announcement of several plant closings left unclear which of two plants (Arlington or Willow Run) assembling large rear-wheel-drive vehicles would be closed, each plant undertook a campaign to convince the company to keep them open. This brazen pressure for local concessions infuriated the UAW and seriously strained relations with GM, while also creating severe conflicts between the workers and local unions in the threatened plants.

Variation has been spurred in local work-rule bargaining in part because management and union bargaining leverage across plants was a function of the degree to which the workforce faced previous or (threatened) future employment reductions. In addition, it was at the local level that labor and management were best able to experiment with new concepts. Furthermore, as was illustrated in the earlier discussion of team-leader selection procedures, for many work-rule issues there was no obviously superior national solution but rather a variety of solutions that fit particular local preferences and the detailed requirements of particular technologies or work processes.

Consequently, as the focus of collective bargaining has been shifting to the plant level, so has power within the national union, although this power shift has been both gradual and unsettling. Local union leaders do enjoy the greater authority and responsibility they gain along with the elevation in the importance and intensity of local bargaining. Yet, these role shifts can overwhelm local union officials who are suddenly being asked to evaluate financial statements and engage in long-term business planning.

While they enjoy the associated increase in authority, local union leaders still often look to the national union for guidance on how to respond to management initiatives. But the national offices of the UAW are not particularly well prepared to provide the coordinating role needed to protect and educate local union officers. The national offices of the union lack expertise in work restructuring, and it is difficult to redirect resources within shrinking union budgets (which have been declining along with employment and unionization). Moreover, national officers of the UAW have been reluctant to forcefully address local work restructuring issues because those issues are so controversial within the union, given the differences in opinion and interests that exist over teams and other work-rule issues among workers and union officers.

Moreover, given the long-standing dominance of the Reuther coalition within the national offices, the UAW does not have a tradition of active debate at the national level regarding workplace issues to draw on when it has been pressed to take positions regarding management initiatives.[37] Although the national company-wide collective bargaining agreements facilitate local workplace initiatives through the outsourcing, quality, or employment security-related local committees they authorize, the national union generally leaves it to local union officers to make policy regarding work restructuring. For example, the UAW has never adopted a formal position regarding team systems, in contrast to the German metalworking union (IG Metall), which developed and pushed a particular version of group work.

Even if the national officers of the UAW had wanted to alter the union's internal structure to respond to the demands of the more decentralized mode of collective bargaining, this would have been no simple matter. In the union's traditional administrative structure, the key individuals that serve as the liaison between the national offices of the UAW and the auto plants are the international servicing representatives (the "servicing reps"). The traditional role of the servicing reps is to monitor local bargaining so as to ensure that the local unions do not violate national standards and to communicate up from the plant when the locals, for example, seek the national union approval required to conduct a local strike.[38] As such, the traditional role of the servicing reps is largely to monitor local bargaining.

Given the greater involvement of plants in work-rule bargaining and business issues, however, it would have been advantageous for the servicing reps to shift to educating both local union officers and higher national union officials about the experimentation (including successes and failures) at the local level. But few servicing reps want to carry out such a new coordinating role in which they communicate information upward inside the union as frequently as they constrain wayward locals.[39] Such a coordinating role might put the international reps in the awkward position of seemingly criticizing national union policy when they find local practices that either do not fit with or work better than national policies. The role problems created for the servicing reps by the decentralization of bargaining and the resulting increased variation in plant-level bargaining illustrate how these pressures challenge traditional union administrative structures.

The result is that local branches of the UAW have ended up with a lot of discretion regarding workplace issues. This discretion is spurring experimentation and variety in local work-rule changes. Yet, the absence of forceful national coordination of work-rule bargaining also opens the door to managerial-led whipsawing in which plants are played off against one another in survival contests when excess capacity and production cutbacks shift bargaining power to management, as is illustrated by the Willow Run–Arlington competition (described above).

### PROBLEMS FOR MANAGEMENT FROM INCREASED VARIATION AND DECENTRALIZATION

Management typically initiates the workplace changes discussed in this chapter in an effort to improve costs, quality, and production flexibility in their plants. Data from assembly plants suggest that on average, Japanese-oriented work practices have led to improvements in production costs and product quality (MacDuffie 1995a). Yet, some U.S. assembly plants have attained relatively favorable production costs without resorting to such methods (Babson 1995b). These plants have retained many traditional work and industrial relations practices but have modified the practices incrementally by gradually increasing, through informal channels, the amount of worker (and union) involvement in plant operations. In some cases, increased worker input has come in these plants through the greater use of suggestion programs. In these "incrementalist" plants, job classifications have often been simplified and reduced, although not through the introduction of team methods. Cost improvements also have come in the incrementalist plants (as in the Japanese-oriented plants) through changes in management methods that reduce the number of parts and simplify the assembly process as well as through improvements in technology. (The same is true for plants that radically restructured work organization.)

The successes achieved in plants that adopted an incremental approach to work restructuring have created doubts within the ranks of both managers and union officers as to whether more extreme work-practice changes are necessary to maintain profitability and employment (Lee 1996). These doubts have been enhanced by the fact that more radical work practice reform efforts did not always work out well in the auto assembly sector. For example, the introduction of formal team systems in GM assembly plants in the early and mid-1980s led to declines, and not expected improvements, in productivity on average, even though a few assembly plants in GM had team systems that did substantially improve performance (Katz, Kochan, and Keefe 1987). The teams may not have been able to improve productivity in all cases because their plants did not always substantively increase worker involvement in decision making, and workers and unions in many plants resented having introduced teams in response to management's threats to otherwise close the plant. Incrementalism in changing employment relations also was promoted by the financial success of Ford in the late 1980s and Chrysler in the early 1990s, which seems to have stemmed primarily from successful product design, not from particularly successful work practices.[40]

Thus, managers and unionists were not convinced by the late 1990s that work-practice initiatives were essential for financial success, and they were confused about whether and how changes in work practices would affect economic performance. This confusion helps explain why there has been (and continues to be) so much variation in the initiatives being pushed by management. Given that corporate (and central union) officials are uncertain of the advantages of a particular work practice, the initiative for change is typically left to plant-level actors. This shifts the locus for change to the plant level.

Overall, management benefited greatly from the shift toward locally driven workplace initiatives because they led to lower costs and improved product quality, even despite confusion about the sources of improvements. Yet, when demand for Big Three products improved and capacity constraints tightened in the early 1990s, management at some plants lost its bargaining leverage, and localized bargaining turned back into a process of union-led whipsawing. This was well illustrated by events in the early and mid-1990s at GM, when the UAW conducted a series of strikes at parts plants. A strike at the Dayton brake plant of GM in the spring of 1996 led to the closure of nearly all of GM's assembly plants (Blumenstein and Christian 1996: A3). Then, a fifty-four-day strike in the summer of 1998 at two plants in Flint, Michigan, stopped production at GM. This strike escalated into a national confrontation after GM management initially refused to grant the sort of investment and employment guarantees that had been provided in previous local disputes, although GM eventually relented and did provide such guarantees as part of the settlement terms (Bradsher 1998).

The specific issue that precipitated each of these strikes varied, but the common thread of these local strikes was efforts by the UAW to acquire more extensive employment security guarantees at the plant level. The union had bargaining leverage usually because the plant was the sole supplier of a particular part or because of production pressures following strong market demand for a particular model. In the 1990s, the typical outcome of these strikes included the hiring of additional workers, explicit employment targets, and commitments for specific investments in machinery and capacity (Bureau of National Affairs 1996b: D6, and 1994: A12–15). These local agreements and pledges improved the limits on outsourcing and guaranteed minimum employment levels the UAW had gained in periodic company-wide contractual improvements (Bureau of National Affairs 1996c: D-3).

The round of local strikes at GM in the 1990s provide a clear illustration of the increasing importance of local issues concerning work organization and work practices. Local issues were more central to collective bargaining because it was at the plant level that productivity, product quality, and the extent to which the workforce was assured that it could continue working at a particular plant, were all determined. In the past, the UAW and one or another of the Big Three firms occasionally had long strikes concerning wages or fringe benefits during the negotiation of company-wide ("national") collective bargaining agreements, as in 1945, 1947, and 1970 (Katz 1985). The fifty-four-day strike in the summer of 1998 was the most telling illustration of how a local dispute, and not a company-wide contractual issue, could now halt production at GM and elsewhere.

GM management appeared to be surprised by how local disputes were producing costly production shutdowns. Yet, it should not have been surprising that the more decentralized structure emerging in the Big Three could be used by the UAW to its advantage when bargaining power shifted to the union's advantage. Management would have benefited by reflecting on the lessons provided in their own bargaining history, in particular, the way corporate officials had helped national offices of the UAW increase their influence over local negotiations in the first place (by acquiring the right to approve all local contracts in the early 1950s) (Katz 1985: 133). The round of local strikes at GM shows that even though management generally benefits from bargaining decentralization, management faces great difficulty in coordinating its interests in a more decentralized bargaining structure, a problem that is analogous to the issues that confront national unions, as discussed above.

Thus, even though it retains a relatively high level of unionization, especially in the assembly sector, the broad trends underway in employment relations in the auto industry are very similar to the trends in the U.S. economy. The same employment patterns are spreading in the auto industry as elsewhere in the U.S. economy. In addition, in the auto industry, as in other parts of the U.S. economy, the process of employment relations is becoming more informal and decentralized and includes the spread of practices such as contingent compensation.

Developments in the telecommunications industry, analyzed below, clarify the degree to which these commonalities extend to a service-oriented industry making use of advanced information technologies.

### RESTRUCTURING IN THE U.S. TELECOMMUNICATIONS INDUSTRY

As compared to the auto industry, the U.S. telecommunications industry has faced more limited international competition and does not confront Japanese transplants. Nevertheless, the variations in telecommunications employment relations are very similar to the auto industry.

The major pressure for change in employment relations in telecommunications over the past ten years came from industry restructuring and a steady stream of major technological innovations. Changes in employment relations include sizable employment contractions associated with corporate downsizing; the growth of a large, nonunion sector in an industry that historically had been heavily unionized; a decentralization in the locus of collective bargaining that has increased the variation in employment terms in the remaining unionized sector across and within firms; the growth of low-wage competition that has led to concessionary pressures on union standards; and uneven experimentation with new forms of work organization and employee and union involvement in decision making. The scale of corporate restructuring and technological changes heightened the pace and the extent of employment-related changes and makes the telecommunications industry a particularly noteworthy case.

The restructuring of the Bell system has been at the center of the changes in the U.S. telecommunications industry. As Jeffrey Keefe and Karen Boroff report, "Throughout the twentieth century the Bell System was the telephone industry, a public utility organized as a unified natural monopoly" (1994: 304), providing both local and long-distance services for most Americans. The key firms in the Bell system were AT&T Long Lines, provider of long-distance telephone services; the Bell Telephone Companies, spread throughout the country as providers of local telephone services; Western Electric, a subsidiary of AT&T that manufactured almost all the telephone equipment used by the Bell System; and Bell Laboratories, America's premier research laboratory with a research budget that surpassed the total research budget for the rest of U.S. industry (305).

Prior to being broken up through a divestiture demanded by the federal Justice Department in 1984, AT&T was the world's largest private employer, with more than 1 million employees.[41] At divestiture, the twenty-two Bell operating companies were split off from AT&T (the other main parts of the Bell system remained within AT&T) and reorganized into seven regional operating companies (RBOCs).[42] In the same time period, GTE was transforming itself into the "eighth RBOC" by merging with Contel (Keefe and Boroff 1994: 323).

After divestiture, AT&T underwent a series of corporate reorganizations and extensive downsizing. These changes and shifts in the composition of employment (described below) led to enormous declines in the number of unionized employees at AT&T. The cutbacks announced by AT&T in early 1996 were projected to reduce unionized employment at AT&T (including employment at the two firms split off from AT&T) down to eighty-two thousand, which is less than one third the number of unionized jobs at AT&T at divestiture (1984) (Batt and Keefe 1997: 52–54).

Much of the reduction in unionized employment at AT&T has occurred through involuntary layoffs. From 1984 to 1992, AT&T laid off 62,006 unionized employees, while another 45,285 unionized employees accepted voluntary severance offers, and an additional 25,709 unionized employees left through attrition (deaths, normal retirement, and quits) (Batt and Keefe 1997: 54). Employment reductions in recent years have also taken place at the U.S. RBOCs and at telecommunications firms in other countries, but only at AT&T did these reductions include involuntary layoffs (Katz 1997).

Although employment declined substantially, as of the late 1990s, AT&T retained a large share of the long-distance telephone service market; however, it faced intense competition from MCI (fiercely antiunion) and Sprint (largely nonunion). The RBOCs, in turn, were facing increasing pressure from new entrants, some of whom merely resold leased telephone lines and were advantaged by lower labor costs. Meanwhile, the expansion of cellular telecommunications services led to corporate restructuring (a number of the RBOCs teamed up or paired with a long-distance company to create cellular networks), and new services provided over either cable lines or the Internet loomed as potential major competitive challenges for telephone service providers.

### The Telecommunications Equipment Industry

The telephone equipment side of the industry has also experienced major changes. AT&T, in part through its Western Electric operations, has always been a major player in the U.S. and international telecommunications equipment businesses. In the 1990s, AT&T's leadership position in the U.S. and international telecommunications equipment sectors faced intensified competitive pressure from six other multinational firms: Northern Telecom (Canadian), Siemens (German), Alcatel (French), Ericsson (Swedish), NEC (Japanese), and Fujitsu (Japanese) (Keefe and Boroff 1994: 318). To enhance their ability to sell telecommunications equipment to competitors in the telephone services side of the business, in late 1995 AT&T announced that it would separate itself into three companies focused respectively on network services, equipment, and computers (with the latter primarily operations that previously had been acquired through AT&T's takeover of NCR). Shortly thereafter, plans were announced to reduce employment at these three companies by a combined seventy-five thousand employees, through either voluntary severance or layoffs.

### Divestiture and Telecommunications Collective Bargaining

The divestiture of AT&T has led to a decentralization of collective bargaining and subsequent increases in variation in the outcomes and processes of collective bargaining. This decentralization and variation arose as the RBOCs started pursuing a variety of business and employment relations strategies and the focus of employment relations in turn shifted downward within both AT&T and the RBOCs.

Decentralization occurred within a bargaining system that had by the early 1970s become very centralized. Responding to strong pressures from the Communication Workers of America (CWA) and AT&T's own interests in coordinating a national telephone system, the traditional collective bargaining structure involved a heavy role for the corporate officers of AT&T and national union officers. AT&T and its Bell operating companies bargained at two levels prior to divestiture. At the first level, called "national bargaining," Bell system-wide agreements were reached on wages, benefits, and employment security. At the second level of bargaining, "local bargaining," individual Bell operating companies bargained with local union leadership over work administration and work rules (Batt and Keefe 1997: 61–62).

A centralized bargaining structure fit with high levels of union representation in the Bell system and the strong influence of national-level officials within the respective telecommunications unions. In 1983, before divestiture, unions represented 55.5 percent of the entire workforce in the telecommunications industry, with nearly total representation of operators and field-service technicians (who install and repair equipment and maintain network phone lines) and heavy representation among customer service representatives (who handle billing, complaints, and service requests) (Batt and Strausser 1998). The two major unions representing telecommunications employees are the CWA and the International Brotherhood of Electrical Workers (IBEW), whose relationship with each other has oscillated between rivalry and cooperation over the post–World War II period. In contrast to most U.S. private-sector unions, many unionized employees in the telecommunications industry perform administrative and technical jobs, not manual labor.

The break-up of the Bell system is leading to increased variation in employment relations by fragmenting a formerly coordinated national administrative structure and by creating the preconditions for intense competition between AT&T and the RBOCs. Yet, even with divestiture, the CWA and IBEW might well have been able to more successfully limit the ensuing variation in employment relations if those unions had not confronted pressures emanating from the increasing nonunion employment in the telecommunications industry. This growth was in part a consequence of divestiture but also was driven by factors independent from the corporate reorganization of the Bell System.

### Growth of Nonunion Telecommunications Industry Employment

Nonunion employment has grown dramatically over the past ten years within AT&T and the RBOCs, and it grew even more sizably through the entry of new nonunion firms into the telecommunications industry. By 1996, unions represented only 28.7 percent of the workforce in the industry (whereas unionization was 55.5 percent in 1983) (Batt and Strausser 1998). Not all employees are eligible for coverage by the National Labor Relations Act. Of all "union eligible" employees in the telecommunications industry, 71.9 percent were union members in 1983; 45.7 percent were union members in 1996.[43] The scale and path of union membership decline differs across the various sectors of the telecommunications industry.

*Nonunion Long Distance Telephone Services Employment.* As AT&T reorganized and downsized, the level of unionization in the company dropped dramatically, and it is likely to drop even further as a result of AT&T's split-up into three companies. Some of the decline in union jobs occurred through AT&T's acquisition of nonunion businesses such as American Transtech (the largest U.S. telemarketing service) and AT&T Universal Card (the second-largest credit card company).[44] Increased managerial employment that stood outside the formal bargaining unit and simultaneous disproportionate declines in employment across the ranks of the CWA or IBEW-represented workforce has been another critical factor behind the decline in unionization in AT&T's services segment. Forty-seven percent of AT&T employees in 1990 were classified as either managerial or supervisory and thereby outside the jurisdiction of federal labor laws. This figure had stood at 29 percent in 1980 (Keefe and Boroff 1994: 331).

The opening of the long-distance market, a development spurred by judicial decree and the development of new technologies based on cellular, microwave, or computer-based transmission, paved the way for nonunion firms to enter this segment of the telecommunications industry. MCI emerged as AT&T's greatest long-distance rival. MCI has proved to be an intensely antiunion company, frequently moving its operations when a union drive surfaces and conducting intense campaigns opposing unionism where representation elections have been ordered.[45] For its nonmanagerial employees, MCI follows an employment-relations pattern based on low wages, with a high degree of temporary and subcontracted labor. As a result, MCI has historically experienced very high levels of employee turnover (Keefe and Boroff 1994: 335). MCI's nonunion strategy will be strengthened through its recent merger with the fiercely nonunion WorldCom.

Sprint has similarly aggressively resisted unionization in its long-distance operations and followed a low-wage employment strategy with heavy use of temporary, subcontracted, and other forms of contingent labor. Sprint did, however, acquire a significant body of union-represented employees when it merged with Centel, a sizable local independent telephone company (Keefe and Boroff 1994: 336).

*Nonunion Growth in the "Local" Telephone Service Sector.* The share of employment in the local telephone services sector that was unionized started declining in the early 1990s as nonunion competitors to the RBOCs began to chip away at their monopoly of local telephone service provision. This competition was particularly intense in large urban areas as small, nonunion telephone service firms began to either lease existing telephone lines, lay their own fiber-optic cable, or serve large corporate customers with other technologies. The corporate segment of the telephone service market is technologically the easiest segment to enter and historically has had relatively high profit margins. Examples of these nonunion new entrants include MFS and Teleport (later purchased by AT&T)[46] (Batt and Keefe 1997: 48).

The share of "occupational" employment that is unionized within the RBOCs began to fall in the early 1990s as these companies started to outsource various segments of their business to nonunion firms.[47] Many of the RBOCs, for example, started to subcontract production of their yellow pages (telephone listings and advertising) to nonunion subsidiaries or external firms.[48]

A particularly contentious issue that has arisen between the RBOCs and the CWA and IBEW is the union status of employees that lay the fiber-optic cable linking households to the trunk lines (which earlier had been changed over to fiber-optic cable). The RBOCs started to outsource (subcontract) this work to lower-wage nonunion firms in the early 1990s, and then the CWA and IBEW pushed to bring this work back in house. A variety of bargaining outcomes have followed across the RBOCs concerning this matter. At Bell Atlantic, this issue was at the center of the bargaining impasse reached with the CWA in 1995, after the IBEW had agreed to a lower rate of pay for crews that would perform cable-laying work in one geographic region of Bell Atlantic on terms that were unacceptable to the CWA, which represented the same type of employees in other regions of Bell Atlantic. At BellSouth, the cable-laying work was first outsourced and then brought back in house after the CWA had proved to the company that it could carry out the work cost effectively.

The downsizing of union-represented employees at the RBOCs has not included involuntary layoffs but rather has been accomplished through early retirements and other voluntary severance that has been spurred by enhanced retirement or severance benefits.[49] Furthermore, aggressive downsizing was initiated later at the RBOCs than at AT&T (starting in earnest in 1994 at the RBOCs). Nevertheless, the downsizing of the RBOCs weakened the CWA and IBEW by, among other things, reducing the unions' dues-paying membership.

### Growth of Nonunion Employment
### in the Telecommunications Equipment Industry

Leading competitors to AT&T in the U.S. telecommunications equipment industry are Northern Telecom and Siemens, two large multinational corporations respectively based in Canada and Germany. Although the blue-collar forces within both these companies in their home countries are represented by unions, in the United States both companies operate largely nonunion. Northern Telecom was once recognized for its positive labor-management relations in Canada, but in the United States it has been pursuing an aggressive union-avoidance strategy. Northern Telecom opened new plants in the United States (often in the South or in rural areas) on a nonunion basis, often using a low-wage employment strategy in those plants or, in a few cases, previously acquired unionized facilities. In the late 1970s and 1980s, through decertification election procedures bolstered by extensive union-avoidance campaigns, Northern Telecom eliminated union representation in several of its U.S. plants (Keefe and Boroff 1994: 333–34).

The telecommunications equipment industry increasingly has been shifting to the provision of computer or information services. The professional or technical employees who carry out such work in the United States have very low levels of unionization outside AT&T and the RBOCs. Thus, the fastest growth in telecommunications equipment employment is occurring in industry segments where unions have little representation and little hope for future success at organizing.

*Unionization and Wage Trends in the U.S. Telecommunications Industry*

The net effect of the trends discussed above is a substantial and continuing decline in unionized employment in the U.S. telecommunications industry. Total employment in the industry fell only slightly from 1,153,476 in 1980 to 1,126,450 in 1996, but these declines are small compared to the declines in the number of unionized jobs.[50]

Just as the telecommunications industry's relatively high levels of unionization prior to divestiture of the Bell system contributed to the relatively low levels of income inequality found in the telecommunications industry as compared to other U.S. industries, clearly, declining unionization was a key cause of the extensive income inequality that has been appearing in the telecommunications industry in recent years. Furthermore, income inequality grew even more in the telecommunications industry than it did in the U.S. economy as a whole. Among clerical workers in the telecommunications industry, from 1983 to 1996, wage inequality rose by 25.5 percent, compared to a 7.5 percent growth in income inequality among all clerical workers in the United States.[51] By 1996, the ratio of the earnings of clerical workers at the 90th and 10th percentiles in the earnings distribution was 2.75, close to the 2.95 ratio for all clerical workers in the United States. (Note that the 90/10 ratio had stood at 2.19 in the telecommunications industry in 1983.) For telecommunications sales workers, wage inequality increased by 44 percent from 1983 to 1996. By 1996, the 90/10 wage ratio for sales workers in telecommunications was 5.58, higher than the comparable ratio for sales workers in the United States as a whole. (In 1983, the 90/10 for telecommunications sales workers had stood at 3.88, far below the comparable ratio of 4.67 for all U.S. sales workers.)

Growing unionization contributed to low real-wage growth as well as to growing income inequality. For example, the median real weekly earnings of nonunion clerical and sales telecommunications workers fell by 19.8 percent from 1983 to 1996, while over the same period the real median weekly earnings of nonunion technical telecommunications workers fell by 11.9 percent. It is telling that even in the face of an alleged shortage for highly skilled technical employees, the real weekly earnings of nonunion technical telecommunications workers at the 90th percentile of the earnings distribution fell by 6.9 percent from 1983 to 1996.

There has been much discussion of the possibility that cable television companies will begin to provide telephone services, a possibility heightened by passage of the Telecommunications Act of 1996. Although some local cable TV companies are unionized, only about 5 percent of eligible cable workers are union members (Batt and Keefe 1997: 55). So if the RBOCS (or AT&T) lose out to the cable companies as technological advances and regulatory changes allow the provision of telephone and television services over the same transmission lines, this will speed the already rapid declines in union representation in the telecommunications industry.

### Employment-Relations Variation in Unionized Telecommunications Firms

In the unionized parts of the telecommunication industry, the extent of variation in employment relations has increased dramatically since the divestiture of AT&T. One contributing factor is the shift away from the highly centralized bargaining structure that had traditionally maintained a high degree of similarity in the terms of collective bargaining agreements at AT&T and the RBOCs. Cross-company variation in business strategies, as well as corporate variation in strategies toward employee relations and differences in the tenor of the labor-management relationship, helped produce variety in the employment relations strategies pursued by AT&T and the RBOCs after divestiture. Post-divestiture variations in the business strategies pursued by the RBOCs include differences in the extent to which each company has been subcontracting or downsizing, and the RBOCs also differ in the extent to which they have been expanding internationally.

Increased variety also is appearing across the various businesses within each of the unionized telecommunications companies, in part as a result of the movement toward more decentralized organizational structures that seek to introduce a profit-center orientation. Wide variation exists also in the extent to which low-wage, alternative suppliers or subcontractors are available (or utilized) as suppliers of the services or equipment traditionally produced by the respective unionized firms.

Employment relations also are becoming more decentralized and more variable inside AT&T and the RBOCs since the adoption of managerial workplace initiatives that, at least in broad terms, bear many similarities to initiatives being implemented in the U.S. auto industry. As in the auto industry, these managerial initiatives shift the focus of employment relations to the shop floor through the use of team systems and other mechanisms to increase workforce involvement in business decisions. Variation has been increasing between and within the unionized telecommunications companies through several different channels.

*Weakening of Pattern Bargaining between AT&T and the RBOCs.* As described earlier, in the early 1970s the Bell system adopted a coordinated two-tiered bargaining structure in which wages, fringe benefits, and employment security issues were set at the national level. As Rosemary Batt and Jeffrey Keefe (1997) note, "As a result, a telephone technician working in New York City received the same relative wage increases whether he or she worked for the local operating company, New York Telephone, or AT&T. . . . In a similar manner, vacations, pension benefits, health care coverage, and insurance benefits became more standardized across the System, regardless of the employing Bell Operating Company" (61). After divestiture, the CWA failed in its efforts to retain national bargaining but was more successful at continuing company-wide bargaining over wages, fringe benefits, and employment security (and other key issues) within AT&T and the RBOCs.

The CWA and IBEW pressed hard to retain pattern bargaining between AT&T and the RBOCs in the company-wide bargaining that occurred in 1986, 1989, 1992, 1995, and 1998. The unions were most successful at retaining similarity in the level of wage increases, although even here, some differences appeared in the increases provided each year.[52] For example, in 1994, the base wage increases ranged between 1.68 percent at BellSouth to 3.9 percent at AT&T, and wage increases at Southwestern Bell were provided on a dollar per hour, and not percentage, basis. Over the life of the 1998–2001 contracts, base increases vary very little, although there is some variation in the timing of annual increases.

More sizable differences appeared across AT&T and RBOC contract settlements after 1986 with regard to the COLA clause and the component of the pay package that is provided on a contingent basis. Many of the RBOC collective-bargaining agreements include contingent pay through profit-sharing plans or team awards. AT&T has been providing stock shares but the NYNEX contract did not include any such contingent component, reflecting the opposition within the regional offices of the CWA in the NYNEX jurisdiction to contingent pay.[53]

In its 1998–2001 contract, AT&T extended the use of contingent compensation by introducing a new "performance award" for union members based on the same business-success measures used in a similar program for managers. Union-represented workers will get bonuses if AT&T meets certain targets for earnings per share, revenue growth, and reductions in selling, general, and administrative costs (Bureau of National Affairs 1998b: A-11).

There also have been significant differences across the companies in the contractual health-care provisions concerning matters such as whether and the extent to which second opinions or managed care are required, and the degree, if any, to which retired workers have had to co-pay for health coverage (Keefe and Boroff 1994: 350, 352). A bitter four-month strike occurred at NYNEX in 1989 over health insurance coverage, a strike largely won by the CWA and IBEW (Batt and Keefe 1997: 64).

In the area of employment security, perhaps the widest variation appears in the terms of the contracts AT&T and the RBOCs have with the CWA and IBEW.[54] Employment security has become a major issue in RBOC and AT&T collective bargaining as a result of the sizable downsizing at all of these companies and because of declining union membership. The variation that appeared in the 1995–1998 employment security clauses at NYNEX, Ameritech, and BellSouth illustrate the variation appearing regarding this subject. At NYNEX, extensive joint-training options were provided along with early retirement and pension enhancements. While the latter were common to agreements reached at the other companies, the amounts tended to be smaller than those provided in the NYNEX contracts, and the form of these benefits varied much. Ameritech was distinguished by the negotiation of "hometown" area transfer opportunities, while the BellSouth agreement included a novel clause extending CWA jurisdiction over "buried cable" work (Communications Workers of America 1995).

A particularly contentious labor-management issue are the differences that exist across AT&T and the various RBOCs in the language in their labor agreements concerning union recognition and the procedures for employees in unorganized facilities to gain union recognition. The CWA and IBEW strongly prefer that card check recognition be available to all unorganized workers, which avoids the need for representation elections by authorizing union representation if a majority of employees sign cards expressing a desire for representation. The unions are particularly anxious to gain card check in the new lines of business that are being formed within the telecommunications companies, including their cellular operations. This issue is especially important in light of the active pace of mergers occurring in the telecommunication industry, which has led to the acquisition of previously unorganized firms, such as Teleport, by traditionally organized telecommunications firms (in Teleport's case by AT&T) and the limited success of unions in expanding their representation through the normal election procedures. Among the telecommunications companies, SBC has the most liberal card check rights.[55] The procedures vary across the other companies, with AT&T agreeing to a form of speedy elections with arbitrator oversight in its 1998–2001 contract with the CWA and the IBEW (Bureau of National Affairs 1998: A-11).

### Within-Company Variation in Unionized Employment Relations: Workplace Initiatives at BellSouth

The evolution of participatory processes at BellSouth, one of the RBOCs, illustrates both the depth of the experimentation with worker involvement in the unionized telecommunications industry and the wide variation in work organization appearing within a single company.[56] BellSouth has experimented with two approaches to employee involvement. One entails participatory management through a total quality management (TQM) program. The other involves self-directed work teams. As Batt (1995a) notes, "Differences in the two (approaches) center on the extent to which firm decentralize decision-making to middle and lower level managers versus front line workers to achieve enhanced competitiveness in customer service delivery" (6). While under participatory management, lower- and middle-level managers retain decision-making authority with respect to customer service; the self-directed teams involve few lower and middle managers and shift many of their responsibilities to front-line employees.

Service areas doing comparable tasks at BellSouth vary greatly in terms of their use of and approach to employee involvement. Batt's (1995a) survey reveals that as of 1995, 12 percent of BellSouth's employees had participated in a quality action team or other problem-solving team (parts of the TQM program), while 5 percent of the workforce in network and customer services were participating in self-directed teams. Her research shows significant variation in the nature of self-directed teams (and in the performance of these teams) in the network versus customer service areas. She also shows that in the face of downsizing, from 1996 on, many of these participatory initiatives waned at Bell South. Although not as well documented, there was evidence of related developments in other telecommunications companies (Batt 1995b).

INCREASED INCOME INEQUALITY IN THE UNITED STATES

Pay is perhaps the most important employment outcome, and here there is clear evidence of growing income variation in the United States. Increased variation has been particularly apparent in income distribution trends. After 1979, there was a "sharp acceleration in the growth of earnings inequality, particularly among men" (Levy and Murname 1992: 1333). Although increasing income inequality is a trend common to many countries, the increase is particularly large in the United States. Evidence is accumulating showing that a mixture of market and institutional factors (most important, the low level of unionization and decentralized structure of collective bargaining) have caused income inequality to rise and help explain why the rise in equality is so large in the United States (Blau and Kahn 1996; Freeman and Katz 1995).

As Richard Freeman and Lawrence Katz (1995) note in their review of income trends in OECD countries, "Only in the United States, however, has the rise in inequality associated with quite large declines in real wages for low-wage workers (even those in year-round, full-time employment)" (4). Blau and Kahn (1996) find that the relatively high wage variance and greater spread at the bottom of the wage distribution are particularly pronounced in the nonunion sector of the U.S. economy.[57] In our view, the relatively large growth in the low-wage employment pattern described in column 1 of Figure 1.1 is the source of a significant part of the wage distribution trends noted by Blau and Kahn and thus a key explanation of why U.S. income inequality has been growing relatively rapidly.

In addition to the scope of the inequality, another unusual feature of recent U.S. income trends is the fact that since 1970s, earnings inequality has increased steadily within groups defined by education, age, experience, and gender. Levy and Murname (1992) find that "growing differences in the wages paid by different firms to workers with the same measured characteristics play an important role in explaining the increases in within-group earnings inequality" (1368). In other words, individuals with the same demographic characteristics and other attributes that normally are associated with earnings similarities have been increasingly earning divergent amounts. Consequently, although some of the increased income inequality may well have been caused by growing differences in the earnings of members of different demographic groups, for example, differences in the earnings of the highly educated versus those with low levels of education or the earnings of young versus old workers, an explanation for increased income inequality must also account the growing income differences *within demographic groups*.

The increased use of contingent compensation procedures in both the union and nonunion sectors discussed earlier in this chapter likely is one of the mechanisms through which these growing differences have appeared across firms. Evidence of the role played by contingent compensation as a vehicle through which inequality has been expanded is provided in data showing a strengthening of the relationship between individual performance and pay. For example, data on pay increases associated with different levels of individual performance from Hay Associates show that "in 1989, the increase associated with the highest level of performance was 2.5 times larger that the increase associated with the lowest level. By 1993, that ratio had risen to a factor of four." (Cappelli 1995: 22–23). The elevation in the importance of performance-based pay and declines in union coverage and strength also may well have contributed heavily to the measured declines that have occurred in the returns to seniority experienced by employees that have stayed with the same employer in recent years (Chauvin 1994).

The evidence presented in this chapter suggests that increased variation in employment relations has made a sizable contribution to increased earnings inequality. Unions have traditionally served to standardize wages and other employment conditions within and across enterprises, and union decline very likely has contributed to earnings inequality by lessening union pressure for standardization.

The evidence mentioned above of higher variance and a greater spread at the bottom of earnings distributions in nonunion versus union sectors also suggests a direct link between the employment patterns described in Figure 1.1 and rising U.S. income inequality. In particular, the growth in low-wage employment practices in the United States likely has contributed to these characteristics in income distribution.

The detailed descriptions of changes in the auto and telecommunications industries discussed in this chapter also illustrate the numerous mechanisms through which increased variation in employment relations is appearing. If better statistics were available documenting the national distribution of work practices and employment relations, these data would probably also reveal growing variation and help explain the growing inequality evident in national income statistics.

SUMMARY

Variation in employment relations is increasing in the United States as a product of the growth in nonunion employment and the existence of a variety of union and nonunion employment patterns. The auto and telecommunications industries are distinguished by their high levels of union representation (which are declining) but not by the processes through which variation in employment relations is appearing. The breakdown of pattern bargaining across firms and industries in the union sector, and the spread of contingent forms of pay and associated greater reliance individualized rewards, are all contributing to increased variation in pay. These changes in pay practices have contributed to the unusually large increases in income inequality in the United States.

Although team systems have spread and operate as a critical part of the HRM and joint team-based patterns, more traditional forms of work organization continue in firms following the low-wage, bureaucratic, and New Deal employment patterns. Meanwhile, work-practices variation is being spurred by a decentralization in managerial and corporate structures. Management is eager to pursue this decentralization and link it to more direct involvement of the workforce in business decisions and new communication strategies. However, in union settings, when bargaining power has shifted back toward labor's advantage, decentralization has not so clearly worked to management's advantage. The labor movement has occasionally been able to use decentralized bargaining to whipsaw management; more often than not, union weakness has been both a precondition and consequence of collective bargaining decentralization. Decentralization, more direct management-employee communication, and increased employee (and union) involvement in business decisions all have contributed to the wide variation in work practices.

No one employment pattern is dominating in the United States, in part because management is unsure of the performance advantages of the various employment patterns. Management's indecisiveness has been fueled by the mixed objective evidence regarding performance effects and the seemingly close linkage between the effects of employment practices and business (and labor) strategies. What is most striking about U.S. developments is the wide variation appearing *within and across* employment patterns.

NOTES

1.  Differences between the union and nonunion sectors are highlighted in Kochan, Katz, and McKersie (1994).
2.  On the leveling effects of union compensation policies and practices, see Freeman (1980, 1982).
3.  Unions did grow in the public sector, particularly from the early 1960s to the mid-1970s. This growth included sizable representation of white-collar and professional-

sional employees, such as school teachers, social workers, and police officers (Burton and Thomason 1988).

4.    Other surveys have found less extensive use of team systems. For example, the 1994 EGW-NES national survey of establishments found that 12 percent of nonmanagerial workers participate in self-managed teams (National Center on the Educational Quality of the Workforce 1994: 3).

5.    An earlier (and more narrow) data set reported by Voos and Eaton (1992) find that the union sector used teams and participation processes more extensively than the nonunion sector.

6.    Topologies of industrial relations patterns with some similarities to this scheme are provided in Edwards (1979) and Fox (1974).

7.    This human resource management pattern developed in a few nonunion firms in the 1950s and had roots in earlier corporate policies of the 1920s (often labeled welfare capitalism) (Kochan, Katz, and McKersie 1994: 47–80).

8.    For example, see the history of personnel policies followed by Sears in Jacoby (1997).

9.    What we refer to as the Japanese-oriented work system has similarities with the "lean" work system described in Applebaum and Batt (1994: 33–37).

10.    For evidence on the role of the founding executives, see Foulkes (1980).

11.    For analysis of how these changes in bargaining structure were similar to the types of decentralization underway in other countries, see Katz (1993).

12.    Decentralization of collective bargaining began to occur earlier in some industries, as noted in Kochan, Katz, and McKersie (1994).

13.    The political functions served by pattern following in wage setting and the use of "wage rules" are discussed in Katz (1985: 27–29).

14.    Also see Kochan and Osterman (1994) for discussion of the factors leading to slow diffusion of work innovation in the United States.

15.    A large research literature (reviewed in Katz and Keefe 1992) examines the effects of changes in work organization on plant-level economic performance.

16.    The work practices in the German transplants are not clear at this time, because these plants have only recently begun production.

17.    Although the unionized Mitsubishi plant in Illinois is now solely owned by a Japanese company, it was at one time owned jointly by Mitsubishi and the Chrysler Corporation.

18.    These figures are the maximum hourly wage rates for production workers. When first hired, workers at the transplants and at Big Three auto plants receive lower hourly wage rates that are increased stepwise over time according to fixed schedules. The transplant figures cited in the text were collected at the respective plants during interviews, while the General Motors figures are reported in an unpublished wage series maintained by the UAW.

19.    The company has plans to shift to a bonus based on a combination of individual and plant performance, but Georgetown managers are hesitant to introduce individual variation into the bonus system. The latter was conveyed to Harry Katz in a personal communication with Paul Adler in March 1996.

20.    General Motors estimates that total (wage and fringe benefit) hourly costs at General Motors versus the Toyota and Honda transplants were, respectively, $44.23, $29.86, and $27.36 in 1994. These estimates are provided in an unpublished internal report of General Motors.

21.   In this system the grievance procedure with binding third-party arbitration serves as the end point of contract administration, although disputes concerning production standards, new job rates, and health and safety issues are not resolved through recourse to grievance arbitration. Rather, the union retains the right to strike over these matters.

22.   These concessions were negotiated in three rounds of bargaining conducted under pressure from the U.S. Congress, which had just agreed to provide Chrysler with loan guarantees.

23.   These figures are from an unpublished wage and COLA series maintained by the research department of the UAW.

24.   For a while, there were differences in the way profit sharing was calculated in the Big Three profit-sharing plans. Under pressure from the UAW, in response to pressures from disgruntled workers at GM, the profit-sharing formulas were standardized across the three companies.

25.   See Katz, Kochan, and Keefe (1987) for evidence regarding the problems GM had with the introduction of teams.

26.   Chrysler management also has been pushing "progressive operating agreements," which differ from the modern operating agreements in that these plants do not change work organization and worker and union roles as formally as MOA plants (MacDuffie 1997).

27.   See Milkman (1997) for developments at Linden.

28.   The GM Tarrytown and Arlington assembly plants use strict seniority to select hourly team leaders.

29.   In this procedure, seniority is the determining factor if candidates have equal assessment scores. The GM Lansing agreement outlines such a procedure.

30.   Disputes over team-leader selection have occurred at transplants such as the Ford-Mazda Flat Rock and Ford Dearborn plants (Babson 1995a).

31.   Time clocks and factory gate restrictions have been eliminated in a number of plants to convey a spirit of increased worker autonomy and responsibility.

32.   Saturn, a subsidiary of GM, is a complex of plants in Spring Hill, Tennessee.

33.   In a small percentage of Big Three auto parts plants, workers are represented by unions other than the UAW, such as the IUE or the IAM.

34.   The largest independent auto parts producing firms as of the mid-1990s are Borg Warner, Budd, TRW, and Rockwell International.

35.   At both Dana and Budd, union organizing drives at nonunion plants have sometimes been a source of much controversy. At one point, the Dana Corporation was ordered through a court injunction to follow the neutrality pledge it had signed with the UAW in 1976 in the aftermath of a union-organizing drive held in one of its plants in 1980. See Bureau of National Affairs (1982) and Rose and Suris (1996: A-3).

36.   These adjustments fit the pattern outlined in Katz and MacDuffie (1994: 205–8). Also see Cutcher-Gershenfeld and McHugh (1994) for evidence regarding the diversity in employment relations surfacing across auto suppliers.

37.   The UAW does have a tradition of vibrant debate at the local (often plant) level regarding work-rule issues. Candidates for local union offices often campaign for office on the basis of their views regarding work restructuring.

38.   According to the UAW's constitution, local unions are required to have the approval of the national union to conduct a local strike (Katz 1985: 33).

39. The reluctance of many servicing representatives to take on a new role has been revealed to us in informal interviews conducted with these representatives over the past ten years, although there are some exceptions to this pattern.

40. In the mid- and late 1980s, Ford benefited from the success of the Taurus, the Explorer, and strong-selling truck models, while Chrysler's success in the 1990 was driven in large part by the success of their minivan, the LH model, and various truck lines.

41. Jeffrey Keefe and Karen Boroff (1994: 305) note that "with $138 billion in assets, it (AT&T) was the wealthiest private institution in the world; its profits totaled $7.3 billion (annually), and it ranked first in corporate net income.... Its revenue amounted to almost 2% of U.S. GNP, and its investments accounted for over 9% of U.S. domestic investment. The local Bell companies provided over 80% of the U.S. local telephone service, while AT&T Long Lines handled over 95% of long-distance calls."

42. The RBOCs are Ameritech, BellSouth, Bell Atlantic, NYNEX, Pacific Bell, Southwestern Bell, and USWest.

43. These figures are derived from analysis of CPS data by Rose Batt and Michael Strausser.

44. Nonunion equipment firms were also being acquired by AT&T, as described below.

45. The only unionized division of MCI is Western Union International, represented by the Teamsters. This division had already been unionized at the time of its purchase from Xerox in 1982 (Keefe and Boroff 1994: 335).

46. Teleport was acquired by AT&T in 1998, and the future representation status of its employees remained unclear in light of the telecommunications unions' interest in organizing Teleport's employees and the new quick election procedures provided in AT&T's 1998–2001 collective-bargaining agreements. See our later discussion of the new contract language at AT&T.

47. Occupational employment refers to employees covered by the National Labor Relations Act and excludes managerial employees.

48. After Bell Atlantic purchased the nonunion National Telephone Directory corporation in 1993, the company began to shift work from its unionized yellow page subsidiary to this new entity (Spalter-Roth and Yoon 1995: 11).

49. A sizable number of middle-level managers were involuntarily laid off at the RBOCs as at AT&T (Batt and Keefe 1996).

50. These figures are the total number of employees in SIC 4813. Figures are from the Current Population Survey, various years.

51. This and other statistics about earnings distribution trends cited in this paragraph and the paragraph that follows are from Batt and Strausser 1998.

52. The annual base wage increases for 1986 to 1994 for AT&T and the RBOCS are listed in Keefe and Boroff (1994: 350).

53. In 1997, NYNEX merged with Bell Atlantic. Since the various parts of the merged companies continued to maintain separate labor contracts with the CWA and IBEW, below we refer to the "NYNEX" collective-bargaining agreements.

54. There were also significant differences in union security terms. In some of the RBOC contracts with the CWA or IBEW, the union is granted automatic accretion of certain jobs, or in other cases, management pledges neutrality in any future orga-

nizing campaigns that might occur in subsidiaries of the company. The terms and coverage of these union security clauses varies significantly across the RBOCs (see Communications Workers of America 1995).

55. Card check and other union representation rights were a key part of the settlement that ended a CWA-led strike against Bell Atlantic in August 1998 (Pristin 1998).

56. The following description of events at BellSouth draws heavily from Batt (1995a).

57. This result holds even after controlling for the influence of measured (i.e., human capital) characteristics (Blau and Kahn 1996).

# 3

# United Kingdom

The system of industrial relations in Britain has undergone a transformation during the past twenty years, though without resulting in a new, dominant model. The traditional arms-length and largely adversarial unionized model, which bounded employment practices for most of the postwar period, has declined substantially. Union membership and collective bargaining coverage hemorrhaged throughout the 1980s and 1990s, and a substantial expansion of nonunion employment followed. Even where a unionized model remained intact, multiemployer bargaining essentially disappeared; there has been a decentralization to the firm or establishment level; and a range of employment patterns are emerging.

Indeed, the form and nature of decentralization in Britain has been significant. Together with other institutional influences, such as radically altered labor laws and weak structures above the level of the workplace (including trade union organization), employment practices within individual firms are increasingly unbounded and insulated from external influences. This "isolated decentralization" has greatly facilitated growing employment variation in Britain.

In addition to growing nonunionism, a second source of variation has accompanied decentralization—a transformation of traditional employment patterns as firms have sought greater flexibility and improved productivity. New forms of work organization include teams, greater task and functional flexibility, and contingent pay systems. Nevertheless, while some firms have moved away from the traditional adversarial model and adopted a joint team-based approach with their unions or a human resource management

70

model, others have sought either nonunionized or weakly unionized work-places, where the emphasis has been increasingly placed on reduced costs and numerical flexibility.

The substantial restructuring of working practices and employment patterns has thus added variation among unionized companies, owing to programmatic differences in changes to traditional employment patterns. At the same time, the weakening of institutions has helped generate a correspondingly rapid inequality in earnings, even though real wages have continued to rise for workers throughout the income distribution. The United Kingdom has thus been like the United States in experiencing relatively rapid growth in both employment system variation and income inequality as compared to other countries. However, the institutional structure of industrial relations has undergone greater alteration than elsewhere.

## GENERAL INDUSTRIAL RELATIONS DEVELOPMENTS IN THE UNITED KINGDOM

Among the countries analyzed in this volume, the United Kingdom stands out historically because of the general absence of legal support for employment relations. Otto Kahn Freund (1959) described the British system of industrial relations as one of "collective laissez-faire." In this system, legislation played a passive role: rather than defined rights or obligations of employers and unions, statutory immunities exempted unions from the application of common law, which remained hostile to collective organization.  Furthermore, labor law did not establish general minimum standards (for example, of wages or hours), and the government intervened only to address such employment relations issues as health and safety, where collective bargaining was limited, or in low-paying industries, where voluntary collective bargaining had failed to take root and wages councils established minimum pay rates (Brown et al. 1997: 70).

This voluntarist tradition of collective bargaining also extended to contracts, which are generally not legally binding. However, voluntarism did not exclude the importance of the state's role, which was significant in supporting the principle of collective self-organization, even though it did not prescribe the form, level, or structure of collective bargaining (Brown et al. 1997). Labor strength rested on more than its market power, and indeed "throughout the twentieth century... the British state has provided crucial political resources for employers and trade unions.... Until the late 1960s the role of successive British governments was primarily seen in the encouragement of collective bargaining and the creation of bargaining institutions through direct pressure on unions and employers, and use of the public sector as a model 'good' employer" (Howell 1995: 164).

Most industry-level collective-bargaining institutions were, indeed, established as the result of government action and persuasion, and such multiemployer bargaining made it easier for unions both to gain and extend recognition. From the late 1960s to 1979, state concern with collective bargaining remained, though there was also direct encouragement of trade-union membership and strength. Among white-collar workers, for example, recognition was principally the response to direct or indirect government policies (Howell 1995; Bain and Price 1983).

Government policies therefore helped spread trade unionism and collective bargaining, and multiemployer agreements tended to cover basic rates of pay, terms and conditions, and dispute procedures. These external agreements thus tended to bound the extent of variation in Britain. Nevertheless, the absence of a juridified system of industrial relations, and the comparatively highly decentralized organization of unions, meant that the workplace has historically also played a significant role in defining employment relations. Indeed, the system of unpaid and voluntary trade-union representatives in the workplace (shop stewards) is particularly well developed in Britain.

The importance of shop stewards was reinforced by the use of piece-rate payment systems and workplace supplements which were negotiated and implemented locally. By the time the Royal Commission on Trade Unions and Employers' Associations (the Donovan Commission) reported on the state of Britain's industrial relations problems in 1968, an informal system of factory-level bargaining involving shop stewards was commonplace. The Donovan Commission concluded that this informal system co-existed alongside the formal system of industry-wide agreements. Consequently, by 1968 multiemployer bargaining was beginning to establish more of a safety net (affecting the pay of those earning the minimum), rather than setting the floor of basic rates for all workers, as in Germany or Sweden. Wage drift and a growing disparity with industry pay rates thus resulted (Sisson and Brown 1983; Gospel 1992).

The fragmentation and informality of local bargaining was further exacerbated by multiunionism within plants, with shop stewards negotiating for work groups; the predominance of custom and practice over written agreements; and the autonomy of shop stewards from their trade-union organization. Although variation therefore certainly existed, this remained strongly bounded, and the unionized system contained common practices and procedures. Furthermore, the evolution of the system throughout the 1970s accentuated these commonalities.

The 1970s witnessed a decline in piece-rate pay in favor of time-based methods with a reduced emphasis on the variable bonus element. Together with the effect of incomes policies, this tended to reduce informal and frag-mented bargaining, which became more centralized within the firm, while often remaining bound by basic conditions established in industry negotia-tions. Simultaneously, the shop-steward movement expanded very substan-tially, so that stewards were present in almost all unionized workplaces, the principal exceptions being small firms and areas of private-sector services.[1] Shop steward organizations became more formally integrated into union structures and, in many companies, were provided with facilities by man-agement, who took their lead from models of "good" industrial relations es-poused by the state and others, as well as from increased statutory rights for stewards (Terry 1983).

The workplace has played a key role in British industrial relations. De-spite the absence of formal agreements, the importance of custom and practice, the lack of statutory rights underpinning representation, and vari-ation in bargaining power over work organization, the British system also exhibited very common features. The traditional arms-length and adversar-ial model of unionism included shop-steward organizations that were per-vasive and, by 1979, had become more centralized, formal, and profes-sional. Indeed, "shop steward organizations appeared broadly similar wherever they were to be found.... In other words, [there had been a] 'con-vergence' in industrial relations practice across the manufacturing and pub-lic sectors" (Terry 1983: 71, 88). That is, despite the historical and com-parative importance of firm-level structures and processes in determining the shape and outcome of local bargaining (Edwards et al. 1992; Marsh 1992), common practices restricted the extent of variation and helped es-tablish a common model. Indeed, "every unionised firm seemed to practice a similar Donovised routine and to show no inkling of alternative ways of looking at industrial relations" (Dunn 1993: 178).

### Increasing Pressure on Unions

From the late 1970s on, both the formal and informal structures of em-ployment relations in the United Kingdom have experienced many of the same pressures as in other countries. Technological change aside, Brown et al. (1997) note a weakening of the labor market and a tightening of prod-uct markets: unemployment averaged 4 percent for the fifteen years before 1980 but rose to 9 percent for the next fifteen years; manufacturing im-ports, which had accounted for 26 percent of domestic demand in 1980, rose to 45 percent by 1995. These factors, combined with the decline of manufacturing employment from 31 percent to 18 percent between 1979 and 1997, have undoubtedly contributed to an erosion of the industrial power base of unions.

Along with these economic pressures, legislation initiated by successive Conservative governments since 1979 has also challenged the institutions of industrial relations. Paul Davies and Mark Freedland note that the "government saw no legitimate place for collective bargaining in the regulation of labour relations, except perhaps at enterprise level to help management achieve its goals" (1993: 657). The effect of legislative changes have been to end the tradition of collective laissez-faire and voluntarism, weaken trade union power and collective bargaining, help restore managerial prerogative, and contribute to the individualization of the employment relationship.

Among the changes to labor law, the restrictions on trade-union immunities under common law have been especially important: secondary action has been made illegal, thereby confining a dispute to the workplace with a grievance; the definition of a "trade dispute" that establishes issues about which unions can legally strike has been narrowed; an increasingly tightly regulated system of pre-strike ballots has been required, potentially within each workplace of a single employer; and unions have been made liable for unlawful industrial action. Beyond this, provisions for statutory union recognition, introduced in 1975, were removed. This has combined with restrictions on lawful industrial action to significantly constrain the ability of unions to obtain recognition, or to support claims at other workplaces or employers. Indeed, employers now have substantial latitude in determining the conditions of recognition, a practice that would be illegal in countries such as the United States or Germany.[2] Similarly, the effect of changes to industrial relations law has "facilitated the breakup of [multiemployer] industrial agreements by making it more difficult for trade unions to mount nationwide disputes" (Brown et al. 1997: 72).

The decollectivization strategy of the Conservative governments went further than legislation and, at least as important, included "the withdrawal of support for collective bargaining, union recognition, and full employment, all of which were crucial props to union strength" (Howell 1995: 167). Additional policies have included ending tripartite organizations, privatization, compulsory competitive tendering in the public sector, and, indeed, changing notions of what the public-sector model of a "good" employer meant. Together, these have helped end the presumption that collective bargaining was a more favored or legitimate form of industrial relations and have certainly facilitated alternative employment practices.

Thus, these factors not only weaken trade unions but also contribute to growing variation among organized and unorganized workers. Furthermore, employers are now even entitled to introduce individual (or "personal") contracts that specify different employment conditions and wages, a policy that can discriminate on grounds of union membership and even be used to actively encourage deunionization. Beyond this, legislation has also weakened the position of the unorganized. Thus, in 1980, Schedule 11 of the Employment Protection Act, which allowed collective agreements or "going rate" terms and conditions to be extended to unorganized workers (similar to provisions still existing in Germany), was abolished. Likewise, wages councils, which had set minimum pay on an industry-wide basis for unorganized workers, and historically covered 10–15 percent of the workforce, were first weakened and finally abolished in 1993, though a minimum wage was reintroduced by the Labour Government in April 1999.[3]

The new environment of harsher economic conditions, a changing composition of the workforce, legal changes, and government and union policies have combined with and facilitated a shift in managerial preferences and strategies. The cumulative effects have included substantial declines in union membership and recognition, an even greater decline in collective bargaining coverage and consequent growth of the nonunion sector, a growth in the individualization of pay and employment conditions throughout the economy, and significantly more variation in systems and outcomes of employment relations. This dramatic erosion of existing institutions has led John Purcell (1995) to conclude an "end of institutional industrial relations" in Britain.

### Declining Union Membership and Coverage

Although the weakly regulated system in Britain ultimately proved very fragile, both unionization and collective bargaining coverage appeared strong before 1979. During the 1970s, for example, there was a rise in union membership density and a broad strengthening and normalization of many union structures, including shop-steward organizations. Many large companies were also constrained by the predominance of multiemployer, industry-wide bargaining.

The decline in union membership and the corresponding growth in nonunionism, has been dramatic (Table 3.1). From a level of 41.3 percent in 1960, union density rose to 48.2 percent by 1970, and with legislative support it climbed further to its peak of 53 percent in 1979. It then dropped steeply to only 40 percent by 1990, and to only 30.2 percent by 1997. Total membership loss has been in excess of 5 million, or more than 40 percent, and levels are now at their lowest since 1945. This has contributed to a continuing trend of union mergers, and by 1997, some 82 per-

**Table 3.1.** Trade Union Membership (in 000s) and Density (in %)

| Year | Union Members (UK Total)[a] | Union Members in Employment in Great Britain (Certification Officer)[b] | Union Density (Certification Officer)[c] | Union Members in Employment in Great Britain (LFS)[d] | Union Density (LFS)[e] |
|---|---|---|---|---|---|
| 1960 | 9,835 | 8,852 | 41.3 | | |
| 1965 | 10,181 | 9,163 | 40.5 | | |
| 1970 | 11,178 | 10,060 | 48.2 | | |
| 1975 | 12,184 | 10,966 | 49.4 | | |
| 1980 | 13,289 | 11,960 | 52.9 | | |
| 1985 | 10,821 | 9,739 | 46.6 | | |
| 1990 | 9,947 | 8,952 | 40.0 | 8,854 | 38.1 |
| 1991 | 9,585 | | | 8,633 | 37.5 |
| 1992 | 9,048 | | | 7,999 | 35.8 |
| 1993 | 8,700 | | | 7,808 | 35.1 |
| 1994 | 8,278 | | | 7,553 | 33.6 |
| 1995 | 8,089 | | | 7,275 | 32.1 |
| 1996 | 7,935 | | | 7,215 | 31.3 |
| 1997 | | | | 7,117 | 30.2 |

[a] Total union membership in the United Kingdom (i.e., Great Britain and Northern Ireland) reported by unions to certification officer. Source: *Labour Market Trends* (various years) and Metcalf (1994).
[b] Certification officer figures, adjusted to include only union members currently employed in Great Britain (i.e., excluding unemployed, self-employed, and those in Northern Ireland). Source: Metcalf (1994: 127).
[c] Previous column divided by the employees in employment. Source: Metcalf (1994).
[d] Data from Labour Force Survey. Includes union members in current employment source in Great Britain only and is consistent (in inclusions, though not source) to Metcalf's adjusted certification officer figures. Source: Cully and Woodland (1998).
[e] Previous column, divided by employees in dependent employment. Source: Cully and Woodland (1998).

cent of members were concentrated in just seventeen unions. Membership declines have also been especially marked in traditional strongholds of unionism, including among male employees, manual employees, and production industry workers.[4] Indeed, union density in production industries is now comparable to that in service industries.

In the private sector, density in 1997 was only 20 percent, although it has remained stronger in the public sector, at 61 percent (Cully and Woodland 1998). The sharp decline in overall union membership, particularly in the private sector, has also resulted in substantial variation among industries. Density is particularly low in retail trade, hotels and restaurants, and construction, though highest in previously privatized industries such as electricity, gas, water, and communications.

Although there have been dramatic falls in union membership density in the United Kingdom since 1979, its relative ranking among OECD countries has changed little (Brown et al. 1997).[5] However, the falling membership density has been accompanied by a collapse of multiemployer bar-

**Table 3.2.** Employees Covered by Collective Bargaining in Britain (in %)

| Year | Total | Private Sector | Public Sector | Pay Fixed by MultiEmployer Bargaining |
|------|-------|----------------|---------------|----------------------------------------|
| 1961 | 67 |    |    | 45 |
| 1970 | 68 |    |    | 35 |
| 1978 | 70 |    |    | 30 |
| 1984 | 71 | 52 | 95 | 20 |
| 1990 | 54 | 41 | 78 | 10 |
| 1997 | 36 | 32 | 88 | NA |

*Sources:* For collective-bargaining coverage, see Milner (1995) from various sources (1961–1978); Workplace Industrial Relations Surveys (1984 and 1990) (see Millward et al. 1990), and *Labour Force Survey* (see Cully and Woodland 1998). For multiemployer bargaining, see Brown, Marginson, and Walsh (1995). The exact dates differ slightly.

*Notes:* The 1997 data from the Labour Force Survey used here represents collective-bargaining coverage in firms employing twenty-five or more employees. This allows greater comparability with the WIRS data, which excludes firms with fewer than twenty-five employees.

The decline in public sector collective bargaining coverage between 1984 and 1990 reflects the government's withdrawal of bargaining rights for nurses and teachers.

gaining and an even greater decline in collective-bargaining coverage, one larger than at any previous time. The predominance of collective pay settlements had emerged post-1945, when approximately 80 percent of employees were covered by either collective bargaining or statutory wage-setting machinery, such as wages councils (Milner 1995; Brown 1993). Of the firms engaging in collective bargaining, the majority reached agreements in a multiemployer framework.

However, a gradual erosion of this pattern of multiemployer bargaining began in the 1950s, and firms increasingly supplemented industry agreements at the plant level. This led to the development of a range of bargaining practices by 1968, and to the conclusion of the Donovan Commission that "two systems" of industrial relations co-existed side-by-side. Although the additional layer of substantial informal workplace bargaining created a variation in outcomes, these continued to be at least partly constrained by the existence of the formal multiemployer bargaining, and collective bargaining itself still dominated (see Table 3.2).

By the end of the 1970s, more than 70 percent of the workforce had their pay directly influenced by collectively bargained procedures. When wage councils are included, fewer than 20 percent of the workforce had their pay set unilaterally by employers. The strengthening of the collective-bargaining system thus occurred despite the shift of emphasis from multiemployer to firm-level bargaining.

The nature, extent, and pace of change did, however, alter dramatically during the 1980s and 1990s. Coverage in the increasingly decentralized bargaining structures now does not extend much beyond union members and is lower than in the 1930s. When the declines during the 1990s are combined with the abolition of the wages councils in 1993, collective pay-setting machinery affects the pay and conditions of fewer workers than perhaps even in the 1920s (see also Milner 1995: 69). The implication has been that "the rise of nonunionism over the last 15 years is even more marked than the haemorrhaging of union membership...previously suggested" (Milner 1995: 87).

Table 3.2 illustrates the substantial declines in collective-bargaining coverage in the private sector in particular. The combined public and private sector coverage was only 36 percent in 1997. Yet even these data drastically overstate the true picture by including (for comparability reasons) only firms with at least twenty-five employees. Since collective-bargaining coverage among smaller firms was only 7 percent in 1997, total private-sector coverage was just 22 percent. The decentralized bargaining system has produced a remarkable overlap between union membership and employees covered by collective bargaining. Labor Force Survey data indicate that overall, only 14 percent of nonunion members have their pay determined by collective bargaining; 18 percent of union members do not.[6] This overlap illustrates a key effect of decentralization, namely, the increasingly concentrated nature of both unionization and the effects of collective bargaining, in sharp contrast to the other countries we analyze, such as Germany.

### Decentralization of Bargaining

At the time of the Donovan Commission, multiemployer bargaining was eroding, though it remained central. The bargaining structure was more complex because employers supplemented multiemployer bargaining with informal negotiations at the workplace. The erosion of industry agreements continued during the 1970s, and they subsequently became of little importance. Between 1984 and 1990, multiemployer bargaining fell from covering 40 percent of manual employees to only 26 percent, and to only 10 percent of employees in total (Millward et al. 1992). The decline has continued in the 1990s, though at a slower pace.

Particularly significant in the decentralization of bargaining structures was the collapse of the engineering national negotiations in 1990, with other important agreements ending—in banking, docks, newspapers, slaughterhouses, steel, food trade, cotton textiles, buses, water, and electricity. Few firms now belong to employers' associations: only 20 percent of firms in private-sector manufacturing are members, and 10 percent in private-sector services (Millward et al. 1992). Membership is stronger where some multiemployer bargaining still exists, principally industries with small employers, including building and engineering construction, electrical contractors, commercial printing, footwear, and textiles. However, even in industries such as textiles, membership amounted to only 32 percent in 1990, composed primarily of small employers, while the associations continue to decline. Furthermore, where multiemployer bargaining remains, in perhaps three quarters of cases it sets only minimum employment conditions.[7] In the paper and board industry, for example, average gross weekly earnings are twice the nationally agreed rates, reflecting local bargaining supplements, bonus schemes, and overtime (Beaumont and Harris 1993).

Where bargaining has remained intact after the collapse of multiemployer bargaining, there has not been more fragmentation in bargaining at the plant level but rather a slight increase in the importance of single-employer, multiplant bargaining. This is particularly so in the service industry, given the smaller size of service firms. This pattern seems to reflect companies' desires to avoid whipsawing by unions, maintain pay comparability, and, for corporate managers, retain tight control over plants. Nevertheless, the pattern is complex and varied, with a broad distribution of plant- and company-level bargaining. In the expanding nonunion sector, where union whipsawing is not a threat, data from the 1990 Workplace Industrial Relations Survey (WIRS) indicates that plant-level determination of wages has increased significantly and is considerably the most important (Millward et al. 1992).

Nevertheless, even where bargaining is apparently "local," there is significant evidence that senior managers maintain control, either directly or through budgets. An extensive 1992 company-level survey of firms with more than one thousand employees found that even in companies with formally decentralized pay arrangements, corporate managers were involved in lower-level negotiations in two thirds of cases (Marginson et al. 1993).[8] The complex bargaining structures in Britain have, therefore, allowed more room for company- and plant-level variation in pay-setting arrangements.  Furthermore, formally decentralized bargaining structures that are controlled by corporate headquarters may help to fragment union organizations and make it harder for coordinated action to be taken by workers but also protect against union whipsawing.

### Concession Bargaining and Growth of Contingent Pay

The trend toward decentralization has also been connected to the expansion of concession bargaining in the 1980s. Throughout that decade, and in response to heightened environmental pressures, consistently one third of collectively bargained wage settlements involved changes in working practices. The most common were the removal of restrictive practices and the introduction of new technology, flexibility agreements, and incentive pay (Ingram 1991a).

Even where there has been stability of procedural clauses in collective-bargaining agreements, work organization has become more flexible through changes in substantive clauses, either because of flexible job descriptions or greater managerial prerogative in determining job tasks (Dunn and Wright 1994). There has also been an important shift in the management of work organization, with agreements not simply attempting to buy out old work practices but also involving a broader range of tasks, such that "the logic of flexibility is replacing the rules and procedures associated with 'custom and practice' which had hitherto held sway" (Edwards et al. 1992: 26). That is, management has been largely successful in its goal of reasserting prerogative on the shop floor. The 1990 WIRS survey, for example, indicates that agreements limiting management flexibility of work organization are clearly a feature of older workplaces and that the number of issues regulated jointly by management and unions has declined.

Although management was clearly intent on extracting concessions in working practices and reasserting its prerogative, unlike in the United States and Germany, concession bargaining has not involved reductions in pay. Indeed, Ingram (1991b) found higher wage settlements associated with productivity concessions. More generally, real wages have grown faster than at any time in the postwar period (Bayliss 1993), though pay increased more slowly for unionized than for nonunionized workers. The setting of pay at the firm or establishment level has thus also been linked with reforms in work organization, the introduction of greater flexibility, and the introduction of individualized pay systems.

The cumulative effect of the decline of multiemployer bargaining, decentralization, derecognition, and the development of new pay systems (including the individualization of pay) is part of a process of fragmentation dating to the 1950s. However, "even set against this background, the extent of the changes in the second half of the 1980s seems to have signalled a qualitative shift in patterns of pay determination" (Beatson 1993: 413). Incentive pay schemes have become especially widespread and include individual performance-related pay, skill- or competency-based pay, and profit-related pay.

Historically, individual performance-related pay (IPRP) and appraisals in Britain were confined to management, a practice that has changed. A 1997 Institute of Personnel and Development (IPD) survey found that 40 percent of firms used IPRP for management employees, and 25 percent for nonmanagement (IPD 1998). However, it is also significant that nearly 60 percent of these organizations had introduced the schemes in the previous five years, while few had discontinued them. In addition, there was evidence of substantial experimentation, with 30 percent of firms having undertaken "radical" reforms to their pay schemes to link them more closely to key organizational objectives. The proportion of pay that was contingent remains limited, with a median of 4 percent, though the mean was 10 percent. These schemes thus do have the potential for creating an important degree of variation in pay determination both among and within firms, which can greatly increase the individualization of the employment relationship.

Performance-related pay, and in particular merit pay, seem to have become more common from the mid-1980s onward, especially in medium and large employers (Beatson 1993). Furthermore, a growing number of companies use merit pay as the sole basis of wage increases, including Marks and Spencer and the Burton Group in the retail sector, and a wide range of companies in the financial sector especially. In the case of Barclays Bank, for example, such a scheme has been controversial and involved industrial action by its unions.

The IPD survey revealed that team-based pay for 8 percent of both managerial and nonmanagerial employees, and skill or competency-based pay for 6 percent and 11 percent, respectively. The growth of these schemes is new and includes such examples as Bank of Scotland, Blue Circle Cement, Pilkington Glass, Pirelli Cable, Cummins, BHS, and Michelin. Gainsharing programs, such as at Owens Corning and BP Exploration (BPX), have developed as firms have sought to introduce performance pay schemes that are tied to team working, performance improvements, and employee involvement and motivation.[9] In the case of BPX, employees' gainshare bonus can amount to up to 15 percent of pay.

Profit-related pay schemes have also become widespread in Britain, existing in more than one third of organizations for both managerial and nonmanagerial employees (IPD 1998). These schemes are especially common in engineering, retail distribution, and financial services. The growth of profit-related pay has been dramatic during the 1990s. Between 1990 and 1994 there was a sevenfold increase in the number of private-sector employees covered, rising to 2 million.[10] While much of the growth has resulted from legislative encouragement and favorable tax status, in many cases (such as at Lloyds Bank, Philips Electronics, and British Aerospace MA Division), at least 20 percent of pay is converted into a profit share.

New pay systems have been used in some companies to break away from collective bargaining and develop an individualized employment relationship (Smith and Morton 1993, Brown et al. 1998). William Brown et al. found that firms that derecognized unions were more likely to link pay rises to individual performance, with the goal to "increase the dispersion of pay, both within grades and between hierarchical levels...recruiting less skilled labour at lower rates than before, as well as increasing rewards for higher skill levels" (1998: i). As such, this individualization of employment contracts "may be increasing the segmentation of the labour market" (29).

Despite these practices, new pay systems have also "involved shifting the relationship with trade unions to a more co-operative, consultative basis. There are very few examples of modern performance pay systems being developed via adversarial distributive bargaining" (Kessler and Purcell 1995: 358). Thus, the introduction of new pay systems itself reflects changing patterns of employment relations, whether individualized or collectively. However, the reassertion of managerial prerogative has been reflected in a more aggressive stance to unions themselves, as indicated by the growing pattern of union derecognition.

### Increasing Union Derecognition

Union derecognition had previously been unheard of in Britain and during the 1980s occurred principally as an opportunistic response to union weakness and low density at individual establishments. It was also limited to supervisory, professional, and managerial grades, with these workers commonly being placed on individual contracts. Nevertheless, evidence from WIRS panel data indicate that 11 percent of manual employees and 10 percent of nonmanual employees experienced either active derecognition (as a result of managerial action) or passive derecognition (as a result of union member apathy) (Beaumont and Harris 1995). Among a sample of larger companies, Geroski et al. (1995) found between 14 and 15 percent of companies had undertaken at least partial derecognition. Much of this derecognition followed the collapse of the engineering industry's national bargaining agreement, when small firms in particular chose to establish nonunion employment practices (Millward et al. 1992).[11]

However, there was a step change in the extent of derecognition from the late 1980s into the 1990s, marking a substantial shift in managerial strategies (Claydon 1996). Between 1989 and 1993, for example, the proportion of derecognitions confined to specific grades of employees fell from 55 percent to 39 percent, with a correspondingly significant increase in unions for production workers being derecognized.

Derecognition has been especially common in publishing and printing, chemicals and petroleum, engineering and vehicles, and wholesale and retail distribution. Companies derecognizing unions include Esso, BP, Mobil, Shell, Monsanto, and Pfizer. Indications are strong that derecognition in these companies has not been reactive or opportunistic but rather strategic and purposive. This has included placing selected groups and senior grades of employees onto individual contracts, before derecognizing technicians, craftsman, and also manual-process workers at many plants (Claydon 1996; Gall and McKay 1994; Greg and Yates 1991). At Esso and Exxon plants at Fawley in 1993, for example, process operators were given base-pay rises of 10–13 percent and other increases in return for signing personal contracts.

Although in some such instances derecognition has been part of a strategy of introducing a human resource management approach to employment relations, in others the objective has been cost reduction and implementation of a low-wage pattern. In printing and publishing, this latter approach has included a two-tier wage structure and elimination of any institutionalized "voice" mechanisms for employees (Gall 1998). Derecognition has thus been used to directly introduce greater variation in employment practices.

Increasing variation and individualization of employment practices is therefore clearly becoming more important as multiemployer bargaining breaks down and union derecognition increases. However, the very limited extent of unions winning recognition agreements at newer workplaces since recognition became entirely voluntary in 1980 is probably of greater significance. In 1980, unions were recognized in 45 percent of newer establishments, though by 1990 this figure had fallen to only 24 percent. Even where unions have gained recognition, they have done so primarily through management support, predominantly granted in multiplant firms where the unions are recognized elsewhere; it is now not normally given in formal agreements, a practice unlike that in more well-established firms (Millward 1994).

The key role of management attitudes for securing union recognition was confirmed by the 1998 Workplace Employee Relations Survey (WERS). While unions were recognized for some purposes in 45 percent of all workplaces, this rose to 94 percent where management had a favorable view of unions, and density to 62 percent. In workplaces where management had an unfavorable view of unions, recognition was only 9 percent and density 7 percent. Despite this, "in a significant proportion of workplaces with union recognition, management is not supportive of a union role in joint negotiation, or even joint consultation" (Cully et al. 1998: 17). The scope of bargaining is thus narrow and management prefers to communicate directly with employees, rather than through a union channel. Among the most significant changes between 1993 and 1998, "management were much more likely to have consulted with employees (57 percent) than unions (32 percent of workplaces with recognized unions). Moreover, in 41 percent of cases there was no union involvement at all" (18).

Greater variation has also been introduced as firms made greater use during the 1980s and especially the 1990s of temporary working, fixed-term contracts, agency work, and casual work. Between 1992 and 1996, these categories increased from 9.9 percent of the workforce to 12.9 percent.[12] This growth in an almost exclusively nonunion, low-cost workforce has been boosted by the substantial contracting out of such services as catering, cleaning, and maintenance, in both the public and private sectors. Between 1993 and 1998, one third of establishments contracted out work previously done in-house, while contractors to one third of these establishments included employees previously directly employed by the company (Cully et al. 1998). In the public sector, this development corresponds to changing notions of what constitutes a "good" employer and to legislation to require compulsory competitive tendering. Yet, there is also an increasing use of temporary and fixed-term contracts for professional employees: 5 percent of workplaces employ professional workers on a temporary basis and 15 percent on fixed-term contracts (ibid.).

### New Work Practices and Employee Involvement

A shift in employers' approach, away from the traditional collectivist model to one of individualism, is clearly evident. However, no alternative model has emerged as a substitute for trade-union representation. An increasing range of companies make use of an HRM model, though many other nonunion firms have instead adopted a low-wage approach, with little consultation of employees. Equally, some unionized companies have used elements of HRM to individualize the employment relationship without full derecognition of unions; others have moved away from a traditional adversarial relationship and adopted a partnership role with their unions.

All of these approaches reflect a shift from the historically dominant adversarial pattern, which has been categorized by John Purcell as "bargained constitutional" (Purcell and Ahlstand 1994; Purcell and Sisson 1983). Certainly some variation has always existed, particularly in sectors with low unionization and among small firms (though the extent of small-firm variation has been limited by the unusually high concentration of large firms in the U.K. economy).[13] Indeed, the patterns (or styles) of employment relations identified by Purcell are drawn along similar lines to the ones we make here.[14] However, the notable feature of employment relations in Britain has been the substantial variation in styles since the early 1980s.

The overall use of consultative committees, for example, declined between 1984 and 1990, illustrating that no dominant, integrated HRM model has emerged, and indeed, these were more common where a union was recognized than where it was not. The role that such committees play also varies, while in unionized workplaces the role of the union has declined, with most representatives on committees being chosen through nonunion channels (Millward 1994).

There has, however, been more use of team briefings, quality circles and other problem-solving groups in Britain in the 1980s and 1990s, as employers have attempted to increase the flexibility of labor and employee involvement. Team briefings increased from 36 percent of workplaces in 1984, to 48 percent in 1990, and 61 percent in 1998.[15] The use of problem-solving groups and quality circles also increased significantly, from 35 percent of workplaces in 1990 to 42 percent in 1998 (Millward et al. 1992; Cully et al. 1998). This increasing adoption indicates the extent of experimentation, even if autonomous work groups have not had a wide impact.

By 1990, semi-autonomous work groups were used in only 2 percent of establishments. By 1998, 65 percent of workplaces reported that most employees were in formally designated teams, with 5 percent in semi-autonomous teams where they were given responsibility for a specific product or service, work together, jointly decide how work is to be undertaken, and appoint their own team leader. Furthermore, the 1998 WERS found that "training, teamworking, supervisors trained in employee relations matters and problem solving groups are all associated with one another. In combination this group of practices might be construed as a model of direct employee participation in decision making" (Cully et al. 1998: 11).

In many other workplaces, however, management has sought to increase its own shop-floor prerogative (for example, through the ending of so-called mutuality or status quo agreements in engineering), and expand flexibility and downward job enlargement (Geary 1995). Certainly, the changes that have occurred have included widespread reductions in grading structures and the division of labor, as well as contractual clauses displacing detailed job descriptions with the recognition of managerial discretion (Dunn and Wright 1994).

The evidence does not, therefore, suggest the general adoption of a "high commitment" model but, equally frequently, the retention of managerial supervision (Gallie and White 1993). However, the pattern of both unionized and nonunionized companies adopting diverse approaches, with both HRM and what we describe as a low-wage approach evident, is also confirmed in greenfield site establishments set up since 1980 (Guest and Hoque 1994, 1996), and among nonunion firms in high-technology industries (McLoughlin and Gourlay 1992).

Furthermore, widespread case-study evidence shows companies undertaking substantial work reorganization, including introducing cross-

functional and problem-solving teams, eliminating job boundaries, and removing supervisory levels (Storey 1992). This pattern of development and
experimentation with new systems of work organization is consistent with
the more recent patterns of expansion in other countries in this volume,
and there is evidence indicating that new practices have increased during
the 1990s.

Companies that have adopted a nonunion HRM model of employment
relations include representatives from a broad range of industries, and include BP Chemicals, Plessy, Whitbread, Marks and Spencer, Rank Xerox,
IBM, Digital, and Hewlett-Packard, and parts of other companies, such as
Esso and Motorola. BP Chemicals is representative of a company that has
moved to derecognize its unions (the TGWU and AEEU) in adopting an
HRM approach and, like Esso, is notable because its relationship with
unions was traditionally relatively cooperative. Other such companies, including Barclays Bank, have not derecognized their unions but, in adopting
a more cost-conscious and downsizing approach, have produced a more adversarial industrial relations climate. In contrast to these, the extent of diversity is also illustrated by the development of joint team-based models.

### Joint Team-Based Patterns

The end of national, industry-wide bargaining in the water industry in 1989
and privatization illustrate the growing variation among firms within a
single industry. After threatening its unions with complete derecognition,
Northumbria Water granted them the right to represent their members in
disciplinary procedures but not to negotiate pay. Instead, the unions were
given only one of eight employee seats on a new company council, which
has responsibility for pay determination (Ogden 1994).

Such company councils, which have become more common since their
introduction at Toshiba's plant in Plymouth in 1981 (Trevor 1988), typically do not have bargaining rights. Rather, the company council is a consultative body of employee representatives, that receives and discusses company information and aims to reach a consensus on employment practices,
including pay. The final decision, however, generally rests with the company. This structure of employee representation thus seeks to insulate the
firm from the influence of any external organization and to enhance the
plant or company focus of the (possibly incorporated) employee representatives. As such, the representative body may function either as a company
union or as a quasi-nonunion.

In contrast to attempts to marginalize unions and move away from collective employment relations, Hyder (formerly Welsh Water) shifted from

its traditional arms-length and adversarial relationship and adopted a joint-team based approach in 1990.[16] Hyder's partnership approach has included an employment security guarantee, profit-related pay, greater flexibility of work organization, skill enhancement, the decentralization of authority to work groups, and single-table bargaining for the four recognized unions.

The consequence of the partnership approach has been a dramatic change in the role of trade-union representatives within the company. Although union membership amounts to 85 percent of the workforce, the focus of union activities has shifted from grievances to joint problem-solving. Equally, however, the role of the human resource function shifted as responsibility for employment relations has been increasingly decentralized to operational managers. There has also been an increasing decentralization of authority to work groups on issues including the organization of work, budgets, and logistics. Although the partnership agreements have coincided with increased outsourcing, the union has had more of an influence on this than in other utilities.

Other strongly unionized companies that have moved from an adversarial approach to joint team-based employment practices include British Steel, Pirelli Cable, SmithKline Beecham, Blue Circle, Tesco, Kimberly-Clark, Castle Cement, Transco, and Scottish Power. These companies have sought greater flexibility in the deployment of labor and reduced demarcations, increased use of (often semi-autonomous) team working, greater skill development and training, and various forms of contingent pay. Many of these joint team-based practices have taken a considerable length of time to evolve. However, they reflect the goal of increasing employee involvement from a largely adversarial starting point, though in heavily unionized environments.

As in Hyder, the adoption of joint team-based patterns has also involved new approaches for the unions involved. However, the diversity of management approaches to restructuring work, the substantial decline that unions have endured during the 1980s and 1990s, and the absence of any institutionalized security through legal rights in the workplace or to bargaining recognition have also resulted in substantial caution on the part of unions. This has been reflected in the response of the Trades Union Congress (TUC) to HRM practices.

Having consistently opposed a set of managerial policies that they viewed as inimical to unions and as worsening the terms and conditions of employment, the TUC altered its stance in 1994. Following the report of a task force, they recognized the distinction between companies attempting to marginalize unions and adopt a low-cost approach, and those wanting to work in partnership with employees. The TUC consequently adopted a policy of constructively engaging employers to encourage them to adopt a cooperative approach with unions. This was taken further in 1997 with a "New Unionism" agenda for partnership, utilizing the slogan "Partners in Progress." Unions are thus responding to the diverse employment patterns by actively promoting the joint team-based approach, even though that, too, requires a restructuring of their workplace strategies.

## SUMMARY

Throughout the postwar era, state encouragement for collective bargaining, a tight labor market, and the predominance of multiemployer bargaining all helped trade unions extend their representational influence throughout the economy (Howell 1995). The demise of these three elements since 1979 has had a drastic effect on union representation, as discussed above. This outcome has been brought about only in part by changes to elements of the institutional structure of British industrial relations. What is at least as important, these changes have interacted with other preexisting institutions and, in doing so, have highlighted the fragility and consequences of the system as a whole. In particular, decentralized, workplace-based unions have been unable to extend any influence beyond their isolated sphere or to coordinate among spheres.

The decline in the strength of unions in Britain is, however, easily witnessed on a range of measures. The decline of private-sector unionization to only 20 percent, and of collective-bargaining coverage to 22 percent, attests to that. However, despite the resulting dramatic rise in nonunionism, a broad range of employment patterns are emerging. Some unionized companies have moved away from the traditional adversarial industrial relations practices and adopted a partnership approach, whereas others have sought to derecognize the unions. Furthermore, while Britain is often characterized as a low-wage economy, even in the nonunion sector, human resource management practices have become substantially more widespread.

## DEVELOPMENTS IN THE AUTO INDUSTRY

The most striking feature of the auto industry in Britain since the early 1970s has been the substantial collapse in production, followed by a more recent revival. Passenger-car production, for example, fell from a peak of over 1.9 million cars in 1972 to fewer than 900,000 cars a decade later. Dur-

**Figure 3.1.** Production in the U.K. Auto Industry

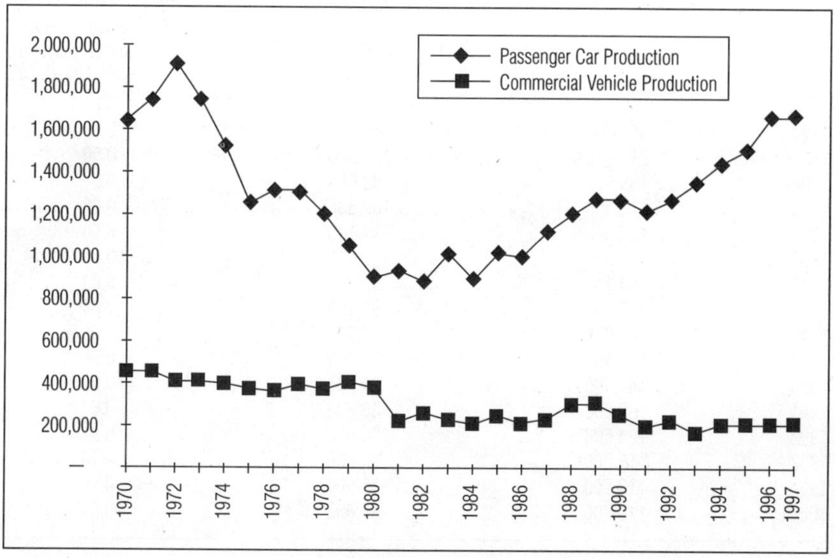

Source: *Census of Production,* Office of National Statistics (U.K.) (various years).

ing this period, exports of cars similarly collapsed, falling from more than 40 percent of production to less than 20 percent; a similar collapse occurred in the production of commercial vehicles.

However, since its nadir in 1982, production has undergone a substantial recovery, and by 1997 nearly 1.7 million cars were produced (Figure 3.1). There had, furthermore, been a strong recovery in exports of both cars and commercial vehicles, to 57 percent and 44 percent, respectively. This recovery of the U.K. auto industry has been strongly assisted by the addition of Japanese transplants. Nissan, Toyota, and Honda all established assembly plants in Britain between 1986 and 1992, and by 1996 they were collectively producing more than 450,000 cars for the European market.

The 1980s collapse of auto production was accompanied by a corresponding decline in employment among both assembler and supplier companies. Between 1979 and 1985 alone, combined assembler and supplier employment in the auto industry fell by 44 percent. Although employment then stabilized somewhat, by 1995 the total decline since 1979 was 53 percent (Table 3.3). The decimation of the British auto industry hit all of the "traditional" mass manufacturers—Rover, Vauxhall (General Motors), Ford, and Peugeot Talbot.[17] Indeed, employment among these producers

**Table 3.3.** Employment in the U.K. Auto Industry

| Year | Assembler Employment | Supplier Employment | Ratio of Supplier to Assembler Employment |
|------|----------------------|---------------------|-------------------------------------------|
| 1979 | 290,100 | 157,000 | 0.54 |
| 1980 | 261,700 | 146,500 | 0.56 |
| 1981 | 214,800 | 121,300 | 0.56 |
| 1982 | 189,500 | 108,000 | 0.57 |
| 1983 | 170,900 | 102,600 | 0.60 |
| 1984 | 164,300 | 98,100 | 0.60 |
| 1985 | 153,300 | 97,400 | 0.64 |
| 1986 | 144,100 | 92,200 | 0.64 |
| 1987 | 142,200 | 91,100 | 0.64 |
| 1988 | 144,000 | 91,500 | 0.64 |
| 1989 | 140,400 | 96,100 | 0.68 |
| 1990 | 142,400 | 94,700 | 0.67 |
| 1991 | 132,000 | 88,200 | 0.67 |
| 1992 | 124,500 | 86,000 | 0.69 |
| 1993 | 115,200 | 80,800 | 0.70 |
| 1994 | 113,700 | 85,500 | 0.75 |
| 1995 | 116,700 | 94,600 | 0.81 |

*Source: Census of Production,* Office of National Statistics (U.K.) (various years).
*Note:* There is a series break between 1992 and 1993 due to a change in SIC classification.

fell from 284,000 in 1979 to only 83,100 in 1997, an average of more than 70 percent in eighteen years. Even Ford, where employment has held up best, witnessed a 42 percent reduction. But Rover, the principal British company, has seen employment plummet by more than 80 percent from a peak of 199,500 in 1970 to 38,750 in 1997. During this time it has undergone a succession of ownership, including being nationalized, privatized through sale to British Aerospace, 20 percent owned by Honda, and finally, in 1994, bought by BMW. The introduction of Japanese transplants has supported both production and employment in Britain, though by 1997 Nissan, Toyota, and Honda's combined employment was relatively low at 10,600.

The collapse of Britain's auto industry was closely related to its historical weaknesses and problems characterized as the "British disease." This included low productivity growth, weak management, and a strongly adversarial relationship between unions and shop stewards on the one hand, and management on the other. This difficult relationship was, in turn, manifested in a bad strike record, with a preponderance of unofficial strikes led by shop stewards. Moreover, the industry had a reputation of "hire and fire" employment practices; overmanning was widespread; restrictive practices were operated by multiple unions, with strong demarcations of work among unions; the organization of work further contributed to low functional flex-ibility; and both productivity and quality were poor (Marsden et al. 1985).

### Decentralization in Employment Relations in the Auto Industry

The voluntarist nature of British industrial relations, the importance of cus-tom and practice in the workplace, and the decentralized organization of unions and shop-steward movements historically removed important forces producing a common system of employment relations. In the absence of in-stitutional regulation, centralization, or coordination, the British auto in-dustry reflected much of the rest of the economy in exhibiting some varia-tion in industrial relations outcomes and processes. These affected both the organization of work and the structure of bargaining.

The British operations of Ford, for example, stressed (in the abstract at least) managerial prerogative. In contrast, by the 1970s, Rover had inher-ited a range of different plant-level work organization and industrial rela-tions traditions, which were frequently subject to "mutuality," that is, an em-phasis on the status quo and the need for shop stewards to approve changes before their introduction (Marsden et al. 1985).

However, although there were important differences among companies in the details of work organization, the underlying pattern of employment relations traditionally had considerable similarity. This common pattern in-cluded a limited role for the internal labor market; the widespread accep-tance of custom-and-practice agreements even at Ford; a high level of job fragmentation and demarcation, shop-steward power, and restrictive prac-tices; and the limited imposition of (even contractually agreed) managerial prerogative. Furthermore, a strongly adversarial pattern of employment re-lations dominated the industry.

The 1970s also witnessed a convergence of formal employment practices throughout the industry. Rover, in particular, made strident efforts to elim-inate plant-level variation in work organization and pay systems. By the be-ginning of the 1980s it had largely achieved its goals, including the intro-duction of centralized (company-level) pay bargaining, a "measured day work" pay system, interplant pay parity, and group-wide incentive schemes (Marsden et al. 1985: 30–31).

Although multiemployer, industry-wide bargaining had become the pre-dominant wage setting in Britain by 1945, this never included the auto in-dustry. In addition, the decentralized organization of unions prevented co-ordination in bargaining among companies, and the industry was never characterized by U.S.-style pattern-setting arrangements. Rather, the auto industry was characterized by "independent" company bargaining, and although Ford has sometimes been viewed as the pattern setter for the engineering sector, and indeed more broadly, the evidence to support this is minimal.

In Ford, bargaining traditionally took place exclusively at the company level, with full-time national union officials. Similarly, in 1971 Vauxhall centralized pay bargaining conducted by a joint national committee. In contrast, however, Rover's historically fragmented growth through mergers of independent companies led to an equally fragmented bargaining system, decentralized to (and even sometimes within) plants.

The historically decentralized system of bargaining among companies also reflected their different payment systems. Thus, Ford and Vauxhall not only avoided plant-level bargaining but also avoided the piece-rate pay systems that fueled the shop-floor bargaining in Rover plants. Although Ford was able to avoid the disruption and the fractional disputes that resulted from such bargaining, its adversarial industrial relations was nevertheless characterized as a "ball and chain" approach, and fostered local conflict as well as national pay disputes over pay parity in the industry in 1969 and 1971 (Beynon 1973; Darlington 1994). As a consequence, Ford's practice of negotiating exclusively with the national trade union leadership was eroded during the 1970s as plant convenors were incorporated into the bargaining structure. By 1978, all convenors were included, and they were in a majority, though bargaining remained centralized.

Rover had a variety of decentralized bargaining systems in the early 1970s. The practice of local negotiations led to wide variation in, for example, disputes procedures, while pay issues centered on piece-rate bonus systems. Local negotiations, conducted in an often strongly adversarial relationship between unions and management, tended to promote persistent intra- and interplant union-led whipsawing. In this process, shop stewards made particular use of mutuality, or the principle that emphasized the status quo and required union agreement on changes to work practices.

Rover management moved progressively toward a more centralized bargaining structure and a new payments system throughout the 1970s, in an effort to assert managerial control. The company's aims included common review dates for wage increases and group-wide grading, pay structures, and incentive systems. As part of their attempt to increase the degree of centralization, in 1976 Rover incorporated the terms of the engineering sector industry-wide negotiations into their agreements. This was done even though Rover did not have provisions for company-wide bargaining, and industrial-relations issues were principally settled at the plant level. Progression toward greater centralization was, however, resisted with stoppages from the shop floor, where mutuality facilitated continual and widespread leapfrogging.

The move toward greater centralization culminated in the unilateral imposition of common practices through the "Blue Newspaper" package of managerial reforms of 1980. These proposals ended mutuality, established the right to manage unilaterally, reduced more than five hundred job classifications into five company-wide grades, and confirmed the centralization of bargaining. They were resisted by shop stewards in particular, who recognized the implications of this change in terms of a loss in their power. Nevertheless, although the unions did not agree to the changes, workers reluctantly accepted the revised centralized bargaining structures, as well as revisions to the grading structure (Marsden et al. 1985; Scarborough and Terry 1996). At the same time, Rover withdrew from its short experience of using the engineering sector agreement, in order to establish its own industrial relations framework.

By 1980 there was, therefore, substantial similarity in bargaining structures among companies even without pattern bargaining, and company-level bargaining has not included the involvement of national union officials to coordinate negotiations. Nevertheless, pay and grievances were negotiated on a centralized basis, and the previous importance of shop-steward bargaining power was eroded. Piece-rate pay systems, once common, ended, and while Ford did not operate any output-based pay incentive schemes, those at Rover, Vauxhall, and Talbot were nonnegotiable (Marsden et al. 1985: 114).

The auto industry in the United Kingdom had, therefore, experienced a convergence of employment relations by 1980 into a common pattern, one that included arms-length adversarial industrial relations and a decentralized workplace structure with important roles for shop stewards. Indeed, the dominant employment pattern strongly reflected that in much of British industry. However, variation has subsequently been growing with vertical disintegration in the industry, the addition of only quasi-unionized Japanese transplants to the traditional manufacturers, and programmatic differences in work organization.

### Vertical Disintegration and Declining Unionization in the Auto Industry

The dramatic decline in auto industry production from its peak in 1972 reached a nadir in 1982, and has subsequently made a significant recovery. This latter period has seen a substantial restructuring of work organization and industrial relations within the core assemblers. However, Mari Sako (1997) has also identified a spectacular degree of vertical disintegration in the industry (see Table 3.3, which shows the ratio of supplier to assembler employment rising from 54 percent in 1979 to 81 percent in 1995).

**Table 3.4.** Distribution of Employment by Plant Size in the U.K. Auto Industry

| Plant Size (Number of Employees) | Employment 1981 | Percentage Share 1981 | Employment 1993 | Percentage Share 1993 |
|---|---|---|---|---|
| 1–99 | 17,700 | 14.6 | 16,200 | 20.1 |
| 100–299 | 13,600 | 11.2 | 16,900 | 21.0 |
| 300–499 | 11,200 | 9.3 | 15,100 | 18.7 |
| 500–999 | 19,600 | 16.2 | 18,300 | 22.7 |
| 1000+ | 59,000 | 48.7 | 14,100 | 17.5 |
| Total | 121,100 | 100 | 80,600 | 100 |

*Source:* Mari Sako 1997 (from Business Monitor, *Census of Production,* Office of National Statistics [U.K.][various years]).

The vertical disintegration has, however, actually been more dramatic than indicated by her aggregate data. In particular, it has also been associated with a remarkable shift in the size of supplier plants (Sako 1997: 8) (see Table 3.4), with an extremely strong trend toward smaller plants and a corresponding decline in large plants. Thus, the employment share of plants with fewer than five hundred workers has increased from 35 percent to 60 percent, though this subgroup has had near-even growth across plants of different sizes. The largest decline has been in large suppliers, or those employing more than one thousand workers, though again the trend to smaller plant sizes is clear across the spectrum of supplier firms.

The emerging contrast between large assembly and small supplier plants in the U.K. auto industry has had an important effect on variation in employment relations for two particular reasons. First, it has accentuated the trend to lower levels of unionization, and second, it has also resulted in greater variation in wages.

As in British industry as a whole, union density in the auto industry has been on a decline since 1989 (see Table 3.5). Although assemblers remain fairly strongly unionized, the decline is nonetheless significant and may in part reflect the relative expansion of employment in the Japanese transplants (see below). Although no data indicate that union density has declined more rapidly among supplier firms, the lower level of density is notable. Since vertical disintegration has clearly helped shift employment into a more weakly unionized sector, it has almost certainly helped to lower union density within the industry.

Unfortunately, the data series is neither long enough nor sufficiently detailed to indicate specifically how the trend to smaller plant sizes has contributed to lower union density. Nevertheless, for the private sector as a whole, data from the annual Department of Trade and Industry Labor Force Survey clearly show lower levels of unionization in smaller plants. It

**Table 3.5.** Trade Union Density in the U.K. Auto Industry

| Year | Assembly | Suppliers | Great Britain Union Density (percent of all employees) |
|---|---|---|---|
| 1989 | 75 | 55 | 39.0 |
| 1991 | 69 | 50 | 37.5 |
| 1993 | 64 | 46 | 35.1 |
| 1994 | 69 | 45 | 33.6 |
| 1995 | 68 | 46 | 32.1 |
| 1996 | 63 | 47 | 31.3 |
| 1997 | 57 | 43 | 30.2 |
| Percentage Change 1989-1997 | -24% | -22% | -22.6% |

*Source:* Sako (1997) and Labour Force Survey, Department of Trade and Industry (various years).
*Note:* There is a discontinuity in the data series between 1993 and 1994, due to a change in the industrial classification.

is, therefore, probable that the trend to smaller firms has lowered the level of union density throughout the 1980s and 1990s.

The decline in unionization and consequent growing variation in the supplier industry is illustrated by the experience of Unipart. Until 1987, Unipart was a division of Rover and had been subject to common terms and conditions. In 1987, however, it was bought out by its management, which then established a relationship with the Japanese supplier company Yachiyo Kogyo. Unipart subsequently made a concerted and explicit attempt to introduce nonunionized Japanese-oriented employment practices, which included quality management programs, quality circles, continuous improvement, teams with flexible deployment of labor by a "team leader" who fulfilled the role of supervisor, direct communication, performance-related pay (based on appraisal), and common status for all employees.

However, Unipart managers also viewed its two unions, the Amalgamated Engineering and Electrical Union (AEEU) and the Transport and General Workers' Union (TGWU), and particularly shop stewards from the latter union, as resistant to such new practices. Consequently, in 1992, Unipart derecognized both unions, even though they represented more than four thousand workers and had density levels above 90 percent in some divisions, and 40 percent among office workers.

Although component suppliers have not made other substantial moves to derecognize unions, wage inequality across auto suppliers has been growing because of vertical disintegration in the auto industry. At the same time, the decentralized bargaining structure within the industry (as, more generally, in the United Kingdom), the lack of strong union coordination, and the increasing insulation of firms from external union influences has also produced significant wage disparity among the core assemblers.

### *Bargaining-Process Variation and Pay Outcomes across Auto Assemblers*

As described above, multiemployer pay bargaining was never a feature of the auto industry in Britain, though by 1980 centralized bargaining had been introduced within each company. Since then, however, both the outcomes and processes of wage determination have become increasingly varied across the auto industry.

Key unions in the auto industry, and in particular the TGWU, the principal industry union, have traditionally adopted a decentralized organizational structure, with substantial autonomy for shop stewards and plant convenors. During the 1970s, this policy of decentralization was reinforced. As unions have been weakened within auto plants during the 1980s and 1990s, and as employment levels have collapsed, the unions have found it increasingly difficult to exercise even the strong informal coordination of bargaining outcomes among companies. This trend has been exacerbated by financial strains within the unions themselves and changes in labor law. Just as significantly, however, unions have no common bargaining cycle to coordinate. In 1982, Rover signed a two-year contract, a cycle that also applied to Jaguar and Land Rover. However, when Ford, Vauxhall, and Peugeot Talbot moved to two-year contracts in 1985, an alternative bargaining cycle was created. The irregularity of the bargaining cycle was increased further in 1996, when Vauxhall signed a three-year agreement.

Variation in wage determination has been expanded, in particular, by the Japanese-transplant assembly operations of Honda, Nissan, and Toyota. The addition of these firms to the traditional core manufacturers has introduced nonunion bargaining structures into the industry, while also weakening the common pay practices that had developed by the early 1980s.

Nissan and Toyota have adopted very similar mechanisms to both accept unions and simultaneously minimize their role. Each company signed a single-union agreement with the (now) AEEU. In each company, union representation rights were extended beyond production workers to include (in the case of Toyota) senior group leaders and senior engineers, and excepting only senior managerial ranks. However, despite an apparently broad bargaining unit, the single-union agreements also substantially limit the union's representational role and power, in a manner that would be illegal in the United States or Germany.

 Both single-union agreements concede exclusive managerial prerogative over production methods, manpower planning, temporary hiring, work standards, sourcing, workforce communication, recruitment and training, and transfer and promotion. Although these provisions certainly limit the role of the union and are particularly unusual in restricting union communication with members, of even greater importance is the union's lack of bargaining rights. Rather, companies retain the right to establish wages and other terms and conditions through a company council.

Toyota and Nissan operate their company councils on very similar principles, much like those of other Japanese plants in Britain, such as Toshiba (Trevor 1988). The Toyota company council (termed the Members' Advisory Board) includes ten elected employee representatives, out of a total of eighteen council members. These employee representatives may or may not be union members. The union does not have any representatives, of right, on the council, and neither does the union bargain on behalf of the workforce. Indeed, although the council considers terms and conditions, employee members on the council are not permitted to express a mandated or group position on any issue under consideration but rather must reach a conclusion on what is in the best interests of the company (Toyota 1991). This limits the potential role for the union in establishing policy for representatives on the council, who happen also to be union members. In addition, the council is the only forum available to discuss such matters as wages, and it operates through consultation with worker representatives rather than through negotiation.

The aim of the council is to reach agreements through consensus, and although disagreement can be pursued through conciliation and arbitration (but not strike action), the final decision rests with the company, though in the case of Nissan there is a provision for final offer arbitration. The consequence of the single-union agreement, and the severely constrained role of the union at both Nissan and Toyota, thus adds significant diversity to both employee representation and wage determination processes.

Whereas Nissan and Toyota represent a form of quasi-nonunionism, Honda chose to operate its Swindon plant on a fully nonunion basis. Honda opened an engine plant in 1989 as part of its then joint venture with Rover and an assembly plant in 1992. Initially, the company stated that no decision on unionization was appropriate until after it had recruited a workforce; since beginning operations, however, it has resisted attempts at unionization and has indicated that it does not see a potential role for unions within the plant. While Nissan's decision in the early 1980s to sign a single-union deal and establish a company council can clearly be regarded as an attempt to protect against the possibility of more independent and aggressive unionization becoming established after production had started, Honda's decision in the 1990s reflects the perceived decline in union power. In particu-

**Table 3.6.** Auto Industry Pay in Britain (in pounds per week)

| Company | Assembler Base Pay[a] | Assembler Variable Pay[b] | Assembler Total Pay | Craftsman Base Pay[c] | Craftsman Variable Pay[b] | Craftsman Total Pay |
|---------|------------------|---------------------|---------------|-----------------|-------------------|--------------|
| Ford    | 257.48 | 20.50 | 277.98 | 303.42 | 9.59  | 313.01 |
| Jaguar  | 278.90 | 26.91 | 305.81 | 297.48 | 26.91 | 324.39 |
| Nissan  | 255.72 | -     | 255.72 | 291.36 | -     | 291.36 |
| Peugeot | 244.22 | 11.00 | 255.22 | 272.35 | 8.00  | 280.35 |
| Rover   | 269.92 | 2.89  | 272.81 | 297.23 | 2.89  | 300.12 |
| Toyota  | 242.70 | -     | 242.70 | 282.09 | -     | 282.09 |
| Vauxhall| 263.22 | 54.24 | 317.46 | 293.94 | 54.56 | 348.50 |

*Sources:* Company figures, 1996.
[a] Equivalent to Ford Grade 2.
[b] Inclusive of attendance pay, productivity pay, linework bonus, and profit-related pay, as appropriate.
[c] Mechanical and Electrical Craftsman, equivalent to Ford Grade 5.

lar, as general trends in the United Kingdom indicate, the granting of new recognition agreements has become much less frequent and derecognition more common. In light of this, Honda has resisted establishing even a company council to consult with the workforce.

The representation structures at Nissan and Toyota, and nonunionism at Honda, clearly add variation to the process of wage determination. Beyond this, new pay systems are leading to greater diversity. However, although both Nissan and Toyota's contracts allow for individual performance-related pay, neither company has taken advantage of this flexibility, as indicated by Table 3.6, nor has Honda. However, both Nissan and Toyota have an annual appraisal system to determine an employee's progression along the pay scale, with first-line supervisors playing a particularly strong role in the assessment.

Profit-related pay schemes have added further variation to pay outcomes and are now in use at Vauxhall, Rover, Peugeot, and Rolls Royce, though not at Ford, Toyota, Nissan, or Honda. The higher variable pay indicated in Table 3.6 for Vauxhall reflects significant profit-related payments, which amounted to 901 pounds (approximately 1,440 dollars) for each worker in 1994, as well as a substantial plant-based variable productivity bonus of more than 1,600 pounds (2,560 dollars). The case of Vauxhall, and also that of Rover, where a profit-sharing scheme was introduced in 1988, illustrate that these schemes have the potential to increase pay variation in the industry.

Further variation was allowed in 1998 at Vauxhall, when the union agreed, under the explicit threat of a plant closure, to a new contract that included the very novel practice of linking pay to the exchange rate. If the pound to deutsche mark exchange rate falls from 2.99 to 2.7 for two consecutive months, then pay raises are to be increased by 0.5 percent. In return for employment guarantees, this contract also provides for new employees to be hired at only 80 percent of full rates, with an equalization period of five years. Furthermore, the two-tier employment structure includes new employees receiving five fewer vacation days per year. The agreement thus emphasizes how pay is being explicitly linked to company performance and the ability to pay, and becoming increasingly varied.

As Table 3.6 indicates, pay rates significantly vary for equivalent grades of workers among auto companies, with the Japanese transplants being relatively low payers, as are the small operations of Peugeot.[18] The different bargaining structures and negotiating timetables have also, for example, created variation in hours of work. Standard hours vary from thirty-nine at Ford, Nissan, Toyota, Honda, and Peugeot, to thirty-eight at Vauxhall (negotiated in 1996), and thirty-seven at Jaguar (itself now a subsidiary of Ford), and only thirty-five at Rover, following the introduction of an annual hours contract in late 1998.

However, the vertical disintegration of the auto industry in Britain and the trend to employment in smaller plants have resulted in even greater wage inequality. Utilizing data of wages in assembler and supplier firms, Sako (1997) has identified a growing wage gap (see figure 3.2). The wage gap for operatives in the supplier firms in particular has increased from their earning 96 percent of assembler wages in 1979 to only 72 percent in 1995. The decline in wages for administrative staff has been smaller, from 83 percent to 73 percent. With a growing proportion of the industry now employed in supplier firms, this shift has clearly increased wage inequality between auto workers in the assembly and supplier firms (Sako 1997). Furthermore, overtime at supplier firms also fluctuates substantially more than at the assemblers, indicating that these firms are seen as buffers.

The explanation for the growing wage gap between assemblers and suppliers is significant for the future development of wage inequality in the whole industry. Sako (1997) notes that the relative decline in supplier wages has less to do with slow growth of wages there than it does with the particularly rapid growth in wages at assembler firms during the period examined. Indeed, supplier wages increased in line with manufacturing industry more generally. However, the particularly rapid growth in assembler wages is also associated with very rapid productivity increases. During the period 1979–1992, real labor productivity increased by 1.8 percent annually at supplier plants but by a massive 6.1 percent annually at assemblers.

The growth of assembler wages thus seem to reflect an increasing emphasis on firm-level performance. Indeed, the TGWU has adopted an explicit

**Figure 3.2.** Wage Gap between Assemblers and Suppliers

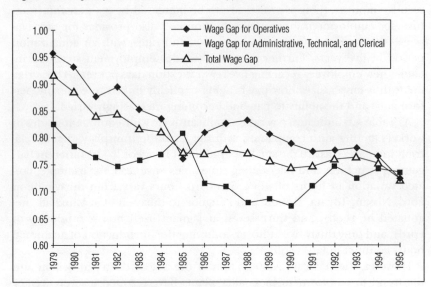

Source: *Census of Production,* Office of National Statistics (U.K.)(various years); See also Sako 1997.

negotiating stance of linking wage increases to firms' ability to pay and to increases in productivity, director's pay, and cost of living. This policy clearly contrasts with an earlier emphasis on pay parity for workers throughout the industry and pattern bargaining. Moreover, the focus on the firm reinforces the "isolated decentralization" that is leading to more general variation in Britain. Although the policy certainly has the potential to bring advantages to assembler workers, it has not done so for those at supplier firms (Sako 1997: 26–29).

Beyond pay, however, variation among the auto companies has also grown as they have each adopted strategies to reorganize work and introduce greater flexibility in the use of labor in particular. As the companies have transformed their industrial relations and work organization, program-matic differences have emerged in their employment practices and rela-tionships with trade unions.

*Team Working*

The traditional auto companies have followed broadly similar objectives of substantially increased flexibility, reassertion of managerial prerogative, changes to grading structures, lessening of skill demarcations to reduce the need for craftsmen, and elimination of the principle of mutuality (Marsden et al. 1985). In their quest to achieve these goals, auto manufacturers have adopted different approaches to employment relations both in the initial stages of transformation and subsequently. This can be observed clearly in the widespread experimentation with team-working practices. Where team working has been introduced, there has been programmatic variation in the structure of the teams and the roles team leaders play. This variation relates closely to the different employment patterns we identify.

At Ford and also Vauxhall, changes in work organization in the early 1980s required stronger implementation of existing agreements that already stressed managerial prerogative rather than substantial contractual changes. At Rover, however, more fundamental changes to contracts were required, and management adopted a strongly adversarial approach in the early 1980s including the unilateral imposition of the Blue Newspaper. While this policy clearly entailed an adversarial confrontation with shop stewards and unions, there were also elements of accommodation as well as attempts to bypass stewards and communicate directly with the workforce. However, Rover never sought to eliminate unionism, and during the 1980s and 1990s this initially adversarial approach has evolved into a strong example of a partnership with the unions and workforce.

### A Joint Team-Based Approach at Rover

The reorientation of Rover's objective, from re-establishing managerial control to one of greater participation, occurred in the mid-1980s. But given the strongly adversarial history of industrial relations and the previous unilateral managerial action, it took considerably longer to realize. Programs such as "Working with Pride" (which included elements of team work and quality circles) and the subsequent total quality management program were resisted by the unions. They viewed these programs as a threat to job control and employment security, as well as to union control over communication with the workforce.

Nevertheless, during the 1990s in particular, substantial progress has been made toward a cooperative and joint team-based relationship, formalized in the New Deal agreement passed by a minimal majority in 1992 but subsequently strengthened greatly through commitment to the reality of this joint approach. Of particular importance for the unions and workforce has been their increased confidence in the pledge of no compulsory redundancies and the use of retraining rather than short-time working. The positive effects of the change is evidenced by the view of senior management that the workforce and unions at Rover are perhaps more cooperative and flexible than at BMW, which has owned Rover since 1994, even if productivity remains significantly lower. Both the principal unions, the AEEU and the TGWU, argue that the New Deal was a momentous change toward greater partnership and one that has both protected and indeed enhanced union power, despite the initial fears of many in the unions and the workforce.

For Rover, the impetus toward a joint team-based approach was the belief that substantial productivity improvements during the 1980s had been achieved through technological change and the fear of job losses (which had been continual), though without significant improvements in work organization or flexibility (Scarborough and Terry 1996). Rover concluded that this source of productivity improvement was reaching its limit, and that greater gains and flexibility required a more cooperative and less threatening environment.

The resulting New Deal agreement in 1992 established single-status employment; removed all restrictive practices; introduced a single-grade pay structure for all employees, with advancement by means of skill acquisition; and provided a unique job-security guarantee based on the willingness of employees to undertake retraining and redeployment. As Scarborough and Terry note, "The New Deal does represent an apparent transformation in the industrial relations of a company with a long-standing reputation for adversarial and bitter relationships" (1996: 19). The partnership approach, with improved communication and consultation between the company and the union, has been of central importance and is illustrated in Rover's approach to team working.

Although team leaders at Rover are elected by team members, subject to the leaders' meeting certain skill proficiencies, the unions feared that the operation of teams would undermine both the position of shop stewards and the role of the union. Both management and unions have thus supported the separation of team leaders' and stewards' functions, and both have sought to ensure the continuing centrality of the unions. As Andrew Mair (1999) has noted of the Swindon body plant, "On every issue management now approached the factory's trade union representatives directly to discuss the best ways to implement change" (260). In this respect, the unions have increasingly been viewed as key resources for facilitating and implementing change, and the unions have had extensive access to information.

In view of this participatory approach, Rover has not sought to impose a detailed model of team working. Rather, it has established principles of the joint approach and encouraged the decentralized implementation of the

**Table 3.7.** Team Leader Selection and Payments

|  | Teams Leader Selection | Team Leader Payments |
|---|---|---|
| Ford | Appointed | 10 percent of basic grade |
| Jaguar | Appointed | 10.73 percent (grade 2); 11.44 percent (grade 5) |
| Honda | Appointed | Supervisory Grade |
| Nissan | Appointed | Supervisory Grade |
| Peugeot | Elected | 5 percent payment above grade |
| Rover | Elected | Higher grade worth 30 pounds per week |
| Toyota | Appointed | Supervisory Grade |
| Vauxhall | Appointed | 9 percent payment above grade |

*Sources:* Company figures, 1996.

most appropriate practices at and within the Longbridge, Cowley, Solihull, and Swindon plants. This decentralized approach has been reinforced by reductions in managerial ranks, which have resulted in a "downgrading of the bureaucratic interest in the standardisation of policy and practice" (Scarborough and Terry 1996: 35). Evidence from both the Cowley and Swindon plants highlights the variability of the detailed operations of teams within plants and also that of team leaders (Scarborough and Terry 1996; Mair 1999). However, this approach of placing less emphasis on precise rules also requires a change in union operations. Nevertheless, Andrew Mair notes that "the significant strategic role being played by the trade unions in the management of change towards teamwork appeared to be giving the unions a certain level of influence over the precise form teamwork should take" (1999: 283).

Although the elected team leaders are paid at the rate of a higher grade, worth 30 pounds (48 dollars) per week (see Table 3.7), their role is not extensive, even acknowledging that it varies between teams. Team leaders have neither managerial nor disciplinary powers, they can be deselected if the team is dissatisfied with them, and their role is carefully differentiated from that of both supervisors and shop stewards. To avoid a clash of roles with stewards, team leaders do not have the role of spokesperson, which remains with the stewards. At the same time, the role of supervisors has been amended to that of a facilitator focused on quality and process improvement, rather than on production volume (Scarborough and Terry 1996; Mair 1999). The amended role of supervisors has been made easier by the absence of any individual performance appraisal at Rover.

Teams in Rover are relatively self-managing and generally are created around natural work groups. In an attempt to end any remaining demarcation constraints, teams were given responsibility for quality and basic maintenance. As jobs become broader and include elements of multiskilling, teams typically decide the extent of job rotation. Furthermore, at the Swindon subassembly unit they became involved in the development of both skills and training matrices, as well as in all aspects of planning involving the facility and work processes (Mair 1999). By 1995, team members at the Swindon plant were being encouraged to become polyvalent within their teams, with the opportunity to learn as many tasks as desired. This was associated with both the enlargement and enrichment of jobs. But even though teams in some production areas have also been able to set their own pace of work, in assembly operations they have substantially less production autonomy, given the pre-specification of tasks. Nevertheless, the commitment to a joint approach to change has differed importantly from that at Vauxhall and Ford.

### A Piecemeal Approach at Ford

Among the traditional auto companies in Britain, Ford historically placed the greatest emphasis on managerial prerogative, though by the 1970s it was equally characterized by extensive job demarcations, rigid work organization, and an adversarial relationship with unions. Like Rover, Ford initially adopted an aggressive approach to imposing managerial prerogatives, increasing flexibility, and introducing rationalization and efficiency measures. This strategy led to a two-week strike in 1981, though subsequently Ford sought to develop less adversarial industrial relations (Darlington 1994).

Ford's strategy included a series of programs, in particular the "After Japan" and "Employee Involvement" initiatives in the 1980s, which achieved important successes in enhancing flexibility. Between 1979 and 1990, Ford reduced the total number of separate job categories from 577 to only 58, contained within five grades of labor, while at the same time introducing flexibility clauses, eliminating job controls, and enhancing the extent of managerial prerogatives and the rights of supervisors (Dunn and Wright 1994; Mueller 1992a; Starkey and McKinlay 1989).[19] The majority of these changes occurred through the 1985 Pay and Working Practices Agreement, which essentially bought out restrictive practices and demarcation lines by giving workers an 18.5 percent pay increase. However, this agreement did not itself establish a strategy of either a reassertion of managerial prerogative or a cooperative approach to work restructuring at the plant level.

Despite achieving increasing flexibility, however, Ford has been less successful at instituting a cooperative employment relations climate. During the 1980s, Ford faced a contradiction between its simultaneous goals of employee involvement and its determination to reassert and retain managerial prerogative, especially at the plant level. This contradiction inhibited the consistent and successful implementation of the After Japan and employee involvement initiatives. More generally, it limited cooperation and the development of a joint approach, while also ending in a number of local disputes (Starkey and McKinley 1989; Darlington 1994).

The contradiction also constrained shop stewards from becoming more cooperative, though previously militant union attitudes at plants such as Halewood have softened as union officials have increasingly favored cooperation over a strongly adversarial approach. This conciliatory attitude of the unions has certainly been connected to reduced union power at Ford, reduced employment levels, and to threats of plant closures. Nevertheless, a joint partnership approach has not emerged. Given the history of adversarial industrial relations, and the contradictions in Ford's new approach to flexibility, shop stewards have feared that such initiatives as quality circles were designed to bypass the union. Consequently, stewards boycotted the early work reorganization initiatives and sought to retain control over jobs.

Darlington (1994) also points out that Ford's continual downsizing has clearly constrained the potential for cooperation. In contrast to the employment security guarantees provided at Rover, in 1992–1993 Ford threatened compulsory redundancies to meet its goal of a smaller workforce. Although the strong opposition forced Ford to back down, the threat highlighted the extent to which Ford was prepared to go to obtain cooperation. At the same time, however, Ford has been less interested in adopting a team-based work organization than Rover. Indeed, the organization of production remains relatively traditional, and the introduction of team leaders and elements of team working have not fundamentally changed the organization of work.

Teams play only a limited role in Ford. By 1996, few workers in assembly operations were organized into functioning teams. Furthermore, although teams were initially intended to contain eight to twelve workers, the average size has exceeded twenty. The organization of work remains traditional, and Ford's principal goal has been to increase flexibility in the deployment of labor, and to integrate direct and indirect production tasks. This goal was facilitated by the 1989 integrated manufacturing team agreement and subsequent plant-level negotiations, though limited use has since been made of that or of corresponding multiskilling in Ford's "total productive maintenance" program. There is also little job rotation, according to the unions, because of team members' lack of interest.

In line with the limited restructuring of work, the role of team leaders at Ford plants is considered part of the traditional career ladder within the plant—to assist foremen. Indeed, team leaders have replaced the previous system of lead operators and, before that of charge hands, though with some additional responsibilities. Correspondingly, as Table 3.7 indicates, Ford appoints team leaders to an enhanced rate of pay following a selection process that includes both tests and interviews.

This historical continuity of team leader roles at Ford is primarily a consequence of the continuing traditional organization of work, albeit with much greater flexibility. Team leaders provide stock and tooling, establish schedules, organize maintenance work, ensure quality, and provide basic training, supervision, and relief within the work group. Although there are formal restrictions on team leaders undertaking a disciplinary role, they typically supervise and direct work acting as the foremen's assistant. At some plants, such as Dagenham, a reduction in foremen since 1993 has accentuated this role. In contrast to Rover, the unions remain concerned that teams will undermine the role of shop stewards, since there are no provisions to ensure the unions' institutional security.

Negotiation for work reorganization at Ford has increasingly been subject to decentralized bargaining, in contrast to Ford's historic preference for national negotiations. The total productive maintenance program, for example, was negotiated locally with plant convenors and without the knowledge of officers from the national unions. In the view of the national unions, plant-level negotiations reflect the delegation of operations to plant managers, the weakening of the shop-steward organization at the plant level, the ability of management to whipsaw plants over fears about employment security and future investment decisions, and the lack of structural mechanisms within the national union to coordinate or even gather accurate information about plant-level activities. Although the national union has introduced new procedures to exchange plant-level information, it has found control hard to reassert.[20]

This decentralization has enabled Ford to whipsaw plants into, for example, outsourcing. Restrictions on the nature of such changes reflect the strength of the local union. At Dagenham, for example, the TGWU was able to ensure that seat production remained unionized when it was outsourced to Johnson Control, an antiunion company. Furthermore, in response to Johnson Control's demands for a "Japanese transplant model" company council, the TGWU was able to ensure representation by shop stewards on the council proportional to union membership (currently some 90 percent) and thereby prevent the form of company unionism evident at Nissan and Toyota. Nevertheless, where the union has been weaker, such as at Halewood, where the limited success of the Ford Escort has left the plant in a more precarious position, the union has been less successful in restricting the form of outsourcing.

Overall, Ford's approach to work reorganization has been somewhat piecemeal and uncoordinated, with restricted ambition. Ford has relied on an essentially traditional organization of work, enhanced by increased labor force flexibility, though without developed team-working structures. Furthermore, although Ford has made attempts to lessen the historically adversarial bargaining relationship, unlike Rover it has not committed itself to a joint team-based approach. Nevertheless, the company still reports that Dagenham saw the largest increase in productivity in Europe in the five years from 1991.

### Constrained Partnership at Vauxhall

General Motor's British company, Vauxhall, sought many of the same goals as Rover and Ford during the early 1980s—the reassertion of managerial prerogative, reduced job demarcations, and increased labor flexibility. However, it has taken a gradualist and decentralized approach to a common corporate model of team working at both its Ellesmere Port and Luton plants. This model of extensive team working recognizes a central role for the union. In contrast to Rover, however, the union's role is constrained by managerial prerogative, without any attempts to construct an extensive partnership relationship.

Vauxhall's initial reassertion of managerial prerogative included the prolonged "We Will Manage" strike at the Ellesmere Port plant in 1979, when the company attempted to reassert long-standing procedural agreements that had not been enforced during the 1970s as "shop steward bargaining and custom and practice encroached further into areas of previous managerial prerogative" (Marsden et al. 1985: 32). Yet, although this strike occurred at the start of a period that saw Vauxhall cut employment by one third in the four years prior to 1983, the company did not attempt to press its short-term bargaining advantage. Rather, Vauxhall also sought to cooperatively increase flexibility.

Changes to work organization during the 1980s included compressing the grading structure for semi-skilled production employees, classifying craft workers into only two categories (electrical and mechanical), progressively reducing job demarcations and securing agreement for semi-skilled production workers to undertake minor maintenance work. In contrast to Ford, however, Vauxhall also enhanced job security: in 1984 it agreed not to enforce redundancy resulting from technological change or new work practices, while in 1987–1988 it provided employment security for the life of the contract.[21]

Although these changes indicate the progress Vauxhall has made, the institutional security of the union remained unclear. Thus, in 1988, the unions rejected a package of proposals entitled "Meet the Challenge," which included team work, because the revised pay structures were unsatisfactory and because the proposals made no reference to the role of the trade unions (Fisher 1995). The constrained nature of Vauxhall's relationship with its unions was illustrated in the dispute settlement. Although this settlement confirmed the central role of unions in work reorganization, at the same time the company took steps to restrict the effectiveness of shop stewards, thus bypassing structures through which the latter exercised power.

The pattern of constrained partnership is also reflected in the agreements to implement teams within Vauxhall. Two plant-level contracts on team working were negotiated in 1990 and 1992, which despite plant-level bargaining were largely identical and corresponded to a corporate model.[22] The decision to conduct decentralized negotiations reflected the company's belief in a progressive, incremental implementation strategy rather than a differentiated and localized model. Consistent with this, the unions view the illusion of decentralization and local managerial autonomy as facilitating management-led whipsawing of plants on work organization issues and the company's ability to take advantage of the weak coordination by unions across plants. Thus, the first team-working agreement was reached at Ellesmere Port after six months of negotiations in return for securing investment in a new V6 engine plant and a 5 percent *plant-specific* wage increase. This agreement, and the plant wage premium, in turn led to successful negotiations being extended to Luton, on the same terms.

The Vauxhall team-working model explicitly recognizes the central role for unions and is couched in cooperative language that establishes a framework of joint union-management regulation that allows the unions to bargain change and have a "considerable impact upon the character and direction of these new workplace institutions" (Stewart 1995: 7). At the same time, however, the model reflects continued union reticence concerning team working, the removal of demarcation lines (with a reduction in occupational classifications from thirty-seven to seven), and other new managerial practices. Thus, the unions simultaneously view the changes as a damage-limitation exercise in what Thomas Murakami (1995b) has characterized as a "them-and-us attitude" between unions and management, and one of institutionalizing the role of the unions in the new structure.

The structure of teams illustrates the constrained nature of partnership at Vauxhall. Although the company and union jointly established criteria for the appointment of team leaders, the union plays no role in their selection; team leaders receive a 9 percent pay premium; and their responsibilities include some commonly associated with supervisors (Murakami 1995b). These responsibilities include performing all jobs within the team;

providing training; overseeing quality, cost, productivity, job rotation, and performance; and regulating matters internal to the team, including disputes. The union regards team leaders as "mini-managers" and, unlike team members, whose movement within the plant is guided by contractual provisions, the movement of team leaders is determined solely at the discretion of management. Furthermore, the role of team leaders replaces that of the traditional charge hands, who date back to 1941, were also appointed by management, received additional payment, and were part of the normal career ladder. Significantly, 80 percent of the initial team leaders were former charge hands, this being a deliberate company policy (Murakami 1995b).

Team leaders are not responsible for disciplinary action or reviewing performance. However, Murakami's research both confirms that workers perceive team leaders as being aligned with managers and establishes strong worker support for the election of team leaders. Nevertheless, both the company and unions were in clear agreement that team leaders should be appointed without union or worker input into the decision.[23] Once again, this agreement illustrates the constrained partnership that has evolved at Vauxhall. The company was opposed to election, fearing that the power of shop stewards would increase, while the union was anxious to avoid any confusion of roles between team leaders and shop stewards, which the union feared would arise if they were elected.

The unions' strategy was thus to ensure that their own role and that of shop stewards remained intact, and that there continued to be a single source of employee representation. This reticence to adopt a stronger partnership relationship reflects the unions' concern for their institutional security. The consequence of the unions' policy of establishing a clear separation of team leader and shop-steward roles was, however, that a significant number of shop stewards were required to resign their posts when applying for appointment as team leaders. Nevertheless, the unions continue to fear that team leaders will simultaneously play a supervisory role and also undermine the role of the union.

In contrast to these fears, evidence from both Murakami (1995b) and Stewart (1995) at Luton and Ellesmere Port, respectively, shows that thus far, the distinctive role of the union has remained intact. The formal agreement on teams, which specified the role of team leaders, has preserved the unions' role as the pivotal communication channel and allowed union representatives to be present at team-leader training sessions, if not to attend all team meetings. In addition, shop stewards (rather than team leaders) remain the central communication channel at Vauxhall and receive extensive company information. The centrality of the union role is evident in various ways: the union can veto a percentage of applicants to the plant; the company formally encourages union membership; and the union is consulted closely on a wide range of plant issues. Furthermore, there is a no-compulsory-redundancy pledge and a commitment to increased redeployment of labor within the plant, as well as an agreement to consult the union before any use of contractors.

Team working itself has been introduced extensively at both Ellesmere Port and Luton, particularly among production workers. At Ellesmere Port, for example, teams of approximately ten workers have been formed around natural work groups, with no demarcations, responsibility for routine maintenance, and workers undertaking all tasks in their section. Although the extent of team autonomy varies, it is generally limited, as is job rotation. Stewart reports that rotation "is possible only under the sanction of the team leader in negotiation with the shop steward" (1995: 4), illustrating the continued role of shop stewards, whereas Murakami (1995) notes that at Luton, the limited rotation has sometimes been ordered by management. In part this reflects the continued constrained partnership between the union and management. Institutional structures have been established to facilitate a cooperative relationship, but the tensions resulting from pressure to increase plant performance, continued employment reductions and recent increases in outsourcing and temporary contracts, and the removal of job controls have left the union uncertain of its security and future limits to managerial prerogative.

### A Japanese-Oriented Employment Pattern

All three Japanese transplants in the United Kingdom have adopted similar Japanese-oriented employment practices. These include tightly structured teams organized around standardized work processes, a strong role for managerially appointed and hierarchical team leaders, a high degree of managerial prerogative, and a key role for supervisors. Despite different policies on unionization, practices are similar. Thus, while Honda has adopted a clear nonunion approach, both Nissan and Toyota formally encourage employees to become members of the AEEU. In 1996, unionization rates were estimated by the union to be 40 percent in each case, though more than 95 percent among manual workers in the traditional auto companies. Nevertheless, the role of the union is very limited not only with respect to bargaining, as discussed above, but also on the shop floor, in establishing work organization and in the operation of team-working structures.

The weakness of the shop-floor union role at Nissan and Toyota results from the single-union agreements that concede exclusive managerial prerogative on work organization and the deployment of labor. Rather than incorporate a union voice, principles of work organization can only be discussed by the company council, though even then, management holds sway, together with the appointed team leaders and supervisors. The effect is to marginalize the role and influence of the union, though much more fundamental was Nissan's agreement prohibiting shop stewards within the company. Although this restriction was later conceded, shop stewards still have no representational role within Nissan.

Flexibility is also ensured by the absence of any job descriptions or demarcation lines. Together with the extensive use of teams, there is thus substantial freedom to deploy labor according to a plant's needs. At Honda, this flexibility includes a blurring of the divide between blue- and white-collar jobs (Mueller 1992b).

In all three transplants, team leaders are selected by management and are appointed as a different grade employee (Table 3.7). This selection is regarded as promotion into the first rank of management (Mair 1994; Mueller 1992b). Despite single-status employment, team leaders consequently play a central role as supervisors of their team and, along with first-line supervisors, were among the first employees to be recruited. Team leaders are expected to be multiskilled employees and are responsible for the performance of the team and of team members (or "associates"). Their greater authority over team members includes oversight of the individual appraisal systems at Toyota, Nissan, and Honda. These appraisals affect workers directly through performance-related wage increases, as opposed to bonuses. At Nissan, the continual appraisal process influences employees' progression on the pay scale and is linked to the achievement of objectives agreed between an employee and the supervisor (Garrahan and Steward 1992a, b).

In addition, supervisors have an unusually strong position at Nissan because they are responsible for final hiring decisions during the recruitment process. Indeed, this was designed to enhance their authority, and their responsibility extends beyond such personnel and appraisal decisions to budget setting, the scheduling and organization of work, and coordination with team leaders.

Although team size varies from five to seven at Toyota and from ten to fifteen at Nissan, the organization of team work is similar. In particular, teams are typically organized around specific production tasks; job rotation is formally encouraged by management; publicly displayed skills matrices are used; and team leaders are integrated into teams and are expected to provide cover for absent employees. Production tasks are clearly defined, with minimal production autonomy for either the team or team leader, and task times at Toyota are even reportedly established with advice from Japan. Furthermore, although team meetings are frequent (often daily), they are also very short, often lasting only a few minutes.

In an important contrast to Rover, none of the Japanese transplants provide employment security guarantees, though they state a preference for stable employment levels. The contracts at Nissan and Toyota, furthermore, establish procedures for layoffs, which at both firms require four weeks' notice. To meet lower than anticipated demand in 1993, Nissan did indeed seek volunteers for a redundancy program, though there were no involuntary redundancies. At Toyota, the contract requires the company to take into account volunteers, length of service, skills, and also the employment and performance record of the workers in determining layoff procedures. Although the Members' Advisory Board at Toyota, must be consulted on layoffs, as is done on other issues, no consultation or agreement is required with the union itself.

## SUMMARY OF AUTO DEVELOPMENTS

The auto industry in Britain has moved substantially from its adversarial tradition, which characterized all companies in 1979. Japanese transplants have added substantial variation to working practices and also to bargaining procedures and the form of worker representation in the industry. However, the sources of variation run much deeper than that, as is seen in the extent of vertical disintegration, the corresponding trend to lower unionization rates throughout the industry, and the growing wage disparity between assemblers and suppliers.

Beyond these sources of diversity, as the traditional companies have restructured their working practices and industrial relations, programmatic variation has emerged. There is no consistent approach to employment practices in Britain, but substantial room for strategic choice has been demonstrated within the unionized segment of the industry. However, the reticence of unions at Ford and Vauxhall to endorse new practices illustrates that this is not a one-way choice. Rather, it highlights how the absence of union institutional security can actually hinder the adoption of a joint team-based approach when unions fear that such a path might actually be a sham to undermine their representational structures within plants.

## THE TELECOMMUNICATIONS INDUSTRY

In contrast to conditions in the auto industry, developments at one firm—British Telecom (BT)—dominated the evolution of employment systems in the British telecommunications industry. The privatization of BT in 1984 and the subsequent deregulation of the telecommunications market has produced one of the most open market structures among industrialized countries. Although BT still dominates this market, competition is increasing, particularly from the nonunion network provider Cable and Wireless Communications (CWC).[24] In addition, nonunion cable TV franchises, themselves mostly subsidiaries of U.S. telecommunications companies, also offer telephone services.[25]

The new market entrants have brought a variety of nonunion employment patterns to an industry historically characterized by complete unionization and a highly regulated, strongly consultative, public-sector employment pattern. While there are examples of low-wage employment practices in some of the new cable TV companies, emerging employment patterns in the telecommunications industry range from nonunion human resource management patterns to Japanese-oriented systems and joint team-based approaches. This variation is not simply found among companies: rather, there is increasing variation of employment patterns applied within BT.

*Developments at BT*

The pace of technological and organizational change within BT has been substantial. Together with significant downsizing, corporate reorganizations have led to a shifting emphasis among centralization, decentralization, and divisionalization, while work restructuring has been extensive. Furthermore, privatization and deregulation have been instrumental in bringing about substantial change and variation in the employment relationship within BT.

BT has traditionally been nearly completely unionized among both non-managerial ranks, represented by the Communications Workers Union (CWU) and managers, represented by the Society of Telecom Executives (STE).[26] Since privatization in 1984, both unions have lost substantial numbers of union members, owing to workforce downsizing and greater corporate reluctance to recognize STE representation of managers. Along with continual restructurings, this has adversely impacted the position of both unions, though particularly the STE.

Downsizing has, however, been at least as important in altering the balance of power between the unions and management. Employment reductions resulting from corporate policies, technological change, deregulation, and competition amounted to almost 50 percent. Employment fell from 241,000 in 1984 to 116,493 in April 1998, with more than 90 percent of this decline occurring after 1990. Operators have been the hardest hit, with their numbers falling by some 88 percent, followed by technicians, for whom employment declined by more than 55 percent. Managerial employment, by contrast, saw greater stability, experiencing only a 23 percent reduction, while clerical employment also fell by 23 percent. Among clerical workers there has, however, been a strong shift in employment away from traditional office jobs toward sales, marketing, and new call centers.

The substantial downsizing has, however, been achieved without the company resorting to compulsory redundancies, though it has cost BT 3.5 billion pounds (5.6 billion dollars), or an average of two years' salary per person in severance payments. Nevertheless, the specter of compulsory redundancies has been a constant pressure on the union. Together with technological change, which has created a substantially more robust technical network, this has contributed to a significant decline in union power. The decline has been exacerbated insofar as before privatization, the unions' power base was supplemented by political influence. But, the unions' political influence has waned, while privatization has also brought a hardening of management's industrial relations approach.

### The Internal Reorganizations of BT

Prior to privatization, BT had been characterized as subject to "over-centralisation, poor delegation and slow decision-taking" (Carter 1977: 66). This situation changed as the removal of layers of bureaucracy, the introduction of a customer-oriented organization, and an increased emphasis on profits became the principal objectives of BT management from the early 1980s onward. To realize these objectives, BT initially restructured by decentralizing operations. In 1983 it adopted a geographic structure based on thirty districts, acting as semi-autonomous profit centers.

The decentralization of managerial decision making aimed to increase operational flexibility and thereby improve local productivity and responsiveness to customer demands. To achieve this objective, districts were granted greater freedom in their technological operations and their ability to reorganize the workforce. However, the local reorganization of work led management to push for renegotiation of the previously rigid and hierarchical job structures contained in jointly agreed "telecommunications instructions" and, therefore, a revision of the old centralized bargaining structures. The BT unions were, in contrast, intent on retaining common work practices throughout BT and strongly resisted a decentralization of bargaining on any issue.

### Decentralization of Bargaining at BT

Despite union resistance, the changing management structures did increase local variation in operational practices and work organization, as well as generate significant conflict over work organization. Nevertheless, when district-level managers circumvented and renegotiated elements of national agreements, both the unions and the corporate industrial relations unit found that, in practice, they had only limited sanctions available to implement the national-level agreements.

The more aggressive managerial style encouraged by privatization, new commercial pressures, and decentralization to districts contributed to the first-ever national strike in 1987. In addition, low morale and union frustration at the increased local pressure for bargaining decentralization also underlay the friction and deteriorating industrial relations climate.

In the aftermath of the strike, however, the geographic decentralization and variation reached its height. Decentralized bargaining became more formal through the introduction of "framework agreements" on more flexible structures of work organization to supersede the previously rigid telecommunications instructions. Thus, managerial power appeared to be ascendant. However, management gained less from this decentralization than it hoped. Decentralized negotiations on the so-called Blue Book, or repatterning agreement, proved to be a substantially greater task than expected, and the union (CWU) attempted to coordinate its own policies across all local districts. Yet variation did emerge where management and local union branches adopted different strategies to the reorganization of work practices.

Although elements of variation helped improve BT's market orientation, it also produced substantial detrimental operational side effects, leading senior BT managers to lament that it should be a "network," not a "patchwork." In addition, the lack of operational coordination inhibited the migration of new technology and work practices and also contributed to a lack of consistency across the company and a deterioration in performance.

BT responded with a massive reorganization in 1991 that introduced a greater degree of divisionalization than had been evident before, including the establishment of three principal divisions to manage business customers, residential customers, and the network, respectively. BT also reduced the layers of management from twelve to six. However, an oscillation between centralization and decentralization has continued in the 1990s, as it did in the 1980s. There have been several reorganizations of the business customer division, as well as a merging and reorganizing of the networks and residential customer divisions, a process that continued into 1998. The continual restructuring of the corporate organizational structure reflects an internal conflict and tension. On the one hand, BT's objective has been to reduce bureaucracy, create a market-oriented structure, and allow operational flexibility to facilitate greater divisional variation, despite union opposition. On the other hand, BT has also felt pressure to improve both the level and consistency of performance and operational coordination, which has implied reintroducing greater commonality (and centralization) in working practices.

For the unions, the reorganizations of corporate structure initially created the difficult task of aligning their own structure to decision makers within BT, given the historically centralized system of bargaining and centralized union organization. Ironically, the unions' eventual success in decentralizing their organization created difficulties for both the union and the company following the subsequent recentralization. After local union branches had gained a greater direct voice in negotiations on work organization issues, they were reluctant to see this diluted in a return to corporate centralization. Local branches even rejected national union proposals for amended union structures, although these structures would have facilitated greater interaction between union officials and appropriate management decision makers.

A more general union reluctance to adjust its structures to those of the company has also followed from the continual corporate reorganizations, since the union has feared that the benefits of matching the corporate organization would only be temporary. For the company, the legacy of their temporary decentralization and continual reorganizations has been to increase the difficulty of introducing corporate-wide changes in working practices, even in a period of substantial managerial prerogative.

### Changes in Pay Structures and Collective Bargaining Coverage of Managers at BT

Traditionally, all staff in BT were members of unions, and their pay and conditions were bargained for them annually in a highly centralized public sector system, involving joint consultation and "fair comparison" pay determination. Although bargaining was technically separate for managerial and nonmanagerial groups of staff at the time of privatization, all workers received parallel pay rises until 1986, when BT introduced greater fragmentation into the bargaining structure. Negotiations for technicians and clerical grades has since been formally separate, though with only small differences in pay emerging. BT has also been unsuccessful in its underlying goal of introducing performance-related pay for nonmanagerial workers. However, BT has introduced substantially greater changes in managerial pay structures. In particular, it has derecognized the STE for bargaining the pay of a significant portion of managers, as well as introducing a performance-related pay system for all managers.

In 1984, at the time of privatization, 588 senior managers were on individual contracts (so-called personal contract grades, or PCGs). In 1990, BT decided to push increasing numbers of managers onto nonunion, individual contracts, both by threatening to withhold increases if this transfer was not agreed to and also by offering a company car if managers did agree. Despite BT's substantial employment reduction, by 1997 there were 10,260 managers on individual employment contracts, reflecting a substantial move away from collectively bargained employment conditions. Pay increases for these managers consist of a base-rate rise and a nonrecurring bonus, both being theoretically wholly related to individual performance. Incrcases are based on the performance of the company, the performance of the manager as measured against individually agreed objectives, and an external, market-based element. In 1993, for example, the pay award for PCGs averaged 2.52 percent, with a range from zero to 11 percent, the nonrecurring bonus, which can potentially amount to 25 percent of base pay, averaged 3,835 pounds (6,135 dollars), with a range from zero to more than 6,000 pounds (9,600 dollars).

Beyond derecognizing the STE for these senior managers, BT has fundamentally changed the bargaining relationship and pay system for all other managers. In 1984, BT introduced a limited performance-pay system, though with pay primarily service-based (Ferner and Terry 1997). In 1987, the service-based progression was replaced by an appraisal-based system, though the significant performance-related pay element existed alongside a generalized annual increase. In 1993, however, BT introduced a entirely performance-related system, closely akin to that for PCGs. Pay increases for managers are now based on the achievement of a range of competencies, agreed to in individual reviews at least quarterly, which form the basis of the annual performance review. Pay increases and a bonus paid to some managers are related to this appraisal, according to a matrix negotiated by BT and the STE.

This represents a profound change in the bargaining relationship between the company and managerial union, with pay increases critically dependent upon line managers and BT unilaterally deciding how its overall budget for pay increases is distributed. The STE's role in this increasingly individualized structure has been minimized, reflecting BT's underlying drive to marginalize the STE management union and operate an HRM system among its managers.[27] Indeed, in interviews senior managers in BT regarded this change in pay structures as having "struck at the heart of the bargaining relationship with the STE." As such, BT is developing a human resource management employment pattern with respect to even its unionized managerial employees.

An equally fundamental change in pay structures among management ranks occurred with new performance-related pay systems for field managers, who supervise the field-based technical staff in the residential customer division. In addition to their base pay, field managers have a performance-related pay system linked to the achievement of a set of measured objectives (rather than annual appraisals). Initially, performance-related pay amounted to up to 25 percent of base pay, though this was increased in 1996 to a maximum of 33 percent. However, the more significant aspect of the field managers' pay system is its relationship to their supervisory role. In particular, field managers' pay is now dependent not directly on their *own* performance but rather on that of the field technicians they supervise (discussed further below).

### Work Reorganization at BT

Historically, employment at BT was based on a bureaucratic structure of complex and hierarchical job demarcations, with rigid divisions among hierarchies, strong internal labor markets, and joint regulation of staffing ratios, supervision, and work processes. These were contained in tight national agreements (Batstone et al. 1984). Similarly, changes to grading structures were subject to extensive joint consultation and negotiation between BT and the unions. Following the 1987 national strike, substantial changes were made to the grading structure. The telecommunications instructions, which had established these work rules and employment patterns, were abolished and replaced with the Blue Book. This agreement introduced substantial flexibility into the grading structure, including a significant increase in multiskilling.

The flexibility of the Blue Book has reduced the need for renegotiation, despite massive, ongoing technological change. It has also facilitated BT undertaking multiple attempts to reorganize its workforce to drive up productivity. However, none of the range of work patterns that have been introduced have demonstrated clearly superior results. In part, the alternative experimental patterns that have emerged reflect divisional variations in employment relations, though there are also various experiments with different employment systems within individual divisions.

### Changing Roles of Field Managers

The most widespread employment system in the residential customer division at BT corresponds to our Japanese-oriented pattern, with close supervision, standardized jobs, and individual performance appraisal. Three elements are central to this new and changed organization of work: a new field manager supervisory system, with an unusual performance-related pay system; standard job times and the measurement of field technicians' performance against these; and a new job distribution and allocation system. These changes represent a coherent strategic shift in the employment relationship for these workers.

Historically, field managers spent only 20 percent of their time in the field and 80 percent on administrative duties. Although most of the work of field technicians has long been individualized, from the early 1970s on, there was a senior technician (ST) with a "chargeship" role, primarily coaching and problem solving with other workers. In the early 1990s, BT decided against expanding the chargeship role of these technicians, which would have increased the ratio of workers to field managers. Instead, BT moved to largely eliminate this post and introduce a substantially tighter supervisory role for field managers.[28] This change consisted of the establishment of field support offices, to allow field managers to spend 80 percent of their time in the field, with a significant expansion in the number of field managers.

### Performance Management of Field Technicians

The second critical element in this employment system was the introduction of a measurement system to assess the performance of field technicians. Traditionally, there had been minimal measurement of jobs in BT and no individual (or indeed group) productivity-based performance assessment. However, the "Field Effectiveness with Quality" program involves establishing standard times for all jobs—so-called quality task times consisting of both job quality and productivity elements. The performance of individual field technicians is assessed by field managers on a weekly basis against the achievement of the standard times, with both in-progress and retrospective reviews to assess the quality of work.

In addition to this unprecedented increase in performance measurement, the quality management system (QMS) introduced at BT for the first time established detailed and extensively documented company-wide procedures for how jobs were to be completed and include the establishment of a national "documentation center."[29] The continuous improvement program associated with both the field effectiveness standard times and the QMS system is a centralized and top-down process with, at least in theory, strictly limited local discretion. The structure is instead intended to ensure consistent working practices, to facilitate centralized process and procedure improvements being quickly and easily disseminated throughout the company.

The introduction of the new tightly supervised work organization pattern has also been associated with new working-time arrangements, which have introduced significantly greater flexibility in start and finish times. Furthermore, a new automated job allocation and distribution system (the work manager) has facilitated real-time analysis of individual field technicians' performance on any given job. The work manager thereby increases the practical relevance of standard times within BT.

The performance-related pay system for field managers is critically dependent not on their own direct performance but rather on that of the field technicians they directly supervise (with a ratio of approximately 1:15 field managers to field technicians). Indeed, the performance pay of field managers includes a component based on the sales achievements of field technicians, even though such selling is strictly voluntary for the field technicians. Although BT was unsuccessful in overcoming union opposition to the introduction of performance-related pay for field technicians, technician performance does constitute a central component of a restructured and much more detailed annual performance review. Furthermore, one-to-one performance reviews are held with field technicians at least monthly.

The agreement between BT and the CWU on the Field Effectiveness program was in part a concessionary bargain by the union on work practices, centering on BT's agreement not to double the number of subcontractors used internally and not to "surplus" (and therefore lay off) any workers as a result of productivity improvements caused by the ongoing work reorganization. Instead, workers were to be transferred to BT's "capital uplift" program for improving the quality of the local network, with a corresponding one-for-one reduction in the use of subcontractors. Although introduced in the field activities of the residential division, the principles of the field effectiveness program have been extended more generally in BT.

This case thus provides an example of an area where management has been able to effectively use its enhanced power to whipsaw the union despite the integrated nature of production in the telecommunications industry. Although the form of whipsawing between manufacturing plants evident in the auto industry, and the more general use of outsourcing, have been either not possible or much more difficult in the telecommunications industry, there are nevertheless also trends in this direction.

### Increasing Use of Contingent Workforce

The first steps that BT made to focus on its core telecommunications services occurred in the late 1980s when BT withdrew from manufacturing. The company sold Mitel, BT Fulcrum, BT Marine, BT Consumer Electronics, and its label operations. The trend to greater outsourcing was extended as BT contracted out its catering, cleaning, reprographics, and security operations. By 1996, BT had adopted a new, divisional strategy on downsizing and the use of contractors and agency staff. These resourcing decisions are now decentralized to divisional and business unit managers, to be made on the basis of a "total labor cost" approach, rather than the previous "headcount" reduction approach (CWU 1998). This change has contributed to a substantial increase in the use of contingent workers.

Contractors and agency staff have increased from approximately 10,000 in 1984 to 21,725 in 1997. Taking into account the ongoing downsizing, this represents an increase from 4.2 percent to 17.4 percent of the workforce, and included 7,583 agency staff, 6,720 outsourced jobs, and 7,422 subcontract workers. The most dramatic example of BT's adoption of a low-wage employment pattern using contingent workers occurs in its call centers. In this area of growing employment, 85 percent of employees were agency workers in 1997. These call centers have experienced especially high turnover and other employment relations problems.

BT has, furthermore, extended its use of employment of contract labor into other core areas of work, including switchboard operators and field technicians. During the 1990s, the use of contract field technicians has increased from 6.5 percent of this employment category in 1991 to 13.4 percent in 1997. These contract field technicians are employed in such activities as the installation of information technology on customers' premises (CWU 1998).

The consequence of these changes has been a substantial decline in the role of unions in determining pay and conditions. When BT was privatized in 1984, significantly fewer than 1 percent of employees had their basic terms and conditions established other than by collective bargaining. By 1997 this had risen to 29 percent.

### Participatory Efforts at BT

Despite these general moves to introduce more contingent workers and a closely supervised production organization in an industry more commonly associated with high discretion among skilled field technicians, BT has also made attempts to introduce joint team-based (participatory) approaches. These are efforts to address the problems of a demotivated field force, where skills have been underutilized and productivity gains limited. Within BT's residential division, for example, team-based pilots were introduced in 1994–1995 and tested more seriously in 1996.[30] They involve the potential of giving field technicians more scope in introducing local initiatives, greater responsibilities for work scheduling, control of the overtime budget, team working through local geographic "patch" working and increased communication among individual technicians (including the use of mobile phones for the first time), and greater flexibility for the technicians to determine the extent of multiple skilling negotiated in the 1987 Blue Book. Associated with these changes has been a reduction of BT's increasing "command and control" management style, with greater emphasis on managerial support and coaching.

An earlier and at least initially more substantial introduction of the joint team-based approach occurred in the business communications division in the early 1990s. In response to BT's active contemplation of franchising its customer premise equipment (CPE) activities, a divisional agreement was reached with the CWU. The relevant CPE section of the business division adopted a strategy of substantial consultation and communication with the union, which the union has regarded as a "phenomenal industrial relations event, a velvet revolution," and "verging on industrial democracy" (interviews).

The division and union agreed to significant changes in work organization, which included more flexible working time practices, the extension of sales activities for technicians, a "virtual team" relationship between technicians and sales staff, and team-based incentive pay. This incentive pay is confined to the technicians, not managers, with the deliberate intention of managers adopting a more supportive team leader approach than is evident with field managers. The introduction of this new structure of work organization led to the elimination of BT's franchising proposals (with the corresponding possibility of compulsory redundancies) and the agreed reduction in subcontracting.

The concessions made by the union for the extra employment security included more flexible working practices and especially the active participation of technicians in sales activities. Also of particular importance, the union allowed an exception to be made from their previously strict opposition to contingent pay. The initial success of this employment pattern in terms of additional sales revenue and the favorable response of employees encouraged expansion of the practice. Yet doing so also created significant internal conflicts within the union.

The official union policy against many of the concessions made in this agreement (and particularly contingent pay) clashed with national union officers' realization that concessions were necessary to ensure BT involvement in that market segment. This had consequent implications for employment security; also at issue were the substantial improvements and quality of the industrial relations practices and the generally very positive responses of those employees involved in the teams, given their greater discretion and participation. For the national union officers, the issue thus became in part how to facilitate a decentralized and yet controlled work experiment, encouraging and actively supporting what they perceived as a remarkably positive shift in industrial relations practice, while simultaneously upholding official union policy.

The variation of employment patterns emerging within BT illustrates the uncertainty of the performance advantages of each system, together with different divisional preferences and strategies. In general, the residential division has adopted the "hardest" style of industrial relations, including the least use of consultation with unions. By contrast, the business customer division has adopted a considerably more participatory style, establishing more extensive and detailed joint consultation structures with national and "zonal" (though not individual branch-level) union representatives.

An initial underlying motivation among BT managers for the various employment-relations approaches was the different levels of value added among residential and business customers. At the very least, in the late 1980s many managers within the low-value-added residential customer division believed that they could not afford a "cosy" industrial relations approach. Managers also believed that a speed-up of work was required and that the potential downside risk from an adversarial stance was low. With higher value-added work, the business customer division potentially bore higher risk from an unsuccessful and resisted speeded-up approach, but also might have more to gain from participation.

Despite the implementation of what seemed to be elements of economic and production logic, management of both divisions has questioned the short- and long-term advantages and costs associated with different employment patterns. This "performance uncertainty" was enhanced in the residential customer division during the 1990s in particular because productivity improvements were thought to have resulted only from technological change and not from improved employee performance, despite the greater flexibility achieved.

This uncertainty has clearly promoted more significant variation and experimentation, with divisions simultaneously adopting joint team-based approaches alongside Japanese-oriented practices. However, strategic choice has also governed the adoption of particular patterns. This has included key individuals (for example, in instigating the partnership approach in the CPE operations), as well as management reactions to perceived (local) union attitudes. Indeed, local union militancy in areas such as London has unquestionably reinforced an adversarial management stance. Furthermore, despite the very progressive views of national union officers, they have been constrained by formal union policy established at annual conferences. The adoption of joint-team based practices have been constrained by some of these policies, creating a dilemma for many national union officers.

### Negotiation and Consultation Structures

Historically, joint consultation committees were used extensively in BT, established under the Whitley system of public-sector industrial relations. Indeed, between 1978 and 1980, the post office (of which BT was then a part) was the site of an experiment into industrial democracy, with union representatives on the board (Batstone et al. 1983). However, even independent observers noted substantial problems with the Whitley system. Thus, for example, Batstone et al observed that the "wheels of joint consultation and negotiation...ground exceedingly small; they also ground exceedingly slow" (1984: 144).

In the post-privatization period, BT has progressively moved to narrow the range of consultation and negotiation with the unions, particularly following the first national technicians' strike in 1987, when BT felt that its structure of direct communication with the workforce was significantly lacking. Its attempts to rectify this, particularly with group briefings as part of its total quality management program, have combined with a reduction in local (branch-level) union access to managers to lessen the role played by unions.

Consequently, the unions attempted to revitalize the consultation process at the national level through a proposal in 1992 for a "New Dialogue," which bore (coincidental) similarities to AT&T's "Workplace of the Future" agreement. This proposal sought to create a flexible system of consultation not rooted in the Whitley tradition but rather "in today's commercial imperatives" (NCU 1992). BT rejected the proposal, essentially deeming it unnecessary in the context of a weaker union. Instead, BT continued to reduce the number of paid full-time union representatives. Yet, in interviews, even senior national union representatives remark that BT management avoided fully exploiting the loss of union power, significantly because a consistent application of employment policies throughout the company provided continued advantages. Nevertheless, the trend to a divisionalization of BT has been reflected in diverging union consultation structures among divisions.

Corresponding to divisionalization and a decline in consultation there has been a substantial decline in the importance of the industrial relations function in BT and a transfer of responsibility to operational managers.

This shift was most evident in the 1994 "service value analysis" review of the personnel function, which recommended a 46 percent cost reduction of this support activity, with protections to prevent any "ballooning" of the function at the operational level. The reorganization included an increase in the subcontracting of support functions, further adding to the variation of employment patterns.

Initial indications were that operational managers were finding it difficult to contain the demands on the industrial relations function at the operational level. Operating managers often were not well trained for or did not have adequate resources to handle the expanding array of industrial relations issues they were confronting. At the local level, both administrative and industrial relations tensions resulted.

At the national level, the scope of bargaining within BT has been significantly narrowed, with BT management confining an increasing number of topics to the "consultation only" realm. Furthermore, where bargaining occurs, BT has introduced the distinction between agreements on principles and those on processes, and it confines negotiations to one or the other. The intent has been to restrict the substance of all agreements, thereby to increase the flexibility of contracts and to avoid local union negotiators being able to grieve on the details of contracts and policies. Examples of the increasingly restricted nature of negotiations included bargaining over the Network Administration Implementation Program for reconfiguring the structure of the network, where BT purposely resisted making any formal agreement. Likewise, the "Release '92" redundancy program, under which some thirty-five thousand employees left the company, was negotiated in a total of five weeks and restricted to five pages, since BT bargained only on the substance of the package and not on the principles.

Beyond this, the recentralization of power in BT from 1991 on is increasingly associated with greater divisionalization, with responsibility transferred to operational managers. This has been so with the introduction of new working-time arrangements in both the residential and business customer divisions, such that contracts now vary by division; the introduction of new working practices, such as the Field Effectiveness program and the use of teams in the customer premise equipment section of the business customer division; and the reorganization of technology and work practices in the network division. Indeed, the corporate industrial relations function plays no role in the implementation of agreements, and grievance disputes can only be escalated within a division. This revised bargaining structure increases the importance of operational managers within divisions and restricts the role of industrial relations managers at the corporate level. In turn, more varied employment patterns are emerging within BT.

*Problems Created by Variations in Work Practices at BT*

An important objective and conflict for BT has been ensuring consistent operational practices throughout the organization while also boosting performance and responsiveness to customers. In part, this objective for greater consistency reflected a response to the variation from BT's decentralization of its management structure in the mid-1980s. The subsequent variation in work practices led to a variation in performance also, though it did not enable BT to identify productivity, cost, or quality advantages associated with particular employment practices. The variations in employment patterns themselves reflected both differing management objectives, strategies, and perceptions, and also differing degrees of local union strength and militancy.

Given BT's strategic desire to provide a highly consistent level of service throughout its operations, it was anxious to avoid the resulting variation in service performance. Yet BT has continued to face a deep, underlying conflict between its desire to decentralize responsibility to operational managers, to increase responsiveness to customers, and to experiment with new forms of work organization, on the one hand; and to maintain consistent performance and to rapidly disseminate new working practices and technology throughout the company, on the other. This conflict has been compounded by the use of bureaucratic QMS systems, which greatly increased the demands for common, centralized, and closely documented working practices.

*The Nonunion Employment Pattern at Mercury*

Cable and Wireless Communications (CWC), the dominant rival network provider, has focused its operations on establishing competition in the City of London and in long-distance and international networks. By 1995, CWC had acquired an approximately 50 percent share of telecommunications market in the City and a 29 percent share of the international market. In the national business market, BT's share had fallen to 83 percent, while it was 93 percent in the residential market, where cable TV companies have provided the dominant source of competition. In mid-1998, CWC had 11,500 employees, with the cable TV companies estimating total employment (including network construction) of 16,000 at the end of 1996.[31] Neither CWC nor any cable TV companies recognize any unions.

CWC's employment practices differ substantially from those in BT and closely correspond to our human resource management pattern.[32] Indeed, it has deliberately avoided establishing any internal grade structure as part of its policy of establishing an explicitly individualized employment relationship. There are thus no official pay ranges for jobs titles, which are used simply used to establish "organizational understanding" and "status." Instead, local line managers set pay levels and increases based on the company's ability to pay, market value, and individual performance. All pay increases in CWC are based on an individual's annual performance appraisal, which is in turn related to an individually negotiated performance contract, which includes both job-specific appraisals and a competency review. CWC claims to base pay entirely on merit, with no fixed pay scales or maxima, and from 1994 allowed individuals flexibility in how their performance was to be assessed. As part of the individualization of the employment relationship, staff do not receive information on the mechanics of the performance assessment and pay levels. In line with this employment structure, all communication within CWC is individualized, while additional overtime without pay is part of the regular employment contract.

In 1996 CWC did, however, introduce an "employee involvement forum," which reflected "a managerial preference for weaker forms of employee participation which may dilute or serve as an alternative to union-based systems of representation." This forum "provides no institutional role for unions, specifically excludes discussion of contentious issues such as pay, benefits and grievances, and allows the chief executive to veto agenda items proposed by employees" (Heery 1997: 101). This "forum," which bears a resemblance to the company councils at Nissan and Toyota, had one third of its twenty-one employee seats unfilled at its inaugural meeting.


SUMMARY OF TELECOMMUNICATIONS DEVELOPMENTS

A growing trend in nonunion employment patterns has thus emerged in the telecommunications industry in Britain from liberalization and the entrance of new telephone and cable TV competitors to the highly unionized BT. Along with new variation in working practices, there has also been a significant expansion of variation within BT. The effective derecognition of unions among managerial ranks has been one manifestation, though it has by no means been confined to this. Taking advantage of its heightened managerial prerogative and the introduction of new technology, BT has also experimented with a range of employment practices.

An important explanation for the diversity that has emerged has been the uncertainty over the performance results of different patterns, in both the short run and especially the longer run. This uncertainty has been reflected in BT's increasing concern for the possibly detrimental effects of the extremely low employee morale that has resulted at least in part from the new, tightly supervised employment patterns. Yet, the widespread uncertainty over the value of changes in work organization, as distinct from the introduction of new technology, has resulted from the failure to realize productivity gains from these changes. Indeed, operational conflicts have arisen from attempts to decentralize managerial structures, leading to an oscillation between centralization and different forms of decentralization. Matching this uncertainty, BT has attempted to introduced a range of work experiments in the joint team-based approach, which often coincide uneasily alongside more aggressive top-down, management-dominated practices.

### INCOME INEQUALITY IN THE UNITED KINGDOM

After a compression of the wage structure during the 1970s in Britain, growing inequality began to occur in the late 1970s (in contrast to the United States, where it began at the end of the 1960s), and has been dramatic since, with few signs of slowing. Polarization of the wage and income distribution is consistent across a broad range of measures, with there being little wage growth for the bottom 10th percentile and rapid real wage growth at the 90th percentile (Machin 1996; Leslie and Pu 1996). Furthermore, this increase in inequality appears to be permanent in that it does not represent an increase in the instability of earnings but rather an increase in inequality of earnings across individuals. There is increasing variation between workers with differing education levels (with a rising skill premium evident), a widening age-related differential, and also greater variation among occupations, including manual and nonmanual workers within manufacturing (ibid.). Yet a further similarity with the United States is that the polarization of earnings represents as much intragroup variation as it does intergroup variation. That is, there is also a substantial growth of intragroup inequality, reflecting a greater variation among workers with the same education, age profile, occupation, and sectoral employment. This trend is particularly large for the lowest educational groups.

The sharp decline in manufacturing and corresponding growth in the service sector are insufficient to explain the general pattern of income polarization. Although the service sector, where unions have been weaker, has consistently had greater variation in wages, there has been a greater rise in income inequality inside the manufacturing sector than within services in the 1980s (Schmidt 1995). Although evidence points to some increase in income inequality owing to changes in demand patterns for particular groups of workers, "an important part of the 1980s rise in wage inequality can be attributed to the weakening of labor-market institutions" (Machin 1996: 61). The rapid decline in the rate of unionization and the weakening of unions is paramount, and there is an association between the faster decline of unionization rates in manufacturing than in services, and the faster growth in inequality in manufacturing. Gosling and Machin (1995), Schmidt (1995), and other studies have consistently found that declining unionization explains 20 percent of the growth in wage inequality.

The massive fall in unionization and collective bargaining coverage, and the substantial decline in national and industry pay-setting arrangements, have significantly increased firm-level wage variation. It has also reduced unions' ability to compress within-firm wage profiles. This contrasts significantly with the 1970s, when (in contrast to the United States) rising unionization was associated with growing wage compression. The pattern of a particularly sharp rise in variation among the lowest educational groups is also consistent with a growing decentralization of bargaining. Developments in Britain well illustrate the finding of Blau and Kahn (1996) that a principal effect of decentralized bargaining structures is to lower the relative earnings of workers near the bottom of the wage distribution, while also increasing wage inequality within the union sector.

Additional labor market changes include the weakening of wages councils from the mid-1980s (and their elimination in 1993) and the erosion of the closed shop. Wages councils set minimum wages for industries such as retail, catering, and hairdressing, covering 2.5 million workers. Machin notes that although the greater polarization of earnings was not associated with a decline in labor's share of national income, evidence of the increasing power of employers in the labor market is illustrated by rising corporate profitability and rate of return, and a corresponding fall in the capital-output ratio (1996: 61).

## Conclusion

The changes in industrial relations institutions in Britain since 1979 and the declining role of unions in particular have facilitated substantial variation in employment patterns. Certainly, multiemployer agreements were historically important for unions (along with state encouragement) in extending collective bargaining coverage, thus helping unions gain recognition in new firms and thereby limiting the extent of nonunionism. Wages councils similarly helped limit variation in pay outcomes. Within this framework, and combined with tight labor markets, the essentially fragmented and decentralized structure of unions did not undermine or limit collective representation. The strong reliance of plant-level unions on management support and resources, on unpaid lay shop stewards rather than a union organization utilizing full-time paid officials, and the voluntarist nature of industrial relations also did not have adverse consequences for unions. However, more significantly, the seemingly decentralized and laissez-faire system produced comparatively little variation, and during the 1970s whatever variation existed, in fact tended to decline.

But changes in labor law since 1979 have compounded the demise of multiemployer bargaining and served to isolate industrial relations and employment practices within individual firms and even plants. In significant contrast to Germany and other countries discussed in this book, the highly decentralized organization of unions in Britain and their reliance on managerial resources at the local level have inhibited the possibility for coordinating employment practices and pay across plants and firms. Rather, the fragmented institutions of British industrial relations have served to increase the diversity of outcomes. Furthermore, this fragmentation gives management greater opportunity and flexibility to shape employment practices at the local level.

The bans on secondary picketing and, ultimately, any secondary action, together with the narrowing of the definition of a trade dispute, were particularly important. These provisions limit the sphere within which unions can legally act at the firm level, thus isolating (or insulating) the firm from the influence of external unions and were used successfully during the 1980s in disputes at Messenger, P&O, and News International. Similarly, during the engineering unions' campaign for a shorter working week during 1989–1990, these prohibitions constrained the unions to campaign only at the level of the individual firm.

The law's impact in insulating individual employers from coordinated union action is particularly noteworthy in comparative terms. In addition, however, the historically decentralized organization of unions in Britain has also limited the potential for interfirm and even interplant coordination. Indeed, British unions have been structured, organized, and funded to an unparalleled extent around unpaid volunteer activists (i.e., shop stewards) and organized with highly decentralized, fragmented, and relatively autonomous structures at the workplace level (Terry 1995). The central importance of shop stewards, over and above national unions, had been settled in favor of the former by the 1960s, and was reinforced both de facto and by the strategic choices of unions during the 1970s.

This fundamentally decentralized structure, with weak national unions and uncoordinated workplace organizations, relied substantially on employer resources. Yet, during the 1980s and 1990s, employers have become more confident in resisting unions, including withholding resources. National unions, under increasing financial stress from collapsing membership, have not been able to lead a reform of this organizational structure. As a result of a weaker labor movement, it has been increasingly difficult for unions to coordinate or extend policies across plants and firms or limit management's ability to more concertedly shape employment practices at the firm level. With weakening local union structures came the extraction of concessions, a greater plant focus, and the emergence of greater variation.

Indeed, in contrast to the other countries we analyze, the weaknesses of union organization in Britain are significant. Unlike the United States, for example, contracts have not been legally enforceable; even where employers accept union recognition, there are no mandatory subjects of bargaining; and at the plant level, unions rely more heavily on employer resources. Some single-union recognition agreements, the so-called beauty deals struck at companies such as Toshiba, Nissan, Toyota, and elsewhere, limit the topics of union representation and even exclude pay. Such agreements, which would not be possible in other countries, illustrate the real possibility of plant syndicalism in Britain.

The substantial employment system variation in Britain has not, however, simply been the result of unions being unable to constrain management to a joint team-based approach. Such a pattern of employment relations had not previously been common, and unions themselves have displayed considerable nervousness over the implications of that approach. In particular, unions have feared the threats that team-working structures might pose to their shop-floor representational structures. The absence of worker rights has thus compounded other institutional features that leave substantial room for the influence of the strategic choices of labor and management.

However, despite plant-level isolation in the British decentralized structures, there has been much commonality in the way the spread of nonunion, HRM, and Japanese-oriented employment patterns has increased the diversity in employment relations in the United States and Britain. In addition, there is much similarity in the growing variation within both union and nonunion sectors in the two countries.

Developments in the British auto and telecommunications industries also mirrored those of their U.S. counterpart industries. In the British auto industry, for example, a joint team-based approach was instituted at Rover, while at Ford and Vauxhall, respectively, piecemeal and constrained partnerships appeared. Variation in employment systems extended to the use and form of teams, pay systems, and employment security practices. Exacerbating the variation in work practices was the wide variability in the detailed operation of teams and other work practices at the shop-floor level in all these firms. At the same time, the Japanese-owned nonunion and company-union auto transplants followed a Japanese-oriented employment system, with a strong role for company councils and supervisors.

In the British telecommunications industry, variation in employment systems was spurred through the entry of nonunion firms (including Cable and Wireless Communications) that challenged the historical dominance of BT. Meanwhile, within BT, many managers no longer have their employment terms collectively bargained as they shift onto individual employment contracts. For these managers, as well as other BT employees, HRM employment practices were on the rise as management sought a more direct and flexible relationship with employees. Even where collective representation persisted at BT, more decentralized and, in some cases, joint team-based approaches spread.

In other British industries, even wider variation appeared in employment patterns, in part due to the lower levels of union representation as compared to the auto and telecommunication industries. Derecognition and limited union organizing among new firms led to general and significant declines in union membership and coverage. HRM and, in a few cases, Japanese-oriented work systems spread (as in the auto and telecommunications industries) as management sought more direct communications and gained the flexibility to adjust work organization and pay more quickly in response to market pressures.

Perhaps because of their previous strength, unions in Britain have found it particularly difficult to develop a coherent or coordinated response to the many strategic initiatives being taken by management. Auto unions exemplify the ambivalence British unions feel toward the spread of human resource management and participatory practices. And although their reaction to derecognition and the increased individualization of employment relations has been somewhat more forceful, British unions there as well have met with little success in slowing these trends. In the end, the British labor market, like that in the United States, is exhibiting growing income inequality and the declining influence of collective representation.

## NOTES

1. By the end of the 1970s, shop-steward organizations existed in 73 percent of manufacturing establishments with more than fifty employees. The pattern was similar in the public sector, and these organizations were becoming increasingly common among the white-collar workforce. Furthermore, the role they fulfilled in the

workplace was similar: recruiting for the union, staffing workplace committees, conducting health and safety and job evaluations, representing workers in disciplinary hearings, and bargaining over pay and conditions (Terry 1995).

2. The Employment Relations Bill, introduced by the Labour Government in January 1999, aimed to restore statutory recognition rights. It is noteworthy, however, that the 1998 Workplace Employee Relations Survey (WERS), indicates that the effect of this legislation is likely to be limited: only one percent of workplaces have a majority of employees as union members, but no union recognition arrangements (Cully et al. 1998). Furthermore, restrictions would remain on the ability of unions to pursue recognition agreements, and employers would retain comparatively large discretion in determining the conditions of recognition.

3. At the time of their abolition, wages councils covered some 2.5 million workers, principally women, and often those in part-time employment. The minimum wage which the Labour Government restored in April 1999 was set at a rate of 3.60 pounds (5.75 dollars). The Low Wage Commission calculated that this would directly affect the pay of two million workers.

4. Between 1989 and 1997 alone, density among male employees fell from 44 percent to 32 percent, while in production industries it fell from 45 percent to 31 percent. During the same period, density in service industries fell by only 6 percentage points (Cully and Woodland 1998).

5. Britain's "league position" for union density among OECD countries between 1970 and 1995 remained near the midpoint in spite of the collapse of membership. Its ranking increased from 9th to 10th between 1970 and 1980 despite a rise in membership during these years. Between 1980 and 1995, Britain's league position increased only one additional place, to 11th (Brown et al. 1997, Table 2, p. 74).

6. In the private sector, however, fewer than 10 percent of nonunion members have their pay and conditions set by collective bargaining, while approximately 25 percent of members do not. Only in the public sector does collective-bargaining coverage now extend to a significant number of nonunion members.

7. "The Changing Role of Employers' Associations," *IRS Employment Trends* (January 1994): pp. 4–13, and (May 1994): pp. 10–16; Marginson et al. 1988.

8. The Warwick company-level, industrial relations survey (CLIRS) found that nonunion companies were less likely to have decentralized pay negotiations than union ones. This difference from the 1990 WIRS data may reflect the large firm size in the CLIRS survey.

9. "Gainsharing at Owens Corning Building Products," *Pay and Benefits Bulletin*, No. 418 (February 1997): pp. 2–6, and "Gainsharing at BP Exploration," *European Industrial Relations Review*, No. 269 (June 1996): pp. 24–28.

10. "Spectacular Growth in PRP Continues," *Pay and Benefits Bulletin*, No. 373 (April 1995).

11. This shift to greater individualization of the employment relationship is also indicated by the CLIRS survey with one in five companies reporting that recognition had been wholly or partially withdrawn (Marginson et al. 1993).

12. "The Changing Nature of the Employment Contract," *IRS Employment Trends* (July 1997).

13. In Britain, large and multinational firms account for a higher proportion of production and employment that in almost all other OECD countries. In 1987 half

of manufacturing employees worked for companies employing one thousand or more, and a quarter worked in firms of ten thousand or more (Edwards et al. 1992).

14. In addition to the "bargained constitutional" style, Purcell's typology identifies two styles, termed "sophisticated human relations" and "sophisticated consultative" which are closely akin to our human resource management and team-based patterns, respectively. A "traditional" (cost minimization, antiunion) pattern corresponds to our low-wage pattern. Purcell utilizes a typology with two dimensions: the commitment of management to an investment in employees as a resource to be developed, and the degree of (and approach to) collectivism in the firm. Using these two dimensions, Purcell also identifies two intermediate categories: nonunion paternalists, and co-operative, unionized "modern paternalists" (Purcell and Ahlstrand 1994).

15. The data in the 1984 and 1990 Workplace Industrial Relations Survey's and the 1998 Workplace Employee Relations Survey are not strictly comparable owing to a change in the survey question. However, the data indicate the use of "regular meetings with junior management" including team briefings.

16. "Hyder Maintains Long-Term Partnership," *IRS Employment Trends,* No. 662 (August 1998): pp. 12–16.

17. Rover has operated under a progression of names during its history, the result of its creation through the acquisition and merger of a host of smaller companies. It has thus been known as Austin and Morris, BMC, BLMC, British Leyland, and Rover. For ease and consistency, the current name of Rover is used.

18. Unfortunately, no data is available from Honda, which, unlike the other auto companies, does not share this information with fellow manufacturers.

19. Frank Mueller (1992a) reports that on paper, there were 3,200 job titles in 1966, while between 1,400 and 1,800 could be distinguished in practice. The progressive task of eliminating these demarcations over a significant number of years can thus be observed.

20. In a similar vain, the AEEU has also established a new committee, the National Committee for Cars and Commercial Vehicles, and a structure to coordinate information, union activities, and policies across companies and plants. Before the mid-1990s, there had been no such coordinating mechanism.

21. This did not, however, preclude either voluntary redundancy or natural wastage.

22. One small difference between the Ellesmere Port and Luton plant agreements is that the latter establishes voluntary attendance at team meetings outside normal working hours and contains different wording through which the union would agree to the criteria for the company to select team leaders.

23. The electrical section of the AEEU had wanted elected team leaders, with the job rotating, and they also supported the appointment of shop stewards as team leaders. Neither the engineering section of the AEEU nor the TGWU supported this stance.

24. Cable and Wireless Communications (CWC) was formed as the result of a merger of four companies in 1997. Until that time, Mercury, a subsidiary of Cable and Wireless (C&W), was the principal competitor to BT. However, in June 1997, it merged with three cable TV companies: Bell Cable Media, NYNEX Cablecomms, and Videotron.

25.   By 1994, some 86 percent of cable TV provision was by North American companies, while sixteen full public-telephone operator (PTO) licenses had also been issued for companies offering an alternative telecommunications network.

26.   The Communications Workers Union was formed in 1995 from a merger between the Union of Communications Workers (UCW) and the National Communications Union (NCU). The NCU had previously represented workers in BT and the UCW workers in the postal service. The NCU had itself been a federated union with an engineering and clerical section.

27.   BT has, indeed, actively contemplated fully derecognizing the STE on more than one occasion. Partly through the intervention of the CWU, BT desisted, instead choosing to adopt a marginalization strategy. Following a ballot on industrial action in negotiations in 1996, the STE did acquire greater visibility of the post hoc distribution of wage increases to allow individual managers to assess their comparative standing. Nevertheless, BT retains essentially unilateral control of the distribution of pay increases.

28.   The choice not to use ST chargeship grades to "supervise" employees was related in particular to BT's fear of the disadvantage of what would happen in cases of industrial action and whether these senior technicians, who are not managerial employees, would perform a strong enough supervisory role to tackle poorly performing staff.

29.   Historically, telecommunications instructions established processes to be carried out for most jobs, such as standards to be maintained, and interaction with control, dispatch, or planning departments. However, they involved no monitoring capability and did not contain details of the actual procedures to be carried out in completing particular jobs. They thus contained an important qualitative difference from the QMS system.

30.   Original proposals using the term "self-managed teams" had to be altered, owing to unacceptable connotations of this term at BT. In response to ongoing debates within the company of how to improve morale and productivity, this term was later revived.

31.   Because CWC was formed by a merger between Mercury and the cable TV companies Bell Cable Media, NYNEX Cablecomms, and Videotron, employment for 1998 in the rest of the cable TV industry may now be lower than this figure.

32.   The following material is based on practices at Mercury before the merger to form CWC. However, Mercury's employment policies have, in fact, been adopted by the new company.

# 4

# Australia

The major changes in employment practices in Australia in recent years have much in common with those occurring in the other countries noted in this volume. This commonality has arisen despite the distinctive character of Australian employment relations.

Australia entered the 1980s with one of the most centralized systems of employment, relations founded upon state and federal tribunal awards stipulating minimum wage and other employment conditions. In the late 1980s, the decentralization of employment relations that began with the spread of enterprise bargaining has brought, among other things, greater variance in employment relations. In Australia, as in other countries, this decentralization is taking place within the context of declining union membership. Yet, union membership in Australia still stands at a relatively high base, and the labor movement was well represented in a Labor government that held office from 1983 until 1996. Furthermore, in contrast to most other countries that had abandoned such policies, for many years under the Labor government, an accord between the federal government and the labor movement sustained a national incomes policy.

Nevertheless, the patterns of work practices that are growing in Australia have much in common with the patterns those of other countries. Institutional factors are influencing the ways and the extent to which those trends appear in Australia and the consequences for Australian employees. For example, the continuing presence of national awards and the Australian Industrial Relations Commission (AIRC) have helped limit low-wage employment practices.

136

BROAD DEVELOPMENTS IN AUSTRALIA

*The Highly Centralized Traditional Tribunal Award System*

Employment relations in Australia since early in the twentieth century have been distinguished by heavy reliance on "industrial tribunals" and a compulsory arbitration system that operates at the federal level and in four of six states (Dabscheck and Niland 1981: 305–7). In this system, wage minimums (and sometimes wage increases) and other employment conditions have been set in the national and industry "awards" issued by the industrial tribunals (see Table 4.1). Awards set the same pay and working conditions for approximately nine thousand separate job classifications throughout the country (Gregory and Vella 1995: 205).

Industry- and, in some cases, firm-level collective bargaining traditionally provided supplements to these awards (including "overaward" wage payments) and devised the specific terms for their implementation.[1] Australia also has been noteworthy for its craft- or occupational-based unions, a union structure that influenced both the wage award system and the supplementary industry- and firm-level collective bargaining.

Over the years, there had been some oscillation in the extent to which awards and the AIRC influenced employment conditions. In the late 1960s, for example, some unions took advantage of tight labor markets and the resulting increases in their bargaining leverage to expand their direct negotiations with employers, and they used those negotiations to gain very favorable employment terms. However, in 1975 the AIRC reasserted its authority and introduced wage indexation and this halted the spread of local bargaining (Lansbury 1978).

**Table 4.1.** Award Coverage in Australia

|  | Federal & State Awards[a] | Federal Awards Only | State Awards Only | Neither/ Don't Know |
|---|---|---|---|---|
| All Workplaces (20 or more employees) | 22 | 21 | 51 | 6 |
| Employment Size 20–49 | 17 | 24 | 51 | 8 |
| 500 or more | 41 | 18 | 36 | 5 |
| Industry |  |  |  |  |
| Manufacturing | 40 | 28 | 28 | 4 |
| Communication | 3 | 92 | 0 | 5 |

*Source:* Callus et al. (1991: Table A90, p. 318).
[a] All figures are the percentage of workplaces with a particular type of award. The data are from a sample of 1962 workplaces.

### A Downward Shift toward Enterprise Bargaining

A more significant shift to decentralized employment relations has been spurred by national wage cases (cases determining wages or wage increases for all workers covered by federal awards) and the AIRC's decisions in these cases. In August 1988, a national wage case decision instituted a "structural efficiency principle" that encouraged lower-level negotiations to modify wage awards so as to "improve economic efficiency and provide workers with access to more varied, fulfilling and better paid jobs" (cited in Rimmer and Verevis 1990: 1).

In the 1988 decision, the commission stated that the goal of lower-level bargaining and the restructuring of awards was to "establish skill related career paths; eliminate impediments to multi-skilling; create appropriate relativities within the award and at the enterprise; ensure that working patterns and arrangements enhance flexibility and efficiency; include properly fixed 'minimum rates' for award classifications; and address any discriminatory provisions contained within the awards" (cited in Rimmer and Verevis 1990: 1).

This was followed in 1989 by a national wage case decision requiring "award restructuring" involving negotiations at the industry or firm level that could include productivity bargains, issues related to the implementation of wage changes, and associated changes in work rules and work practices. A 1991 national wage case decision explicitly promoted "enterprise bargaining" (Lansbury and Niland 1995: 63–65).

Although the Australian labor movement officially had generally supported the movement toward enterprise bargaining (for reasons discussed below), unions became alarmed when the Industrial Relations Reform Act of 1993 allowed enterprise flexibility agreements (EFA) to take the place of enterprise agreements.[2] The critical feature of an EFA versus an enterprise agreement was that unions did not have the right to be a party to an EFA. Rather, the employer had the power to draft an EFA.[3] The employer was then required to take reasonable steps in informing and explaining to employees the terms of the EFA and its possible effects. In addition, the employer had to secure the genuine agreement of a majority of employees at the time the EFA was applied.

The overall effect of these wage decisions and other economic pressures has been to increase the extent of industry-, firm-, and plant-level collective bargaining. Some of this decentralized bargaining has followed as part of labor and management's efforts to satisfy the specific requirements of the industrial relations commission concerning the structural efficiency or award restructuring case decisions. Firm- or plant-level bargaining has varied much across firms and industries (and time), and in the academic community there is disagreement over the degree to which recent decentralizations in the structure of collective bargaining merely extend previous and more informal forms of plant- and firm-level bargaining.[4] Nevertheless, the overall trend was strongly toward a more local (and often enterprise-level) determination of wages and other employment conditions.

*Australian Unions' View of Union Structure and Enterprise Bargaining*

The central union federation in Australia, the Australian Confederation of Trade Unions (ACTU), has supported the expansion of enterprise bargaining. As Bray (1991) notes, the ACTU "favored a decentralization of bargaining towards the enterprise level provided this occurred within a strong centralized framework (at national and industry levels)." The union movement's support for enterprise bargaining was encouraged by strong unions that saw enterprise bargaining as a way to make up for ground they would lose from wage restraint imposed by a union-government accord, possibly through negotiated improvements in non-wage employment conditions. The accord, which began right before federal elections in 1983, initially "envisaged federal government support for full wage indexation in return for the unions pledging to make 'no extra claims' for wage increases" (Lansbury and Niland 1995: 62).

Although the accord was modified several times after 1983, the terms were honored with rare exceptions, by the unions. As Davis and Lansbury observe, "Those unions seeking to press for wage increases outside the Accord have found themselves isolated and their campaigns have usually proved unsuccessful" (1994: 112). Furthermore, the wage rates tied to specific job classifications closely followed the national pay rates determined by the AIRC (Lansbury and Niland 1995: 66).

As the accord continued through various extensions, labor and others in Australia increasingly became concerned that enterprise bargaining would exacerbate the weak position of low-skilled, female, and other disadvantaged workers. In response, the later phases ("marks") of the accord provided special increases for these workers. Mark VIII of the accord, adopted in 1995, provided three "safety net" pay increases (through dollar per hour increases) for workers that did not achieve at least the equivalent through enterprise bargaining and other special increases for low-paid workers (Newsletter Information Services 1995b).

The accord, however, was ended by the government of John Howard after its electoral victory in March 1996. Even bigger changes in Australian employment relations are underway as a consequence of legislation promoted by the Howard government (discussed below).

*Trend toward Union Consolidation*

The trend in union structure in Australia runs somewhat counter to the bargaining decentralization resulting from enterprise bargaining. Since the late 1980s, the ACTU has strongly promoted union consolidation.[5] Union amalgamation has involved the merger of craft- or occupational-based unions into either multiskill or, in some cases, industry-wide unions or, in other cases, the formation of loose groupings of unions.[6] From 1991 to 1993 alone, the number of trade-union affiliates in the ACTU declined because of amalgamations from 126 to 72 (Gardner 1995: 41). Bargaining centralization (and, it was hoped, the further spread of enterprise bargaining) also was encouraged by situations where multiple unions represented employees: the 1992 amendments to the Industrial Relations Act required these unions to form a single bargaining unit (for single businesses) (Peetz, Preston, and Docherty 1992: 43).

Consolidation of union structure did help facilitate enterprise bargaining by reducing union jurisdictional issues. In turn, it became easier for labor and management to negotiate job classification consolidation and introduce team working and other forms of "functional flexibility"—issues that commonly arise in enterprise bargaining (Rimmer and Verevis 1990).

The ACTU's push for union consolidation was stimulated by an influential report, *Australia Reconstructed,* from a group of key union officials who, after a study trip abroad, encouraged emulation of the relatively centralized union structure common in northern European countries (Australian Council of Trade Unions and the Trade Development Council 1987). Thus, although the ACTU initially endorsed enterprise bargaining, it did so with the expectation that the accord and union consolidation would provide a strong central framework under which enterprise bargaining would proceed.

The ACTU's support for enterprise bargaining also was consistent with the view held by some in the Australian labor movement that although union membership was relatively high, unions in Australia were in fact relatively weak at the workplace level given their historical reliance on the tribunal system to improve employment conditions.[7] It was hoped that the spread of enterprise bargaining would counteract this weakness by creating a local foundation for more active shop-floor unionism (Bray 1991). Even in the face of this concern, the Australian trade union movement (and the ACTU in particular) has supported the spread of enterprise bargaining which is noteworthy because central unions in other countries have generally opposed movements in their own countries toward more decentralized bargaining (Katz 1993).

Not all Australian unionists are enamored with either union consolidation or the spread of enterprise bargaining. These fears have been heightened by the declines in union membership of recent years. Whereas 41 percent of Australian workers belonged to unions in 1989, as of 1996, only 31 percent of workers were union members (Australian Bureau of Statistics 1990, 1996).

Some Australian unionists also worry that enterprise bargaining will lead to fragmented and co-opted unionism. Unionists were particularly alarmed by the labor law changes (discussed below) promoted by the Liberal Party after its 1996 electoral victory that made it easier for employees and management to create individual employment contracts and, in the process, avoid union representation.

### Management's Preference for Enterprise Bargaining

The management community in Australia has strongly supported enterprise bargaining, a view consistent with the support for more decentralized bargaining expressed by managers in other countries. At the same time, there have been differences among managers. The influential Metal Trades Industry Association, for example, long was prepared to accept a continuing role for the award system in a system of "managed decentralism" and only later shifted its support to a more fragmented form of bargaining decentralization (Lansbury and Niland 1995: 69). In contrast, the strongest promoter of enterprise bargaining, the Business Council of Australia (BCA), favored a quick dismantling of the award system and emulated the more aggressive deregulatory policies being adopted in New Zealand (Sheldon and Thornthwaite 1993; Lansbury and Niland 1995: 68). While the deregulatory policies preferred by the BCA have never been adopted in full, changes adopted in 1996 after the Conservatives' electoral victory go a long way to meeting the desires of management.

### Workplace Relations Act of 1996

Passed under a newly elected conservative government (led by the Liberal Party), the 1996 Workplace Relations Act makes numerous changes in the award system. Awards are to be simplified down to twenty matters and take on more of the status of safety nets underpinning enterprise agreements. Arbitration by the AIRC will be limited to the 20 allowable matters, unless there are "exceptional circumstances." Furthermore, formal provisions allow for individual contracts to be known as Australian workplace agreements (AWAs).[8] AWAs are not reviewed by the AIRC but rather by a new body, the office of the employment advocate. The employment advocate can refer a workplace agreement on to the AIRC for vetting only where doubts exist regarding compliance with the law.

Although both the AIRC and the employment advocate will still apply a no-disadvantage test in their respective reviews of agreements, the nature of the test was altered by the 1996 legislation. The 1996 act provides that the relevant award *as a package* be used as a benchmark, and the public interest can now be considered in the application of the no-disadvantage test to AWAs.[9]

While previously permitted enterprise flexibility agreements (EFAs) were seen as a mechanism for allowing employers to reach formal agreements with employees as a group in nonunion or lightly unionized settings, AWAs provide the possibility of individual contracts that will essentially replace union-negotiated consent agreements.[10] In the past, unions could present themselves as the representative of the workforce, negotiate a collective (i.e., enterprise) agreement, and gain certification of that agreement from the AIRC without formal approval from the workforce. The 1996 act, however, abolishes the automatic right of unions to bargain collectively on behalf of employees in all workplaces where there are some union members.

Furthermore, the act allows for nonunion certified agreements and requires that all collective agreements be approved by a "valid majority" of employees. As of October 1997, there were 181 nonunion certified agreements (and only 11 percent of nonunion workplaces with five or more employees had a written agreement) (ADAM Report 1997c: 20). The new legislation allows for rejection of a union-negotiated agreement to open the way for negotiation and eventual approval of a nonunion certified agreement. In effect, this would provide a route for union disenfranchisement.[11]

Although the national award system will continue in Australia and the AIRC will continue to administer and vet enterprise agreements (certified agreements in union and nonunion workplaces), the role of the commission is likely to be seriously weakened under the new act. The intent of the 1996 act is clearly to increase the role of individual contracts and reduce the role of the AIRC. At the same time, the actual spread of AWAs will depend in large part on how aggressively Australian employers promote their adoption.

It also remains to be seen how strong a role the employment advocate will play in the review and vetting of AWAs. The federal government is providing rather limited funding (A$12 million in 1997) to staff and operate the Employment Advocate office, which will limit the role the employment advocate could play in restricting the contents of AWAs.

Early experience with AWAs suggests that few, if any, AWA applications were actually being refused based on their failure to meet the no-disadvantage test.

By February 1998, of the 1,175 AWAs refused by the office of the Employment Advocate, all were refused for procedural reasons, not for failure to meet the no-disadvantage test. (A total of 15,750 federal AWA applications had been received by the AWA.) In addition, the AIRC had yet to refuse an AWA (ADAM Report 1998: 13).

The importance of the 1996 act has been strengthened by Australian state governments that have been making changes to their state award systems similar to the changes adopted at the federal level (except for New South Wales) (Buchanan et al. 1997: 17–21).

*Spread of Enterprise Bargaining*

All these legislated changes from the late 1980s on helped spur formal and informal enterprise-level collective bargaining in Australia. By 1994, a majority of workplaces reported "that they had introduced some changes through negotiations with unions or with employees in the proceeding year" (Department of Industrial Relations 1995: xxvi). Large and unionized workplaces are the most likely to have agreements in place. As of 1995, 63 percent of employees in workplaces with at least twenty employees were covered by an enterprise agreement (Department of Industrial Relations 1995: 185).[12]

One of the ways the federal government has spurred the diffusion of enterprise bargaining has been by successively lessening the AIRC's oversight over enterprise agreements. The Industrial Relations Reform Act of 1993, for example, eliminated the requirement that the parties demonstrate productivity improvements in order to gain commission approval of enterprise agreements that include pay increases. And as described earlier, the AWAs allowed under the 1996 act are vetted by an employment advocate and not by the AIRC, unless there are unusual circumstances.

These factors have led recently to a downward shift, to the plant level, in the negotiation of enterprise agreements. For example, while in 1994 only 22 percent of federally registered enterprise agreements were largely made at the worksite level, in 1995, 60 percent of comparable agreements were made at that level. Another indication of the downward drift in enterprise bargaining is the finding by the 1995 Australian Workplace Survey of a significant increase in single-site (rather than multiple-site) enterprise agreements (Department of Industrial Relations 1995: 66, 81). The involvement in enterprise bargaining of managers from the workplace also rose substantially. (By 1995 workplace managers were involved in 83 percent of the cases where bargaining occurred.) Reciprocally, the involvement of managers beyond the workplace declined in enterprise bargaining (Department of Industrial Relations 1995: 83, Table 3.2).

Workplace union delegates are struggling to cope with this downward shift (to the workplace level in many cases) within enterprise bargaining. In one survey, 48 percent of union delegates report that they either have no bargaining skills or that their bargaining skills are not good enough (ADAM Report 1996a: 19, Table 3.3).

*The Contents of Enterprise Agreements.* Productivity improvements and reference to performance indicators are central features of enterprise agreements. Forty-two percent of enterprise agreements pursue productivity enhancement through such measures as the establishment of performance indicators or the linking of pay increases to improved performance. In manufacturing, an even larger fraction of enterprise agreements (88 percent) contain references to performance indicators (ADAM Report 1994: 17).

The specific content of enterprise bargaining varies much across work sites. Pay rates, work hours, and training are the most common issues addressed in enterprise agreements, as reported in Table 4.2. Joint consultative committees, often given responsibility for establishing and monitoring performance indicators and assisting the processes of organizational change are also common, as noted by the 63 percent of federal agreements that have such a committee involved in developing productivity measures (see row 12, in Table 4.2). Data from the periodic workplace industrial relations surveys shows that the proportion of workplaces reporting ongoing consultative arrangements through joint consultative committees doubled over the 1990 to 1995 period, from 14 percent to 33 percent. (Morehead et al. 1997: 189).

Enterprise bargaining has served as a vehicle to discuss the work reorganization being spurred by the same technological and market pressures common to workplaces in other countries. As noted in the ADAM Report (1997b: 22), semi-autonomous work groups and performance pay are being adopted in Australia, generally in frequencies that are comparable to the frequencies cited earlier for the United States (see Chapter 2).

There are also numerous reports of shop-floor and plant-level negotiations that involve significant changes in work organization (Davis and Lansbury 1996). Some of the cited cases involve team systems of work and large reductions in job classifications. At some sites, team work is associated with the introduction pay-for-knowledge schemes and more extensive worker participation (Mathews 1994). Frequently at these sites, participatory processes contain many if not all the elements of the joint team-based pattern described in our categorization (see column 4 of Figure 1.1).

Mathews (1994) describes a variety of cases fitting what he refers to as a social technical production system. A central role is played by joint labor and management forums through which workplace changes are negotiated and

**Table 4.2.** Issues Covered in Enterprise Agreements, as Reported by Workplace Managers

|  | Agreements Addressing an Issue (in %) |
|---|---|
| Pay rates | 94 |
| Performance appraisal/pay | 45 |
| Work hours | 81 |
| Penalty rates | 50 |
| Discipline and dismissals | 48 |
| Work practices or work organization | 65 |
| Retrenchments or redeployments | 44 |
| Occupational health and safety | 52 |
| Training | 68 |
| Leave arrangements | 63 |
| Child care or family leave arrangements | 47 |
| Consultation or negotiation arrangements | 63 |
| Grievance handling procedures | 60 |

*Source:* AWIRS95 main survey reported in *Enterprise Bargaining in Australia: 1995 Annual Report* (Department of Industrial Relations, 1996).
*Note:* The population comprises all workplaces with 20 or more employees with collective agreements (certified or EFAs) made since January 1994 under the Industrial Relations Act of 1988.

monitored at these sites. This is well illustrated by the team structures at ICI's Botany chemical complex, which include joint (composite) site and plant review teams, work teams, and skill-based career structures (Botany Site Combined Review Team 1995; Mealor 1996, 1997). A joint team-based pattern is also well illustrated by developments at BHP Steel and Australian Post (Baird and Lansbury 1996: 146–59; Kelley and Underhill 1997: 158–84).

Although case studies by Mathews, Mealor, and other researchers cite the performance advantages of this approach, it is important to note that many Australian workplaces have not adopted increased worker and union participation. In an analysis of enterprise agreements negotiated in 1995, researchers at the University of Sydney note a slowdown in the spread of innovative human resource practices through enterprise bargaining. In 1995, only 26.1 percent versus 47.6 percent of pre-1995 enterprise agreements have clauses that deal with some aspect of work organization. Furthermore, while 15.7 percent of earlier enterprise agreements had provisions for teamwork, only 2.2 percent of 1995 agreements have such provisions (ADAM Report 1996a: 15).

At the same time, direct employee participation schemes are often introduced independently of enterprise bargaining. The percentages of workplaces reporting team building, autonomous work groups, and total quality management in 1995, respectively, was 47, 43, and 37 percent (Morehead et al. 1997: 189). These percentages are much higher than the amount of these activities reported in enterprise agreements, respectively, 12, 3, and 2 percent in 1995 (ADAM Report 1997b: 23).

Furthermore, it is becoming clear that work reorganization often places additional burdens on employees. This is revealed by the majority of Australian employees who believe that the range of tasks they perform has increased over the previous twelve months, and the majority of employees who also believe that the level of job stress and work effort have increased (Department of Industrial Relations 1995: Table 16A).[13]

Enterprise bargaining shifts greater responsibility to plant-level managers, although it is not clear that Australian plant-level managers are adequately equipped to handle these new responsibilities. From case studies of workplace bargaining in a variety of industries, Lansbury and MacDonald (1992) uncover a high degree of head office (i.e., corporate) involvement in nonstrategic matters at the plant level. Furthermore, they warn that the further devolution of responsibility for employee relations "may leave relatively inexperienced plant management exposed to strong unions, ultimately requiring centralized controls to be reimposed by corporate headquarters" (Lansbury and MacDonald 1992: 218).[14] Thus, although management in Australia, as in other countries, has been a strong supporter of more plant-level bargaining, plant-level management may well have difficulty handling the responsibilities created by this shift, especially in environments where bargaining leverage strengthens labor.

While enterprise bargaining is spreading in Australia, so is the use of individual contracts. An estimated 30 percent of employees in 1996 were neither covered by awards nor collective bargaining agreements, and hence their employment conditions were determined by individual contracts (ADAM Report, 1996b: 15, Table 2.1). The diffusion of individual bargaining is also indicated by the fact that 47 percent of all surveyed managers in 1995 reported at least some bargaining between workplace managers and individual employees (Department of Industrial Relations 1996: 20). In some firms, individual contracts are associated with a human resource pattern of work practices.

## THE DIFFUSION OF EMPLOYMENT PATTERNS

### A Human Resource Management Pattern

Nonunion or lightly unionized Australian firms have adopted individualized work practices that are supported by extensive communication policies and strong corporate cultures. Although there was always some use of these policies in Australian firms, the successful adoption of these practices by American firms and recent legislative changes in Australia appear to have spurred the diffusion of this approach. For example, in Australia, as in the United States and other countries, HRM practices are found in IBM and other large firms in the information technology industry (Shadur 1997: 142–44).

A key advantage of the HRM pattern in the Australian context of traditional wage awards is that the pattern includes individualized pay procedures that are often linked to performance appraisal systems. Individualized pay gives Australian managers a mechanism to avoid the rigidities inherent in wage awards. Furthermore, jobs tend to be relatively broadly defined, thereby enhancing functional flexibility. Optus, described in the discussion of the Australian telecommunications industry, has received much publicity for its use of these procedures. Other firms, such as Toys-R-Us and Channel 9 (a television broadcast firm in Sydney), also illustrate the HRM pattern (Campling et al. 1996).[15]

Through adoption of the HRM pattern, the firms achieve advantages that include broader job classifications, more working-time flexibility, and individualized pay procedures. These policies are preferred to the employment conditions provided in the awards governing these firms and their employees. Furthermore, managers are able to avoid union involvement in the determination of employment conditions.

In the nonunion and lightly unionized firms that are adopting an HRM pattern, there is some variation in consultative procedures involving employees. For example, Optus and Channel 9 aggressively strive to maintain direct communication between managers and employees and to avoid any form of consultation between groups of employees and managers. Toys-R-Us, while also seeking to limit the unions' role, does maintain consultative processes through which managers communicate with employees in group forums (including "team-talk" meetings) in addition to one-on-one communication channels.

### The Low-Wage Employment Pattern

In addition to firms that follow joint team-based or HRM employment patterns, Australia also has firms that follow either traditional unionized or low-wage employment patterns. To document these practices and the diversity in employment relations within each of these categories, we rely on data from the Australian Workplace Industrial Relations Survey.

Callus et al. (1991: 148–75) categorize Australian workplaces in terms of whether workers are represented by unions and whether any unions are active, and the extent to which management systematically structures its relations with employees. With these criteria, 20 per cent of workplaces and 9 per cent of employees fall within a category labeled "informal" workplaces. According to Callus et al., "Management at these workplaces was likely to be completely autonomous and adopt a case-by-case approach to managing employees, with few formal procedures or rules on industrial relations management" (1991: 57). Furthermore, these informal workplaces have high levels of voluntary turnover and do not pay as well as other workplaces in their respective industries.

These policies are very similar to the practices followed by firms using what we label as the low-wage employment pattern (see column 1 in Figure 1.1). The key difference is that the Australian award system, by imposing minimum wage and other employment conditions, limits the degree to which firms following this pattern can take advantage of their market power and pay low wages. By providing a lower bound on the employment terms in the low-wage ("informal") workplaces, Australian institutions, in particular the award system, limit the variation in employment conditions and thereby produce outcomes that contrast particularly sharply with the outcomes in the less restricted U.S. labor market.

### A Traditional Labor-Management Relations Pattern

The Australian Workplace Survey also shows that a significant number of workplaces follow a more traditional labor-management relations pattern. Callus et al. categorize 21 percent of workplaces and 50 percent of employees as either "reactive" or "active" bargainers. These workplaces have collective bargaining and management is "structured in its relations with employees" (Callus et al. 1991: 157). Even with these common attributes, sizable differences exist within firms that follow this pattern, between workplaces where the union is relatively inactive and bargaining only occurs when the need arises (over such matters as discipline or health and safety issues) versus workplaces where the union is active, with union representatives "often engaging in both wage and non-wage bargaining." In the latter, it is found that "management-union relations are more strained or conflictual than at other workplaces" (Callus et al. 1991: 171).[16]

### CONTINUING INFLUENCE OF THE AWARD SYSTEM

The role of labor market institutions in Australia is well illustrated by the continuing influence of awards, the AIRC, and the employment advocate, despite the expansion of enterprise bargaining. National surveys of enterprise bargaining regularly report that enterprise agreements most often complement and do not replace awards (see, for example, ADAM Report 1993: 1). Recent enterprise bargaining is even less likely to replace awards completely than did earlier enterprise bargaining.[17] Furthermore, if an individual contract were to be reached under the new AWA procedures described earlier, there is at least the possibility of serious review of the terms of such a contract by the government-appointed Employment Advocate office. In contrast, there is no analogous monitor of the terms of individual contracts in the United States or the United Kingdom.

So far, the continuing role of awards has served to moderate the influence of work-practice patterns in Australia. The award system appears to have limited the number of firms that are pursuing practices similar to the low-wage pattern and to have provided a floor on wages and other employment conditions in firms with low-wage patterns. At the same time, it remains to be seen if the spread of AWAs and the further extension of enterprise bargaining leads to a more serious deterioration in employment conditions.

## DEVELOPMENTS IN THE AUTO INDUSTRY

The changes in recent years in the Australian auto industry are much like those seen in other Australian industries, although the auto industry has faced particularly strong economic pressure from realignments within the world auto industry. Key pressures for change in the Australian industry have included changes in tariffs and taxes which have exposed once highly protected production facilities to heightened international competition, and a substantial increase in the presence of Japanese auto companies in the market place and in the ownership of assembly operations. Efforts to restructure and rationalize the industry have precipitated many of the changes occurring in the structure and conduct of employment relations.

Nevertheless, like other Australian industries, a key factor shaping and to some extent constraining changes in employment practices in the auto industry is the heavy role traditionally played by the national award system, which provided occupational wage increases and a relatively centralized bargaining system that complemented these pay awards. Another institutional factor affecting the evolution of employment relations is the complete unionization of the auto assembly sector and the modest growth in nonunion employment in the auto parts sector.[18] Furthermore, a relatively high percentage of white-collar employees are unionized.[19] In particular, the award system and the high levels of unionization serve to limit the spread of low-wage competition in the auto industry and thereby narrow the range of changes in employment systems.

Institutional constraints aside, recent years have seen strong movement toward more decentralized collective bargaining, and this, in turn, has helped spur a wide variety of changes in work organization, pay methods, and skill development. In addition, at the workplace level, the changes occurring in Australia bear many similarities to changes taking place in other countries through the emergence and spread of joint team-based and Japanese-oriented work practice patterns.

### Movement toward Enterprise-Level Collective Bargaining in the Auto Industry

Like other Australian industries, earnings and work conditions in the auto industry have long been heavily influenced by the decisions of the national AIRC through the issuance of national awards providing occupationally based wage minimums and other employment standards and the involvement of the commission in the resolution of industrial disputes. Under the award system, the auto industry developed industry-level collective bargaining involving numerous occupationally based unions. Industry bargaining traditionally was supplemented by company-level collective bargaining agreements that included overaward payments. Within this traditional structure, shop-floor labor-management relations were relatively underdeveloped, and formal channels for regular union-management or worker-management interaction were limited.

This system began to shift in the 1980s, as it did in other sectors of Australian industry, when company-level collective bargaining began to intensify and focus on work restructuring issues and workplace problems.[20] The negotiation of job classification consolidations, for example, became a common feature of company agreements in this period. In addition to work restructuring, common topics that began to surface in company-level collective bargaining were employee and union involvement processes focused on skill enhancement.

Further changes in collective bargaining were spurred by efforts to link pay increases to productivity, initially via the two-tier wage system introduced by the AIRC in March 1987 (Lansbury and Bamber 1997: 221). The commission's approval of second-tier wage increases was made conditional on productivity and skill enhancement, thus providing a strong incentive for auto labor and management to expand their discussion of workplace issues and shift the focus of collective bargaining downward to the enterprise level. Workplace issues also became a more central part of the commission's awards. For example, in 1987, an auto industry award simplified job classifications and altered many work practices.

Two-tier (industry and company) bargaining followed in 1988 and 1989 under the impetus of commission-imposed deadlines and conditions associated with the payment of second-tier wage increases. Two-tier bargaining included development of training programs within the auto companies, including the vehicle industry certificate (VIC), the industry-wide skill certification system (discussed in more detail below). Consultative mechanisms concerning work organization and training issues expanded at the enterprise level, and numerous joint working parties were established. Although at first the changes in work practices across the auto companies were very similar, over time, company- and workplace-level discussions increased the variation in work practices across and within the auto companies.

### *Auto Assembly Employment Relations*

*Wages.* Enterprise agreements have been negotiated since 1992 at the four assembly companies—Ford, General Motors-Holden, Toyota, and Mitsubishi.[21] The timing, duration, and level of wage increases provided in the successive rounds of enterprise bargaining conducted at the four companies have varied, as outlined in Table 4.3.

In addition to variation in the amounts provided for wage increases, companies vary in the manner and degree to which wage increases have been linked to productivity and quality. A common aspect of the enterprise agreements covering all four assembly operations is the inclusion of language stipulating that improvements in productivity and quality are a necessity in light of increased international competition and the relatively poor past performance of the Australian plants. Explicit productivity and quality improvements are stipulated in some enterprise agreements, and in certain cases, wages are paid as a direct function of productivity achievements. Productivity targets typically have been stated in terms of vehicles per hour. An exception to this trend was Toyota's 1992 enterprise agreement, in which the productivity target included indicators based on worker participation in continuous improvement activities and other industrial relations performance measures (Newsletter Information Services 1994: 71–74).

Most often, the particular productivity targets were met and the system operated smoothly, but when the performance targets were not met, labor-management conflict followed. For example, during the term of the 1992 Toyota agreement, when productivity targets for the first half of 1993 were

**Table 4.3.** Wage Increases at Australian Auto Assembly Plants, 1992–1996 (in %)

| Month/Year | GM-Holden | Toyota | Mitsubishi | Ford |
|---|---|---|---|---|
| July 1992 | | | 3.0 | 3.0 |
| August 1992 | 3.0 | 3.0 | | 2.0 |
| December 1992 | | 1.25 | | |
| February 1993 | | | 2.0 | |
| March 1993 | 2.5 | | | |
| April 1993 | | 1.25 | | |
| August 1993 | | 2.5 | 5.0 | 3.0 |
| December 1993 | 2.5 | 2.3 | | |
| June 1994 | | 1.5 | | |
| August 1994 | 5.0 | | 4.5 | |
| December 1994 | | 1.5 | | |
| January 1995 | | 3.0 | | |
| April 1995 | | 1.0 | | 5.75 |
| July 1995 | | 1.5 | 3.0 | |
| April 1996 | | | | 5.75 |
| August 1996 | 5.75 | 5.25 | 5.75 | |
| TOTAL | 14.0 | 18.8 | 17.5 | 16.0 |

*Source:* Unpublished document, GM-Holden, 1996.
*Note:* Additional "at risk" or "skill related payments" of 1 percent, 1 percent, and 5 percent were, respectively, provided at Holden, Toyota, and Ford during this period.

not met while targets for the second half of the year were greatly exceeded, disagreement ensued between labor and management over the effect on performance-based payments, and an industrial action followed. Toyota management ultimately decided to make—but defer—the first productivity-based performance payment.

A formal productivity-pay linkage also was used on a trial basis in the 1992 enterprise agreement at GM-Holden, which formally tied a piece of the scheduled wage increase to the size of quality improvements.[22] As at Toyota, a heated labor-management disagreement ensued at GM-Holden over the payment of the quality-linked component of the wage increase. Both sides came to doubt whether a team spirit and continuous improvement were being promoted through the performance-pay linkage (Bamber and Lansbury 1997: 222).

A relatively tighter pattern in wage setting returned with the negotiation of wage increases ranging between 5.25 and 5.75 percent in all four enterprise agreements in 1996. Meanwhile, the auto unions have been pressing for greater standardization in fringe benefits. In the mid-1990s these efforts included the issue of long-service leave, a benefit that varies across companies partly because the laws differ in each Australian state. South Australian legislative provisions for long-service leave are the most generous and unions have been pushing with some success to have these more generous provisions extended to auto workers in Victoria and New South Wales.

Also, as in other Australian industries, there has been a substantial consolidation in the auto industry across the large number of occupationally based unions that traditionally provided workers with representation. Management favors this consolidation because it simplifies discussions concerning work restructuring (in part by reducing the likelihood of union jurisdictional rivalries) and the administration of collective agreements. The ACTU strongly has backed union consolidation as a necessary step to rationalize the Australian labor movement. Through mergers, the number of unions in the auto industry has been greatly reduced, and the remaining unions participate in the negotiation of enterprise agreements at the assembly plants as a single bargaining unit. At the same time, the industry has not achieved the style of representation found in other countries (such as Germany and the United States).[23]

*Training and Skill Development.* Skill development has been a central issue in the enterprise-level discussions over productivity improvements and work restructuring. Both management and the unions have sought ways to ensure that workers possess the skills necessary for the expanded jobs they are being asked to handle, jobs that are broadening owing to such factors as classification consolidation, greater use of on-line inspection, and the spread of team methods of work organization. In the 1970s, the ACTU became a strong voice in favor of skill upgrading, and their advocacy of enhanced training contributed to the development the VIC. The standards built into the VIC were especially attractive to the labor movement in light of extensive corporate restructuring, which heightened workers' concerns regarding the portability of their skills in the face of plant closings and threats of further corporate restructuring.

All the assembly companies adopted pay-for-skills programs and linked these programs to the VIC, although the form of these programs and the amount of resources devoted toward training across the companies varied.[24] The Mitsubishi enterprise agreement, for example, outlines a pay-for-skills systems that includes three skill groups for production workers and skill levels (two or three) in each skill group (Mitsubishi Motors Australia Ltd. 1995). Wage rates vary as much as 8.9 percent across the three levels within the top skill group and vary 21.5 percent from the lowest skill level (level 1 in group 1) to the highest skill level (level 3 in group 3). Production workers at the highest skill level receive the same wage rate as entry-level craft workers in the company (Mitsubishi Motors Australia Ltd. 1995: Schedule A).

*Team Systems of Work Organization in Auto Assembly.* In all four auto assembly companies, the number of joint activities involving union officials, workers, and managers has increased sizably. In each of the enterprise agreements there is much discussion of and some similarity in the specific language concerning the need for increased consultation, greater information sharing, and less recourse to formal dispute resolution procedures. The composition of the joint committees that provide this consultation and worker-union involvement, however, varies much across the companies.

One of the clearest ways cross-company variation appears in employee relations concerns the use and form of team systems. Three of the four companies (Toyota, Ford, and Mitsubishi) have a formal team system. The system has not necessarily led to widespread team working. Rather, in the Australian auto plants, as in other industries and countries, work practices vary across work groups in any given plant.[25] Furthermore, operating procedures differ across assembly plants that use teams, and this variation resembles the variation found in team operations in the U.S. auto industry. The Ford Australia assembly complex uses "natural work groups," in which hourly team leaders are selected by a joint assessment procedure jointly designed and administered by union officers and managers (Ford Australia 1995: 10). In the Toyota assembly operation, in contrast, hourly team leaders are selected by management with no union input, a procedure the union dislikes intensely.[26] Toyota's use of standardized job assignments also differs from Ford's approach to teams.

At Toyota, teams are a part of a pattern of work practices that is very similar to the Japanese-oriented approach described in column 3 of Figure 1.1. The strong influence of the parent firm is obvious here. The personnel director at Toyota reinforced this influence by noting that although it is well understood that the unions (and some workers) oppose having team leaders appointed by management, this was a basic part of the Toyota system that corporate management at Toyota (in Japan) was not willing to abandon.[27]

At the other assembly plants, each respective parent multinational corporation has had a heavy influence in the design of work practices, even though local discretion is permitted concerning the detailed implementation and operation of those practices. At Ford Australia, for example, there is a slow but gradual diffusion of a joint team-based approach. Plant teams are very similar to the natural work groups in Ford's American plants, and workers and the union exercise the kind of independent influence in plant affairs that is found in the joint team-based pattern. The natural work groups in Ford's Australian plants extend concepts that had been introduced in the mid-1980s through employee involvement groups, which also had numerous similarities with a program being adopted in Ford's U.S. plants.[28]

The GM-Holden assembly operation agreed to a phased introduction of work groups in a July 1996 work organization agreement. These work groups initially were introduced into two work areas in pilot programs (Holden-F.V.I.U. 1996). Traditionally, the GM-Holden assembly operations had relied heavily on a suggestion program to elicit worker input into problem solving. Furthermore, although the GM-Holden plant has not used a formal team system, it has features in common with the joint team-based approach, including joint committees and the sharing of information with union officials. GM-Holden also has long made use of leading hands, or senior workers who serve as leaders in a work area and receive higher pay as compensation. The leading hands at GM-Holden tasks carried out by hourly team leaders at the other plants. Leading-hand systems predated team leaders at the other assembly plants and were previously used (and at GM-Holden still used) to accomplish duties now performed by hourly team leaders. The July 1996 agreement introducing teams at Holden provides that all leading hands be given the opportunity (and sufficient training) to make the transition to work group leader (Holden-F.V.I.U. 1996: 9).

A distinguishing feature of the evolution of employee relations in the Australian auto assembly plants is the complete unionization of those plants including the two Japanese transplants. In principle, the management of Toyota could have tried to operate the Altona assembly plant, which was a greenfield facility, on a nonunion basis. The Mitsubishi plant had been purchased from the U.S.-based Chrysler Corporation and was a unionized facility when Mitsubishi acquired it. But like Toyota, Mitsubishi could have pursued a different investment strategy and sought to operate on a nonunion basis in Australia. Likely, the strength of the Australian labor movement and the existence of a Labor government at the federal level dissuaded Toyota and Mitsubishi from pursuing a nonunion strategy of the sort followed by Japanese transplants in the United States (and by Japanese transplants in the United Kingdom).[29]

### Employment Relations at Auto Supplier Firms

*Captive Parts Plants.* The parts operations owned by the companies that also own assembly facilities (captive auto suppliers) in Australia are all unionized. Employee relations have been evolving in these plants in a direction very similar to that emerging in the auto assembly plants, although the timing and extent of work restructuring varies much across the plants.[30]

Work practices at the GM-Holden engine plant illustrate the range of work innovations adopted at auto suppliers. The 1994–1996 enterprise agreement governing the GM-Holden engine plant provided for "synchronous work unit groups" that include hourly team leaders (GM-Holden 1994: 38). The agreement also included wage increases of up to 2 percent for the achievement of productivity objectives specific to each work area.[31] A joint steering committee operates in the plant in a manner very similar to the joint committees of the team-based pattern outlined earlier, and in other ways, the engine plant's employment system closely resembles this pattern.

Joint labor-management committees and other features of the pattern are also found in Ford's internal plastics plant. In the late 1980s, this plant developed employee involvement committees that were very similar to initiatives then underway in Ford's U.S. plants (Lansbury and MacDonald 1992: 148–77). In 1992, the plastics plant went on to adopt a natural work group structure very similar to a work reorganization being adopted in some of Ford's U.S. plants.[32]

*Independent Auto Parts Plants.* A high fraction of the independent auto parts plants are unionized, and whether or not the plants are unionized, earnings are supported by the national award system. Both high unionization and the award system have produced relatively modest earnings differentials between the auto assembly firms and the independent auto parts firms, and especially modest differentials when contrasted with the sizable differentials in the United States. In Australia, average earnings (for full-time nonmanagerial workers) from 1985 to 1993 in the independent parts firms (sector 3234 in the Australian industrial code) ranged between 86 percent and 99 percent of the earnings of workers in the auto assembly firms (sector 3231 in the Australian industrial code). [33]

Cellular and team systems were also being introduced into independent auto parts plants in the late 1980s and 1990s. One example is the Bendix Mintex plant (Australia's largest supplier of automotive friction materials), where team working has been linked to the introduction of manufacturing cells (Mathews 1994: 105–30).

Overall, employment practices in the Australian auto industry are changing in ways that fit our analytic framework, with variety expanding through the employment patterns described in Figure 1.1. At the same time, the high levels of unionization and the continuing influence of the Australian award system have constrained employment system variation in the auto industry.

## AUSTRALIAN TELECOMMUNICATIONS RESTRUCTURING

The same institutional factors also have constrained the variation that has been appearing in the Australian telecommunications services industry, although by historical standards there has been much change in employment relations. Furthermore, the specific changes in pay and other work practices in the telecommunications industry are much like those implemented in the Australian auto industry, even though the work tasks of the two industries are different.

The provision of telecommunications services and equipment in Australia has long been dominated by Telstra, a highly unionized, government-owned enterprise. In recent years, Telstra has undergone a series of corporate reorganizations in response to competition from a second carrier, Optus, and efforts to make the firm more consumer oriented and technologically sophisticated. An analysis of the changes in employment practices must take into account both the decentralizing and centralizing movements within Telstra in recent years. In addition, employment relations in the telecommunications industry have been influenced by enterprise bargaining at the two firms.

The national award system and the occupationally based unions heavily influence employment relations in the telecommunications industry, as they do in other Australian industries.[34] Nevertheless, employment patterns in Australia's telecommunications industry, for example, Telstra's joint team-based approach and Optus' human resource management pattern, have many similarities to those of other countries.

### Structure of the Telecommunications Industry and Employment Relations

Telstra (formerly Australia Telecom) is the dominant provider of telecommunications services and is a sizable manufacturer of telecommunications equipment. Although the federal government remains a dominant shareholder of Telstra, in March 1997 Telstra was partly (25 percent) privatized, through a public stock offering and there have been heated debates surrounding the possibility of further privatization of Telstra, especially after the Liberal Party's 1996 electoral victory. Another important telecommunications service firm besides Optus, which received a second carrier license in 1991 and captured large shares of the cellular and domestic markets, is Vodaphone, which competes in the mobile telecommunications services market.

As late as 1987, Telstra management had negotiated with twenty-eight unions and each bargaining round included fifteen separate negotiations with these unions or with groups of unions. Shortly thereafter, however, substantial consolidation occurred within the occupationally based telecommunications unions. By the mid-1990s there were three unions representing employees at Telstra—CPSU, CEPU, and AFMEU.[35]

Management's efforts to exclude senior managers from the national award system also spurred employment changes. Until the early 1990s, only twelve jobs at Telstra were exempt from industrial awards and union representation. Then, in 1992, Telstra removed one thousand senior managers from coverage by unions and awards and shifted these employees to individual contracts. The company later offered individual contracts to another four thousand executives. A dispute followed over the latter, and Telstra shortly thereafter replaced the corporate director of industrial relations who had overseen this reclassification.

In 1992, following the national movement toward enterprise bargaining, Telstra negotiated separate enterprise agreements with its three unions, and there has been discussion of the possibility of shifting to a single enterprise agreement. The enterprise agreements spurred joint labor-management discussion of how work practices could be modified to meet productivity and quality (service) objectives. Substantial changes have been made in the 1990s to increase the flexibility of labor deployment, including the consolidation of one hundred job classifications into six classifications.

At Optus, in contrast, only 10 percent of employees are unionized, and very few of these are managerial or supervisory employees. In 1992, Optus negotiated an enterprise agreement with the CWU (one of the unions that later, through merger, formed the CEPU). After federal legislation had been changed to allow enterprise flexibility agreements, Optus became the first major firm in Australia to negotiate an EFA in 1994.[36] The adoption of an EFA fit Optus' style of focusing on individualized relations with its employees and using work practices that closely follow a human resource management pattern (see below).

### Employment Relations Changes at Telstra

*Decentralization and Recentralization.* Driving the changes in employee relations at Telstra have been a series of decentralizing and recentralizing corporate reorganizations. The oscillations within the corporate structure started after a report by the McKinsey Consulting Group in 1988 recommended that Telstra be decentralized into a divisional structure so as to link businesses more closely to various product markets and to increase the firm's customer focus. This decentralizing campaign culminated in 1992 with the creation of six business units and one service unit. Employment relations were decentralized to fit with the more decentralized corporate structure in that year, when industrial relations responsibilities were distributed to twenty-two bargaining units across the firm. At the same time, a counter-centralizing movement occurred within the firm's corporate and employment relations structures through the weakening of the formerly powerful state branches of the firm, in favor of corporate officers and more standardized corporate policies.

As at auto and other Australian firms, Telstra has tried to link pay more directly to corporate performance, and as at other firms, these efforts were not always successful. In an effort to promote more customer responsiveness, the 1992 enterprise agreements at Telstra included two bonus payments, of A$500 and A$1,000, to be paid out if specified corporate performance targets were met. But when the performance target for the first (A$500) payment was not met, labor-management disagreements led to negotiations between management and the unions, which culminated in the payment of A$200 in lieu of the $500 bonus (Bamber, Shadur, and Simmons 1997: 146).

By 1994 the virtues of decentralization were being questioned, and Telstra took some steps to recentralize its corporate structure. Recentralization of the employee relations corporate staff followed in 1995 because this meshed with corporate restructuring and also because corporate officers were dissatisfied with the outcomes of bargaining unit-level negotiations. Management felt that the company's short-lived experience with bargaining across twenty-two separate units had been exceedingly costly, for the unions were able to "leapfrog" gains from one unit to another. In addition, management complained of costly and inefficient pay increases through increases in job classifications and excessive promotions to higher pay grades within given classifications.

Managers claimed that leapfrogging had resulted from central control of bargaining unit discussions, which allowed the unions to outmaneuver managers, who were constrained by a more decentralized organizational structure. Moreover, management asserted that the decentralized managerial structure led to a lack of coordination, particularly in network operations, through varying engineering maintenance practices, for example.[37] Management's recentralization of employee relations in 1995 also conveniently fit with efforts to downsize corporate staff in the employee relations area, as well as in many other corporate functions, as part of re-engineering initiatives then being launched at the company.

*Workplace Changes.* At the workplace level within Telstra there has been a gradual although somewhat limited diffusion of work practices similar to the joint team-based pattern described in column 4 of Figure 1.1. Joint labor-management discussion of work practices intensified at Telstra with the emergence of enterprise bargaining in the early 1990s. Despite recentralization of corporate employee relations responsibilities, labor's involvement in business issues expanded. For example, workers and union officers

**Figure 4.1.** Participative Implementation Framework

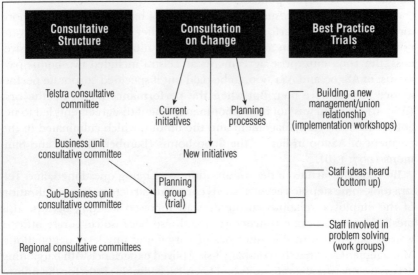

*Source:* Telstra 1996, unpublished document, Melbourne.

have been drawn into discussions of service problems through the participatory approach initiated in 1994. The participative framework at Telstra incorporates an array of joint committees, including business-unit consultative committees and work groups that address specific problems as part of best practice trials (see Figure 4.1). One best practice trial addressing customer service work recommended giving customer service representatives both sales and after-sales responsibilities so as to avoid the inefficiencies of the fragmentation produced by old work patterns.

It is telling that union officials at Telstra complain of being understaffed as they try to participate in the new workplace consultative committees.[38] This staffing problem appears to have arisen in part because the telecommunications unions have not adapted their formal administrative structure to the corporate reorganizations or the consultative programs. Rather, the unions retain a geographically and state-based administrative structure developed for Telstra's old organizational structure. As noted elsewhere in this book, telecommunications unions in other countries similarly have been sluggish in modifying their administrative structures (when they, too, have faced radical changes in the structure of the corporations they are bargaining with) and in expanding shop-floor consultative forums.

The committee structure within Telstra's participative framework (outlined in Figure 4.1) is very similar to AT&T's Workplace of the Future program and includes the sort of processes common to the joint team-based pattern. Except for a few best practice trials, however, Telstra has not made extensive use of formal team systems.

At one point, the unions' and the workers' voices were enhanced through the inclusion of an assistant secretary of the ACTU (and Telstra former employee) on the firm's board of directors.[39] At the same time, top management made it clear that the participative approach was a mechanism for enhanced *consultation* and not a device for "co-determination."[40]

The changes in the employee relations structure at Telstra reflected management's efforts to maintain a separation between the negotiation of pay, occurring at a central level as part of enterprise bargaining, and more localized workplace problem solving. Telstra management did not want to be drawn into potentially costly productivity bargaining, as it claims occurred with bargaining unit discussions from 1992 until the 1995 reorganization. Yet, the best practice trials and other workplace joint discussions may ultimately be constrained by this separation of pay and work practice discussions, because this separation may inhibit the creation of adequate rewards for effective practices.

The tenor of labor-management relations at Telstra toughened shortly after the national election of a conservative coalition government in 1996. For example, Telstra replaced Ian Macphee, who had fostered many of the earlier participative efforts, with a new director of human resources and a few associates who, in their former jobs at the company Rio Tinto, had challenged the unions by dealing more directly with employees. Then in 1998, Telstra management announced that it would strive for a new enterprise agreement that would not include any special provisions outside the twenty matters listed in new Workplace Relations Act. Through this narrow approach, management hoped to eliminate what it termed "restrictive practices" and "outdated allowances" (Ross and Bamber 1998).

As in the large telecommunications companies providing services in other countries, Telstra has been rapidly introducing new technology and changing the content and location of the jobs of many of its employees. For example, customer service representatives and maintenance technicians have been affected by the creation of mega-service centers and the increased use of computer-mediated work.

In contrast to the adjustments within U.S. telecommunications firms (AT&T and the RBOCs), nonunion employment has not expanded at Telstra through the creation or greater use of nonunion subsidiaries or subcontractors. The firm did create a new subsidiary, Visionstream, to handle the introduction of fiber-optic cable. Yet, after negotiations with its unions, Telstra agreed that all Visionstream employees would be union members, including those hired through subcontractors to lay new fiber-optic cable. Although they gain the benefits of union representation, these employees are hired on a temporary basis and do not receive the employment security commitments and associated benefits provided to regular Telstra employees.

Whether the recent hardening in management's approach to employment relations lasts at Telstra remains to be seen. In the past, the tenor of labor-management relations, along with Telstra management's strategy toward organizational structure, have oscillated greatly. Thus, although institutional factors have constrained variation in employment patterns in the Australian telecommunications industry, by effectively limiting nonunion alternatives, this has not brought stability to labor-management's relationship at Telstra.

*Employment Relations at Optus*

Although nonunion employment is limited in the Australian telecommunications industry as compared to some of the other countries examined in this volume, Optus, the corporate challenger to Telstra, is a significant exception in that it is nonunion. Optus possesses many characteristics of the human resource management pattern described in column 2 in Figure 1.1.[41] The company promotes a strong corporate culture in its recruitment and communication policies, and jobs are defined somewhat more broadly than those at Telstra for similar work. For example, broader job classifications allow a closer integration between customer service and technical staff. Job flexibility also is promoted through extensive corporate communications and open-floor office layouts. Fitting with this approach, pay increases are determined by individual performance appraisals, and little use is made of seniority-based or across-the-board increases. Employees of the same classification can receive different wages, and within a span, top-performing employees can earn up to 30 percent more than the rate set at the bottom end of the span (Newsletter Information Services 1995a: 32–34).

Optus management prefers to communicate with employees on an individual basis and avoid collective employee relations processes. This direct communication is facilitated by the level of union representation at Optus, which has never been higher than 10 percent of the workforce.

Optus management also has taken steps to effectively limit the role of unions in determining employment conditions. In 1992, Optus negotiated an enterprise agreement with the Communications Workers Union (CWU), which represented the bulk of the employees who belonged to a union. Although this enterprise agreement provided for more flexible work and pay arrangements than those at Telstra, Optus took advantage of federal legislation allowing the creation of an enterprise flexibility agreement without a union acting as a direct party to the EFA. Optus secured employee consent to their EFA through a vote in which 89 percent of those voting supported the EFA (with 85 percent of eligible Optus staff voting).[42]

At that time, federal legislation required the AIRC to vet and certify EFAs. The commission had to be satisfied that the EFA did not "disadvantage" or "discriminate" against employees and was not contrary to the "public interest."[43] The Optus EFA was approved by the AIRC, over the strong objections of the CWU. Optus management later took advantage of changes in federal legislation to entirely eliminate collective procedures in the firm's employment relations.

For comparable job duties, the level of pay and other employment conditions at Optus are similar to those at Telstra, with a few minor differences. For instance, work hours are 38 per week at Optus and 36.75 at Telstra; Optus provides family-leave benefits but Telstra does not.[44] The distinctive feature of Optus' personnel policies is not the level of rewards they produce but rather the degree to which policies are tailored to promote an individualized rather than collective relationship between employees and management.

Although Optus is an interesting example of the nonunion human resource employment pattern, it is important to keep in mind that to date, Optus has acquired a relatively small share of the total telecommunications market in Australia. It is perhaps even more noteworthy that Optus' employment practices have not been imitated by a large number of other employers in the industry.

Overall, the trends in employment outcomes and processes in the Australian telecommunications industry, like the auto industry, fit the national movement toward more localized collective bargaining, steady erosion in the coverage of union representation, and growing variation in employment patterns. These and related trends have been moderated by Australia's particular institutional legacy, but the trends are significant nonetheless and very consistent with shifts in the other countries we analyze. As described below, the trend in Australia's income distribution similarly involves growing variation moderated by institutional factors.

## INCOME DISTRIBUTION TRENDS

The national award system and other institutional factors long produced a lower level of wage inequality in Australia than that found in the United

States and many other countries. In fact, Australian wage inequality for men and women is close to the degree of inequality found in Sweden (Freeman and Katz 1995: 13, Table 2). At the same time, the Australian income distribution has exhibited many of the same trends that have emerged in other advanced industrialized countries. For example, since the mid-1970s, Australia has experienced a sizable decline in middle-income jobs and has experienced sizable growth in employment at the higher and lower extremes of the earnings distribution (Gregory and Vella 1995: 205–26).

Real wages had grown rapidly in Australia in the early 1970s, but the various phases of the national accord (and an economic recession and trade problems) later helped reverse this trend. Average real wages fell by 10 percent between 1983 and 1989 and rose marginally after 1989. (The Accord was adopted in 1983.) By 1994, average earnings were just above the 1976 level (Gregory and Vella 1995: 208). The awards provided in the various rounds of the accord often allowed for uniform percentage pay increases. However, one factor that has increased the dispersion in actual earnings, even in the face of these uniform increases, is that promotion rates have differed sizably across firms (Watts and Mitchell 1990).

A decline in union density has contributed to the growing income inequality. Between 1986 and 1994 alone, union density declined from 50 to 38 percent for male employees, and from 39 to 31 percent for female employees. Borland (1996) finds that the decline accounts for approximately 30 percent of the increase in earnings dispersion for male employees but had smaller effects on female earnings dispersion. Borland (1996) also finds over this period sizable increases in earnings variation within the nonunion sector. The latter may have been caused by the increasing variation in work practices and the diffusion of the diverse nonunion patterns described in our categorization, although neither Borland nor other researchers have explicitly tested the influence of employment relations patterns on Australian income distribution trends.

Has enterprise bargaining served to disadvantage employees that are in a relatively weak position in the labor market and, in particular, increased male/female earnings differentials? The Australian federal government's 1994 report on enterprise bargaining shows mixed evidence, depending on which wage series is analyzed, regarding the trend in the male/female earnings ratio over the early 1990s, and no clear evidence that enterprise bargaining has worsened relative labor market outcomes for female workers (Department of Industrial Relations 1994: 239–43).

Although Australia's accord and the award system helped maintain a relatively compressed earnings distribution, they did not protect Australian workers from the effects of the same income distribution trends that have appeared in most advanced industrialized countries. It is likely that if Australia had had labor market institutions more like those found in other countries, then market and trade pressures would have made the income distribution even more inegalitarian.

Summary

Noteworthy historical characteristics of Australian employment relations include relatively high levels of unionization, a politically strong labor movement, a national award system, and the strong authority granted to government-appointed bodies to oversee collective bargaining. These institutional factors have shaped the timing and procedures of changes in employment practices. The judicial and formal nature of the Australian award system, for example, clearly led to a slower emergence of plant (or enterprise)-level bargaining as compared to the United States or Britain, where management's push for decentralized collective bargaining was even less encumbered. The political and organizational strength of the labor movement also affected the distribution of employment patterns. While nonunion and Japanese employment practices were spreading, the rate of diffusion was slower than that found in the United States, for example. That the Japanese-owned automobile assembly transplants retained union representation provides a pointed contrast to American practices.

Yet, despite this unique institutional context, the workplace changes in Australia are strikingly similar to those of other countries. The same four employment patterns emerging in other countries are also spreading in Australia, and within these patterns the same practices, teams and contingent compensation, have been increasingly adopted. In addition, union membership has declined substantially; the process of collective bargaining has become more decentralized and more informal; and there has been significant growth in individualized employment contracts. So while Australian institutions produced a more limited range of variation, the fundamental direction and process of change in employment systems has not been altered by these institutions.

Legislative changes made in 1996 will likely speed the diffusion of individual contracts and union decline. As a result, employment patterns and work practices in Australia are likely to become even more similar to those now found in the other English-speaking countries.

1. The 1990 Australian Workplace Industrial Relations survey reveals that 68 percent of all workplaces paid overawards and in manufacturing, 81 percent of employees receive overawards (Callus et al. 1991: 241).

2. The 1996 Workplace Reform Bill, described in more detail later, eliminated EFAs but does allow nonunion consent agreements and individual contracts.

3. This account of EFA procedures draws heavily from Pragnell and O'Keefe (1994: 3–4).

4. This has spurred a debate in the Australian industrial relations community regarding the advantages of "managed decentralism," versus either retention of the old tribunal-arbitration system or a more comprehensive shift to "enterprise bargaining" (Lansbury and Niland 1995; Bray 1991).

5. The Industrial Relations Act of 1988 and amendments to that act in 1990 increased the minimum size of federal unions. This was intended to help promote union amalgamation and deter the proliferation of small, craft-based unions (Davis and Lansbury 1994: 102).

6. There are now nineteen clusters of unions (or "super unions"). Some of these involve fully merged unions, while others involve loose groupings of unions.

7. For evidence regarding the weakness of unions on the shop floor, see Lansbury and MacDonald (1992).

8. Individual contracts existed under the previous legislation, but the new bill adds formal provisions for individual contracts as a separate "stream" in the system.

9. Section 170xa (2) of the 1996 bill provides that an agreement disadvantages employees if it "would result, *on balance,* in a reduction in the *overall* terms and conditions of employment" (emphasis added). This allows the individual provisions of an AWA to be below the requirements of an award.

10. Note that there never was significant use of EFAs. Employers complained that the administrative procedures were too cumbersome, and they also disliked the fact that previous legislation allowed unions to formally oppose an EFA before the AIRC.

11. This point was made to one of the authors by Ron Callus and is also discussed in ADAM Report (1997a: 28–29).

12. This enterprise agreement could have been written or verbal, and registered or unregistered.

13. This evidence is consistent with findings from the United States showing that team systems often induce workplace stress.

14. Lansbury and MacDonald (1992) note the similarity in their findings with Marginson et al.'s (1988) analysis of British developments.

15. Channel 9 does not have either an enterprise agreement or an EFA as management does not feel the need for a certified agreement.

16. It is not possible with the AWIRS data to tell how many of the unionized workplaces have adopted work practices similar to what we have categorized as the joint team-based approach, nor can we tell from these data how many of the unorganized workplaces use policies similar to what we label the HRM approach; the categories Callus et al. (1991) use differ somewhat from our categories.

17. ADAM Report (1995: 2) reports that 1995 enterprise agreements are less likely to replace awards as compared to earlier agreements.

18.    The percentage of the workforce in the motor vehicles and parts industry that were union members declined from 67.4 percent in 1986 to 52.6 percent in 1993. These figures are reported in Kitay (1997: 35) and are derived from unpublished figures collected by the Australian Bureau of Statistics.

19.    For example, Lansbury and MacDonald (1992: 151) report that in 1991, more than 50 percent of the white-collar employees at a Ford plastics plant are unionized. The unionization of white-collar employees in the auto and other industries, however, has declined substantially in recent years.

20.    Some decentralization of collective bargaining was introduced in the auto industry earlier in the mid-1970s, when General Motors began to sign separate collective-bargaining agreements with the auto unions and no longer participated with the other auto assembly companies in joint negotiations.

21.    An assembly plant owned by Nissan closed in 1994, and for a few years the GM-Holden plant was operated in a partnership with Toyota.

22.    The Customer Satisfaction Participation Reward Program is described in GM-Holden (1992: 15–17).

23.    For example, six and four unions, respectively, signed the GM-Holden and Ford 1995 enterprise agreements in Australia. The Vehicle Builders Employees Federation of Australia is the most important of the auto unions.

24.    In interviews, union officers claimed that some assembly companies invested heavily in pay-for-skills programs (which they liked), while other companies did not.

25.    For evidence, see Simmons and Lansbury's (1996: 80–100) account of the team system at the Ford plants in Melbourne.

26.    The unions' strong preference for the Ford team structure and dislike of the Toyota approach was conveyed in an interview with Ian Jones, national secretary, Federation of Vehicle Industry Unions, Melbourne, Australia, August 16, 1995.

27.    Interview with Peter Holland, personnel director, Toyota Altona Plant, Altona North, Victoria, Australia, August 17, 1995.

28.    Compare the description of Ford Australia's employee involvement program in Lever-Tracy (1990) with Ford's U.S. program described in Katz (1985).

29.    Toyota's assembly and parts plants in Georgetown, Kentucky, for example, operate on a nonunion basis, while the NUMMI assembly plant jointly owned by Toyota and GM is unionized. See Chapters 2 and 3, respectively, for discussion of the union status of U.S. and U.K. auto assembly plants.

30.    A substantial fraction of the output of these parts plants are exported, which reflects the small scale of the Australian assembly operations.

31.    There are also a 5 percent and 4 percent wage increases during the first and second years of the agreement.

32.    The introduction of work groups at Ford's Australian plastic plant is described in Mathews (1994: 173). These teams can be compared to the teams found in Ford's U.S. plants described in Katz (1985: 79–85).

33.    These figures are total ordinary earnings and include award wages, payments by result, and overawards, from an unpublished survey conducted by the Australian Bureau of Statistics.

34.    A number of the occupationally based unions in the telecommunications industry have members only in that industry.

35.   The full names of these unions and the types of employees that they include as members are, respectively, the Community and Public Sector Union (white-collar employees including customer service representatives and office clerical staffs); Communications, Electrical and Plumbing Union (technicians and maintenance staff); and the Automotive, Food, Metals and Engineering Union (drivers and other miscellaneous craft positions). The CPSU and CEPU represent more than 90 percent of unionized employees at Telstra.

36.   EFAs are described more fully later in this chapter.

37.   These complaints were conveyed in an interview with the Employee Relations Task Force, Telstra, August 17, 1995, Melbourne.

38.   This was conveyed by Ian McLean, state secretary, CEPU, in an interview conducted in Brisbane with one of the authors, August 22, 1995.

39.   That person was Bill Mansfield who, along with the rest of the Telstra main board, is appointed by the federal government. After the election of the conservative government in the spring of 1996, Mansfield was removed from the Telstra board.

40.   In a summary of the remarks of Frank Blount, CEO of Telstra, a company newsletter states, "Neither senior management nor the unions envisages that the Statement of Intent of the Participative Implementation Framework document amounted to 'co-determination'" (Telstra 1995: 2).

41.   Fifty-one percent of Optus is owned by a consortium of two Australian insurance companies; the other 49 percent of the firm is owned by two international telecommunications companies, BellSouth (U.S.) and Cable & Wireless (U.K.).

42.   These figures are reported in Bamber, Shadur, and Simmons (1997: 139).

43.   For example, the AIRC initially disapproved the Toys-R-Us EFA on the grounds that the agreement had not been adequately explained to the workforce (Campling et al. 1996: Appendix, p. 127). The commission also exercised its authority over EFAs when in 1994 Arrowcrest's initial EFA was rejected on grounds that it included a buy-out of two weeks of annual leave, which the commission felt violated the public interest. An amended EFA that conformed to the commission's preferences was eventually approved (Newsletter Information Services 1995a: 3–4).

44.   The longer hours at Optus were said to be a trade-off for certain pay advantages. These differences are described in Bamber, Shadur, and Simmons (1997: 141–47).

# 5

# Germany

The "German model" of industrial relations has become renowned for the strength of its inclusive unions, the extensive coverage of its sectoral collective-bargaining system, and the dual structure of broad employee rights exercised through works councils and supervisory boards. During the 1980s these elements combined were seen to be key in preserving the strength of the labor movement, facilitating controlled decentralization, and limiting the extent of variation in the economy (Turner 1991; Thelen 1991). Union membership was indeed considerably more stable in west Germany during the 1980s than in most other industrialized countries, and unions were able to preserve greater strength and centralization.

Nevertheless, membership did decline, and after an initial boost in 1991 following unification of the two Germanys, the subsequent decline has been significant. During the 1990s, moreover, variation in employment practices has been increasing in a weak labor market; corporate and work organizational restructuring has been extensive; and eastern Germany has experienced massive economic turmoil following unification. The growing pressure for variation is also evident in the strains on the industry-wide collective bargaining system in both west and east Germany, as well as at the workplace.

### GENERAL INDUSTRIAL RELATIONS DEVELOPMENTS

The German model of industrial relations is characterized by its legalistic (or "juridified") structure and dualism. The division of roles between the eleven broad and inclusive industrial unions on the one hand, and works councils with strong codetermination, information, and consultation rights on the other, is clearly established in law.[1] On the employers' side there is a similarly strong division between employers' associations and firms. Yet this legalism does not define the precise roles of unions, works councils, employers' associations, and firms but rather sets the limits within which they operate. Thus, although a division of responsibilities remains, it has also evolved over time. Despite the widespread perception of substantial stability in overarching institutions, the system continues to be subject to important changes in the balance among its component parts. These changes have, in turn, been an important factor in the increasing variation in employment outcomes and processes within Germany.

The challenges and threats to German institutions include declining union membership; increasingly strident demands from firms within employers' associations for changes in the collective-bargaining system, and for greater flexibility and diversity at the firm level; fewer firms belonging to even the most important employers' associations, such as Gesamtmetall; and increasing variation being introduced both directly and indirectly as a result of the unification of east and west Germany. As a result of these pressures, framework agreements are much more common in sectoral collective-bargaining accords facilitating a decentralization of decision making from unions and employers' associations to works councils and firms. This decentralization has been accompanied by a growth in plant-level diversity, though the decentralization itself has been both a cause and an effect of the pressure for greater variation.

Nevertheless, the variation in employment systems becoming apparent in Germany is more controlled than in the United States and the United Kingdom in particular. Even though German industrial relations institutions have become somewhat weaker, an important element of the growing flexibility has been negotiated within existing institutions. For example, framework agreements and opening clauses are defined at the sectoral level and then applied locally. Such institutional flexibility in part explains the resilience of German institutional structures, because change can be both more subtle and more liable to discrete "steps" than in the United States and Britain.

For example, firms are subject to significant limitations on their ability to "break the bonds" of industry-wide collective bargaining, though there are important examples of this indeed happening. Equally, there are extensive limitations on the ability of firms to introduce either an HRM approach or a low-wage nonunion approach, given that the legal rights of works councils inhibit firms from bypassing employee representatives to communicate directly with workers, as is increasingly the case in the United States and the United Kingdom. Instead, and especially in large firms, works councils have extensive rights to company information not only at the workplace level but also through their presence on the supervisory board and the establishment of an economic committee providing information on the market position of the firm.

The cumulative effect is to constrain firms' actions and to make a joint labor-management approach to employment relations more likely. Consequently, the degree of variation in employment systems is not as great as in other countries, and in particular we find little evidence of moves to a nonunion model. However, it is also important not to underplay the change occurring. Within Gesamtmetall, for instance, an increasing number of firms have called for reforms in the system of Flächentarifvertrag (industry-wide pattern bargaining). This debate developed during the second half of the 1980s and has become more vehement in the 1990s. The pressures for variation demanded by firms have, on the one hand, loosened the bonds of collective agreements, thereby allowing much more firm-level variation. The collective-bargaining round in 1994 was particularly significant in this respect. On the other hand, these debates also portend further reforms in the collective-bargaining system.[2]

### The Collective-Bargaining System

Describing the experiences of the mid- to late-1980s, Kathleen Thelen argued that "the challenges labor now faces require some organizational rethinking on the part of central unions, but no dramatic restructuring" (1991: 234). The decentralization from unions to works councils was occurring both because of greater working-time flexibility (itself prompted by the unions' success in reducing the length of the working week) and a greater emphasis on qualitative bargaining goals (such as the reorganization of work, employee participation, and the humanization of work).

As Table 5.1 indicates, membership in the DGB union federation fell during the 1980s, after density had reached a peak in 1981. However, the declines have been significantly sharper in the 1990s. Between 1991, when total membership reached its peak, and 1997, the DGB lost more than 3 million members, or 27 percent. Of this, 1.25 million members have been lost in western Germany and, more dramatically, more than 2 million in eastern Germany.[3] The collapse of union density in the east and the steep decline in the west have been spread across all unions, with the metalworking (IG Metall), chemicals (IG Chemie), post and telecommunications (DPG), and public sector (ÖTV) unions all losing more than 20 percent of

**Table 5.1.** Trade Union Membership and Density in Germany

| Year | Total All Unions (%) | DGB Union Membership (000s) | Union Density (DGB) Total (%) | Union Density (DGB) West (%) | Union Density (DGB) East (%) |
|------|------|------|------|------|------|
| 1970 | 36.1 | 6,712.6 | 31.6 | 31.6 | |
| 1975 | 37.3 | 7,364.9 | 32.2 | 32.2 | |
| 1980 | 38.3 | 7,882.5 | 33.7 | 33.7 | |
| 1985 | 36.0 | 7,719.5 | 31.2 | 31.2 | |
| 1988 | 36.4 | 7,797.1 | 30.3 | 30.3 | |
| 1989 | 36.7 | 7,861.1 | 30.5 | 30.5 | |
| 1990 | 38.0 | 11,564.9 | 32.7 | 30.4 | 39.4 |
| 1991 | 38.5 | 11,800.4 | 33.1 | 29.6 | 42.2 |
| 1992 | 36.9 | 11,015.6 | 31.3 | 28.9 | 38.2 |
| 1993 | 34.9 | 10,290.2 | 29.4 | 27.6 | 35.2 |
| 1994 | 33.5 | 9,768.4 | 28.0 | 26.8 | 32.0 |
| 1995 | 32.4 | 9,354.7 | 27.0 | 26.2 | 29.0 |
| 1996 | | 8,972.7 | 26.2 | 25.9 | 27.3 |
| 1997 | | 8,623.9 | 25.5 | 25.5 | 25.9 |

*Sources:* Total union density and DGB union density from Fichter (1997 and unpublished), Jacobi et al. (1998), DGB, and authors' calculations.
*Note:* As of 1991, DGB East includes Berlin-West.

their membership (Table 5.2). HBV, the commerce, banking, and insurance union, has been especially hard hit, losing nearly 34 percent of its membership. The decline for these unions has been concentrated in eastern Germany, with IG Metall losing 64 percent of its membership there. Nevertheless, between 1991 and 1997 IG Metall membership declined by some 13 percent even in west Germany.

In contrast to the United States and Britain, it is generally misleading to distinguish between German firms on the basis of whether or not they are unionized, since the structure of industry-wide collective bargaining agreements in Germany constrains the emergence of nonunion employment patterns. German firms, for example, do not need to have in excess of 50 percent unionization rates to be included in collective-bargaining contracts. Rather, belonging to an employers' association typically entails being a party to the sectoral agreement irrespective of the actual unionization rate. Firms find a strong incentive to retain membership in the relevant association to avoid confronting strong, centralized unions alone, especially since unions have a policy of fighting company efforts to avoid union contracts and imposing especially beneficial contractual conditions where they are required to sign a single-company deal.

The extensive coverage of collective bargaining contracts is further ensured by the system of encompassing industry unions and industry bargain-

**Table 5.2.** Individual Trade Union Membership in Germany

| Union | Membership 1991 | Membership 1997 | Percentage Decline 1991–1997 |
|---|---|---|---|
| IG Metall | 3,624,380 | 2,660,951 | 26.6 |
| IG Median | 244,774 | 191,610 | 21.7 |
| ÖTV | 2,138,317 | 1,643,692 | 23.1 |
| DPG | 611,969 | 487,814 | 20.3 |
| IG Chemie | 876,674 | 694,897[a] | 21.0 (est. 26.0)[a] |
| IG BCE[b] | 1,425,032 | 1,012,000 | 29.0 |
| IG Bau[c] | 911,761 | 655,356 | 28.1 |
| HBV | 737,075 | 488,271 | 33.8 |
| DGB | 11,800,413 | 8,623,918 | 26.9 |

*Source:* Zagelmeyer (1998b).

[a] IG Chemie data for 1996. In October 1997, IG Chemie merged with the mining and energy unions to form IG BCE. Authors' calculations estimate a total decline in IG Chemie membership of 26 percent between 1991 and 1997.

[b] IG BCE data include those of IG Chemie, as well as those of the previously independent IG Bergbau und Energie and Gewerkschaft Leder.

[c] IG Bau combines the agricultural and construction unions that merged in 1996.

ing. Although collective bargaining is nominally regionally based, in practice a pilot region is used to bargain an industry pattern contract that is subsequently extended to all regions.[4] Furthermore, pattern setting in Germany is not only interregional, but also strongly interindustry. Most commonly, IG Metall or, alternatively, IG Chemie or ÖTV, establish the pattern. The broad coverage of agreements is further encouraged by the possibility of the federal minister of labor extending industry agreements to all firms, through a "declaration of universal applicability," or AVE.[5] A declaration can been applied where bargaining coverage exceeds 50 percent of employees in a given region. In practice, the clause is infrequently invoked and extends to only approximately 4 percent of pay agreements. It is generally applied only to specific sectors such as construction and retail (Lindena and Höhmann 1989). Nevertheless, potential application of the AVE is important: it encourages firms to retain membership in the industry employers' associations, even where a firm has low levels of unionization. Firms that retain membership must abide by the industry-wide collective-bargaining agreement.

In addition, by leaving an employers' association or by ceasing to bargain with a union, a firm is still bound by existing contracts, which continue to apply unless superseded with a new contract. Thus, labor-market institutions discourage firms from adopting nonunion status and have traditionally resulted in high membership in employers' associations and extensive collective-bargaining coverage. Nevertheless, the pressures for variation in employment practices have led to significant declines in employers' association membership, paralleling those of union membership.

**Table 5.3.** Employer Association Membership in Germany

| Year | Gesamtmetall Membership (Firms)[a] | Gesamtmetall Membership (Employees)[b] |
|------|------------------------------------|----------------------------------------|
| 1970 |        | 73.3 |
| 1975 |        | 70.4 |
| 1980 | 57.5   | 72.7 |
| 1985 | 54.6   | 73.8 |
| 1988 | 50.7   | 71.6 |
| 1990 | 46.4   | 69.4 |
| 1993 | 42.8   | 64.2 |

*Sources:* Gesamtmetall membership, 1970–1985, from Müller-Jentsch (1989), and 1985–1993 from unpublished data collected by Stephen Silvia.
[a] Percentage of firms in west Germany belonging to Gesamtmetall.
[b] Percentage of employees in west Germany in firms belonging to Gesamtmetall.

During the 1980s, the pressure within employers' associations came mostly from smaller Mittelstand companies. These firms stridently advocated flexibility of employment practices and differentiation of conditions by firm size, while some also left the associations. In the 1990s, however, the pressure for more varied and flexible collective-bargaining agreements was heightened when larger employers also began to leave the associations (Lange 1994). Consequently the percentage of the workforce in firms belonging to associations is sharply lower, a pattern that is evident even within the strongly organized metalworking industry employers' association, Gesamtmetall (Table 5.3).

In West Germany during the 1970s, more than 70 percent of employees in the metalworking sector belonged to firms within Gesamtmetall, and this figure increased slightly in the 1980s. However, during the 1990s, Gesamtmetall membership fell, from 71.3 percent of employees in 1989 to 64.2 percent in 1993. When measured by the overall number of firms belonging to Gesamtmetall, the fall has been even greater and, significantly, began earlier, with membership dropping from 57.5 percent in 1980 to 42.8 percent in 1993. This reflects the patterns of debates within Gesamtmetall, with Mittelstand firms leaving during the 1980s, and larger firms during the 1990s as they, too, have sought greater flexibility and variation. Unions and employers admit that this trend of declining Gesamtmetall membership has continued throughout the 1990s, and that similar membership loss has occurred in other sectoral associations.

With declining Gesamtmetall membership, company-level bargaining has been increasing. Between 1989 and 1997, the proportion of valid company agreements among all agreements in west Germany increased from 25 percent to 33 percent. Furthermore, since 1994, 45 percent of newly registered agreements have been reached at the company level.[6] Of equal significance has been the sharp rise in west German firms that reach agreements only at the company level. This increased from fewer than 2,000 in 1989 to 3,606 in 1998 (Zagelmeyer 1998a, 1999).

High rates of sectoral bargaining coverage persist, and this strongly limits variation in employment conditions. Nevertheless, decentralization is also evident here: whereas 51.8 percent of establishments and 69.9 percent of employees in west Germany were covered by sectoral bargaining in 1995, by 1997 this had fallen to 49.0 percent and 65.3 percent respectively. The decline was greatest in mining and energy, transport and communication, construction, and credit and insurance sectors (Zagelmeyer 1999). Although no consistent time series data exist, there are indications that this decentralization is part of a broader trend. Even when combined with the 10 percent of employees covered by company-level bargaining (Bispinck 1997; Kohaut and Bellmann 1997), these data are considerably below the 90 percent traditionally estimated for collective-bargaining coverage in west Germany. Moreover, in east Germany, only 25.7 percent of establishments and 43.9 percent of employees were covered by sectoral bargaining in 1997, while 14 percent of establishments had company agreements.

Industrial relations institutions in Germany and comparatively extensive collective bargaining inhibit both low-wage and HRM employment patterns. And because the German model is based on pervasive unionization (or at least the pervasive effects of unionization), high wage equality, and high skills, the nonunion sector is quite small. Works councils also inhibit the ability to introduce nonunion systems in Germany, since employees are entitled to have plant-level worker representation in any company with five or more employees. Small firms typically do not have works councils, however, and indeed only between one fifth and one quarter of all private-sector firms have works councils, though coverage is greater in manufacturing (Frick and Sadowski 1995; Addison et al. 1997).

The combination of collective-bargaining coverage and works councils gives Germany perhaps the most homogenous system of employment relations of any country. Nevertheless, the number of works councils declined during the 1980s, from 36,300 to 33,000 (Müller-Jentsch and Sperling 1995). The percentage of the private sector covered by works councils also fell from 51 percent in 1981 to 45 percent in 1990 (Mitbestimmung Kommission 1998: 50–51). This rate fell further, following unification, to less than 40 percent by 1994 and may signal increasing employment variation among smaller firms.

A broader set of labor market institutions, beyond collective bargaining, also limit the development of a low-wage, nonunion sector. Wolfgang Streeck, for example, notes the important role of the German training regime. Occupational apprenticeships play a key role in Germany, with about four hundred being recognized by the national government. These involve the "legal stipulation of a 'qualification profile' (*Berufsbild*) which specifies the knowledge and skills one must command to be certified as a member of the occupation. The law also regulates in detail the curriculum" (Streeck 1996: 145). Yet, "de facto training regimes are more like industrial agreements" made between industrial unions and employers' representatives, than they are like government decrees. The implication is that "German-style occupational skills correspond to a particular organization of work and mode of co-ordination of work roles" (1996: 146), including the minimal exercise of formal hierarchical authority, the granting of discretion at work and room for individual judgment, the emphasis on technical competence, and an occupational (as opposed to generalist) work organizational mode.

Rather than firms establishing skill structures, the role of the employers' association, the unions, and the government in Germany limits employment system variation, especially since works councils have a strong influence in retaining the internal job structures of firms. Thus, Streeck notes that "German firms are subject to extensive social regulation by law and industrial agreement; they have less freedom than firms in other countries, notably Britain or the United States, to experiment with work organization." Despite the weakening of external regulation with technological and work reorganization, "a wide range of subjects, from skill profiles to payment systems, to a significant part are not decided by the parties at the workplace alone and will not be in the foreseeable future" (Streeck 1996: 167). It is not just collective bargaining but a broad set of German institutions above the level of the firm that restrain managerial voluntarism and enterprise individualism. Despite of these important societal constraints, however, variation in employment systems is growing.

### Reforms to the Collective-Bargaining System

The late 1980s and, even more, the 1990s have witnessed substantial pressure on the collective-bargaining system and loud calls for its reform. The debate was triggered by the small and medium-sized Mittelstand companies which argued for greater flexibility to adjust conditions to the circumstances of individual firms and for greater variation in outcomes.[7] Commonly advocated reforms include collective bargaining with only genuinely minimum conditions; the creation of broader framework agreements subject to detailed negotiation at the plant level; allowing firms to defer wage increases in return for higher investment or greater employment security; increased flexibility to introduce new methods of compensation, such as profit sharing; wider sectoral and regional variation (especially in such broadly defined sectors as metalworking, which incorporates thirteen industries, including automobiles, machine tools, electrical and mechanical engineering, and shipbuilding); and greater use of opening clauses in sectoral agreements to allow for variation to increase job security, as was recommended by the Council of Economic Experts (Schnabel 1995).

Although decentralization and flexibility generally increased during the 1980s and early 1990s, particularly regarding working time (Thelen 1991), Otto Jacobi has argued that 1994 could be a "turning point in the history of German industrial relations, since far-reaching formal and new substantial elements have been included in collective agreements" for the first time (1995: 47). What was most significant was that these changes, which are seen as granting "cafeteria choices" or "bargaining à la carte," involve the extension and formalization of variation in collective bargaining and employment relations. The most important changes included the introduction of opening and hardship clauses in sectoral agreements, which allow companies to adjust working conditions to specific company circumstances more easily. In some instances individual employees can more freely choose their own terms and conditions. In contrast to the United States and the United Kingdom, these choices are frequently established within the centralized collective agreements, while nevertheless simultaneously allowing greater plant-level flexibility.

As the vanguard to greater flexibility in sectoral collective-bargaining agreements, IG Chemie has certainly led IG Metall. The 1994 chemical industry agreement, for example, permitted companies to hire long-term unemployed workers at up to 10 percent less than the standard sectoral wage rate. During 1996 this permission was extended to other new recruits and apprentices. The latter agreement also provided for especially low wage increases in return for guaranteed employment security. Similar agreements were reached in building and textile sectors, whereas the chemical industry agreement allowed firms to cancel the annual bonus (amounting to a month's pay), if necessary.

Of far greater import, however, was IG Chemie's 1997 agreement to create a "compensation corridor," constituting the first general opening clause on *wages*. This agreement was reached following an employment decline of 60,000 in 1993–1997, and in the face of substantial threats by twenty-six companies, led by Continental AG, the tire manufacturer, to leave the employers' federation. The agreement applies to 590,000 workers and allows works councils to negotiate up to a 10 percent pay reduction in return for employment security or guaranteed investment levels.[8] It also requires more successful companies to establish profit-sharing schemes, to be agreed at firm level with the works council. Additional firm-level flexibility to limit wage increases and allow greater pay differentiation was allowed in the 1998 bargaining agreement.

The chemical sector is the first in Germany to decentralize such decisions to works councils and is pathbreaking in its importance. It equally marks a substantial shift from IG Metall's consistent avoidance of the pressure exerted by Gesamtmetall to introduce opening clauses in sectoral contracts. IG Metall has previously granted pay concessions at the plant level, for example, in the cases of Hagen Batterie and Daimler-Benz Aerospace. It has also signed a "hardship clause" in east Germany (see below). However, the IG Chemie agreement goes much further, especially with the unprecedented freedom and flexibility granted to works councils.[9] Bayer was quick to take advantage of this, making a commitment to DM 20 billion (11.5 billion dollar) investment over five years and employment guarantees for three years, in return for DM 300 million (171 million dollars) in reduced annual labor costs.

Following IG Chemie's lead, opening clauses allowing divergence from sectoral collective agreements to be reached with works councils have become increasingly common (Bispinck 1997). Opening clauses on pay remain controversial, though clauses on working hours and for particular groups of employees have become more acceptable. Other union moves to increase plant-level flexibility include the 500,000 DAG white-collar federation's decision in 1996 to allow firms in financial difficulties to negotiate individual pay agreements with their works councils (IRE 1996). The textile sector has similarly introduced flexibility in the payment of negotiated wage increases, including allowing companies to forgo the negotiated pay raise, if circumstances require. The agreement also introduced an annualized hours system that allows companies to vary the actual hours worked and the corresponding pay levels. IG Metall also proposed the "Alliance for Jobs," which would have allowed additional decentralization and variation in direct return for employment guarantees, though this was rejected by Gesamtmetall.[10] Nevertheless, company-level versions have been developed by an increasingly large number of firms, including Opel, Porsche, Mercedes, Robert Bosch, Deutsche Babcock, and Schlafhorst.

The shift from sectoral collective agreements to plant-level collective bargaining does not remove issues from joint determination nor necessarily reduce the role of unions (Thelen 1991). However, plant-level agreements with works councils have greatly increased variation, particularly in the adverse economic climate of the 1990s, when works councils have often been more flexible than the centralized unions. Indeed, the DGB and IG Metall have become increasingly concerned at the gradual erosion of sectoral collective-bargaining agreements. In particular, concessions granted by works councils frequently vary from and breach sectoral collective agreements. In 1997–1998, 15.6 percent of companies in west Germany and 29.8 percent in east Germany contravened valid collective-bargaining agreements signed with unions. Pay accounted for 37.9 percent of the cases in west Germany and 59.9 percent in east Germany (Schulten 1999; Bergmann et al. 1998). Such concessionary agreements have been particularly widespread in response to actual or threatened employment reductions, and as companies search for greater variation in employment practices (discussed further below). This flexibility results partly from the decentralization of subjects to works councils and also from increasingly overburdened works councils being under increasing economic pressure to make concessions once decentralization has occurred.

An additional source of variation in employment conditions has concerned working time. The central goal of unions in the 1980s, to reduce the working time to thirty-five hours, has only been achieved by IG Metall and IG Median, creating some sectoral variation here. Beyond this, intrasectoral variation in (and flexibility of) working time has also expanded with the creation of annual working-time agreements in the 1994 bargaining round. This represented the culmination of a retreat from the union policy of fixed working weeks and a decentralization of bargaining to works councils, which had its origins in IG Metall's 1984 shorter working week agreement (Thelen 1991). Firms have increasingly tried to push for greater flexibility and the separation of working time and machine-operating time, while simultaneously obtaining cyclical and seasonal variation.

The annual hours agreements are not confined to the metalworking sector, and in 1994 it was the chemical sector that created a "working time corridor" of 35–40 hours without overtime pay. The chemical sector also introduced opt-out clauses in 1994, allowing professional workers to negotiate individual working time, with limits (including hours worked) outside the sectoral agreement (EIRR 1994b). The number of company-based working-time models are increasing, though because working time is a subject of codetermination with the works council, they remain based on a joint-participative approach. Nevertheless, annual hours and flexible working-time agreements reduce works councils' control of overtime, a traditionally important source of bargaining power for the councils (Streeck 1984).

This decentralization and flexibility has been enhanced by firms and works councils jointly agreeing to reduce both working hours and wages, within established limits, in order to increase job security. These agreements extending the "VW worksharing model" (discussed below) were included in the metalworking contract in 1994 and are decentralized to the plant level, rather than involving unions. Within six months, this work-sharing agreement in the metalworking sector had been applied to some 500,000 employees, who saw working time and base pay reduced by an average of 10 percent (EIRR 1994b). This form of worksharing agreement has been introduced in metals, chemicals, wholesale, import and export trades, and other sectors.

### The Union Sector under Pressure

The decentralization of bargaining, the introduction of opening clauses, and the declining unionization and membership of employers' associations have made for greater variation in employment conditions among firms. Yet such trends have also been a response to pressure from firms for greater variation and to break away from existing collective bargaining contracts, to introduce firm-specific employment practices, and to extract concessions. The first substantial example of concession bargaining occurred in 1992 at Lufthansa, one of the few large companies to have a firm-level collective bargaining contract. The package of concessions was estimated to produce DM 3 billion (1.71 billion dollars) in savings in wage costs, as well as reforming pay grades and introducing more flexible working-time arrangements (EIRR 1992a). In return, the unions were able to prevent a decentralization of bargaining structures.

Examples of plant-level concession bargaining have also been increasing, where employees and works councils have agreed to extend working hours beyond the limits established in collective agreements. At Motorola, which is not party to collective agreements, employees agreed to increase working hours without additional pay in 1993, while a significant proportion of its annual pay rise was in the form of a lump-sum bonus. In 1994 Deutsche Bahn introduced an individually based annualized hours scheme. Companies that have extended working time without wage compensation include Ravensburger AG, Continental AG, and Mohn GmbH. In the latter case, wage concessions were also granted, along with the introduction of a profit-sharing scheme potentially equivalent to a full month's pay annually.

The computer industry likewise illustrates growing diversity and pressure on unions from substantial competition and employment levels, which fell substantially in the 1990s, reversing the expansion of the 1980s. Typically, and as in many other countries, the computer industry in Germany is weakly unionized. Furthermore, companies such as Software AG and SAP AG, and manufacturers such as Hewlett-Packard, Texas Instruments, and Digital Equipment Corporation, have not had collective agreements but rather have determined pay by individual agreement.[11] This does not, however, remove institutional influences constraining variation. Roßmann (1994) notes that even where not unionized, works councils can use their influence to add a "norming effect" to the individually regulated agreements within the firm.

In contrast to this picture, however, IBM had traditionally belonged to the metalworking employers' association, Gesamtmetall.[12] To introduce greater flexibility and variability, in 1992 IBM adopted a new corporate organizational structure with five separate business units, withdrew its largest business unit (IBM Informationssysteme GmbH) and three others from Gesamtmetall, and terminated its collective contracts. This left only seven thousand of its thirty-one thousand workforce (in the highly organized IBM Produktion GmbH division) in the metalworking sectoral agreement. IBM's unprecedented action aimed to decentralize decision making to business units, reduce personnel costs, increase working hours to forty a week at the same salary (from the thirty-six hours contractually due to be implemented in April 1993), abandon job guarantees, and what was most important, introduce a large performance-related component to pay. IBM complained that the sectoral agreement in metalworking left inadequate room for individual performance-related bonuses, since 90 percent of pay increases were across the board.

IBM's actions reflected an underlying pressure inside Gesamtmetall for greater variation of employment relations, pay levels, and pay systems. However, it also illustrates the difficulties of derecognizing a union in Germany or of adopting a nonunion status. Leaving an employers' federation and terminating an existing collective bargaining agreement does not nullify the applicability of that agreement under German labor law and the 1949 Collective Agreements Act, because agreements remain in force for all union members until their expiry date. Wage contracts (*Lohntarifverträge*) are typically valid for one year; contracts on working conditions (*Manteltarifverträge*), and payment structures (*Rahmentarifverträge*) usually have a considerably more extensive life.

Second, there is a critical distinction in Germany between collective agreements reached by the company (or association) and union (*Tarifverträge*) and company agreements with the works council (*Betreibsvereinbarungen*). Generally, the works council is prohibited from reaching an agreement with management that has been settled by a collective agreement, even where the works council otherwise has codetermination powers (such as the principles of the remuneration system, including incentive pay).

Even in a sparsely unionized sector like computing, IBM was unable to adopt a nonunion model of employment relations, instead having to sign a company-level agreement with the non-DGB white-collar union, DAG.

While this agreement did add to the extent of variation, by increasing working hours and introducing a new payments system, including salary and
bonus structures that produced an individualization of pay, it did not eliminate union representation. Indeed, the agreement included the nearly unprecedented provision of providing safeguards for the DAG union stewards
(*Vertrauensleute*), including the right to use company facilities (which metalworking agreements do not have).

The IBM case is unusual partly because so few large companies have withdrawn membership in their employers' association, and also because even
within a relatively weakly unionized sector, it illustrates that union contracts
cannot be fully circumvented; nonunionism was itself not an option.
Greater variation in employment practices was nevertheless achieved with
greater individualization of pay and longer working hours.

Siemens sought a similar goal—to reduce labor costs and increase working hours from thirty-five to forty. In 1997, it created five new business units
and contemplated outsourcing twenty thousand jobs to avoid the metalworking sectoral agreement. However, to avoid conflict with IG Metall, in
1998 Siemens agreed to retain an amended sectoral agreement. Labor cost
savings were reached by reducing holiday and Christmas bonuses and introducing annual working time, while performance-related pay of up to 5
percent of wages was also agreed. At Debis AG, Daimler-Benz's financial service and computer company, IG Metall agreed to a further compromise. Debis had previously resisted the application of the metalworking sectoral
agreement as incompatible with the needs of the information services sector. In March 1998, a contract was signed allowing for flexible working time,
enhanced employment security for older employees, rights to five days'
training per year, and, significantly, a new performance-related pay scheme.
This can amount to 10–20 percent of annual income, with half dependent
on individual and half on company performance (Schulten 1998).

Such compromises illustrate the strength of IG Metall in extending collective bargaining to the information services sector. However, they also indicate the union's increasingly pragmatic response to employer demands for
varied employment practices and for individually based performance-
related pay schemes. As such, they represent a gradual erosion of IG Metall's
long-held policy of common employment conditions for all and their increasing acceptance of variation. It may even imply "that the principle of having different collective agreements within one corporation would become
more and more the rule rather than the exception" (Schulten 1998).[13]

Telepac represents an additional instance of a drive to variation in employment relations and the signing of a company-level collective agreement
(*Haustarifvertrag*) rather than the company remaining bound by a sectoral

agreement. The strength of IG Metall and the works council is notable in this case, even where a decentralized company-level agreement was signed. The contract, which included a restructuring of pay and grading, training, job design and work organization, and participation, is based on IG Metall's Tarifreform 2000 bargaining agenda. The result is an extension of the joint team-based approach we describe, with an increase in employee participation and management-worker interaction (for example, through multiple joint committees and grievance rights that extend beyond the level of the works council) (EIRR 1993b). In such cases, even where the drive for flexibility occurs outside sectoral collective bargaining, there are clear examples of an extension of the joint participative approach.

High-profile cases like IBM, Siemens, and Telepac are notable for their rarity inside the German industrial relations system. As such, they provide evidence as much for the stability of the collective bargaining system as for the existence of variation. Yet the cases illustrate the growing process of reform, decentralization, and variation. This variation has not, however, expanded significantly either low-wage nonunion or HRM approaches.

The traditional dominance of the permanent employment contract has been weakening, however. Fixed-term contracts have become more common, at least for new hires. In the mid-1980s, a third of new employment contracts were fixed term, and in certain sectors of east Germany since unification the figure has been above 50 percent (Höland 1995). This practice was facilitated by the 1985 Employment Promotion Law,[14] which has been applied most extensively by small and medium-sized employers. Only slightly more than half of fixed-term contracts made as a result of this law have later become permanent contracts. Also, a significant rise in part-time and agency employment has been evident in Germany since the mid-1980s, though the level remains lower than in most other European countries. Agency employment in particular facilitates variation, since such workers are not covered by collective agreements, have their terms and conditions determined unilaterally by employers, and in 1995 received only 63.4 percent of the pay of an average employee. As such, temporary employment agencies have been described as representing "a 'black hole' of nonunionized and non-collectivist firms in contemporary German industrial relations" (Zagelmeyer 1997a).

### Team Working and Variation

Works councils, the basis of employee representation at the plant level, became more effective forms of interest representation in Germany from the mid-1970s to late 1980s.[15] However, at the same time that demands on works councils from the decentralization of bargaining are increasing, the expansion of team work and quality circles has created additional challenges to works councils as the source of worker representation. Examining increased employee participation in the work process, Müller-Jentsch and Sperling (1995) cite evidence indicating that quality circles were being introduced in 40–50 percent of the largest one hundred manufacturing enterprises in the late 1980s, while by 1990 this was true for 20 percent of service-sector companies (compared with only 5 of 121 of the largest companies in 1985).

Despite this growth, evidence from the automobile and chemical industries shows that team working and quality circles have not undermined the councils but have complemented them instead. Frequently, teams and quality circles are subject to works agreements that show, at least for large firms, "that these procedures of direct participation are not 'unilateral procedures.' In contrast these are in fact 'multi-lateral procedures' which involve management and works councils negotiating the arrangements for the introduction and implementation of quality circles together" (Müller-Jentsch and Sperling 1995: 19). The Works Constitution Act ensures that teams and quality circles cannot be introduced to bypass unions and works councils, so there is little evidence of any nonunion or HRM approach despite the variation. However, the decentralized introduction of new forms of work participation and the importance of plant-level employee representatives in their implementation illustrate a programmatic variation in the precise form of direct participation, though predominantly within the joint team-based model.

This is illustrated by the 1996 chemical sector agreement on team working, the first sectoral framework agreement (EIRR 1996c). The agreement facilitates the decentralized implementation of teams by works councils, while ensuring some autonomy and independence for the team, decentralizing certain management functions, securing the election of team leaders (through a mechanism to be decided locally), and providing for additional training within the team.

Overall, in small and medium-sized German companies there has been greater variation in the introduction of teams, since "works councils do not play an important part in the introduction of quality circles either because often they are only little interested in direct participation or because they consider themselves to be overtaxed by this task" (Müller-Jentsch and Sperling 1995: 19). In small firms, less formal employee participation is created by quality circles and team work.

In either case, participation is adding an important layer to institutional structures: it involves a decentralization of employee involvement in work organization and work practices that was not generated by the trade unions and works councils. While "participation, co-determination and collective bargaining were exclusively the business of representative labor institutions...works councils and trade unions have now accepted the managements' initiatives on direct worker participation" (Müller-Jentsch and Sperling 1995: 26).

New forms of work organization are leading to greater decentralization, involving more actors in the design of work organization, and resulting in more varied employment practices. The increasing involvement of works councils and employees in work and technological reorganization has been further emphasized in the 1990s by companies "decentralizing" and "de-bureaucratizing" organizational and managerial structures (Deutschman 1995). The trend toward local profit centers and decentralized managerial responsibility has made it more difficult for works councils to know who they should bargain with. This is particularly so given the traditionally centralized interaction of works councils with management. However, the councils have generally retained their institutionalized role, and thus participation is typically occurring within a joint team-based approach, rather than substituting for collective institutions.

*Eastern Germany*

With the unification of Germany, the government and its social partners attempted to transfer to eastern Germany industrial relations institutions—collective bargaining and works council legislation, employers' associations, unions, and sectoral collective bargaining structures. However, industrial relations institutions have to be fitted into an economy undergoing an enormous economic restructuring, with substantial job losses and high unemployment.

At the beginning of 1998, for example, employment in the east was only 80 percent of its 1991 level and just over 60 percent of its 1989 level. Official unemployment was more than 18 percent, excluding large numbers of workers in early retirement, on government-run active labor market schemes, or withdrawn from the labor market. A massive economic divide remained with respect to western Germany; in particular, east German GDP per capita was only 57 percent of western levels. Furthermore, the contrast is sharp between the west and the east in industrial structure, with manufacturing industry still accounting for 27 percent of employment in the west but only 16 percent in the east. For east Germany, this pattern reflects the massive deindustrialization following unification, when two thirds of employment was lost in the goods-producing industries.

The economic and industrial conditions in the east have placed great pressure on the industrial relations system. Within eastern Germany the result has been a fragile introduction of the west German institutions, with substantial variation in employment relations patterns. Michael Fichter (1997) has argued that there has been an institutional transfer but not an institutionalization of the west German industrial relations system. Yet, while directly increasing variation in the unified Germany, industrial relations practice in east Germany is also leading directly and indirectly to greater variation in west Germany and threatens to erode the collective-bargaining system. Indeed, Fichter argues that "instead of incremental steps toward the high economic standards prevalent in western Germany, the new Länder are becoming the laboratory for a downward revision of union-won achievements throughout the country" (88).

The different industrial structures in the east and west also highlight another problem. As Otto Jacobi (1995) notes, 80 percent of the membership of IG Metall and IG Chemie are blue-collar workers, and these strong, pattern-setting unions have a forty-year spread in their membership structures. Private-sector services in the west frequently have union density levels below 20 percent. In the east, membership structure is very different. Although it is more representative across industrial sectors, the unions have weaker underpinnings despite now similar levels of density. Deep economic recession in the east, unemployment, and deindustrialization have led to massive membership declines (see Table 5.1). These declines are especially high among those under 25, while the unions have been more successful with old and now (early) retired workers. In 1994, IG Metall, for example, had 600,000 members in industrial sectors, though with only 300,000 employees (Fichter 1997).

The large and systematic differences in union strength and industrial structure between the east and the west substantially weakens both inter- and intraindustry pattern setting in Germany and has thereby fostered greater variation within the collective-bargaining system. For example, the number of firms in eastern Germany that exclusively reach company-level agreements has risen steadily, from 450 in 1990 to 1,765 in 1998 (Zagelmeyer 1999). Simultaneously, the membership of employers' associations has eroded. Between 1993 and 1996, even the proportion of manufacturing enterprises belonging to employers' associations fell from 36 to 25 percent. The proportion of employees covered fell more sharply, from 74 to 56 percent (Zagelmeyer 1997b; Bispinck 1995; Fichter 1997). Sectoral variation is substantial as well; among textile and clothing companies, for example, only 9 percent were members.

Overall, in 1996, some 41 percent of companies paid wage rates that undercut the collective-bargaining agreements, up from 35 percent in 1993.

Even among members of employers' associations, 29.8 percent paid less than the agreed rate (Schulten 1999; Zagelmeyer 1997b). In the words of Dieter Schulte, head of the DGB union federation, such practices clearly threaten to "hollow out" the collective-bargaining system.[16]

The massive variation in productivity and profitability performance among companies in the east poses further dramatic problems inside a collective-bargaining system that attempts to establish general minimum levels of pay and conditions (Schnabel 1995). Fichter argues that this is "potentially disastrous" for the industry-wide collective bargaining system. To introduce more flexibility into collective agreements, in 1993 Gesamtmetall canceled the contract in the metalworking sector. Although IG Metall prevailed in the ensuing strike, the result was the introduction of a "hardship clause" that allowed greater flexibility in cases of especially poor company performance (Turner 1997b and 1998). The impact was initially restricted, since IG Metall adopted a hard line and prevented any decentralization. However, by 1997, approximately one hundred companies, employing seven thousand workers had made use of the hardship clause. This agreement can be seen as a precedent for the 1997 opening clause in the west German chemical industry, though more generally the agreement has encouraged other sectors in the east to adopt more flexible hardship, or opening, clauses. For example, the 1997 sectoral agreement in the construction industry allowed firms to reduce collectively agreed wages by up to 10 percent. Even IG Metall has seen more potential for the adoption of hardship clauses in west Germany.

The more common approach, however, has been for many member firms to ignore legally binding wage contracts, usually with the consent of the works council, a move that placed sectoral agreements under substantial stress (Bispinck 1995; Ettl 1995). While some of these cases have been widely publicized, such as concessions made at Sachsen Zweirad, many have been agreed to informally at the company level. Substantial variation is thus occurring even within the system of collective agreements, which traditionally were considered inviolable in west Germany. Bispinck argues that the trend in east Germany means that avoidance of collective agreements represents "tendencies that are increasing in Germany as a whole, albeit to differing extents" (1995). Lowell Turner (1998) argues that even though such variation is unquestionable, it nevertheless occurs when the collectively agreed rate is used as the norm. Although this is probably true, the practice is nevertheless increasing flexibility and variety, while also allowing the development of some lower-paying sectors, in the east in particular.

Beyond this, "collective bargaining policy practice is distinguished by a high degree of differentiation and consideration for the respective sector-

specific situation" (Bispinck 1995: 72). Thus variation in pay levels is substantial among sectors in the east; "cumulative inequality" is another trend,
with low-paying sectors in the west paying even less in the east. At the end of
1994, even the collectively bargained level of base pay (which excludes often substantial bonuses and does not account for the longer hours worked
in the east) ranged from 100 percent of west German levels to only 57.8 percent in the clothing industry, and 62.2 percent in textiles. After wage increases in 1995, even the chemical sector paid only 74 percent of the western rate.

An added element of pay variation has arisen with the 1993 Employment
Promotion Act (Arbeitsförderungsgesetz). The act increased the pressure
for pay flexibility by offering wage subsidies where previously long-term unemployed workers received no more than 90 percent of the collectively bargained rate. Although challenged by unions, IG Metall, IG Chemie, and IG
Bergbau signed agreements under its provisions (Bispinck 1995; Silvia
1997).

The variation in employment relations extends beyond pay to include the
activities of works councils within firms. Michael Fichter argues that while
unions in the west have expended substantial effort to prevent works councils from becoming syndicalist institutions, they have become so in the east.
Indeed, works councils are "almost zealous about protecting their independence from outside guidance or control, even when they accept the basic
role of the union as the representative of employee wage interests" (1997:
100). The focus has, to a significant extent, been on ensuring the survival
of "their" company. The relative influence of management is thereby increased, especially since works councils accept variations in employment
standards to secure jobs and even the company itself.

Although these developments have not doomed the collective-bargaining
system in the east, they have led to greater variation in employment practices. In a series of case studies, Turner (1998) finds substantial plant-level
diversity in production organization and industrial relations. The codetermination rights of works councils increase the potential for a joint-
participative team-based approach, and Turner observes substantial potential for the continued institutionalization of west German industrial-relations
practices. However, the variation is significant, and alongside cases of
strongly unionized firms, with well-integrated and influential works councils are cases of highly cooperative and weak works councils, as well as weakly
unionized firms outside the sectoral agreements. The degree of diversity is
substantially greater than in the west, and "cases that would be outliers in
the West are less unusual in the East; it is, in fact, difficult to find a real main-
stream in the new eastern states" (Turner 1998: 82).

### THE AUTO INDUSTRY

The trends we have identified throughout Germany are clearly weakening the formal and informal institutions of industrial relations and leading to growing variation in employment practices. Some of these trends, such as declining union and employer association membership, have had little impact in the auto industry. Indeed, that industry has retained its preeminent role within IG Metall, which retains comprehensive membership—about 80–90 percent of the total workforce—including both blue- and white-collar employees, and the auto workers account for approximately 40 percent of total IG Metall membership. Certainly, this should help to limit employment variation in the auto industry.

Nevertheless, other general trends observed in Germany have had an equally strong impact in the auto sector: decentralization from unions to increasingly overburdened works councils, the implementation of more flexible sectoral agreements and opening clauses, concession bargaining, and substantial work reorganization. But there is little evidence from the auto industry, as in the rest of Germany, that nonunion employment patterns are emerging, either in the form of low-wage or human resource management models. This is equally true where the western auto industry has expanded in eastern Germany. Again, as throughout the country, unification has both directly and indirectly stimulated variation, in large part by giving firms the opportunity to experiment on greenfield sites. However, variation continues to be constrained to a joint approach.

The German auto industry is a mix of domestic producers (VW, Mercedes-Benz, BMW, Audi, and Porsche) and the European operations of Ford and GM (which operate as Adam Opel). Except for Volkswagen, all the auto companies are members of Gesamtmetall. Although Volkswagen conducts negotiations on a company basis (through a *Haustarifvertrag*), this long-standing structure does not reflect any attempt to lessen the role of unions, nor does it serve to undermine the existing collective agreements in the metalworking sector. Indeed, VW has frequently been a pattern setter for the rest of the metalworking sector, with above-average pay and conditions (Turner 1991: 119). VW's position is enhanced because the metalworking sector has itself long been the pattern setter for the rest of the German collective-bargaining system.

In contrast to the United States, Britain, or Australia, there have been no recent changes to the structure of the auto industry in Germany, no Japanese transplants to bring growing variation of working practices, nor any development of a nonunion sector. However, Opel and VW have taken advantage of unification to experiment on greenfield sites. When these companies opened new plants in eastern Germany after unification, both plants (Opel Eisenach and VW Mosel) were created as units legally independent from the rest of their respective companies. With this legal structure, the new plants have greater independence from their west German counterparts. They are not, for example, bound by company-wide agreements made by the central works councils. The ownership structure of the two greenfield sites was thus designed to allow greater flexibility and experimentation in these new plants, and to weaken the impact of traditional patterns of work organization and unionization from west Germany. That is, the aim and effect has been to isolate the works councils in the new east German plants from their west German counterparts.

The isolation of the new plants was reinforced because the workforce in both cases was selected after rigorous screening from a large pool of experienced auto workers (VW being established at an old Trabant plant, and Opel at a Wartburg plant). After employment in the east German auto industry collapsed from more than ninety thousand to only forty thousand between 1991 and 1992 alone, the companies clearly hoped to create a strong plant identification. Furthermore, both regions have suffered massive unemployment. Nevertheless, neither case represents an attempt at establishing a nonunion plant. Rather, both plants are members of the employers' association and engage in sectoral bargaining, even if at the lower east German rates of pay and working conditions. Indeed, in VW Mosel's case, membership of Gesamtmetall is unlike that of its parent company, since VW otherwise bargains only at the company level.

The introduction of production facilities in eastern Germany, particularly Opel Eisenach, has varied employment practices in a similar manner to greenfield plants in our other countries. However, even in western Germany, variation in employment relations has accelerated in the 1990s as the German auto industry has increased the pace of restructuring. As in the other countries in this volume, the variation is evident in work organization and other employment conditions as companies react to growing industry pressures, and concession bargaining becomes more important.

### Stability of Formal Structures

A distinguishing feature of the German industrial relations system and bargaining in the auto industry has been the stability of formal institutional structures, even though there has also been a shift of emphasis within these institutions. As described above, bargaining over wages and working conditions, as well as participation in work organization, occurs at two distinct levels: IG Metall conducts sectoral bargaining on behalf of the entire metalworking sector, including the auto industry, formally on a regional basis, though with actual extension throughout the country. Basic negotiated pay rates, wage increases, hours, vacation entitlements, principles of payment systems and grading structures are automatically the same across the principal auto companies, and likewise in supplier firms, which also belong to the metalworking sector. The extensive structure of industry-wide bargaining thus circumvents the need for pattern bargaining observed in the United States and other countries.

The legal structure of industry-wide collective bargaining forbids issues settled between the union and employers' association from being negotiated at the local level, unless explicitly subject to an opening clause. Nevertheless, pay rates are subject to informal bargaining between the works councils and companies, though only above the collectively agreed rates. The overtariff payments are typically negotiated on a company-wide basis, though again they have historically been subject to minimal variation among companies.[17]

For their part, the works councils have a wide range of information, consultation, and codetermination rights, which include the ability to conclude either company-wide or plant agreements (*Betriebsvereinbarungen*) on issues not subject to regulation through collective bargaining. Codetermination rights are particularly extensive on matters concerning personnel issues. The details of shift-working and overtime, as well as the introduction or amendment of team work and other work reorganizations, are examples of issues requiring works council approval. The union has no formal role at the plant level, but because IG Metall members dominate the works councils, its influence is substantial within companies and plants.[18]

This highly juridified process of labor-management regulation has been stable throughout the 1980s and 1990s in Germany. The legal rights of the works council, for example, mean that the variation we describe in the United States on differences in grievance procedures in transplants, or the different bargaining roles played by company councils at Nissan and Toyota in the United Kingdom, where independent employee representation is circumscribed, are not an issue in Germany. Furthermore, with near-parity representation on the supervisory boards (*Aufsichtsrat*) and extensive information, consultation, and codetermination rights, there is also less variation in Germany in the degree to which worker representatives are integrated into plant decision making and the extent of information received.

### Concession Bargaining and Working Hours

One of the most significant features of the German auto industry in the 1990s, and particularly since 1993, has been the extent of concession bargaining. Concession bargaining had been unprecedented in Germany where, even in the period 1973–1981, IG Metall and the works council were able to resist concessions as the trouble hit VW (Turner 1991). During the 1980s, the German auto industry performed comparatively well. Car production rose by 32 percent between 1980 and 1990, exports by 47 percent, and employment by 14 percent. In this buoyant market, IG Metall was able to make significant advances in employment conditions. These included progressive moves to a thirty-five-hour week following IG Metall's extensive 1984 strike and, in 1987, the introduction of a rationalization protection agreement providing employment protection for workers affected by new technology or work reorganization.

The deep recession of the 1990s has, however, seen the German auto industry under greater pressure, with rapidly declining production and employment. From its peak in 1991 to 1995, employment fell by more than 15 percent to 661,000, completely reversing the gains of the 1980s. Although by 1998 it had stabilized at 660,000, employers continued to insist that they were structurally overmanned. For employers, the drive to cut costs has been paramount and has triggered a wave of concession bargaining akin to that in the United States in the early 1980s.

Concession bargaining has taken three forms. First, negotiations have been held at plant or, more usually, company level for lower wages by reducing payments above the sectorally bargained level (that is, to reduce overtariff wage payments, i.e., payments above the minimum set in the sectoral agreements). Second, changes to work organization have been agreed, including some that have reduced cycle times and increased work intensity. And third, working time is more flexible, in particular through the introduction of "annual hours," which stands in opposition to IG Metall's long-held policy of a standard working week. This concession is popular not only because it increases management's flexibility to maintain capital utilization rates but also because it reduces overtime payments (and is therefore in effect a substantial wage concession). Furthermore, it constrains works council control of overtime. In the German context, this concession is particularly significant, since works councils have traditionally used their codetermination rights concerning overtime as a bargaining tool to extend their rights into other areas (Streeck 1984). Thus, concession bargaining has not only affected financial and employment conditions but also the role and power of works councils. For their part, the councils have agreed to significant concessions (and thereby variation in employment practices) principally in return for employment guarantees and to secure investment in German plants.

A feature of the German bargaining structure has been that pay concessions have occurred outside the confines of sectoral bargaining. Instead, they have taken place at the company level through agreed reductions in the company's overtariff payments. Concessions have generally been made in response to management threats of new investment abroad and downsizing at the plant level. While both Ford and Opel have long had production facilities throughout Europe, and thus at least the potential to pressure plants in different countries, this is a new and increasing development among German auto companies. Traditionally, German companies had confined their production facilities to Germany, while inside Germany the production of particular models was generally limited to a single plant. The changing corporate strategy, illustrated by Mercedes' goal of increasing international production from 5 percent at the beginning of 1995 to 25 percent by the year 2000, is allowing firms to whipsaw the works councils into both pay and work practice concessions.[19]

One of the first examples of wage concessions took place at Opel in September 1993. The central works council agreed to limit wage increases for four years between 1994 and 1997 by offsetting some increases agreed by IG Metall in sectoral collective bargaining against the existing overtariff payments. The council also agreed to link the Christmas bonus to a reduction in absentee rates and other cost savings (Opel 1993).[20] In return, Opel guaranteed to increase production in its German factories and avoid layoffs, which had been part of its plan to reduce vertical integration. Rather than this being a one-time agreement, it was renegotiated for a further four years in 1998. The works council agreed to substantial concessions by annually offsetting 1.25 percentage points of any IG Metall collectively bargained wage increase for four years. In return, Opel agreed to guarantee future investments, safeguard employment, and review proposed and existing outsourcing (EIRR 1998). This agreement was reached despite threats by GM Europe to lower employment by 20–30 percent throughout Europe, and by between 9,000 and 14,000 in Germany alone.

Wage concessions and greatly reduced bonus payments were also negotiated at Mercedes for the period 1993–1996, in return for Mercedes' commitment to build its "Baby Benz" car at its new plant in Rastatt (rather than in Britain, France, or the Czech Republic), and to avoid compulsory redundancies for at least two years. This agreement was similarly renegotiated in 1997 for a further four years, but it included an agreement to negotiate a new payment system. Wage concessions at Ford have likewise been substantial. In 1994, the central works council agreed to offset 3.5 percentage points of any sectorally negotiated wage increase over two years; a new agreement in 1997 conceded a further 4 percentage points over the next two years. In Ford's case, rather than negotiate employment security guarantees, the works council secured guarantees concerning investment levels in Germany until the year 2000, extended in 1997 to the year 2010.

Although the pattern of wage concessions being granted by works councils is very similar in the auto industry, the concessions are in fact company based and are distinct from the metalworking sectoral agreement. Furthermore, since the concessions made by works councils refer to payments above collectively bargained sectoral rates, they are having the important additional effect of *reducing* the wage differential between key auto companies and suppliers. The stabilizing effect of pay-setting institutions can be seen in that from the end of the 1970s until the early 1990s, the ratio of pay between suppliers and assemblers in Germany hovered consistently at 85 percent (Sako 1997), despite pressure on suppliers to reduce costs. However, the pay concessions granted in the mid- to late-1990s at assemblers are narrowing the wage differential. This reduced wage disparity results from suppliers making only limited or no overtariff payments and thus having less room to maneuver as the reduction in such payments by the assemblers takes them closer to the sectorally agreed minimum. The difference in profitability rates between assemblers and suppliers has, however, led "to a massive clash of interests" as assemblers have tried to pass cost increases on to the suppliers (Schnabel 1995: 33). Although the structure of collective bargaining has thus limited the degree of variation, it is also encouraging firms to leave the employers' confederations.

The inflexibility in the German system for suppliers, which results from their not making overtariff payments, constitutes a disincentive to aggressively pursue reductions in the degree of vertical integration among the auto assemblers. Nevertheless, a trend in this direction has been observed (Roth 1996b). In certain notable cases, such as seat construction at Mercedes' Bremen plant, management has outsourced functions even while retaining production in the existing plant, and leaving it indistinguishable from other production areas, though with employees receiving reduced wages and benefits (approximately 20 percent lower in the Mercedes case). Similar examples exist at other companies, such as with tube production for air conditioning systems at VW's Salzgitter plant. However, where suppliers such as Stribel have attempted to undercut sectoral conditions, IG Metall has successfully forced them to join the employers' association (EIRR 1995c).

Along with pay concessions the auto assemblers have agreed to changes in working-time arrangements. Indeed, the most fundamental example of concession bargaining occurred at VW in 1993, in what amounted to a substantial political shift by IG Metall and the acceptance of marked variation in employment conditions.[21] Following a sharp decline in sales, substantial short-time work, and planned layoffs of more than 30,000 workers from 103,000 in 1993 to 72,000 by 1995, IG Metall negotiated a reduction in the working week from 36 hours to 28.8 hours, accompanied by a proportionate reduction in pay. In essence, the "VW model" amounted to a 20 percent cut in hours and base pay in return for employment security.[22] The core elements of the model have been extended in additional contracts in both 1995 and 1997, and at a minimum, job security has been guaranteed until 1999. VW and IG Metall have also introduced a working-time corridor to respond to variations in demand, with annual average hours remaining at 28.8 and days off in lieu of overtime. The apparent structural surplus of workers at VW appears likely to make the VW model a long-term feature of the firm's employment relations, despite the gradual attrition of the workforce and an early retirement program introduced in 1997 aimed at 10,000 workers over five years.

The IG Metall agreements at VW extend more deeply into pay systems than the union has accepted at other auto assemblers and again illustrate the union's increasingly pragmatic response to demands for variation. To reduce outsourcing in an attempt to secure up to two thousand jobs, IG Metall in 1997 agreed to the addition of two new low-pay grades, as well as a new two-tiered employment structure.[23] New staff could be hired on exclusively temporary contracts, with wage rates 10 percent lower than for core employees. Furthermore, IG Metall agreed to a new profit-related bonus at VW, worth DM 500 (285 dollars) in 1997. This further highlights the growing variation in pay levels in the auto industry. In 1998, Audi, an operationally independent subsidiary company of VW, also introduced a new and permanent profit-related pay system, agreed with its central works council. However, in contrast to the scheme at VW, initial payments amounted to between DM 1,400 (800 dollars) and DM 2,400 (1370 dollars).

Despite the high publicity of the VW work-sharing model and its underlying principles being broadly extended in the 1994 collective bargaining round, it has not been adopted by the other works councils or companies in the auto industry. Indeed, companies have explicitly rejected this route to addressing problems of excess workers. Yet as a response to VW's crisis, the work-sharing model allowed variation in employment relations within the industry, both in terms of take-home pay and by introducing more options for variation in working hours that were permitted more broadly after the 1994 bargaining round.

A further example of working-time flexibility was the "working-time corridor" agreed to at Opel's Rüsselsheim plant in October 1995 for eleven thousand workers. As at VW, this agreement allows Opel to seasonally adjust its workforce without any financial burden (EIRR, 1995b). This flexibility was conceded by the works council within a section of the plant in response to management pressure concerning a DM 6 billion (3.4 billion dollar) investment for its new Vectra and Astra models.

In spite of being Germany's only auto company not to reduce employment levels in the 1990s, a similar deal was reached at BMW in 1996 in return for employment guarantees (EIRR 1996b). Though the details differ, the BMW agreement is also noteworthy because it again breaches the boundaries set in IG Metall's sectoral bargaining contract. Similar plant-level concessions exist at Mercedes: a 1993 agreement for increased flexibility of working time, plant utilization rates, and payment systems at its new Untertürkheim engine plant (discussed further below); and in 1996 an additional working-time flexibility agreement for the remaining plant employees, together with a 5 percent cut in wages at an axle plant. In the latter two cases, the concessions granted by the works council secured employment guarantees from Mercedes until the year 2000 (EIRR 1996a).

The prevalence of concession bargaining in the mid-1990s has had a greater procedural effect than that generated by the disparate outcomes. Even though IG Metall is the strongest union and the auto industry its strongest sector, it has been difficult for the union to maintain common standards throughout the industry. The concession bargaining has, moreover, accelerated the decentralization of labor-management interactions to central works councils, and even to the plant level. It has also put noticeable pressure on sectoral collective-bargaining contracts, increasing their degree of flexibility. The diversity and concessions are, nevertheless, broader and have included changes in work organization and the introduction of team working.

## INTRODUCTION OF TEAM WORKING

Pressure to introduce team working has a long history in Germany, dating back to wildcat strikes between 1969 and 1973, which were partly a protest against traditional assembly line work (Turner 1991: 104). In the early 1970s, IG Metall adopted a campaign for the "humanization of work," with demands for greater job rotation, job enrichment, and work teams. As a major theme of IG Metall's bargaining agenda, in 1973 IG Metall negotiated an agreement in North Baden-Württemberg to limit the division of labor and establish minimum cycle times of 1.5 minutes. However, IG Metall failed to extend this regional agreement nationally (Markovits 1986: 226–33). Similar, more limited (and largely unsuccessful) experiments to introduce team work were made at VW's Salzgitter plant, and at Ford's Saarlouis plant. Turner (1991) describes two further stages in the development of team work in Germany. Between 1979 and 1985, IG Metall unsuccessfully bargained for change, and from 1985, the union no longer exclusively led the drive toward team work, as management began to develop its own concepts (such as Opel's *Fertigungsgruppen,* or production team, concept). Works councils bargained pilot projects on the basis of principles (*Eckpunkte zur Gruppenarbeit*) developed by IG Metall in the second half of the 1980s.[24]

Turner has characterized the period up to 1990 as one of a "narrow range of variation" in team working, largely as the result of the ability of works councils to constrain managerial strategies (1991: 148). The similarities included not only the involvement of the works councils in discussions concerning the development of teams but also the union-sponsored team-work concepts. IG Metall's twelve-point concept proposed broad task assignment and long cycle times; team autonomy in job rotation, division of work, and quality control and training needs; decentralization of plant decision-making structures; regular meetings; equal pay for team members; and voluntary participation (Turner 1991: 113–14; IG Metall 1992). This strategy of team working closely aligns with our joint team-based approach described in column 4 of Figure 1.1, and was predominant in the pilot projects of the late 1980s.

During the 1980s the German auto industry displayed resilience and strength, following a path of "diversified quality production" (Sorge and Streeck 1988). IG Metall and the works councils' success in bargaining for increased training and skill levels was reflected in the growing numbers of *Facharbeiter* (skilled workers) in production departments and the creation of so-called "system regulators." These workers enjoyed increased flexibility, self-organization, and the relative absence of detailed job descriptions (Jürgens, Malsch, and Dohse 1993; Jürgens 1995; Kuhlmann and Schumann 1997).

These developments had, however, only a small effect on overall work organization, which remained dominated by traditional Taylorist assembly line production methods. Despite IG Metall's interest in promoting its version of team working in the 1980s, teams were slow to develop in Germany compared with the United States in particular. The pilot projects were very limited in extent, with few formal developments until the 1990s. During the 1980s, German auto industry management displayed little interest in IG Metall's concept of team work and instead concentrated on a strategy of automation (Jürgens, Malsch, and Dohse 1993; Turner 1991). Indeed, by 1990 only 4 percent of production workers operated in teams (principally pilot schemes), though by 1993 this figure had risen to 9.5 percent, and by 1994 to 17 percent (Roth 1996a).[25]

Thus, although Turner provides evidence of limited variation across plants and companies during the 1980s, a fourth stage in the development of team work, from 1990 onward, shows programmatic variation in work organization. In the 1990s management has shown interest in team working, though as Table 5.4 indicates, the development has been uneven across the auto companies. Opel and Audi have become the most prominent proponents of team work, whereas Ford, with only 1.6 percent of production workers in teams, has displayed little interest in the concept. Mercedes, Volkswagen, and BMW have adopted a more cautious approach, though the greenfield sites of Opel Eisenach, Mercedes Rastatt, and VW Mosel have had the most broadscale implementation of team work.

Despite these differences in emphasis, however, the responses of corporations have been similar: decentralization in management structures to profit and cost centers; functional integration as an important part of new work organization that has less specialized roles than traditional Taylorism; and team work to increase employee involvement in problem solving and process optimization (Kuhlmann and Schumann 1997). Nevertheless, IG Metall's attempts to develop a common team-work policy have proved unsuccessful in the face of management pressure. Instead, team-work concepts have become more diverse. Gerst et al. thus report that "the shop floor reality in the German automobile industry is characterized by a large array of forms of group or team work" (1999: 368). Essentially, there has been a polarization between the joint team-based approach and the Japanese-oriented approach.[26]

In response to its limited power to impose a common model, IG Metall has accepted a strategy of supporting works councils in local negotiations. This decentralized approach corresponds to the requirements of implementing team work. However, such decentralization has meant that the form of team working varies across plants and companies, and also from the early pilot projects.

The variety of team-working patterns reflects both differing corporate strategies and also the strength of and choices made by local works councils. Although most councils continue to support IG Metall's *Eckpunkte* team work principles, they lack the power to defend those concepts against competing management models, particularly during a period of downsizing in the auto industry and whipsawing among plants.

In several companies, the central works councils have responded by negotiating company-wide agreements governing the introduction of teams. Such agreements have been reached at Opel (excluding the Eisenach plant), Mercedes, Ford, Audi, and BMW; VW has reached only plant-level agreements. However, though the language of these agreements is often similar, the lack of specifics and the decentralized nature of change means that teams continue to take different forms in various plants even where company-level agreements exist (Gerst et al. 1999). The disparity is greater as a result of different company strategies, though Gerst et al. also stress the

**Table 5.4.** Group Work in the German Auto Industry, 1994

| | Employment (Total) | Employees in Groups (Total) | % of Employees in Groups | Manual Worker Employment | Manual Workers as % of Total Employment | % of Manual Workers in Groups |
|---|---|---|---|---|---|---|
| Audi[a] | 32,060 | 16,160 | 50.5 | 23,623 | 78.8 | 68.4 |
| BMW | 57,160 | 9,224 | 16.1 | 35,287 | 61.8 | 26.2 |
| Ford[b] | 31,970 | 430 | 1.3 | 25,854 | 81.0 | 1.6 |
| Mercedes-Benz | 155,230 | 15,700 | 10.1 | 103,538 | 66.7 | 15.2 |
|   Mercedes Rastatt[c] | (1430) | (1,160) | 81.0 | (1,160) | 81.0 | 100.0 |
| Opel | 45,610 | 14,400 | 31.6 | 36,340 | 79.6 | 39.6 |
|   Opel Rüsselsheim[c] | (25,600) | (9,900) | 38.6 | (18,200) | 71.0 | 54.3 |
| Opel Eisenach | 1,920 | 1,640 | 85.0 | 1,640 | 85.0 | 100.0 |
| Porsche[d] | 6,604 | — | — | 3,828 | 58.0 | — |
| VW[e] | 105,310 | 8,423 | 7.9 | 80,667 | 76.6 | 10.4 |
|   VW Mosel[c] | (2,400) | — | — | (2,000) | 83.0 | — |
| | | | | | | |
| Total | 435,870 | 69,122 | 15.8 | 310,777 | 71.3 | 22.2 |
|   (excluding Audi)[a] | | 55,126 | 12.6 | | | 17.7 |

*Source:* Roth (1996a), p. 134.
*Note:* Audi, Ford, Opel, and Porsche as of June 1994; BMW and Mercedes-Benz as of January 1994; VW and Mercedes-Benz Rastatt as of August 1994.
[a] For Audi, group working figures are nominal only. They reflect training for group work rather than the actually functioning groups. These groups have subsequently become active.
[b] Ford for Germany only, excluding Genk (B).
[c] Includes employment in preceding company.
[d] Porsche has no group work, though 80 percent of employees are trained for KVP groups (continuous improvement teams).
[e] VW excludes other forms of work organization, such as "Gruppenkreditvorgabe." Manual worker total includes both direct and indirect functions.

intracompany variation that is emerging at Mercedes. Although the Mercedes company-level agreement "is clearly geared towards self-organized group work," results are disparate because teams are the responsibility of individual production units and there is decentralized bargaining over their implementation (1999: 373).

### Role of Team Leaders

An important illustration of the variation in work organization among companies is the different role played by team leaders and the methods of their selection. At Opel, Mercedes, and BMW provisions for electing team leaders vary. At BMW, these team leaders do not form a separate hierarchical level; and supervision remains at the *Meister* level. At Ford, *Kolonnenführer* (team leaders who perform some tasks previously undertaken by supervisors, are hierarchically above the team, and have a semi-supervisory role) have been appointed by management on a basis agreed by the works coun-

**Table 5.5.** Selection of Team Leaders in the German Auto Industry

| Company | Team Leader Selection Method | Assessment Center | Pay Differential (DM per month) |
|---------|------------------------------|-------------------|--------------------------------|
| Audi | Appointment | Yes | 170 |
| BMW | Election | No | 135 |
| Ford | Appointment[a] | [Yes][b] | 160 |
| Mercedes | Election | No | 120 |
| Opel | Election | Yes | 300 |
| Opel Eisenach | Appointment | Yes | 570[c] |
| VW | Appointment | No | 220 |

*Source:* Derived from an unpublished IG Metall document.
[a] There are provisions for elections with the co-ordination of management, though appointment has prevailed and is favored by the works council.
[b] The system of appointment meant that these employees had already been assessed, though not directly for the new appointment.
[c] DM 570 per month is earned above the highest-paid team members, though on average this represents DM 700 above the average group member.

cil. Similarly, at Audi, appointments are made by management, though with the consensual agreement of the works council. This is similar to conditions at VW, where in some pilot areas the job rotates among team members. At Opel Eisenach, however, the original structure of elections was overturned in favor of management appointments.

Table 5.5 also indicates variations in the use of assessment centers to select team leaders, with these being especially important at Opel Eisenach, Audi, and also Ford. In Opel's west German plants, the works council has ensured that the assessment center plays a minimal role, though in the two years following election, team leaders receive an extra fifty-three days of training. This represents a substantial difference from other companies and again illustrates the variation in the roles team leaders play. Similarly, Table 5.5 indicates variation in payments to team leaders that reflect a combination of higher skill levels and the absorption of managerial tasks by team leaders. At DM 700 (400 dollars) per month more than the average team member, these payments are most striking at Opel Eisenach, where team leaders have a significant managerial role. Yet, in the assembly area of Opel's Bochum plant, team leaders have also absorbed some supervisory functions, and in certain production areas at Mercedes they can play the role of subforeman (Gerst et al. 1999).

Team leaders are not always integrated into production work. At Opel, for example, they are not. At Mercedes, the goal is to integrate them, though at the Rastatt plant, team leaders are freed from production tasks for 30–40 percent of their time. In these cases, the varying organization of team leaders reflects the varying organizations of the teams themselves.

*The Team-Work Experience at Opel*

The essential principles of team work vary less within companies in Germany than in other countries, not simply as a result of company-wide agreements signed by central works councils but also because of the juridified powers of the plant works councils. Nevertheless, team work still exhibits experimentation and variation across plants. The case of Opel, which is the most advanced in the introduction of team work, is instructive. The extent of team work varies from plant to plant and is most advanced at Rüsselsheim, particularly in the assembly area. The development of team work has been evolving, with the Rüsselsheim works council renegotiating the 1991 company-wide agreement in 1994, thus altering the operation of teams. This change demonstrated both the decentralized implementation of team work and the role of the plant works councils in shaping practice.

Opel's company-level framework agreement on team work applies to its Bochum, Rüsselsheim, and Kaiserslautern plants, though the Eisenach plant is excluded. The framework agreement specified the essential structure of teams; for example, that team leaders be elected by team members; that team leaders have no assessment, disciplinary, or supervisory powers; that supervisors should be reoriented to a more supportive role, should coordinate multiple teams, and allow the team greater autonomy over production decisions; that teams should consist of between eight and fifteen members, with flexibility between tasks; that job rotation should be agreed to by both the team leader and the supervisor; and that the weekly team meeting should be scheduled during normal working hours, with the team establishing the agenda, and others (including works councillors or supervisors) attending only by invitation. The agreement also rationalized the pay system, reducing the number of wage groups from forty-two to ten.

Opel was, however, constrained from introducing incentive pay structures and pay-for-knowledge, as it had hoped, because the works council was opposed to wage differentials within teams (Shire 1995: 150–52).[27] Opel was also unable to collapse wage rates for skilled and semi- or unskilled workers into the same scale, owing to opposition from skilled workers. Furthermore, Opel accepted the principle that no redundancies were to result from the operation of teams, while a steering committee was established to ensure that the principles of the framework agreement were enacted (Murakami 1995a). It is clear that the company-wide framework agreement corresponds closely to our joint team-based employment pattern.

The importance of the decentralization of teams was illustrated in 1991–1994 when introduction of teams stalled in the assembly area of the Rüsselsheim plant and led to a renegotiation of the existing agreement.

Teams were reduced from an average of ten to twelve members to six (including the "free-standing" team leader, who does not undertake standard production tasks within the team). A new system for team meetings was introduced (whereby other team leaders from other groups fill in for the team holding a meeting) to ensure at least one hour every two weeks. By mid-1996, there were 956 team leaders, with approximately 65 percent in teams of six members. Within the teams, there is broad skilling, a job rotation and qualification plan, and an increase in team-member flexibility (with approximately 75 percent of workers being able to complete all tasks within a group). However, team working in the assembly area remains on the line, with cycle times of approximately 1.5 minutes, while in the engine and cockpit production areas, off-line production units have been removed, with a return to shorter cycle times and line production.

Within the teams, the works council has emphasized the role of the elected team leader, who has absorbed many of the previous functions of the *Meister*, including coordinating work organization, job rotation and the assignment of work; setting team goals and kontinuierlicher Verbesserungsprozeß, or KVP (continuous improvement) programs; and overseeing relief work, on-the-job training, and quality assurance. In turn, the *Meister*'s role has been redefined as that of a coach, with less direct authority, though with the team leader having adopted a quasi-hierarchical role. Although the number of *Meisters* has not changed and the span of control has remained at between twenty-five and forty, direct supervision has nevertheless been reduced.

In contrast team work at Opel's greenfield plant at Eisenach, in eastern Germany, follows a Japanese-oriented model. The plant was constructed on the site of an old Wartburg auto facility, with production beginning in September 1992. Following substantial new investment, Eisenach is essentially a greenfield site and is legally independent from the rest of GM's German operations. It is not a party to the central works council (*Gesamtbetriebsrat*) and therefore not subject to the company-wide agreements reached by the council on such issues as team-working structures. The works council at Eisenach is also weaker than those in other German plants, and Opel management has been largely successful in creating a strong plant identity. The substantially reduced workforce of two thousand selected from among the old Wartburg employees, and by 1995 160,000 cars were being produced in what Opel management claimed was their most efficient plant (and second in Europe behind Nissan's Sunderland plant).

The legal independence of Opel Eisenach reflected management's intention of introducing a new lean production strategy as a test case for Opel and GM, more broadly. Key production concepts devolved from GM's

NUMMI and especially CAMI operations, with managers also coming from these plants. Eisenach essentially marks a shift away from the traditional German participative production system toward the Japanese-oriented pattern described in column 3 of Figure 1.1.

Teams are organized with five to eight members, with workers belonging to one of two skill categories. Although team leaders were initially elected, the works council agreed to a revised structure whereby leaders were appointed by management, and there is essentially no role for the works council or union. Team leaders are, furthermore, hierarchically above team members, and their extra pay of DM 700 (400 dollars) per month reflects their managerial role. Moreover, the pay structure at Eisenach is different. Since piecework (*Akkordlohn*) and incentive bonus pay (*Prämienlohn*) are the subject of co-determination, Opel chose to simplify the pay structure at Eisenach, paying only a base-pay rate (*Zeitlohn*), thereby reducing the works council's role. Ironically, Opel is reassessing its payment structures at its older plants with a view to making incentive-based pay systems more effective.

Eisenach has a significantly reduced emphasis on automation and a correspondingly greater emphasis on manual assembly on a traditional production line. Rather than the historic German emphasis on skilled workers (*Facharbeiter*), the Eisenach model has focused on a narrowly defined level of common skills (*Jedermanns-Qualifikation*) (Roth 1996a:122). Although the potential for rotation within groups is there, it does not occur through skill broadening. Work tasks are generally restricted, with short cycle times of approximately sixty to ninety seconds, a concentration on production-line work with limited scope for task variation, and the minimal integration of indirect tasks into the line (1996a: 122). Similarly, there is little room for autonomous organization of work, with production tasks being closely defined by narrow rules. Production times are standardized and subject to regular tightening as part of the process of continuous improvement.

The Eisenach model of narrow common skills, low autonomy of work organization, short cycle times, standardized work processes, and greater emphasis on incentive pay represents a shift from the team-working concept promoted by IG Metall. Despite the company-wide framework agreement on team work, Opel has tried to extend this model to its west German plants. However, its success in doing so depends on the relative strength of management and works councils at the plant level. Although the councils have institutionally based power, and additional features of the German industrial-relations system, such as training regimes, certainly constrain management (Streeck 1996), outcomes are disparate in west Germany.

Indeed, Roth (1996a: 143) reports a return to Taylorist team work, for example, with integration of the final stages of engine production, and door and body assembly into existing assembly lines, with a corresponding reduction in cycle times from between seven and twenty-one minutes, to sixty seconds. This has been combined with standardized job assignments. Where such changes are occurring, they add greater variation to the forms of team work present even in older plants. Indeed, high-skilled, autonomous team work is usually confined to indirect, capital-intensive production areas. By contrast, in assembly the tendency is to underutilize existing skill sets, with seven out of ten skilled workers working below their skill levels (1996a: 156–58). Indeed, Roth contrasts the emergence of Taylorist team working practices in assembly, including low task integration, standardized jobs, and a lack of team autonomy, to the pilot projects of the late 1980s. At Opel, such practices are prevalent where management has attempted to extend the Eisenach model into older plants, though variation is frequently apparent where management has been frustrated by the strength of the works councils.

### Broader Variations in Team-Work Practices

A further example of the Japanese-oriented approach is VW's Mosel plant in eastern Germany. It is not as extreme as Opel Eisenach, and the works council plays a somewhat stronger role than at Eisenach, though they bear a close resemblance in the organization of work. Furthermore, although VW has introduced complete team working at Mosel, it has not yet pursued team work at their other plants.

In contrast to Opel, Mercedes has made an attempt to develop a joint team-based organization of work (Kuhlmann and Schumann 1997). In February 1995, Mercedes reached a company-wide agreement with its central works council establishing the principles of team work, based largely on IG Metall's *Eckpunkte* principles (Mercedes 1995). At the Rastatt plant, production was modeled on Volvo's Uddevalla plant. Assembly line production was partly retained, though eliminated for about half of work operations, with significant modifications in other areas. Furthermore, stationary work areas had long cycle times of up to two hours, and on the assembly line, fifteen to forty-three minutes (Jürgens 1995: 304).

IG Metall and the works councils at Mercedes have also been successful at limiting what is perceived to be a dangerous trend at other German auto plants, namely, the tendency for continuous improvement programs (KVP) to be top down rather than team led, with a narrow range of topics open for discussion and limited autonomy for the team. This tendency was perceived as leading inexorably to increasing line speeds at other plants. In response to this, the works council at Mercedes in 1995 successfully reached the first company agreement governing the principles of their continuous improvement program, in particular to allow greater team latitude and autonomy, and to restrict increases in line speed. However, KVP strategies are increasingly widespread in Germany and generally do not conform to Mercedes' approach.

At the firm's Bremen plant, production of the high-value-added SL car is an example of substantial team autonomy and job rotation combined with job enlargement, long cycle times (of between forty-five minutes and one hour, twenty minutes), high skill levels, and low levels of supervision. Large areas of production are operated off-line, with the cars being transported overhead to the work team. The level of team autonomy is, however, lower in other areas of the Bremen plant, where a traditional assembly line operates, and typical cycle times are 2.5 minutes. Although in these latter instances no team autonomy controls the flow of production, there is autonomy with respect to job rotation, broad skilling, and aspects of the production process.

This pattern of variation at Mercedes is backed up by research by Gerst et al. (1999). Although they identify a dominance of self-organized employment patterns within Mercedes, they also identify variation in two case studies from assembly line production. The first is characterized by a high degree of self-organization of work, job rotation, and team regulation of line speed (within tight limits). The second was seen to fail to gain ground against existing Taylorist structures of production on the shop floor as well as negligible self-organization of work, restricted job rotation, and low levels of training opportunities and work flexibility. The team leaders fulfilled the role of sub-foremen and were pressured to achieve team performance targets.

Programmatic variation in the nature of team work is similarly illustrated by an agreement negotiated between Mercedes and IG Metall and the works council to secure a new engine plant at Untertürkheim (EIRR 1994a). This agreement necessitated an opt-out for the plant from the metalworking sectoral agreement while introducing new team working structures and new payment systems. Bonuses of approximately 10 percent of basic pay derived from productivity and plant utilization rates, individual performance based on a three-stage assessment, and team-based performance. In a 1995 agreement, BMW likewise negotiated a new team and payment structure outside the piece-rate based sectoral agreement (EIRR 1996b). The new pay system applies to thirty-six thousand production workers and allows bonuses based on individual contribution to team performance to range from DM 98 to DM 294 (57 to 171 dollars) per month. The supervisor plays an important role in determining this bonus. The framework agreement for teamwork does, however, correspond to the joint team-based approach, and BMW continues to support this approach, preferring not to develop a standardized production model.

As Table 5.4 indicates, Ford has shown little interest in team working, instead preferring a technological strategy and Ford's "total productive maintenance" concept. Ford's increasing tendency to centralize functions in a matrix organization and to develop a world model for product development, supply, and manufacturing systems does not include a centralized model for work organization in general, or team work in particular. Work organization decisions are instead left to local autonomy. In Germany Ford is adopting a slow, bottom-up development of team work, with substantial room for local (plant and within-plant) flexibility. This approach has involved isolated experiments with teams, such as among skilled mechanical production workers in the engine plant at Cologne, which involves the integration of indirect tasks and greater autonomy in work organization (Roth 1995: 13).

There have, however, been negligible attempts to introduce team work in assembly operations in Ford Cologne, though there are pilot programs in the assembly area at Ford's Saarlouis plant. Unlike at Opel, for example, job rotation is minimal at Ford, nor is there a qualification plan. The production organization continues to be very traditional, as do cycle times. A reduction in foremen (and increasing the span of control to about sixty) occurred when *Kolonnenführer* were introduced in the late 1980s (Turner 1991). These generally highly skilled workers continue to be involved in normal production work, though they are released from work for 25 percent of their time to train workers and help problem solve, thus carrying out some tasks previously undertaken by foremen. Although they do not conduct the same disciplinary functions as foremen do, they are selected by managers (usually with the approval of the works councils, which at Ford are very strong) and operate in a largely traditional work structure.

There has also been no common team work agenda at VW, and the early team work pilot projects involving off-line production have tended to stagnate. Work practices have been kept decentralized at and within the plants, with no attempt at a centralized system of work organization. Anne Labit notes that team work is an issue of permanent negotiation at VW, and that "by the end of 1995 it was clear that the IG Metall Union had given up the attempt to negotiate an overall agreement to generalize the experiments conducted under the heading of Gruppenarbeit" (1999: 402). This is reflected in variation among plants, and it is at the plant level that agreements with the works council have been signed. An example of variation is the introduction of team work at the paint shop in Hannover but not in Wolfsburg. Where teams have been introduced at VW's Wolfsburg plant, there is a trend toward increased job rotation, though without the kind of job enlargement that has occurred, for example, at Mercedes. Experiments with longer cycle times and broader skill requirements dating from the late 1980s have not been expanded, while by exerting pressure for concessions (for example, concerning the future production location of models such as the Polo), VW management at Wolfsburg has been able to enter an effective effort-bargain with the works council that involves benchmarking exercises, with a resulting increase in line speed. Labit (1999) also notes the presence of competing models of team work in the Hannover plant.

Although VW has made greater use of quality circles, these are not integrated with production; they operate with a moderator who is appointed by management, and are essentially top-down structures. Supplementing the quality circles is VW's "KVP-quadrat concept," which is also a management-driven continuous improvement concept involving moderators rather than team leaders, and is not directly integrated with production.

### Summary of Auto Industry Developments

The German auto industry has thus been characterized both by increasingly prevalent concession bargaining and a shift to new forms of work organization. During the pilot team working projects in the 1980s, IG Metall successfully limited the degree of variation. Turner (1991) attributed this success to the ability of works councils to constrain management and to impose its own vision of team work, which corresponds to a participatory joint team-based approach. In the 1990s, however, growing company and plant variation reflects the difficulties works councils have had in constraining the more forceful corporate strategies in a hostile economic environment combined with plant and company-level concession bargaining.

Thus, even in this industry, where union strength has continued at a relatively high level, significant variation has been produced by joint team-based approaches, which featured strongly in the early pilot projects, and an emerging trend toward a Japanese-oriented system, most notably at Opel Eisenach. However, despite widespread concession bargaining on pay and working hours, there is no evidence of a shift to a human resource management approach or to union avoidance. The legal rights of works councils make union avoidance in particular extremely improbable, and indeed, the role of works councils has been enhanced by work reorganization, as is illustrated by the multitude of plant-level agreements. Nevertheless, it is increasingly difficult for the union to coordinate the spread of team work practices across plants, while the works councils have been forced to balance goals for the humanization of work and the maintenance of sectoral pay rates with the preservation of jobs and investment in a hostile economic environment.

## DEVELOPMENTS IN THE TELECOMMUNICATIONS INDUSTRY

In contrast to the auto industry in Germany, there have been no examples of concession bargaining or plant-level whipsawing in the telecommunications industry. Indeed, the structure of the industry has historically been very different from that of the auto industry, having been dominated by a single firm, Deutsche Telekom. As a result, the distinction between the sectoral union and the works council has had less relevance. Furthermore, the pressures created in other sectors of the German economy, between firms with different performance levels or operational requirements and broad-based sectoral collective bargaining agreements, have also not been an issue in the telecommunications industry. Indeed, only in 1998 did bargaining for rival telecommunications companies begin to emerge. Nevertheless, pressures to restructure employment practices and to introduce greater variation can also be observed within Deutsche Telekom, though in contrast to our other countries, the institutional strength of employee representation systems again serves to constrain the form of that variation.

Until January 1995, Telekom was a public-sector company with monopoly control over both the telephone network and the cable TV network. As such, Telekom was the third-biggest telecommunications company and the largest cable TV company in the world.[28] However, in 1995, Telekom became a private company, continuing along a path of reform that had begun in earnest in 1989. The first steps of reform, termed Post Reform I, had ended the practice whereby Telekom had been operated alongside postal and banking services within the Deutsche Bundespost (Darbishire 1995, 1997). Furthermore, Post Reform I gave greater independence from the Ministry of Posts and Telecommunications, and increased operational and entrepreneurial autonomy. Reform of the telecommunications industry continued in 1995 with the transfer of Telekom to private-sector status (Post Reform II), and was followed in 1996 by privatization with the sale of a first tranche of shares amounting to some 26 percent of the company.[29]

The process of reforming and liberalizing the telecommunications industry in Germany has included progressively opening the market to competition. Thus, in 1989, Post Reform I introduced competition over value-added network services and mobile services, though not over the voice and network monopoly, which has constituted some 90 percent of Telekom's revenue. Nevertheless, competition within the high-value business customer market has been increasing progressively during the 1990s, particularly through the use of private networks. Deregulation was pushed substantially further in August 1996, when Telekom's monopoly of the network infrastructure was ended. Furthermore, from January 1998, a European Union directive has introduced open competition in voice telephone services throughout the European telecommunications market.

Corresponding to the public-sector and monopoly status of Telekom, the company has traditionally been operated in a highly centralized, hierarchical, and functional manner. Historically, this was true in terms of the organizational and management structure, employee representation, collective bargaining, work organization, employment practices, and employment conditions. The introduction of both actual and forthcoming competition, a growing consumer orientation, and digitalization of the network has prompted the reorganization of the industry, which has, in turn, led Telekom to restructure itself. In doing so, growing variation has become evident. Employment practices in particular have become increasingly varied after Telekom's "Focus '98" restructuring, which includes a divisionalization of the company, decentralization of decision-making, rationalization, and work reorganization.

However, as in the auto industry, the extent of variation in employment practices in the telecommunications industry is still evolving and is more constrained than in the weaker institutional climates of the United States and the United Kingdom. Work practices have thus far remained confined within a joint team-based pattern as a result of the substantial strength of both the union and the works council in Telekom. Moreover, and again in contrast to the United States, the United Kingdom, and Australia, the new entrants into the German telecommunications market are also unionized.

### Corporate Restructuring and Decentralization

Historically, Telekom was organized with a three-tier structure, and in a reflection of the traditional bureaucratic and infrastructural emphasis of the company, decentralized managerial autonomy was minimal. Neither branch offices (*Niederlassungen*) nor regions (*Direktionen*) were historically operated as cost or profit centers, and the management style was one of strict hierarchy in a functional organization. Indeed, Telekom has been remarkable for its degree of commonality in operational practices and work structures throughout the company, the sole exception being variation resulting from geographic circumstances. Adherence to central regulations was perhaps surprising given the lack of local performance indicators, though it is commonly estimated within Telekom that centralization heavily influenced decision making in 95 percent of cases in practice, even if allowing greater flexibility in theory (Darbishire 1997).

Because excessive centralization and lack of local autonomy had become regarded within Telekom as one of its principal weaknesses, in 1994 the company initiated a corporate restructuring. Termed *Telekom Kontakt,* the restructuring was designed to separate the company into business, residential, and network divisions, while simultaneously decentralizing management structures and creating local profit and cost centers. Thus, the 123 branch offices are being given increased autonomy and flexibility through a lessening of centrally determined regulations. The objective is to promote a more proactive management style and to facilitate local variation in operational and managerial practices. The creation of divisions within the company is thought to increase the likelihood of this occurring, since the needs and requirements of the divisions are likely to vary notably.

The Deutsche Postgewerkschaft (DPG) union, which represents 90 percent of both managerial and nonmanagerial employees in Telekom, and the works councils have been concerned precisely that a divisional structure would indeed lead to variation in employment practices, which they strongly oppose.[30] As a result, they forced Telekom to pilot an alternative structure, though ultimately unsuccessfully (Darbishire 1997). The DPG and works councils' desire to prevent the probable spread of employment-system variation was increased by privatization, which changed the legal basis of the works councils of Telekom.[31]

Although employee codetermination and information rights for works councils in both the public and private sectors are the same, within the public sector, works councils are organized on a three-tier, hierarchical, and centralized basis, where authority is vested primarily in the central works council. As a result, agreements reached by the central works council apply throughout the organization. In the private sector, however, works councils have a decentralized two-tier structure, where authority rests primarily at the local level (Darbishire 1995). In large manufacturing industries, such as automobiles, the concentrated nature of production sites means that this latter structure has few disadvantages. However, service industries frequently have multiple and dispersed locations, a situation that creates substantial difficulties for works councils in coordinating policies and practices across work sites. In turn, variation in employment practices is greater in the expanding service sector than in traditional manufacturing industry. This risk of increased variation is particularly problematic in the telecommunications industry, which the restructuring of Telekom compounds by requiring coordination across divisions with different work requirements.

As we find in other countries and industries, employment system decentralization and variation in the German telecommunications industry are promoted by management and opposed by unions. The DPG and works councils in Telekom, like their counterparts in other countries, have sought to avoid any risk of employment system variation and thus have taken steps to mitigate such risks. Their particularly strong institutional and political position, especially during the debates about privatization, helped them negotiate an effective extension of the old works council structure (initially until mid-1997), and to use the DPG shop-steward structure to build new coordinating mechanisms among works councils. Just as important, however, the DPG and works councils have also sought to limit variation by maintaining strong, centralized control. Relevant measures include minimizing the use of works council agreements that could have important implications for employment practice. In contrast to the difficulties faced in other countries, the case of Telekom thus illustrates how powerful and strongly institutionalized systems of employee representation can restrict variation and retain centralized bargaining structures.

### Representation and Bargaining Structures

Changes in German works council structure and activities have made for greater diversity in employment practices, particularly where, as is true of some telecommunications companies, such as British Telecom, employment policies are increasingly determined on a divisional basis. Furthermore, as Thelen (1991) has argued, there has been a general rebalancing of decision making within German employee representation structures, away from unions and toward works councils to facilitate flexibility and adjustment. Within Telekom, however, the DPG has used its strength and authority, as well as its atypical structure, to prevent such decentralization.

The DPG is very unusual within Germany in that it has essentially been a single-company union, representing workers within the Bundespost. The break-up of the Bundespost into its constituent parts has not, however, prevented the DPG from being able to focus unusually strongly on Telekom. In turn, it has been able to restrict the decentralization of decision making to the works councils, and instead retain more extensive use of collective-bargaining agreements. For the union, these agreements have the advantage of being legally stronger, centralized, and applicable throughout the company. There have thus been few agreements reached with the central or local works councils within Telekom. The only two prominent examples are agreements concerning the DELKOS decentralized cost control system, and the DASPO personnel data and management system. In contrast to most other German companies, agreements to restrict redundancies at Telekom, for instance, have been reached with the union rather than the central works council. In addition, the DPG has limited variation within Telekom by conducting very detailed and centralized negotiations governing the restructuring of working practices.

The structure of bargaining between Telekom and the DPG also has been distinguished by the fact that 52 percent of employees are currently *Beamte* (civil servants) and thus have no bargaining rights. The DPG has, however, bargained for other workers together with ÖTV, and attempted to extend these conditions to *Beamte* (Darbishire 1995).[32] The privatization of Telekom and the deregulation of the telecommunications market are nevertheless increasing employment system variation, for at least four reasons. First, the complete separation of the three Bundespost companies has ended the practice whereby they formed a single bargaining unit. Given differences in the degree of, for example, capital intensity and in the growth rates of the postal and telecommunications industries, growing variation in bargaining outcomes is likely. Relatedly, the practice whereby the Bundespost companies bargained alongside ÖTV and the public sector is ending. The principal constraint on this variation is that *Beamte* continue to have their pay set by the government, rather than through collective bargaining.

Second, Telekom is more frequently resorting to performance-related pay schemes. These schemes were first introduced in 1990 after Post Reform I for *Beamte* and were extended to all workers in the 1992 bargaining round. Performance-related pay for civil servants was initially a unique provision to Telekom and the Bundespost, specifically designed to promote pay flexibility and variability.[33] Payment is in addition to the existing salary, is individually based, and can amount to as much as 15 percent of the basic wage.[34] The payments are, however, restricted to 25 percent of employees in any department, a design intended to ensure that the payments are used competitively and that there is differentiation among workers. Experimentation with new forms of performance-related pay schemes has, however, taken place in the DeTeMobil, DeTeCSM, and DeTeSystem subsidiaries. A collective agreement signed between the DPG and DeTeMobil in 1997, for example, included a performance-related pay system for all employees, determined on the basis of individual appraisals and structured on management-by-objectives principles. Telekom hoped to negotiate to extend such a model to all core employees, as it has for senior management.

The third mechanism of generating additional employment practice variation has been through subsidiary companies. Telekom has not, however, sought to create subsidiaries to reduce labor costs through, for example, a low-wage employment pattern. Rather, its motivation has been to introduce greater flexibility and variation by using subsidiaries to circumvent tight *Beamte* employment regulations, which include training, the structure of career progression, functional and geographic mobility, and pay. Telekom has achieved this by encouraging *Beamte* to transfer to subsidiaries, while thereby suspending their status as civil servants, thus allowing it to alter employment conditions.[35]

An average of 75 percent of staff in subsidiaries have been voluntarily transferred from the core of Telekom. These subsidiaries include DeTe-Mobil, DeTeSystem, DeTeMedian, DeTeLine, and DeTeImmobilien. Excluding Global One, the joint venture with France Télécom and Sprint, total employment in these companies exceeded 18,500 in 1997. To maximize the potential for flexibility and variation within the subsidiaries, and following IBM's decision to change union recognition from IG Metall to the DAG, Telekom considered introducing different union representation in its subsidiaries. However, during Post Reform II, the debate concerning the privatization of Telekom, the DPG was successful in establishing the requirement that Telekom is *bound* to negotiate with it not only in the core company but also in any subsidiaries that are formed. The power and rights of the DPG are thus significant in having restricted the ability of Telekom to vary employment practices either through creating nonunion (or more weakly unionized) subsidiaries.[36]

Nevertheless, variation in employment conditions is emerging in these subsidiaries. But the voluntary transfer of *Beamte* to subsidiaries means that flexibility is limited, and employment conditions have to be perceived to be at least as good as those in the core of Telekom. Nevertheless, the subsidiaries have greater flexibility over both the level and form of wages, particularly performance-related pay for managers; they have the ability to use individual contracts; and they are not constrained by *Beamte* regulations governing career ladders.

The DPG reports that the level of unionization in Telekom's subsidiaries is lower than within the core of the company, and although the subsidiaries respect the duty to bargain with the DPG, they have also relied more heavily on agreements with their works councils. In doing so, they have introduced and experimented with new work rules, even though modified work rules are being constrained to follow either a human resource management or joint team-based approach. Furthermore, although a framework agreement with the DPG establishes common pay groupings for all subsidiaries, each subsidiary has separate contracts and pay levels. Thus, Telekom's goal of increasing flexibility in employment practices has been achieved to a degree, though within bounds established by the institutional strength of the DPG and works councils in particular.

In contrast to the telecommunications industry in other countries, no nonunion competitors have yet been established in Germany. Nevertheless, a fourth source of variation has arisen from different forms of unionization among newly forming rival companies. Although the DPG represents all Telekom employees, it is unusual in not being a sectoral union. However, emerging rivals in the telecommunications market have been based on the private networks of utility companies that have aligned themselves with existing (international) telecommunications companies. The principal companies include Otelo Communications (a joint venture among Veba, RWE and BellSouth); Arcor (Mannesmann and Deutsche Bahn); and Viag Intercom (Viag, Telnor, and BT). As with the leading mobile telephone company, Mannesmann, workers in these companies are represented by a range of different unions, among them ÖTV, IG BCE, IG Metall and GdED, the railworkers union. Thus, although new workers in the telecommunications industry continue to be unionized, in contrast to other German industries growing variation in employment conditions is resulting from the application of different (nonsectoral specific) collective bargaining agreements. In June 1998, Otelo reached a first collective agreement with ÖTV and IG BCE for three thousand employees. This differs from the DPG contract and includes a performance-related pay scheme for all employees. The contract also included an opening clause on the level of the annual performance bonus. Similarly, in November 1998, Arcor signed a collective agreement with GdED for three quarters of its 6,500 employees. This contract also differs from the one at Telekom and Otelo.

*Work Organization and Employment*

An important motivation behind Telekom's desire for privatization was to increase its flexibility and diversity in human resource policies, bargaining, and employment adjustment from those in the public sector. Previously, work organization and employment structures had been centrally determined and heavily regulated. Although limitations and restrictions on employment policies that resulted from being a public-sector company applied most directly to *Beamte,* frequently rules were extended to other employees.

Of particular importance were policies governing the structure of career ladders, training, and payment systems. In the civil service, career ladders are separated into four *Laufbahn* (paths), with ports of entry and progression determined by formal training, skills, and qualifications. Progress from one ladder to another is generally severely restricted. Post Reform I did ease some of these regulations, for example, by removing rigid rules governing the ratio of employees in any given hierarchical classification, thereby allowing greater flexibility in the grading and promotion of *Beamte*. Nevertheless, Telekom continued to believe that it was hampered by public sector regulations and thus favored privatization to allow more flexibility in its personnel policies.[37]

The organization of work in Telekom itself traditionally has been and is still centrally determined and regulated, but nonetheless structured on a joint team-based approach. The design of work organization has been reflected in high levels of training, relatively skilled jobs, employee autonomy, and limited supervision. Thus, for example, training for most workers has included apprenticeships for technicians, lasting three to three and a half years of mixed general and specific skills. Even for operators, training has amounted to approximately three months, in contrast to the one to two weeks typical in the United Kingdom and the United States. The emphasis on skills has been similarly extended to additional training, averaging approximately three to four days each year per employee. Although the structure of training is being reformed to meet new technological and customer-service demands, the level of training has not been noticeably reduced.

At the workplace, the emphasis on skills has been accompanied by high worker autonomy and low levels of supervision. Thus, although regulations governing employment and work practices have been extensive, they have in fact not governed the specific procedures required to complete tasks. Indeed, the detailed rules governing work flows and tasks have not greatly affected worker autonomy.[38] In addition, there has been no separation of execution and control in most tasks, and this responsible autonomy approach has been reinforced by an absence of close supervision or control, the minimal use of any decentralized performance measurements, and no forced pacing of work. Instead, field technicians have tended to operate independently, supervised by a team leader (*Gruppe Leiter Servicemonteur*), who services the administrative needs of workers, spending 80 percent of time in an office, with the remaining time focused on support rather than discipline, on quality rather than productivity.

Telekom's history as a public-sector monopoly certainly influenced this strategy of responsible autonomy. Nevertheless, neither growing competitive pressure, performance-related pay systems, nor the introduction of technology increasingly able to monitor and record the productivity of remote-working employees has affected this approach, for at least two reasons. First, the *Beamte* status of half the workforce limits the extent to which performance criteria can be effectively applied, given their particularly strong rights and employment security. Second, the works councils have been able to use their rights to codetermination concerning the introduction of technology capable of monitoring workers' behavior. Thus, works council–company agreements have been reached governing such programs as DELKOS and DASPO to limit the potential use of these systems' data to intensify work practices.

More broadly, workplace data protection laws in Germany generally prohibit the use of electronic data to monitor individual performance, even insofar as the laws allow the use of such data to monitor groups. These constraints have an effect in much of the telecommunications industry where, in contrast to the manufacturing industry, both direct supervision and machine pacing are hard to achieve. These two constraints, together with a workforce whose skills continue to be high, has thus far led Telekom to maintain its high-trust, responsible autonomy approach that is characteristic of a joint team-based employment pattern.

Corporate reorganization, competitive pressures, and technological change are nevertheless spurring changes in work organization, as in other telecommunications companies. Among field technicians, for example, divisionalization has narrowed the range of technicians' tasks to tasks within their own division rather than spanning both residential and some business customers. Overall, however, there has been no deskilling. In 1994, for example, Telekom created a broader employment category, merging tasks previously completed by specialists in provision or repair. The objectives were to increase the flexibility of deployment of labor, to respond to the DPG's desire to broaden tasks completed by these technicians, and to upgrade the (previously less skilled) repair technicians. The work organization of customer service representatives is also changing, though with similar consequences. Traditionally, customer service representatives have been organized in a highly functional manner, with a strongly local orientation.[39]

The work reorganization program within Telekom includes the rationalization and concentration of local offices, and the re-evaluation of the appropriate division of work. The DPG and works councils have, however, successfully pushed to avoid the degree of concentration in operations evident in, for example, the United States and the United Kingdom, and the conception of work remains broad. In particular, Telekom is introducing a system of multiskilled customer service representatives by creating broad sales and service functions that include integrated reception, diagnostic, and control operations. Consequently, there is at least the potential for some broadening of tasks internally.

Work reorganization has not, therefore, caused significant deviation from an employment pattern based on relatively high technical competence of employees, without work intensification or an erosion of worker autonomy beyond that generated through performance-related pay systems. This joint team-based approach is certainly related to the fact that half the employees are *Beamte,* with their permanent status and employment security. Furthermore, *Beamte* rights generally extend to training structures and the skill and complexity requirements of the job; they can be transferred, only to a job of equal status. In addition to this constraint on work organization, Telekom's approach has also been influenced by the strength and involvement of the DPG and the central works council.

Both have been strongly involved in all aspects of work reorganization. Indeed, corporate programs such as Telekom Kontakt and Focus '98 have been negotiated in extensive detail on a centralized basis. The degree of this consultation is related to concerns of worker representatives about the effects of the extensive reorganization on employment practices and employment levels. Much of the detail of specific reorganizations lies outside the codetermination rights of the works council. Nevertheless, the extensive nature of the reorganization allows the council to use its rights concerning, for example, downsizing, relocation of employees, and regrading of employees following the introduction of new technology to negotiate broad programs of restructuring. In other words, council rights and power do not necessarily decline as a consequence of substantial rationalization but can become more effective precisely because of the fundamental nature of work reorganization. Thus, the DPG and the central works council have been able to pursue their goal of ensuring that the reorganization does not have detrimental consequences for the workforce.

The continued power and influence of the DPG and the central works council have had three particular consequences. First, the detailed and centralized negotiation of restructuring programs has meant that change has been slow and that there has been relatively little decentralized experimentation with new forms of work organization. This is well illustrated by the Telekom Service 2000 reorganization of the workforce. Centralized negotiations have produced more than nine hundred pages of regulations that have restricted variation in employment patterns. Second, Telekom has had to eschew cost minimization in favor of revenue enhancement. Third, and related, the DPG has limited downsizing as a requirement for its cooperation with general work reorganization. This strategy has also been significantly influenced by the contractual employment security of much of the workforce, which applies not only to *Beamte,* but also to other workers aged 40 or over with fifteen years of service. Yet, even though technological change is reducing employment, Telekom has had remarkable employment security. Between 1984 and 1994, total employment increased from 191,911 to 225,435. After correcting for eastern Germany, this increase represented little change.

Despite this stability and Telekom's goal of reducing employment, the need for cooperation with the DPG concerning work reorganization led to an agreement in 1994 prohibiting involuntary redundancies for four years during the Focus '98 program, even though rationalizations were directly eliminating eleven thousand jobs. This agreement was subsequently extended throughout the company until the end of the year 2000, as a commitment that even where new digital technology displaced jobs, workers would be found alternative employment.

One of Telekom's principal goals is, however, to reduce employment by 60,000, from 230,000 to 170,000 by the year 2000. Apart from natural attrition, Telekom has sought to introduce expensive voluntary redundancy schemes (costing DM 80–100,000 per person), early retirement, and one-time payments to young *Beamte* to change careers. As a result, employment had been reduced to 191,000 by the end of 1997. Yet, the pattern of employment reduction remains consistent with a joint team-based approach, and Telekom's strategy has been to actively search for new employment opportunities through new business ventures (Darbishire 1997).

The constraints on downsizing have also limited Telekom's ability to adopt a low-wage employment pattern through the use of subcontractors. In response to the employment reduction program and the general employment security of staff, Telekom has been forced to reduce its reliance on subcontractors; as a public-sector company Telekom used subcontractors for 25 percent of its work, principally lower-skilled construction. At the same time, Telekom has increased fixed-term contracts. Thus, although five hundred apprentices were offered full-time employment in 1996, one thousand received only fixed-term contracts.

### Summary of Developments in the Telecommunications Industry

Events at Telekom demonstrate both the pressures for increasing variation and also the constraints from strong institutions, employee representatives, and the special employment status and rights held by half the workforce. Indeed, the DPG has long been one of the strongest unions in Germany, and privatization has not yet substantially eroded the union's strength. Indeed, during the privatization, the DPG was able to secure its right to bargain for workers in all subsidiaries, while employee representatives are also in a uniquely strong position in having equal representation on the supervisory board. These factors have undoubtedly constrained Telekom to a joint team-based employment pattern. Furthermore, worker representatives have limited the variability in work organization by retaining a heavily negotiated and strongly centralized model of change, even though Telekom itself has been striving for greater decentralization.

Nevertheless, employment system variation is emerging. Bargaining is becoming more fragmented as the use of subsidiaries and separate contracts expands. Employment conditions within these subsidiaries remain high, though they are being used to experiment with new working practices, payment systems, and even individual contracts. The subsidiaries also allow circumvention of *Beamte* employment regulations. Yet even within the core of Telekom, the new payment systems are creating variability in employment conditions. Furthermore, the shift of the works council structure to the decentralized private-sector style, together with the divisionalization of the company, are also generating pressure for variation. Beyond this, telecommunications rivals are emerging, and although they are unionized, representation is with unions other than the DPG. Within Telekom, the DPG and the central works council have thus far restricted the variability by using their strength to limit decentralization and local experimentation. The pressures for rapid change are, however, setting limits on the union's ability to continue this practice.

## INEQUALITY OF INCOME IN GERMANY

An important impact of German institutions has been to limit variation in employment practices, for example, through structures of employee representation, levels of training, and the form of work organization. Beyond this, a central feature of the German model has been high wages combined with comparatively little income inequality. As with other outcomes in the labor market, this has resulted from institutional structures within the German economy, including the comprehensive coverage of collective bargaining and the system of pattern bargaining. As discussed earlier, the extensive coverage of collective bargaining is not constrained by the moderate unionization rate and has indeed typically included even very lightly unionized sectors. Consequently, comprehensive industry agreements, though based regionally, extend nationally and also to interindustry pattern setting.

Inter-sectoral wage dispersion in Germany has thus been lower as compared to the United Kingdom, Japan, and the United States, as has the variation among the earnings of workers in small and large enterprises (Streeck 1997). Indeed, the average earnings of workers in small firms has amounted to 90 percent of those in large enterprises. The institutions of industrial relations have constrained the degree of income inequality in Germany, as well as for other labor market outcomes.

Evidence from the auto and telecommunications industries, as well as general trends in Germany, indicate increasing pressures toward variation in employment practices. The trends we have identified include decentralization, concession bargaining, opening clauses, the development of new forms of work organization, and the introduction of such compensation systems as performance- and profit-related pay. These pressures have also been re-flected in debates within the employers' associations; in vocal arguments among firms of different sizes; and in demands for collective bargaining to set only genuinely minimum conditions, to become more decentralized, and to allow greater responsiveness to the circumstances of a particular company.

These trends became obvious in the second half of the 1980s and become particularly so during the 1990s. Correspondingly, the broad institutions of industrial relations remained remarkably intact during the 1980s, with little challenge to the system of collective bargaining, even though there was some decentralization of qualitative issues, including work organization and working hours flexibility. Consistent with this, and the stability of unions through the 1980s, income inequality did not increase during that period.

Abraham and Houseman (1995) find a slight *narrowing* of the overall dispersion of earnings during the 1980s, primarily from a marginal compression of earnings differentials among workers at the bottom of the distribution. They also report no general widening of differentials across education groups or, indeed, widening of the experience- or age-related differentials evident in both the United States and the United Kingdom. Abraham and Houseman's analysis suggests that the relative stability of earnings differentials in Germany is partly due to the rapid growth in a more educated workforce, though they find it harder to explain why supply and demand shifts have not increased the experience wage profile. However, the variation may be less apparent because highly skilled apprentices were substituted for more experienced workers in that decade.

Abraham and Houseman's data indicate that the collective bargaining system prevented wages for less skilled workers from falling, while "institutional factors played an important role in mitigating pressures for greater wage inequality" (1995: 402). That is, the centralized and highly coordinated pay-setting structures extending across regions and industries remained intact throughout the 1980s. This may be the reason for inhibited growth in between-group and within-group earnings. No nonunion pay setting system or institutional transformation evolved that led to greater income inequality.

This pattern of stability in the German income distribution during the 1980s is consistent with our findings. Our evidence suggests, however, that variation in labor market institutions and outcomes has become more prevalent during the 1990s, even if institutions have been more resilient than in other countries. There are indications of similar outcomes for the income distribution. For example, Burniaux et al. (1998) and Dustmann and Van Soest (1997) find little trend toward increased income inequality during most of the 1980s, though some greater dispersion from the late

1980s through the first half of the 1990s. The modest rise in income inequality in Germany may be related to changes "at the extremes of the distribution with progressively smaller movements around the median.... [H]igher-income groups have gained and lower-income groups fell behind" (Burniaux et al. 1998: 12).

This observation is consistent with the findings of Schäfer (1997), who observes that income inequality in Germany has been fostered by atypical employment contracts. In the mid-1970s, 85 percent of employment contracts were full time; by the mid-1990s, this figure had fallen to 67 percent, with 33 percent being "atypical." Furthermore, the proportion of full-time male employees who earn below 68 percent of median wages rose from 31.2 percent in 1980 to 38.6 percent in 1990. Evidence also points to a greater sectoral dispersion of wage increases during the 1990s as sectoral unions have responded in different ways to economic pressure. Between 1990 and 1994 Wirtschafts- und Sozialwissenschaftliches Institut (WSI) data indicate a distribution of compensation increases ranging from 27.9 percent in construction to 16.3 percent in energy, water, and mining, with an economy-wide average of 23.3 percent (WSI 1995). In addition, the evidence clearly indicates a general redistribution of income in national accounts from labor to capital, with profits rising substantially faster than wages, a trend that continued into 1998.

The indications of growing income inequality in German during the 1990s are moderate by the standards of the United States, the United Kingdom, or Sweden. However, recent increases in income inequality in Germany do seem to be related to the pressure that institutions of collective bargaining have been under. Within sectors, this may have been compensated by the general tendency for higher-paying firms to reduce the payments they make in excess of the collectively bargained rates (the so-called *Übertariflohn*), thus tending to increase the degree of wage compression among firms of different size.

Ultimately, the flight from the employers' associations and the resultant modifications of the collective bargaining system are likely to be more significant. Any contraction of collective bargaining coverage would clearly exacerbate income inequality. However, thus far, the centralized system of collective bargaining has remained intact in west Germany, even though the risk of collapse is greater in eastern Germany.

## SUMMARY

The analysis of German institutions of industrial relations in this chapter reveals these institutions' strength and stability. The system of industry-wide bargaining remains overwhelmingly dominant; coverage of collective agreements continues to be ubiquitous; strong, centralized unions have retained their importance; and the juridified system of employee representation at the plant level through works councils remains intact. Furthermore, the councils continue, for the most part, to be well integrated into union structures.

Such stability should not disguise the changes that have taken place, and there has been a weakening of these institutions during the 1990s in particular. These changes include declining union membership, a rebalancing of roles between union and works councils, and some reduction in the centrality of sectoral collective bargaining. In comparative terms, the stability is as noteworthy as these changes and the growing variation apparent in Germany.

Historically, unions in Germany have had a very clear policy of establishing common employment practices throughout industries and, indeed, the whole economy, and in strongly resisting any variation or diversity. This policy has, for example, been reflected in a strong preference for centralized bargaining and for minimal decentralization of bargaining competence to works councils, whether through opening clauses or other means.

Simultaneously, German unions have cooperated closely with works councils. The aim has been to utilize the strong information, consultation, and codetermination rights of the councils to further their joint objectives of establishing and extending a joint-participative approach to employment relations. In this, they have been very successful. While the centralized strength of unions and the rights of works councils have undoubtedly been instrumental in this outcome, unions and councils have been assisted by other labor-market institutions, for example, the jointly regulated apprenticeship training programs and the high level of skills these have generated. Especially in comparative terms, the outcome has historically been to produce very homogenous employment practices throughout the economy, based on cooperation and joint regulation.

During most of the 1980s, unions and works councils were able to resist most pressure for looser regulation, though decentralization did occur on, for instance, working time and qualitative issues of work organization. Even with new work practices, however, unions retained a strong centralized influence by establishing framework practices and coordinating and supporting the actions of works councils. During the 1990s, by contrast, the realignment of employment relations has been more extensive. In particular, there has been greater acceptance of more flexible bargaining institutions, substantially greater decentralization through the use of framework agreements and opening clauses, and more variable outcomes. The terms of the debate in Germany concern whether all this amounts to an erosion or adaptation of the collective bargaining system, without the patterns of diversity being in question.

This decentralization has coincided with unification. Variation is more extensive in the east than in the west and this is observable in the range of models of employment relations, as well as in the relatively weaker institutions of industrial relations. The more varied outcomes in the east do not necessarily imply the demise of the German model of industrial relations, though they do illustrate in a starker form the pressure for a retreat from the uniform outcomes traditionally generated by the industrial relations system.

As in other countries, therefore, firms are demanding greater variation, and forcing modifications in the collective-bargaining system. The causes include "voice" pressure in bargaining and the exit of firms from employers' associations. The greater flexibility in outcomes is exemplified by the 1997 agreement in the chemical sector to establish a compensation corridor, the growing decentralization of bargaining, weakening interindustry pattern bargaining, and the emerging use of profit- and performance-related pay.

Although Thelen (1991) has argued that decentralization of competencies to plants does not necessarily weaken trade unions at the expense of works councils, unions have attempted to avoid just such a move because they felt it would breach their policy of uniform employment practices and would reduce their power. Unions, exemplified by IG Metall, have therefore tried to restrict the degree of flexibility by encasing it within collective bargaining agreements. Their success in achieving this has, however, lessened during the 1990s in particular.

Most unions have increasingly come to accept a more diverse range of employment practices and decentralization that includes increased employee participation at the plant level. Even the highly centralized IG Metall has accepted the need for sufficient decentralization (and implicitly variation) to ensure the preservation of industry-wide bargaining and to introduce greater (but controlled) flexibility to meet the needs of firms.

The importance of the rights of works councils and their links with unions has been a strong constraint on variation in this more decentralized environment. In particular, there has been no real evidence of either nonunion or human resource management-based employment patterns. The variation includes some Japanese-oriented practices, though firms are constrained mostly to joint team-based models. There is, however, programmatic variation among workplaces in the details of the joint team-based approach.

At least three factors help explain the role institutions have played in limiting variation in Germany. First, strong, centralized unions have prevented any substantial weakening of encompassing industry-wide collective-bargaining agreements. Pressure from firms, including flight from employers' associations, has forced looser regulations and more decentralization. Nevertheless, framework agreements negotiated at a centralized level remain intact and constrain the choice of employment patterns at the firm level. As such, centralized contracts substantially limit management's potential to exert strong economic pressure on works councils to force the adoption of syndicalist practices. The importance of the unions' role is illustrated in the near-impossible task firms have found it to avoid union contracts, even if there is some trend toward company-level rather than industry-based collective agreements.

Second, works council rights are not dependent on economic power. Even though the councils have been forced to make concessions regarding both pay and work organization, they have been largely able to resist employment practices that are substantially at odds with the joint team-based approach. As significantly, the unavoidable rights of works councils entitle employee representatives to a strong voice characterized by this pattern, which cannot easily be bypassed. Still, variation within Germany is also limited precisely because of the ubiquitous nature of the councils' rights. They depend neither on the level of unionization, employee militancy, the attitude of the employer, nor any transient shifts in the balance of power. At least in large firms, there is comparatively little variation in the procedures and voice of employee representatives. Regarding the potential weakening of the councils in the future, it is important to note that despite the existence of legal rights, the majority of workplaces have no works council.

Moreover, the works councils do experience economic pressure, as the practice of concession bargaining makes abundantly clear. The trend for large companies to undertake organizational reforms and to create smaller company units also pressures works councils (Silvia, 1993). In particular, the trend makes it less likely that works councillors will have the legal right to be released from active work, while also separating works councillors from managers who take strategic decisions. Furthermore, it reduces the role of worker representatives on corporate supervisory boards, since the creation of small and formally independent companies typically involves fewer seats on the board, as well as more restricted rights. In this way, corporate reorganizations in Germany present a very similar challenge to workers' representatives as in other countries. Yet the legal base of those rights gives works councils greater protection.

The combination of strong centralized and decentralized components is key to the ability of German institutions to constrain variation. The third critical element of the German model is the interaction between these two elements and unions' ability to coordinate among the decentralized units. Even where decentralization has been more substantial, the ability of centralized unions to coordinate between works councils and firms is important in sustaining the joint-team based approach. This coordination role becomes harder, but more significant, in an environment where decentralized implementation of work reorganization is dominant.

The importance of all three elements of the industrial relations institutions is demonstrated by the more extensive variation evident in east Germany. In spite of (or possibly even in part because of) the attempt to transfer west German institutions wholesale to the east, unions have been less successful in becoming institutionalized, and the membership of employers' associations is considerably lower. For their part, works council rights are identical, even if the councils face a dramatically more hostile economic landscape. Nevertheless, diversity in employment practices is greater because works councils are less well integrated into union structures and, indeed, often vehemently protect their independent status. The consequence has been that even where framework collective-bargaining accords exist (and they are by no means ubiquitous in the east), they are less likely to be enforced consistently. This, in turn, has led to greater variation, even beyond the joint team-based and Japanese-oriented approaches. Perhaps the most frightening prospect for unions in west Germany is the real possibility that the more extensive variation in employment systems appearing in the east will spread, through one mechanism or another, through west Germany as well.

NOTES

1.   In October 1997, a series of union mergers reduced the number of unions from fifteen to eleven. The mining, leather, and chemical workers' unions merged to form IG Bergbau, Chemie, Energie (IG BCE), while the textile and clothing union joined IG Metall. In this chapter, we refer to these unions in their previously independent structures.

2.   An important characteristic of the "negotiated adjustment" model of German industrial relations is that change does occur, though it is subject to extensive debate in advance. It is thus a mistake to view stability during a period of debate as a sign of a lack of change, since the direction of change becomes apparent before conclusions as to what formal amendments to the system are to be made. Currently, an outcome of greater flexibility and variation is certainly identifiable as the parties dispute which of a range of models will apply in the future, even if it is not clear to what extent the overall system of sectoral collective bargaining is at stake.

3.   The pattern of declining union membership and density hold when alternative measures and definitions are used. Streeck (1997) quotes figures from 1980 to 1990 of union density for employed members only, which show a sharper fall than that

presented in Table 5.1, though also a slightly different timing for the 1980s. According to Streeck's data, density was stable at 37 percent between 1980 and 1985 and then declined sharply to 32.9 percent by 1990.

4. The traditional pattern-setting areas in the leading metalworking sector have been north Baden/Württemberg, or Lower Saxony. However, shifting strike tactics and the desire to limit possible lockouts by employers in other regions affected by the strike meant that in 1995 IG Metall instead shifted to Bavaria as its pattern-setting region. IG Metall sought to minimize the detrimental impact of legal changes that were made in 1986 to Paragraph 116 of the Labor Promotion Law (*Arbeitsförderungsgesetz*) preventing the granting of federal compensation from the *Bundesanstalt für Arbeit* for workers locked-out.

5. Allgemeinverbindlichkeitserklärung (AVE).

6. These agreements extend beyond pay issues to include broader terms and conditions of employment. Such agreements have a significantly longer duration than pay agreements.

7. Reform proposals have come, in particular, from such groups as the ASU (Arbeitsgemeinschaft Selbstsändiger Unternehmer) and the VMU (Vereinigung Mittelstänischer Unternehmer).

8. After an agreement has been reached between the works council and firm, the bargaining partners retain a right of veto. Furthermore, the agreement states that wages should only be reduced for a limited time period, and although this is not specified, IG Chemie has indicated twelve months.

9. As discussed below, IG Metall retained strong, centralized control over the use of its hardship clause in east Germany and is qualitatively different from IG Chemie's opening clause.

10. The IG Metall proposal, *Bündnis für Arbeit,* aimed to secure low wage increases for guaranteed employment security and even employment expansion. IG Metall offered to allow starting wages below the collectively agreed minimum for limited periods (previously a taboo issue in IG Metall, in spite of its introduction in the chemical sector), working-time flexibility instead of overtime payments, and real wage stagnation in return for employment stability. However, Gesamtmetall ultimately rejected the proposals as providing insufficient cost savings and as not creating enough company-level pay flexibility.

11. In 1993 IG Metall forced DEC to concede a recognition agreement. In 1997 they reached a company-level agreement that included the application of the sectoral wage rates, though abolishing the distinction between blue- and white-collar employees and allowing performance-related pay for certain employees.

12. The IBM case is drawn from details contained within Roßmann (1994); "IBM-Flucht aus dem Arbeitgeberverband: Beispeil auch für andere Firmen?," *Handelsblatt,* July 2, 1992; EIRR 1993a, 1995a, 1995d.

13. An additional noteworthy element in IG Metall's agreement with Debis was that it took the form of a supplementary collective agreement (*Ergänzungstarifvertrag*) to the existing metalworking sectoral agreement (Schulten 1998). Formally, this agreement was made between the union and the employers' association; it is not a company-level agreement. This condition further raises the possibility of a weakening of the homogeneity (and sanctity) of sectoral agreements.

14. *Beschäftigungsförderungsgesetz.*

15.  Kotthoff found that works councils' interest representation was poor and insufficient in two thirds of plants in the mid-1970s, though the figure had fallen to one third by the late 1980s (Kotthoff, 1981, 1994, cited in Müller-Jentsch and Sperling 1995).

16.  Dieter Schulte, head of the DGB union federation, cited in Peter Norman, "Sweet and Sour Experience," *Financial Times,* October 3, 1995, p. 19.

17.  Formally, these overtariff wages are voluntary payments made by management. As such, they are not contractually guaranteed and can also be withdrawn. In practice, however, they are the subject of negotiation between companies and works councils (Streeck 1984), and this has also been reflected in the concession bargaining of the early 1990s.

18.  In the 1998 works council elections, 88 percent of elected works councillors in the auto industry were members of IG Metall. At Opel and VW, membership was close to 92 percent, while although it was lower at Ford (87 percent) and Mercedes-Benz (84 percent), IG Metall still clearly dominated there, too. A broadly similar picture can be observed in all works councils. Furthermore, there is a tendency for nonunion members of works councils to join the union during their term of office.

19.  Current planned production outside Germany by Mercedes includes its new plant in Alabama, where production began in 1997, and its so-called Swatch Car joint venture, where production will be in France. Similarly, VW has production facilities in the Czech Republic through its purchase of Skoda, and in Spain through SEAT. Likewise, BMW has opened a plant in Spartanburg, South Carolina, in addition to its purchase of Rover in the U.K.

20.  Specifically, only two thirds of any sectorally agreed wage increase above 2 percent would be paid. The existing overtariff payment would be reduced to pay for the remaining one third (Opel, 1993). The Christmas bonus is a significant payment in Germany, typically amounting to one month's pay.

21.  This agreement was the first occasion in which IG Metall accepted wage cuts to accompany reductions in working time, something it had long and vociferously argued against.

22.  Bonuses were not proportionately effected by this agreement. After they have been taken into account, the net reduction in pay for workers is closer to 10–15 percent. Although the VW model is frequently described as a four-day week, there are in practice a wide variety of working-time models being used in VW.

23.  The renewed production of shock absorbers for the new Golf and the dismantling of old plant were early examples of increasing in-house production.

24.  The twelve principles of team work were developed primarily by Manfred Muster of IG Metall and the works council at VW. Although subsequently reduced to 10 points by the IG Metall Vorstand, they remain the basis of IG Metall's team-working strategy (IG Metall, 1992).

25.  This figure excludes workers in Audi, where teams had been established, but the teams were not fully operational. If Audi production workers are included, 22.2 percent work in teams.

26.  Kuhlmann and Schumann (1997) and Gerst et al. (1999) use the terms *structurally innovative* and *structurally conservative* as the polar approaches revealed by their research. Their detailed descriptions of these characterizations do, however, correspond very closely to our joint team-based and Japanese-oriented patterns, respectively.

27.  Generally, there have been no significant changes in payment systems, since these negotiations are part of the sectoral collective-bargaining agreement. Ongoing

negotiations to revamp the pay system are taking place within IG Metall's Tarif-reform 2000 negotiations.

28. In 1997, Telekom had revenues of DM 67.5 billion (38.6 billion dollars), some 44 million telephone connections, and 17 million households connected to cable TV.

29. This raised DM 20.1 billion (11.5 billion dollars). In contrast to the privatization of British Telecom, this revenue was available to Telekom, though principally to reduce its high level of indebtedness. Even after these revenues had been accounted for, debt amounted to DM 82 billion (47 billion dollars) at the end of 1996.

30. The DPG exercises considerable control over the works council, since 92 percent of works councillors are members of the union, and the two bodies have long, close, and very well established structural links.

31. Specifically, this resulted from a change in the applicable law from the *Bundespersonalvertretungsgesetz* (Federal Staff Representation Act) to the *Betriebsverfassungsgesetz* (Works Constitution Act).

32. The employment conditions and pay of *Beamte* are established by the *Bundesbosoldungsgesetz*, or Federal Remuneration Act. Pay increases are, however, influenced by those reached in the rest of the public sector, though without there being an automatic link between the two. Furthermore, *Beamte* themselves are prohibited from taking industrial action but retain their status for life and enjoy employment security.

33. In January 1997 the German government passed the Reform Law on the Civil Service (*Gesetz zur Reform des öffentlichen Dienstrechts*). A specific goal of this act was to redesign the remuneration system and introduce performance-related pay, a new performance appraisal system, and a restructuring of career paths so that seniority plays a lesser role and performance a greater one.

34. Thus, for A3 workers, this can amount to DM 2,760 (1,580 dollars) and for B3 to DM 14,760 (8,435 dollars). The total performance-related pay budget can amount to 2 percent of expenditure on personnel.

35. Those *Beamte* who have been transferred have been required to accept a temporary suspension of their *Beamte* status (a so-called *Beurlaub*), to allow the subsidiaries this extra degree of flexibility. This suspension can last five years, at which point the individuals can elect to return to the core company or permanently end their *Beamte* status.

36. The success of the DPG in extending its rights during Post Reform II is significant in a comparative context because it reflected the nature of quasi-corporatism in Germany and, thus, how institutional structures can perpetuate their own strength, even in changing circumstances.

37. Other significant influences on Telekom's desire for privatization included greater freedom in entering international joint ventures, greater distancing from possible political influence in managerial decision making, and the desire to reduce the growing level of corporate indebtedness (Darbishire 1995, 1997).

38. Detailed regulations specify the general tasks of managers and workers within the overall work process. In 1994 there were, for example, some nine hundred regulations concerning the flow of work in network operations alone.

39. Both of these features, of a traditional functional organization and a local orientation, were closely related to limitations in information-processing ability. It is the change in this dimension in particular that is facilitating this reorganization (Darbishire 1997).

# 6

# Japan, Sweden, and Italy

This chapter examines the extent to which and how variation is increasing within employment systems in Japan, Sweden, and Italy. It thereby assesses whether the trends in the countries analyzed in Chapters 2–4 generalize to other advanced industrialized economies. These three countries were selected because the degree of centralized collective bargaining varied enormously as they entered the 1980s. Looking at countries that have such different initial bargaining structures is important because our analysis of the United States, Britain, Australia, and Germany shows that bargaining structure is a critical influence on how and by how much employment practices vary.

Japan has had one of the most decentralized collective-bargaining structures among advanced industrial economies over the post–World War II period as enterprise agreements dominated employment conditions in the private sector.[1] In sharp contrast, Sweden has had one of the most centralized bargaining structures in which a single agreement negotiated between union and employer federations has set the standard for wages and other employment conditions for much of the economy.[2] Italy, historically, has had a middle-range degree of centralization in collective bargaining and pronounced shifts in the locus of bargaining since the early 1980s. Thus, by examining these three countries, we greatly extend our range of comparison.

## BASIC SYSTEM OF EMPLOYMENT RELATIONS IN JAPAN

Employment relations at the workplace level in the private sector in Japan follow the Japanese-oriented pattern described in column 3 of Figure 1.1.

Jobs are standardized, with workers often providing input on refinements in job descriptions and work practices (through the "continuous improvement" process). Wages are influenced strongly by seniority, and are modified by individual skill levels. In addition, annual bonuses are tied to company performance and partly to individual merit evaluations (i.e., performance appraisals).[3]

The net effect is that in Japanese private-sector industries, workers' skills, performance, and attitudes affect pay to a much greater degree than is commonly the case in Western countries. Furthermore, strong intercompany and interindustry pattern bargaining is maintained through the annual "spring offensive" (Shunto) wage negotiations.

Supervisors play a central role in allocating training and promotions, and in the performance evaluations that influence the ability component in workers' wages and the merit component in workers' annual bonuses. Supervisors, some of whom also serve as union stewards, also help channel information up and down the organizational hierarchy.[4] It is the supervisor, for example, who intervenes (typically in an informal manner) to settle individual worker complaints or relay to engineers or higher managers the need to address particular production problems.[5]

Extensive consultation between labor and management occurs through a hierarchy of joint committees. Problem-solving activities include on-line committees (quality circles) and off-line committees that span work groups on a more ad hoc basis. By Western standards, worker and union involvement is extremely informal, though some are contractually defined. Relatively little recourse is made to written or judicial procedures to resolve labor-management disagreements.

Although lifetime employment is a principle that most large Japanese private-sector firms try to adhere to, no explicit legal or contractual guarantees are provided. Severe financial reverses have caused some companies that were previously dedicated to lifetime employment to dismiss workers.

### General Union Membership Decline

Although enterprise unions have maintained relatively stable relations with their management counterparts over the past thirty years, this has not prevented substantial union membership declines in Japan. The fraction of the Japanese labor force that were union members declined from 30.8 percent in 1980 to 22.6 percent in 1997, and there is no sign of an imminent turnaround in this trend. The labor movement in Japan, like labor movements in most other advanced industrial economies, has had great difficulty organizing employees in the growing high-tech and service sectors. The predominance of enterprise unions in Japan creates a special problem for union growth, because existing enterprise unions have few incentives to organize employees in new firms. These weak incentives are apparent in that the fraction of the private-sector workforce newly organized at previously nonunion firms has declined dramatically from the 1980s on (Tsuru and Rebitzer 1995).

Unionism is particularly weak among small firms in Japan. Only 6.7 percent of workers in firms employing less than one hundred workers and 0.5 percent of workers in firms employing less than thirty workers are members of a labor union (Koshiro 1990: 188).

*Reorganization of the National Trade*
*Union Confederation (Rengo) in Japan*

While the growth of nonunion firms has increased the variation within employment relations in Japan, a counter-centralizing drift in the structure of union representation has taken place through the formation of a unified Japanese Trade Union Confederation (the new Rengo). The new Rengo was formed through mergers involving four different national labor organizations, in 1982 and 1989, to strengthen the bargaining position of trade unions and promote policy and institutional reforms. The creation of the new Rengo also signaled the dominance of a moderate faction within the Japanese labor movement, a faction aligned more closely with private-sector unions, in contrast to the greater public-sector orientation found within the old Sohyo confederation (Hiwatari forthcoming).

Although the formation of a unified union confederation made the union structure more centralized, it is revealing that with regard to Shunto wage bargaining, the leadership of Rengo in recent years has been advocating greater autonomy for the various industrial union federations and enterprise unions. In a speech outlining Rengo's goals for the 1994 spring offensive, for example, Mr. Akira Yamagishi, the president of Rengo, stated, "The kernel of the 1994 Spring Struggle lies in activation of the struggle for higher wages *on the basis of industrial self-reliance* [emphasis added]. It is essential that each industrial union formulates and takes responsibility to make its own vital demands by crystallizing the will of all its members" (Yamagishi 1994: Preface). Although this speech and other Rengo policies set the stage for greater variation in the wage demands of industrial unions, subsequent spring offensives have not had this effect. Tsuru (1992: 5) finds a cyclical trend in the variance of Shunto wage increases, yet as Table 6.1 shows, there is no long term trend in the variation of enterprise spring wage increases in the 1990s.

Table 6.1 also suggests that there is no recent general increase in interfirm wage variation; however, there is evidence of growing wage differentials between large and small firms from the late 1970s on (Koshiro 1990: 207). There is also evidence of increased reliance on ability-based pay among

**Table 6.1.** The Variance in Spring (Shunto) Enterprise
Wage Increases, 1971–1995

| Year | Quartile Variance of Wage Increases |
| --- | --- |
| 1971 | 0.07 |
| 1972 | 0.08 |
| 1973 | 0.05 |
| 1974 | 0.07 |
| 1975 | 0.16 |
| 1976 | 0.10 |
| 1977 | 0.07 |
| 1978 | 0.20 |
| 1979 | 0.10 |
| 1980 | 0.06 |
| 1981 | 0.06 |
| 1982 | 0.06 |
| 1983 | 0.15 |
| 1984 | 0.12 |
| 1985 | 0.09 |
| 1986 | 0.14 |
| 1987 | 0.18 |
| 1988 | 0.12 |
| 1989 | 0.11 |
| 1990 | 0.08 |
| 1991 | 0.08 |
| 1992 | 0.11 |
| 1993 | 0.12 |
| 1994 | 0.12 |
| 1995 | 0.10 |

*Source:* Survey of the Labour Policy Bureau, Ministry of Labour, Tokyo, various years.

white-collar employees, as well as similar evidence regarding auto worker
pay (as mentioned above). Morishima (1995: 629), for example, finds
wider use of performance appraisal for middle and senior managers versus
the traditional skill and seniority criteria. Morishima also reports greater individualization in manager promotions and career movements.

At the same time, no significant movement away from the Japanese-
oriented employment relations practices in private-sector firms has been de-
tected.[6] Furthermore, there are still strong commonalities in wage settlements across major firms *within industries*. To the extent that Japanese firms
have diversified their employment relations, they have done so in their subsidiaries and affiliated firms. Nitta (1991: 14), for example, provides examples of this sort of employment relations diversification in the chemical textile industry. Nevertheless, this diversity appears to be rather modest,
especially when compared to other countries.

### Employment Relations at Auto Assemblers

As befits the traditional structure of Japanese labor-management relations, all of the auto assembly companies are unionized, and nearly all the regular employees at these companies belong to the respective enterprise unions. Employment relations at the workplace level in Japanese auto assemblers follow the Japanese-oriented pattern described in column 3 of Figure 1.1.

Individual performance appraisals and company annual bonuses in the industry have led to relatively large, within-plant pay variation across production workers. Pils and MacDuffie (1998: Table 1) find, for example, that the difference between the highest and lowest paid production worker in Japanese auto assembly plants is 205 percent, versus a 25 percent differential in U.S. auto assembly plants. The role of group or individual bonuses differs across the auto assemblers. Toyota, has a group piecework system that complements the standard pay components.[7]

Workers receive generous training, and internal promotion is a chief source of skill generation, as is typical in the other large private-sector firms in Japan. MacDuffie and Kochan (1995) find that Japanese auto assemblers provide substantially more training than do American and European auto firms and make particularly large investments in on-the-job training. Japanese auto workers are expected to learn more than the job they are performing at a given time. Provisions are made for job rotation, the learning of multiple skills, and lifelong learning. The tremendous on-the-job human-capital investment by the auto assemblers and other large private-sector firms is tied to a lifetime employment principle, which helps keep workers in the firm after they receive valuable training.

Since the 1950s, Japan's auto assembly firms have maintained lifetime employment commitments to their regular status employees.[8] Fluctuations in output are compensated through heavy reliance on overtime; adjustments in temporary or secondary employment; and the reassignment of permanent workers to new jobs, work areas, or corporate affiliates. Extensive career planning and guidance are provided to workers as part of this system.

Cyclical fluctuations in output, at least until the early 1990s, had been relatively small, and shifts in output have been buffered by the adjustment mechanisms. Voluntary retirements have been instituted at Nissan and some of the other auto assemblers to reduce employment when sales are sluggish and companies have excess production capacity.

The eleven major auto assemblers all follow the Japanese-oriented employment pattern although work practices vary across firms. Toyota, for example, is known for its relatively heavy reliance on small group activities and multiskilling. Nissan, in comparison, historically has made less use of these practices, preferring instead more centralized union-management consultation and more narrowly trained workers (Cusumano 1985: 316–19; Hiwatari forthcoming). In the mid-1980s, Nissan took steps, including the ousting the strong union leader, Shioji, and introducing more small-group activities, to try to make its work practices more like those at Toyota (Hiwatari forthcoming).

As sales have recently become sluggish, the auto assemblers have increased internal transfers, and as at Nissan, plants or at least parts of operations have been closed. Enterprise unions have become more involved in mediating disputes between workers, especially those in downsized facilities, and corporate management (Hiwatari forthcoming). The enterprise unions frequently have been called on to negotiate quid pro quos in exchange for workers' acceptance of adjustments in transfer rights, compensation, and work hours (Hiwatari forthcoming: 9). In the process, even though unions enter the period with a relatively decentralized enterprise structure, as Hiwatari notes (forthcoming: 35), union structure has, as in other countries, come more and more to "mirror" that of firms, which in turn were becoming more decentralized.

*Wage and Bonus Variation at the Japanese Auto Assemblers.* Table 6.2 reports average percentage wage increases at the major Japanese auto assemblers in 1995. There is little variation in the average wage increase across the companies, with the average ranging only from a low of 2.61 percent at Nissan to

**Table 6.2.** Average Wage (Salary) Increase at Japanese Auto Assemblers, 1995 (in %)

|  | 1995 |
| --- | --- |
| Toyota | 2.83 |
| Nissan | 2.61 |
| Honda | 2.73 |
| Mitsubishi | 3.05 |
| Mazda | 2.71 |
| Isuzu | 2.84 |
| Fuji | 2.94 |
| Daihatsu | 2.94 |
| Suzuki | 2.83 |
| Hino | 2.90 |
| Yamaha | 2.86 |
| Mean | 2.84 |
| Standard deviation | 0.12 |
| Coefficient of variation | 4.32 |

*Source:* Unpublished data collected by the JAW.

a high of 3.05 percent at Mitsubishi. Wage variation was limited even though in 1995, the companies' financial performance varied substantially, with Toyota experiencing a relatively strong year (in terms of sales and income) and Nissan (and other auto assemblers) experiencing net losses in income. Yet, the average wage increase at Toyota was only 100 yen higher than the average increase of workers at Nissan in 1995 (Mori 1995). Furthermore, as indicated by the figures in the second and third columns of Table 6.3, there is no long term trend in the wage variation across the eleven auto assemblers.

Differences are more substantial in the average annual bonus received by auto workers at the assembly firms, as shown in Table 6.4. In 1995, for example, the average bonus was 5.8 months of pay at Toyota and 4.0 months of pay at Nissan (amounting to a difference of 610,000 yen) (Mori 1995). Moreover, columns 2 and 3 of Table 6.5 reveal that variation in bonuses has been rising across the eleven assemblers since 1986.

Although cross-company wage variation is limited, there is evidence that in the 1990s, greater reliance is being placed *within firms* on ability-based pay, and the role of seniority in wage determination is declining. Matsumura (1995), for example, reports that one major auto assembler increased the role of ability in wage determination and introduced a new linkage between pay and personnel rank, in order to reward workers of high ability in cases where advanced abilities could not be displayed through job upgrades because of a scarcity in highly ranked job positions. The union federation in the auto industry, the Confederation of Japan Automobile Workers' Unions (JAW), supports this greater role for ability in wage determination as long as the (enterprise) union is involved developing the criteria for ability

**Table 6.3.** Company Variation in Average Wage (Salary) Increases at the Japanese Auto Assemblers

| Year | Mean Increase | Standard Deviation (of the mean increases) | Coefficient of Variation (of the mean increases) |
|------|---------------|--------------------------------------------|--------------------------------------------------|
| 1995 | 2.84 | 0.12 | 4.32 |
| 1994 | 3.02 | 0.10 | 3.38 |
| 1993 | 3.84 | 0.14 | 3.64 |
| 1992 | 4.89 | 0.15 | 3.12 |
| 1991 | 5.62 | 0.09 | 1.65 |
| 1990 | 5.99 | 0.20 | 3.33 |
| 1989 | 5.13 | 0.16 | 3.09 |
| 1988 | 4.11 | 0.32 | 7.70 |
| 1987 | 3.19 | 0.23 | 7.26 |
| 1986 | 4.60 | 0.39 | 8.50 |

*Source:* Unpublished data collected by the JAW.
*Note:* These figures are computed from annual wage increases at the eleven auto assemblers listed in Table 6.2.

**Table 6.4.** Average Annual Worker Bonuses at the Japanese Auto Assemblers, 1995

|                         | 1995             |
| ----------------------- | ---------------- |
| Toyota                  | 5.8 months of wages |
| Nissan                  | 4.0              |
| Honda                   | 5.6              |
| Mitsubishi              | 5.6              |
| Mazda                   | 4.18             |
| Isuzu                   | 4.9              |
| Fuji                    | 4.6              |
| Daihatsu                | 5.2              |
| Suzuki                  | 5.5              |
| Hino                    | 5.5              |
| Yamaha                  | 5.5              |
| Mean                    | 5.13             |
| Standard deviation      | 0.62             |
| Coefficient of variation | 12.06           |

*Source:* Unpublished data collected by the JAW.

**Table 6.5.** Company Variation in Worker Annual Bonuses at the Japanese Auto Assemblers, 1986–1995

| Year | Mean Annual Bonus | Standard Deviation (of the mean bonuses) | Coefficient of Variation (of the mean bonuses) |
| ---- | ----------------- | ---------------------------------------- | ---------------------------------------------- |
| 1995 | 5.13              | 0.62                                     | 12.06                                          |
| 1994 | 5.11              | 0.52                                     | 10.14                                          |
| 1993 | 5.32              | 0.45                                     | 8.37                                           |
| 1992 | 5.57              | 0.36                                     | 6.55                                           |
| 1991 | 5.51              | 0.54                                     | 9.76                                           |
| 1990 | 5.61              | 0.31                                     | 5.56                                           |
| 1989 | 5.53              | 0.25                                     | 4.45                                           |
| 1988 | 5.40              | 0.32                                     | 5.95                                           |
| 1987 | 5.32              | 0.38                                     | 7.23                                           |
| 1986 | 5.41              | 0.37                                     | 6.86                                           |

*Source:* Unpublished data collected by the JAW.
*Note:* These figures are the mean months of salary provided as annual bonuses at the eleven auto assemblers listed in Table 6.4.

determination (i.e., personal assessments) and the regular personal assessments are shared with the workers being assessed.[9]

### Employment Relations at Japanese Auto Suppliers

Japanese auto assemblers are less vertically integrated than their Western counterparts and rely more extensively on suppliers for product development and just-in-time deliveries.[10] The auto suppliers can be categorized into various tiers; those in the top (first) tier have more dedicated relationships with the respective assemblers. Employment relations at Japan's first-tier auto suppliers tend to include the practices described in the Japanese-oriented pattern.[11]

Employment practices at the second-tier suppliers and especially those at the lower-tier suppliers, in contrast, are a mixture of Japanese-oriented work practices and those of the low-wage pattern described in column 1 of Figure 1.1. Half the second-tier suppliers surveyed by Cole and Yakushiji (1984: 159), for example, do not have a union, whereas all the first-tier suppliers are unionized. Cole and Yakushiji (159) also find that the percentage of employees who belong to the union is higher in first-tier suppliers. Furthermore, the proportion of part-time and seasonal workers is higher (10.9 percent) in second-tier versus first-tier auto suppliers (4.2 percent) (159).

Wages decline, along with degree of unionization, down the auto supply chain. Using figures from Cole and Yakushiji's survey, Howes (1993: 33) calculates that hourly wages in the second and third- to fourth-tier supplier firms are, respectively, 87 percent and 67 percent of the average hourly wages at the first-tier firms. Although the differentials are sizable, they are smaller than auto assembler/parts wage differentials in the United States (see Chapter 2).

Employment relations in the auto industry are representative of the practices found elsewhere in Japan's private sector, particularly the practices of large firms. Public-sector work practices do not, however, generally follow this private-sector pattern, although in recent years public-sector organizations have been pressured to adopt practices more similar to those of the private sector. The telecommunications industry is an interesting case in its own right given its size, and it also provides a telling illustration of a sector in transition between the two styles of employment relations.

### STRUCTURE OF THE JAPANESE TELECOMMUNICATIONS INDUSTRY

Nippon Telegraph and Telephone (NTT) remains the dominant provider of telecommunications services and equipment in Japan even after the 1985 privatization of the company and recent inroads by new entrants to the industry. As at other telecommunications giants around the world, employment relations have been altered in recent years at NTT in response to deregulation and associated competitive pressures as well as pressures produced by technological advances.

In response to these economic pressures the union representing telecommunications employees has expanded its involvement in business decisions at NTT. In addition, employment relations at NTT have become more similar to those of large private-sector Japanese firms and, consequently, to the Japanese-oriented pattern of employment relations. Outside of NTT, nonunion employment in the industry has grown significantly. Thus, the changes in employment relations at NTT have lessened variation in employment relations in the Japanese economy by making NTT's employment relations more similar to those of other large private-sector firms; however, the growth in nonunion employment has increased the variation within the telecommunications industry.

*Employment Relations at NTT:*
*The Traditional Enterprise (Industry) Structure*

Before privatization, NTT's business policies and employment relations were closely regulated by the Ministry of Posts and Telecommunications. The enterprise union at NTT, the Japanese Telecommunication Workers Union (JTWU), has long represented 99 percent of all employees eligible for union representation. (The union in effect represents all blue- and white-collar employees up to and including the rank of section manager.) Given the near-complete monopoly position held by NTT before privatization, the jurisdiction of JTWU at NTT, although technically limited to the NTT enterprise, was in effect industrial in coverage.

By law, prior to privatization, JTWU was not allowed to independently bargain over wages, and wage increases at NTT were closely linked to government wage increases at other public agencies. However, JTWU made up for its weak wage-bargaining position by gaining a heavy influence over the administration of working conditions and work rules at NTT. For example, there were no personal assessments at NTT, and promotions and access to training depended heavily on employee seniority, with a limited role for supervisors' input.[12] In this way, employment relations at NTT were similar to those within other Japanese public agencies. It is interesting to note that this "job control" style of labor-management relations was similar to the traditional employment pattern in U.S. unionized private-sector firms.[13]

## POST-PRIVATIZATION EMPLOYMENT RELATIONS AT NTT

Privatization and ensuing market pressures led to significant shifts in employment relations at NTT. With privatization, JTWU gained the right to bargain directly with NTT management over wages which the union used this to its advantage.[14] Average wages at NTT rose from 90.8 percent of the average wages in all other Japanese industries in 1984 to 105.4 percent in 1992. In 1995, NTT-JTWU bargaining, in fact, took a leadership position in that year's spring offensive (Japan Institute of Labor 1995).

After NTT privatization, JTWU agreed to allow personal assessments, which began to play a role in promotions, although not in wage setting. (The latter contrasts with common practices in Japanese large private-sector firms.) Supervisors at NTT, as at other large private-sector firms, were given more control over worker promotions and access to training. In addition, jobs were broadened at NTT as employees acquired multiple skills. For example, customer service representatives were allowed to follow up on orders and deal with customer complaints.

These changes in employment relations were accepted by JTWU only after NTT management had assured the union and employees that employment security would be provided through the issuance of a statement on employment security (Zendentsu 1995). Employment at NTT did fall, from 304,000 in 1985 to 216,000 in 1993. But there were no involuntary layoffs, and employment reductions were accomplished through regular retirements, attrition, early retirements spurred by enhanced severance payments, and by employee transfers to new NTT subsidiaries (described in more detail below).

After privatization, JTWU became more actively involved in business decision making through business planning decisions rather than merely consultations over the effects of decisions. The joint consultation structure at NTT also has been extended through the creation of more levels of committee meetings, down to the workshop level. In addition, two former union officials were added as "corporate auditors" of NTT (Nakamura and Hiraki 1997: 259).

*Nonunion Growth in the Japanese Telecommunications Industry*

NTT's share of the telecommunications industry declined as a result of the freer market entry provided by telecommunications regulatory reforms. As of 1993, NTT's market share had fallen to 89.9 percent of telephone services, 83.9 percent of leased lines, 36.3 percent of mobile telephones, and 35.5 percent of paging services, from NTT's near-total monopoly in all these service areas as late as 1987 (Nakamura and Hiraki 1997: 234). NTT has created new subsidiary companies to compete in the more open and increasingly diversified telecommunications market. As of 1995, thirty-four thousand NTT employees had been transferred to the new companies, and an estimated 70 percent of these employees work in unionized facilities. Unionization is much lower in telecommunications firms not affiliated with

NTT. For example, most of the new "common carriers" are not unionized (Nakamura and Hiraki 1997: 236).

## INCOME DISTRIBUTION IN JAPAN

As in the overall distribution of employment practices, a moderate increase in variation also is apparent in income distribution. Compared to other industrialized countries, Japan's distribution on entering the 1980s ranked in the middle of the pack in terms of inequality. As of the early 1980s, for example, Japan had less than the high degree of income inequality found in the United States and United Kingdom and more than the limited income inequality found in Sweden and Germany (Freeman and Katz 1995). From 1979 to 1990, male and female wage inequality rose in Japan but not as much as the increases in inequality over in this period in the United States and United Kingdom (Katz, Loveman, and Blanchflower 1995: 27). Consistent with the growing variation in auto annual bonuses, Katz and Revenga (1989) find that *levels* of income inequality and wage differentials in Japan are larger when a more comprehensive measure of earnings that includes overtime earnings and special payments (including bonuses) is used to assess inequality. Yet, Katz and Revenga (1989) also find that *trends* in wage differentials (i.e., a moderate rise in inequality in the 1980s) are not altered when additional aspects of compensation are included in the measure of earnings.[15]

## SUMMARY OF DEVELOPMENTS IN JAPAN

Employment system variation has increased *within* the telecommunications industry and in the Japanese economy in general through nonunion employment. At the same time, the variation was being reduced by the growing similarity of NTT's employment relations to standard private-sector practices. In the auto industry, the greatest source of increased variation in employment outcomes across firms in recent years has been the variation in annual bonus payments.

Within firms, compensation has become more varied owing to performance appraisal and ability-based pay in autos, telecommunications, and other Japanese industries. It is noteworthy that the already relatively decentralized enterprise unions, particularly in the auto industry, were taking on more of a mediating role between workers on the shop floor and corporate management in the process of facilitating workplace adjustments.

Overall, as compared to other countries, Japan has experienced little employment system variation. This attests to the continuing strength of the country's labor market institutions and the relative success of those institutions, which has reduced economic pressure on existing structures.

## OVERVIEW OF SWEDISH EMPLOYMENT RELATIONS

Sweden long has been distinguished by one of the most centralized systems of collective bargaining and by high levels of unionization and wage compression. Although union membership has not declined significantly, the other two distinguishing features of the Swedish employment system have weakened; moreover wages and work organization have become more varied across and within firms. At the same time, variation in employment practices has been tempered by the near absence of either low-wage or nonunion human resource management employment patterns.

### Union Membership and Collective-Bargaining Coverage in Sweden

More than 80 percent of the Swedish labor force belongs to unions, and union membership has declined only slightly since 1987, largely due to the growth of (and somewhat lower union representation in) the service sector. While the LO, a federation of blue-collar industrial and sectoral unions, has long played a leadership role in employment relations and labor politics, from the 1970s on, the hegemony of the LO was increasingly challenged by unions (and union federations) that represented white-collar and public-sector employees (TCO, SACO/SR, and KTK). The growth of the latter helped sustain high levels of union membership, but at times led to union rivalries and the fragmenting of union political and bargaining strength.

Collective-bargaining coverage is also unusually comprehensive. The small number of uncovered firms include a few American-owned computer companies and some employers in hotels, restaurants, and other services (EIRR 1994d: 24–25). Unlike many continental European countries, this high coverage in Sweden does not come from mechanisms that extend negotiated agreements to nonsignatory firms. Rather, "as soon as a union has a member in one firm it has the right to demand negotiations with the aid of strike action if necessary. The firm concerned would then normally affiliate with an employers' federation in order to gain support in the bargaining process" (EIRR 1994d: 24).

### Collective-Bargaining Structure in Sweden

In Sweden's centralized collective-bargaining system, a dominant role is played by the national agreement negotiated between the employers' confederation (SAF) and the LO. Since 1956, the SAF-LO agreement recommended wage increases, stipulated nonwage issues, and often made other detailed recommendations on employment conditions to the national affiliates of the LO and SAF. Sectoral agreements traditionally were then negotiated that often closely followed these recommendations, and company-level bargaining (and agreements) supplemented the sectoral agreements. This relatively centralized collective bargaining produced moderate pay settlements and relatively few strikes (Swenson 1989). In addition, unions used a centralized bargaining structure to implement their policy of wage solidarity (the negotiation of limited intra- and interindustry wage differentials), which was a key part of the "Swedish model."

After 1984, the dominance of the central agreement declined. In 1984, industry-level bargaining completely replaced the SAF-LO agreement. Although in 1985 and 1986 there were SAF-LO agreements, they included more recommendations concerning nonwage issues and fewer stipulations. National wage bargaining was replaced again by industry-level bargaining in 1988. Then in 1989, a two-year national central agreement was reinstituted.

However, neither decentralized industry bargaining in 1984 and 1988, nor more centralized bargaining in the intervening years, were able to slow down a wage-price spiral. From 1991 to 1993, a mediated central two-year agreement (the so-called Rehnberg settlement) that forbid local-level wage bargaining was in force (EIRR 1994d: 24). This agreement was part of a government-promoted incomes policy adopted along with a disinflation policy (Edin and Holmlund 1995: 312). Employers conveyed their intent to break with the traditional centralized SAF-LO agreement in the future by announcing in February 1991 that the SAF would no longer take part in central negotiations and by disbanding the SAF wage-bargaining staff.

Pressures for a more decentralized bargaining structure have been building since the 1980s. Large employers that had previously supported centralized collective bargaining, particularly in the engineering sector and the influential Engineering Employers' Association (which includes the auto manufacturers), strongly have favored a shift toward decentralized collective bargaining. These employers have complained bitterly of heightened international competition pressures and the resulting need for lower labor costs and wider skill differentials (and believe that decentralized bargaining will help respond to these pressures by giving employers more flexibility and bargaining leverage). In contrast, many small employers are less eager to decentralize bargaining, apparently fearing a strengthening of union power if unions had the capability to whipsaw employers and in other ways introduce greater instability in industrial relations. In Sweden, as in most of the other countries analyzed in this volume, throughout those debates the central unions have sought to retain a centralized bargaining structure.

The traditional structure had always included a substantial amount of firm- and plant-level bargaining, which had led to "wage drift" (Swenson 1989; Flanagan, Soskice, and Ulman 1983). For many years, wage drift constituted around half the total wage increases (EIRR 1994d: 24). At the same time, until the erosion of centralized bargaining in the early 1980s, wage drift (and associated market forces) did not significantly erode the solidaristic wage compression promoted in the master national agreements.[16] The effects of wage drift were counteracted in earlier periods by the wage development guarantees included in central agreements.

In the 1993 and 1995 bargaining rounds, the importance of firm- and plant-level bargaining increased as the sectoral (and industry) agreements left the distribution of a sizable share of the negotiated pay increases to be decided by local negotiations between unions and management.[17] The 1993 metalworkers (sectoral) agreement, for example, provided for a 3.3 percent overall pay increase over a two-year period. However, the allocation across workers of this "kitty" was left for company-level bargaining.[18] Furthermore, in contrast to previous practice, the metalworkers agreement stated that any wage drift in the first year that resulted from increased skills and responsibility were not to be deducted from second-year wage increases.

In another break with past practice, the 1993 metalworkers agreement encouraged greater wage variation across individuals as well as company- (and plant-) level pay variation. The agreement provided that "wage increases shall be differentiated on individual or other grounds.... Wages shall be determined on the basis of the responsibility and difficulty of the job tasks and the way in which the individual fulfills these tasks" (cited in EIRR 1993d: 16).

The subsequent 1995 metalworking agreement promoted wage variation even more strongly by leaving the allocation of sizable wage increases to local unions and management. The 1995 agreement provided that only if local unions and management fail to agree on how to distribute the respective kitties would the matter be decided by a national-level arbitration committee (EIRR 1995e: 20).

Spurred by improvements in the Swedish economy, in 1998 collective bargaining proceeded without the acrimony characteristic of the previous ten years, and several three-year sectoral agreements were concluded. The metalworking agreement provides for general percentage wage increases to be negotiated at the local level, subject to guaranteed minimum increases. Provisions for working–time reductions are a central part of the metalworking and other sectoral agreements (EIRR 1998c).

As collective bargaining has been become more decentralized and greater flexibility is being given to local actors to fashion wage allocations, there are some counter-centralizing tendencies in the structure of Swedish collective bargaining. Bargaining in 1993 in the metalworking sector, for example, occurred at a "single table" involving all the unions representing employees in the sector rather than separate agreements traditionally negotiated by each union (or union federation). Although employers in the metalworking industry, as in some other industries, entered the 1993 negotiations with the stated intent to replace all industry-level bargaining with company-level bargaining, their preferences were frustrated by national unions that successfully joined forces.[19] In addition, at the plant level in a number of firms, new forms of union coordination were created through the negotiation of employee agreements that harmonized working conditions across skill and occupational categories, a harmonization that was attractive to both employers and unions.

Simultaneously, cross-firm pay compensation variation was being promoted by profit sharing and/or stock ownership in compensation packages. A 1995 survey found that 34 percent the sampled firms had a profit-sharing scheme and another 12 percent had plans to introduce one (EIRR 1995f: 11).[20] At Volvo, for example, employees can earn almost one month's additional pay in years when the company is making a healthy profit (EIRR 1995g : 19).

### Participatory Processes in Sweden

Local unions increasingly have become involved in discussions with local management concerning work organization and business issues, and in the process, power has been shifting within unions to the local level (Kjellberg 1992: 133). Some of the widening of union and worker involvement in business issues has been spurred by federal legislation promoting codetermination, such as the 1976 Codetermination Act (MBL). Another important piece of federal legislation was the UVA Development Agreement, which in 1982 shifted the focus in joint labor-management activities to productivity-related issues. This shift in focus has been linked to decentralizations within managerial hierarchies.

In contrast to continental European countries, traditionally in Sweden local unions rather than works councils have traditionally been the vehicle through which labor became involved in shop-floor work organization. This resulted from the legally binding codetermination introduced in the 1970s which did not involve the establishment of works councils. Plant-level union locals remain the basic unit of organization: "They represent the labor force in negotiations relating to co-determination as well as wages" (Pontusson 1997: 24). Consequently, Swedish unions have a relatively coordinated structure linking national and local union branches.

This structure may help promote effective trades across wage and non-wage issues by linking wage negotiations and discussions over codetermination and other workplace issues. However, to date, an integrated union structure has not prevented ambiguities from surfacing regarding union roles as employees gain more direct participation in workplace and production issues (Kjellberg 1992: 127–28).

*Work Restructuring*

Highly publicized joint labor-management initiatives in the 1970s focused on the introduction of long-cycle jobs and "social-technical" experiments. Many of these experiments took place in auto plants (Berggren 1992). In the 1990s, however, some of the most far-reaching work redesigns were ended by plant closings. Volvo, for example, closed its Uddevalla (in 1993) and Kalmar (in 1994) car assembly plants (Martin 1995: 272). Uddevalla had been using unusually long job cycles in its auto-assembly process.[21] In addition, Saab closed the innovative Malmo plant and returned to a traditional production process in its Trollhättan plant (Kjellberg 1992: 132).

Although the social-technical experiments were quite bold, they had never represented a sizable share of Swedish employment. The limited scope of the long work-cycle experiments is indicated by the simultaneous increase in the proportion of jobs with relatively low skill content. A survey by the Swedish Metalworkers Union shows that the proportion of engineering jobs requiring few skills and involving physically arduous work increased from 1977 to 1987 (Pontusson 1997: 22).[22]

The range of work reorganization in Sweden clearly was narrowed by the ending of the long job-cycle experiments, yet work restructuring does continue in Swedish plants. In the 1990s, ABB became a noteworthy leader in the introduction of "self-governing" work groups, adopted as part of efforts to decentralize managerial hierarchies, reduce the number of supervisors, and speed product delivery and development (Martin 1995; Berggren 1996: 204). Furthermore, many innovative work-redesign activities were underway in the 1990s with the help of subsidies provided by the Working Life Fund (Berggren 1996: 202–4).

At Volvo and Saab, efforts in the 1990s focused on the introduction of group work. At Volvo's Torslanda plant, for example, the QPE group work included multiskilling and both horizontal and vertical task integration (Brulin and Nilsson 1997). As at auto plants in the other countries we discussed, recent group work initiatives at Volvo are associated with efforts to reduce the number of supervisors and shift the remaining supervisors to a facilitator role. Saab introduced a similar QLEH work group system at its Trollhättan plant in the early 1990s. Another commonality with developments in auto plants in other countries is revealed by the wide variation that is surfacing in the practical implementation of group work across the various departments in the Torslanda, Trollhättan, and other Swedish auto plants (Brulin and Nilsson 1997).

The work restructuring underway at ABB, Volvo, Saab, and other Swedish firms includes the same core features of the joint team-based approach described in our categorization. The ending of many of the highly publicized long-cycle work experiments has, in effect, made contemporary Swedish developments more similar to trends in other countries. Nevertheless, in Sweden, as in the other countries we analyzed, there is considerable diversity in the specific form of new participatory arrangements being introduced at the enterprise and workplace levels in Swedish firms (Kjellberg 1992: 127).

A further similarity with other countries is that along with formal joint labor-management activities, many Swedish firms have recently expanded direct communication between management and the workforce, often through informal channels. A continuing debate within Swedish unions concerns whether these emerging forms of "direct democracy" jeopardize the traditional solidaristic policies pursued by the labor movement at the national level (Kjellberg 1992: 130). Although union solidarity may well be threatened by recent developments, it is important to note that so far in Sweden, as in Italy (described later in this chapter), enhanced direct communication between managers and workers has not been associated with the spread of nonunion employment. As Kjellberg (1992) notes, "apart from some high-technology and service companies, the aim of new management strategies in Sweden—in contrast to the USA—has not been to create union-free enterprises but rather to encourage the union's loyalty to the individual enterprise: a local form of corporatism" (127). Thus, in Sweden there is very limited use of anything similar to the nonunion human resource management pattern.

INCOME DISTRIBUTION TRENDS IN SWEDEN

Worries about the future of union solidarity have been fueled in part by rising income variation. Wage inequality had declined precipitously during the 1960s and 1970s, and Sweden entered the 1980s with the most egalitarian income distribution among OECD countries (Edin and Holmlund 1995: 307). Nevertheless, Sweden experienced shifts in its income distribution in the 1980s and 1990s that bear many similarities to developments in other advanced industrial economies: wage differentials widened from the mid-1980s on, and the degree of wage dispersion in 1991 was back to the mid-1970s levels (Edin and Holmlund 1995: 312).

The labor supply and demand pressures noted by Edin and Holmlund (1995) contributed to the widening income distribution but, clearly, so did the decentralization of collective bargaining and the spread of procedures that linked pay to performance. For example, Volvo took steps in the 1990s to increase the link between workers' pay and measures of economic performance. In 1995, a pay-for-knowledge system was introduced. Pay-for-knowledge increments are in addition to group bonuses (that can amount to up to 10 percent of total pay) and the company bonus mentioned earlier.

### SUMMARY OF DEVELOPMENTS IN SWEDEN

Variation in employment relations in Sweden is increasing across and within firms due to an increasing reliance on performance-linked pay (at the group and individual level) and increased variation in the breadth and depth of work restructuring at the plant level. There is a drift toward deeper union and worker involvement in business decision making at the company and shop-floor levels, even though the extreme experiments with long-cycle work have been abandoned. Although the labor movement has been challenged by these developments and the ending of peak-level bargaining, local unions' authority and involvement has been growing along with the decentralization of wage bargaining and the deepening of local nonwage bargaining.

The increasing individualization and decentralization of wage determination has contributed to the widening of wage differentials. However, Swedish wage differentials and overall income distribution remain remarkably compressed as compared to other countries.

While the structure and nature of union involvement in decision making has been altered from previous Swedish patterns, there is little evidence of HRM alternatives to collective bargaining and little evidence of growth in a low-wage employment pattern. Thus, although unions are struggling to adjust to changes in their role and methods of input, their place in the employment relationship remains relatively secure.

### OVERVIEW OF EMPLOYMENT RELATIONS IN ITALY

Although Italy does not possess the extremely centralized collective bargaining structure found in Sweden, the extent of diversity in employment patterns is relatively narrow given the limited expansion of nonunion employment patterns. Union and worker input into decision making has been altered in many Italian firms in recent years, yet in all but small firms pursuing a low-wage pattern, unions and collective negotiations between managers and worker representatives continue to play a prominent role in employment relations. At the same time, across unionized Italian firms, wide variation is appearing in the nature of union involvement in business issues, a variation that is associated with the diverse production strategies being adopted by these firms. In addition, there have been major shifts in the form and structure of collective bargaining since 1980 that bear many similarities to the changes in the other countries analyzed in this volume.

### Union Membership and "Representativeness"

While Italian trade union membership declined somewhat in the 1980s, these declines have been relatively small compared to the declines experienced in the United States and United Kingdom. Moreover, union membership appears to have stabilized in the 1990s. The three main Italian union confederations—CGIL, CISL, and the UIL—are divided along ideological lines.[23] Their membership as a percentage of the labor force rose from 38.5 percent in 1970 to 49.0 percent in 1980, fell to 39.9 percent in 1987, and as of 1990 stood at 39.3 percent (Ferner and Hyman 1992: 545).[24]

Declining membership in the three confederal unions in the 1980s was not, however, necessarily associated with declines in collective worker representation, as there was a growth in autonomous unions and COBAS (grass-roots committees) (Locke 1995; Ferner and Hyman 1992). Although the autonomous unions and COBAS challenged the "representativeness" of the confederal unions, they did provide forums, often very militant ones, for collective worker input into firm- and plant-level governance. Thus, in contrast to many other countries, central (i.e., confederal) union membership has remained relatively high in Italy. Furthermore, Italian management in the 1980s was at times confronting militant independent worker representative bodies rather than gaining the sort of unilateral authority that managers in other countries acquired through nonunion employment patterns.

The continuing central role of collective representation in Italy had been strengthened earlier by the expansion of employee rights promoted by the 1970 Statuto dei Lavoratori (Workers Statute Law) which reinforced employment security, provided remedies for unjust dismissal, restricted unilateral changes in job definitions, and regulated disciplinary procedures (Ferner and Hyman 1992: 534). The Workers Statute Law also conferred a number of rights on "the most representative unions" at the enterprise level; Italian unions continue to use these rights to play an active role in the works councils that commonly have developed as the forum for employee representation.[25] Furthermore, unions have been strengthened by the common application of the collective contracts signed by the three major unions to workers, regardless of their union status.

In the 1980s, the structure of collective bargaining in Italy did decentralize in a manner that bears many similarities to developments in other countries. The importance of national industry-level bargaining (and collective agreements) declined as the frequency and depth of company, plant, or in some cases territorial, bargaining grew. By 1990, 38 percent of companies concluded a company- or plant-level collective agreement (EIRR 1992c: 24). Although national industry-level bargaining by no means became irrelevant, studies in the late 1980s "revealed that contrary to past practice, local union contracts were the most innovative and important agreements covering workers in industry" (Locke and Bacarro 1996: 12). Company- or plant-level collective agreements addressed the work reorganization and, in some cases, the increased involvement workers were beginning to play in shop-floor decision making through quality circle and team-like initiatives. Various types of work reorganization spread within and across Italian firms (discussed in more detail below).

The shift to more decentralized collective bargaining was linked to the breakdown in centrally negotiated incomes policies during the mid- and late 1980s. Fittingly, the re-establishment of an incomes policy in 1992 shifted the momentum within Italian collective bargaining back to the central level. In 1992, following a proscription within a governmental "protocol," the confederal unions and employers agreed to abolish the *scala mobile* (that had provided cost-of-living payments), impose a one-year moratorium on both firm-level wage negotiations and public-sector collective bargaining, and freeze industrial wages and salaries for a year (Locke and Bacarro 1996: 22).

In addition to being strengthened by the return of an incomes policy, the confederal unions also have reestablished their representativeness on the shop floor. A tripartite agreement in July 1993 replaced the existing plant-level union structures, the so-called Rappresentanze Sindacali Aziendali (RSA), with unitary union structures, the Rappresentanze Sindacali Unitaire (RSU) (EIRR 1994c: 19–22). Although the agreement provides that elections for the new RSU could be contested by any organization capable of gaining at least 5 percent of the employee vote, as Locke and Bacarro note, the three main union confederations gained an overwhelming majority in recent RSU elections—"about 90 percent of all votes in more than 4,000 elections" (1996: 26). The 1993 agreement also spurred company-level bargaining as revealed by recent surveys of bargaining (EIRR 1998a: 25).

Another aspect of the reforms in the RSAs is quite revealing of managers' interest in maintaining coordination across the various levels of union-management relations. The July 1993 agreement provides that only two thirds of the representatives in the new firm-level structures (the RSUs) are elected, with the remaining one third appointed directly by unions that have signed the respective national industry contract. Locke and Bacarro point out that this clause in the 1993 agreement was requested by Confindustria (the employer association) "to establish an institutional link between bargaining agents at the national and plant levels. In other words, the Confindustria wanted to avoid engaging in collective bargaining at the plant-level with union organizations which were not bound by the provisions established in the national industry contracts" (1996:25). Italian management and confederal unions were searching for a bargaining structure that would maintain an effective degree of coordination across various levels and avoid the instability and disorganization that might appear in a more free-for-all decentralized bargaining structure. This is a telling reminder that management does not necessarily benefit from extreme collective bargaining decentralization, as we have noted earlier in this volume.

## PATTERNS OF ITALIAN EMPLOYMENT RELATIONS

The intensification of company- and plant-level bargaining in Italian firms produced wide variation in the tenor of union-management relations and work practices. At some sites, work practices spread that are similar to the joint team-based pattern outlined in our categorization. At other sites, traditional Italian union-management relations prevailed. Although a shift in bargaining power to management's advantage in the 1980s produced employment outcomes that were relatively favorable to management, at many firms this shift was accommodated within the traditional employment pattern; little change occurred in the structure of union-management relations.

Italy also includes a sizable underground (sometimes referred to as "black") economy involving employment practices very similar to the low-wage employment pattern. However, as is described in more detail below, there is very little evidence of practices analogous to the HRM employment pattern in Italy. Furthermore, because of the limited amount of Japanese direct investment (and, we suspect, the continuing strength of Italian unions), there also is little evidence of a Japanese-oriented employment pattern in Italy.

*Low-Wage Employment Pattern*

Low-wage work, typically including substantial employment instability, poor work conditions, little if any union representation, and a heavy role for informal personnel practices unilaterally administered by managers, is common in the underground sectors of the Italian economy. Many of these low-wage jobs are held by women or immigrant workers, who may hold more than one job at a time. It is estimated that the number of "irregularly" employed amounted to almost 5 million in 1980, representing over 20 percent of national employment. Irregular employment is concentrated in small enterprises in manufacturing, agriculture, construction, and private services, and it is disproportionately located in southern Italy. Irregular employment usually involves tax and social security evasion (Italian employers normally make sizable contributions, as a percentage of payrolls, to the social security fund) and labor-rights violations (Ministero del lavoro 1990: 227).

Amin (1989: 244), for example, documents the sweatshop segment in the footwear and leather goods industry in Stella (Naples) among firms employing five to fifteen workers each. The workers in these firms are very young and often female, receive low wages, work long hours, and exhibit high turnover. Union representation is rare in these firms, and they commonly avoid paying social security contributions and other taxes.[26] While the underground economy continues to be sizable and the locus of a distinctly low-wage employment pattern, there is little evidence that this sector represents a growing share of employment in Italy (Erickson and Ichino 1995: 301).

*Joint Team-based Employment Pattern*

In sharp contrast to the low-wage sector, a variety of experiments with team-based work organization and increased worker and union participation in decision making have been occurring in Italy since the early 1980s. Perhaps the most publicized case is the Protocol IRI, a two-year experiment agreed to in 1984 and extended in 1986 between Italy's largest state holding company and the three main union confederations. As Locke (1995) notes, "The Protocol established new institutions aimed at enhancing union participation in firm restructuring efforts" that built on IRI's early legacy as an innovator in employment relations and was influenced by European experiences with codetermination (58). There is also evidence of the spread of quality circles, team practices, and other forums providing more direct involvement by workers and unions in business decision making across other Italian firms (Regalia and Regini 1995: 156–58). Locke (1995: 136–73), for example, describes widely varying workplace and production reorganization strategies in textile firms in Biella.

The use of performance-related pay also increased in the 1980s and 1990s (Regalia and Regini 1995: 149). A 1996 survey finds that 51 percent of firms have some form of variable pay linked to company-specific factors.[27] As compared to other European countries, Italy always had a relatively high use of merit pay, particularly for managers, yet individually determined pay also rose in the 1980s, following a trend apparent in the other countries we analyzed (Ferner and Hyman 1992: 583). In addition, from the early 1980s on, annual bonuses, sometimes in the form of profit sharing or plant-level incentive components, increasingly were being introduced through firm-level collective bargaining (Erickson and Ichino 1995: 275). A further stimulus for performance-based pay was provided by the July 1993 agreement between Confindustria and the confederal unions, which specified that any wage increases provided in company-level bargaining had to be financed through productivity increases or performance improvements. The 1993 agreement followed the abolition of the cost-of-living increases provided through the *scala mobile* (Locke and Bacarro 1996: 12). Furthermore, social security taxes (paid by employers) are partially subsidized where contingent pay schemes are adopted.

One of the most well-publicized recent examples of increased union and worker involvement in decision making, in this case through joint bodies, occurred at Zanussi (a white-goods multinational owned by Swedish Eelctrolux and employing fifteen thousand workers) (EIRR 1992b: 16–17). A "worker-friendly" approach to labor relations was introduced in 1991, and joint committees were established to deal with such issues as work organization, new technology, and job classifications. After a breakdown on negotiations concerning layoffs in 1996, the company terminated the joint committees. Then, in September 1997, the company concluded an agreement with the various unions representing employees to reinstate and solidify the participatory process through the adoption of binding rules and procedures. A key provision in the new rules provides for an external arbitrator to resolve any disputes that might arise in the future concerning the participation framework (EIRR 1997b). The participatory process helped produce an innovative deal between Zanussi and its Italian unions that excludes Italian operations from the parent company's global restructuring plans; in exchange, the Italian unions accepted a series of productivity-enhancing work organization and working-time changes (EIRR 1998b).

Like events at Zanussi, other Italian participatory experiments experienced periods of strain or, in some cases, failed outright. Even the well-publicized IRI protocol confronted implementation problems and labor-management disagreements (Ferner and Hyman 1992: 567). However, these experiments have included a system of work similar to the joint team-based pattern (see column 4 of Figure 1.1).

Although employee and union involvement was generally on the rise outside the low-wage sector in Italy, there were also cases, such as Fiat in the early 1980s (discussed below), where management attempted to gain more unilateral say over the workplace rather than enhance union involvement. Locke (1995: 103–35), for example, contrasts the involvement in workplace restructuring unions developed at Alfa Romeo in the early 1980s with Fiat management's efforts to bypass and exclude unions during the same period.

As in other countries, managers' efforts to deal with employees more extensively on an individual basis expanded in Italy from the early 1980s on, in part through more elaborate direct communication methods. Italian efforts to promote individualized employee relations differ from related efforts in the United States and United Kingdom because in Italy, as Regalia and Regini note, "Attempts to develop a network of direct employer/employee relations based on direct communications policies and quality circles increased, but in the end they complemented traditional collective relations and did not substitute for them" (1995: 159). Ferner and Hyman also report that "direct employee involvement, bypassing the unions, is rare in Italian firms...and this strategy has been adopted only in subsidiaries of a handful of foreign multinational firms" (1992: 586).[28]

## EMPLOYMENT RELATIONS IN THE ITALIAN AUTO INDUSTRY

The Italian auto industry has less employment variation than the U.S. auto industry because nonunion and Japanese-oriented employment patterns are less common. At the same time, there have been significant changes in the locus and tenor of labor-management interactions and strongly contested modifications in pay and other work practices in the industry since the early 1980s.

The dominant automobile producer in Italy is Fiat Auto, which in 1982 had a 12.5 percent share of Western European auto sales and a 71 percent share of Italian auto sales (Altshuler et al. 1984: 167). As a result, our discussion of auto employment relations must include developments in Fiat. In the early and mid-1980s, the strength of the three confederal unions, which had traditionally exercised substantial influence within Fiat, was eroded by managerial efforts to gain control over the right to lay off workers and direct the shop floor. Furthermore, at Fiat, as in other parts of Italy, the confederal unions faced a representation crisis in this period as a result of the growth of autonomous unions (the so-called sindacati autonomi) and COBAS, which provided alternative and often militant collective forms of employee representation. The low point for unionism at Fiat came in 1980 with the "march of the 40,000," in a return to work that defied union leaders who had opposed Fiat management's efforts to lay off a sizable number of workers (Camuffo and Volpato 1994: 5; Locke 1995: 109). In the aftermath of the workers' return to work in 1980, management adopted personnel policies that attempted to move toward an individualized relationship with employees and bypass the unions and collective procedures. Union density at Fiat declined from 32.5 percent in 1980 to 20.5 percent in 1986; "bilateral industrial relations" declined along with union membership ( Locke 1995: 115).

In the mid-1980s, as the firm's economic fortunes recovered, production strategy at Fiat shifted to a focus on the "automated factory," epitomized in the high degree of automation implemented at the restructured Cassino assembly plant. Management became particularly concerned with enhancing internal firm flexibility, in part to satisfy growing demand. To management's surprise, however, problems arose in this automation drive. Fiat came to doubt the wisdom of relying so extensively on technology and began to recognize the need for workplace policies that enhanced the commitment of the workforce toward quality and flexibility objectives. The production strategy of Fiat then shifted, in 1990, toward the integrated factory concept, which attempts to create a decentralized system of production management involving workers and unions in a broad array of decision making and thereby to a large extent reverse concepts promoted through Fiat's earlier efforts to regain unilateral authority and reliance on automation.

The key element of the integrated factory is the elementary technical unit (UTE), a manufacturing cell that governs a segment of the production process (Camuffo and Volpato 1994: 10). In the UTE, direct and indirect labor are supposed to work in a flexible manner to identify and solve problems quickly (EIRR 1993c: 10). The UTE are much larger than the work teams found commonly in other countries' auto industry and vary in size from twenty to seventy workers. The UTE include a key new position of integrated process conductors (in final assembly) and operators (in other work areas). These integrated process conductors/operators help coordinate and facilitate problem solving, but these individuals are not given hierarchical authority (i.e., they are not supervisors). The UTE are not intended to be self-directed units, although the role of supervisors and their links to the integrated conductors/operators remain to be clearly defined.

In addition to the UTE, a wide variety of other worker and union participation processes and work reorganizations have been attempted at Fiat's plants in recent years. There is also extensive variation both within and across Fiat's plants in the depth and nature of the changes occurring. In some plants, such as Rivalta, little decentralized decision making appears to be emerging, whereas at Melfi and some other plants, the movement away from traditional labor-management practices is more extensive (Camuffo and Volpato 1994: 20–21). There are also differences in the way the UTE and other team systems operate across Fiat's plants. For example, Cassino has frequent formal meetings of the UTE teams, while Melfi has are more informal and spontaneous UTE meetings (Camuffo and Volpato 1997). The UTE and other participatory processes have produced a work system with many similarities to the joint team-based pattern, despite the size and unique organizational structure of the teams.

As a sign of Fiat's management's desire to re-establish a strong and reliable role for trade unions, the 1996–2000 Fiat labor agreement was negotiated directly by the various unions that represent workers at Fiat. The RSU were asked only to approve the new agreement.[29]

The agreement created a more elaborate structure for participatory activities. In each of Fiat's "sectors" there will be five joint committees with consultation rights dealing with, among other things, the performance and prospects within each respective sector. At the level of the individual production units, in addition, six joint bodies will be created to consider issues such as quality, training, and "lean production" (EIRR 1996e).

With regard to pay, a new form of variation was introduced at Fiat through the adoption of the Premio Performance Gruppo (PPG) in the 1988 firm-level collective agreement. The PPG has, in fact, remained a fairly small part of total worker compensation. Like the contingent compensation schemes adopted in other countries, the PPG has been the source of some labor-management conflict, as the unions at Fiat have disputed the calculation methods used in the PPG bonus (EIRR 1990: 9). From 1988 to 1993, the PPG payment was nearly constant (at around 1,350,000 lire, which is slightly less than 3 percent of total labor costs) (Camuffo and Volpato 1994: 24). The labor agreement also expanded the range of variation in the performance and added two additional bonus elements, one tied to the group return on investment and the other based on two product-quality indices (EIRR 1996e).

Individual bonuses, merit pay, and pay for performance are also used at Fiat, although they represent a small fraction of worker compensation. These elements of the pay package for blue-collar workers depend on performance appraisals (Camuffo and Volpato 1994: 25). The extent of performance-based pay, like team working, varies across plants. Compensation at the Melfi and Pratola Serra plants is linked more extensively to performance than is the case at other Fiat plants (Camuffo and Volpato 1997).

Following the terms of a tripartite central accord reached in July 1993, collective bargaining in the broad metalworking sector (including the auto industry) in 1993 and 1996 included two interrelated levels—sectoral agreements and company or local deals (EIRR 1997a: 9). The June 1996 sectoral agreement (that ran until December 1998) came only after the federal government made a final "take it or leave it" offer (9). Trying to encourage spread of the sort of contingent pay provided at Fiat, the 1996–1998 sectoral agreement stated that pay increases at the company level could only be a result of agreements linked to company performance.

In the late 1980s and early 1990s, the confederal unions experienced a substantial recovery in their influence, and the unions' role has been altered most where participatory processes blossomed. Union density rose from the late 1980s on to the point that in some plants, such as Cassino and Rivalta, density in 1992 was above 1980 levels (Camuffo and Volpato 1994: Figure 26). It is interesting to note that union density varies substantially across Fiat's plants, from a high of 65 percent at Pomigliano to 35 percent at Mirafiori (in 1992) (Camuffo and Volpato 1994: Figure 25).

Across Fiat's plants, work organization and worker and union roles vary substantially. This variation has much in common with auto plants across the other countries we analyzed. At the same time, the Italian auto industry lacks the HRM or low-wage and Japanese-oriented employment practices found in many other countries.

## EMPLOYMENT RELATIONS IN THE ITALIAN TELECOMMUNICATIONS INDUSTRY

In response to corporate and industry restructuring, employment relations in the Italian telecommunications industry have been changing significantly. However, compared to its counterparts in other countries (but like the Italian auto industry), the Italian telecommunications industry contains a relatively narrow range of employment patterns. Yet, even though employment outcomes span a relatively narrow range, the process of labor-management interactions within the highly unionized industry has been changing in ways very similar to trends in other countries.

The dominant provider of telecommunications services in Italy (and a major provider of telecommunications equipment) is Telecom Italia, a government-owned company.[30] Like other large telecommunications companies around the world, Telecom Italia has undergone substantial reorganization over the past ten years. In 1992, for example, a multidivisional structure, with six business divisions, was adopted. The firm's restructuring has been noteworthy due to the gradual movement toward privatization, the fact that total employment expanded in the company in recent years, and the heavy involvement union representatives have played in discussions surrounding corporate reorganizations.

Although there is talk about future privatization of the company and some small steps giving wider access to the Italian telecommunications market to other firms, Telecom Italia retains monopoly control over substantial segments of the home telecommunications market. As a result, in contrast to the large downsizing at the former telecommunications monopolists in the United States, United Kingdom, and many other countries, employment at Telecom Italia actually grew from 1980 to 1993 (Negrelli 1997: 311). Yet, unsure of what the future would hold, the three confederal unions representing Telecom employees in 1992 negotiated a no-layoff guarantee and an agreement providing a modest number of early retirements (1,500) and employee transfers (Negrelli 1997: 311–14).

The confederal unions represent 60 percent of the employees, and their membership has declined only slightly over the past ten years. Professional and technical employees are represented by unions (with separate collective agreements), and there has been growth in professional associations in recent years (Negrelli 1997: 315). Telecom Italia has generally followed the cooperative and participatory spirit of the IRI protocol (in part because of the firm's formal membership in the IRI group). This has contributed to the spread and broadening of joint consultative committees. Management has sought to complement collective negotiations with direct communications, but as at other Italian firms, this has not jeopardized the influence of trade unions.

Various experiments with team work and multiskilling have been launched over the past ten years, although the use of a formal team system remains fairly modest. Wage bargaining has followed the general Italian pattern, with a heavy role played by the *scala mobile* in the 1980s and a mixture of industry and company-level wage bargaining after 1993. A productivity bonus was introduced in 1986 (as part of a multiyear "collective labor agreement"), which varied between 3.09 percent of contractual pay in 1993 and a high of 6.07 percent of pay in 1989. Overall then, variation in employment relations has been limited in the Italian telecommunications industry and is much less than that appearing in the countries analyzed in this volume.

## Income Distribution Trends In Italy

The strong continuing role played by unions and collective negotiations helped Italy avoid the pressures for income inequality that have been so dominant in other advanced industrial economies since 1980. In contrast to many other countries, in Italy, over the past twenty years there has been a weak trend toward greater income equality (at least in the regular sectors of the economy) (Erickson and Ichino 1995). This equality trend appeared even though Italy's income distribution has been relatively equal. Before 1982, in fact, the extensive automatic cost-of-living increases provided in the *scala mobile* (along with high inflation and the wide coverage of the *scala mobile*) substantially compressed earnings across skill levels within Italian enterprises. The equalizing effects of the *scala mobile* (at least until 1992) offset disequalizing pressures produced by individual superminimum pay increases determined unilaterally (and applied individually) by management and other factors, such as the expansion of performance-related pay that might have otherwise made income distribution trends in Italy more similar to those in other countries (Erickson and Ichino 1995: 282–83).

## SUMMARY OF ITALIAN DEVELOPMENTS

In the face of the variation appearing in Italian firms' employment relations and production strategies Locke claims that the "Italian economy should *not* be viewed as a coherent 'national system' but rather as a somewhat incoherent composite of diverse subnational patterns that coexist (often uneasily) within the same national territory" (1995: 174). His insightful analysis describes how corporate and union strategic choices and the local context in which firms and unions are embedded influenced the evolution of employment relations.

Persistent variation in employment practices is made possible by the lack of a single production strategy (and associated employment practices) that has clear performance advantages. As a result, as Locke notes, "Societies that want to produce industrial goods competitively are not restricted to a single organizational structure or pattern of relations. Instead, production can be organized in several different ways, using different mixes of technology, skills, and organization" (1995: 173). The wide space for organizational and employment system variation found in Italy is similar to the space we noted earlier in the United States and other countries, for in all these countries no production or employment relations strategy is clearly superior. Locke's argument about the inappropriateness of a national system applies to Italy and is even more fitting with regard to other countries.

While the variation appearing across Italian firms in workplace and production reorganization is quite large when compared to early periods in Italy (and may well call into question the appropriateness of national models of industrial relations), as compared to some of the other countries analyzed in this book, Italy nevertheless has less variation in employment patterns particularly because it lacks nonunion HRM and Japanese-oriented patterns.

## LESSONS FROM THE THREE COUNTRIES

Even with wide differences in their traditional structure of collective bargaining and distinctive labor market traditions, in Japan, Sweden, and Italy employment practices are changing in ways that have many commonalities with the trends we analyzed earlier. Perhaps the most significant commonality is that the same four key patterns of employment described in Figure 1.1 are growing in each country. This and other commonalities appear even though the three countries have distinctive traditional characteristics of employment relations, including the heavy enterprise (decentralized) focus in Japan and the contrasting heavy centralization found in traditional Swedish collective bargaining.

At the same time, trends in these three countries reveal the important influence of existing labor market institutions as these institutions shape how and the extent to which variation is appearing in each country. For example, in Italy and Sweden, the continuing strength of labor unions and labor laws have limited expansion in employment patterns that exclude union representation. Consequently, while HRM practices that bear many similarities to those found in other countries are spreading in Italy and Sweden, these work practices usually are complementing, not replacing, collective-bargaining procedures. Thus, institutions are influencing the distinctive country-specific traits in the pace and nature of employment-pattern diffusion.

In Japan, the nonunion sector is spreading, even in the telecommunications industry. Nevertheless, Japanese institutions have exerted their influence by limiting low-wage employment in the private sector as the traditional Japanese (private sector) pattern of employment relations continues to dominate. The institutions differ in Sweden, but there as well the growth of low-wage employment practices has been relatively limited.

In Italy and Sweden, significant variation has emerged in work organization, including diversity in the use and form of team systems. Worker and union participation in business decision making is expanding, although the depth and consequences of that involvement vary much across and within firms. In Japan, the continuing dominance of an employment pattern that already included a strong role for work groups and shop floor-level worker participation has limited the diffusion of new practices. As is the case else-where, unions in the three countries are having a difficult time responding to the growth of nonunion practices as well as the changes in union roles implied by the spread of more participatory work organization.

Across employment patterns in the three countries the use of contingent and individualized pay has grown in a manner that bears many similarities with developments in other countries. Like the other countries, the three have wide variety in the form of those pay procedures, and unions are hav-ing a difficult time adjusting to the variation in earnings appearing across and within firms through the diffusion of these procedures (particularly in Sweden).

The spread of contingent and more individualized pay has contributed to increased income inequality in the three countries. At the same time, the relatively modest diffusion of new employment patterns has helped to pro-duce relatively modest increases in income inequality, especially when com-pared to developments in the United States.

So, with very different starting points, especially with regard to the degree to which collective bargaining has been centrally determined, Japan, Italy, and Sweden exhibit the growing internal variation ("divergences") com-mon to the other four countries we have examined. Developments in Japan, Italy, and Sweden also show that institutions continue to modify the extent and form of the growing within national employment systems. Next, we as-sess these "converging divergences."

NOTES

1. As discussed below, Japan does not have a purely decentralized collective-bargaining structure (in its private sector) given the influence of the annual spring offensive, through which heavy pattern following links wage determination across enterprises.

2. We do not report on developments in the Swedish telecommunications sector given our limited access to that sector and limited available materials in English.

3. The functioning of the performance assessment (satei) system for blue-collar workers is described in Endo (1994).

4. The relatively strong and extensive roles played by supervisors in Japan is em-phasized in Shibata (1995).

5. Group complaints, in contrast to individual complaints, tend to be resolved through the enterprise union (see Shibata [1995: 192–95]).

6. There is no comprehensive survey of work practices in Japan of the sort found in the United Kingdom and Australia, which are discussed elsewhere in this volume.

7. The standard pay components include pay for ability (based on individual per-formance appraisal), pay for age, and skill-based pay grades.

8.   In the 1960s and 1970s, Japanese auto assemblers made extensive use of temporary employees not on regular status (Streeck and Katz 1984).

9.   The JAW's position was expressed in an interview with Mr. Yuji Kato, assistant general secretary, JAW, October 6, 1995, Tokyo, Japan. Mr. Kato also confirmed the findings reported in the paper by Matsumura discussed above. Mr. Kato estimates that the relative importance of age and ability at the company shifted, respectively, from 8:2 to 6:4 in 1992.

10.   Japanese auto assemblers tend to source parts from a smaller number of suppliers while maintaining more dedicated relationships with those suppliers (Cusumano 1985).

11.   For a highly informative analysis of working life at a Japanese auto parts plant, see Cole (1971).

12.   At one point, personal assessments had been tried at NTT, but they were discontinued after worker and union complaints.

13.   Job-control unionism is defined in Kochan, Katz, and McKersie (1994).

14.   Gaining the right to engage in free collective bargaining over wages was one of the key reasons JTWU supported the privatization of NTT (Nakamura and Hiraki 1997).

15.   Within-firm pay differentials and career paths in Japan are examined and compared to those in the United States in Brown et al. (1997: 106–15).

16.   "From the early 1970s until the erosion of central bargaining in the early 1980s the variances of log frame wages exhibit the same pronounced downward trend as the dispersions registered in the market" (Hibbs 1990: 75).

17.   Edin and Holmlund (1995: 332) find that the role of industry-specific factors in wage setting rose in the 1990s, as indicated by the increasing importance of variables such as lagged industry profits in estimated wage equations.

18.   This agreement was also noteworthy because for the first time in the postwar period, no extra money was set aside for distribution to the lowest-paid workers.

19.   Clearly, the unions' temporary unity was motivated by their interest in avoiding full-fledged company-level bargaining.

20.   For evidence on the spread of profit sharing and stock ownership also see Kjellberg (1992: 108); Pontusson and Swenson (1996: 21).

21.   The Uddevalla plant was subsequently reopened to produce a specialty vehicle in a joint effort with a British investor.

22.   This deskilling may have been influenced by sectoral shifts in the composition of employment (Pontusson 1997: 22).

23.   As Ferner and Hyman (1992: 543) note, "For almost all its existence the Italian trade union movement has been ideologically divided."

24.   Evidence regarding stabilization and some sign of union membership rejuvenation, at least in the auto industry, is provided in Camuffo and Volpato (1994) and is discussed earlier in the auto section of this chapter.

25.   See EIRR (1992c: 17) for a description of the union and employee representation rights provided in the Workers Statute Law.

26.   Amin (1989) contrasts the sweatshop firms with those in two other segments of this industry ("modern small factories and craft firms") that respect the wage and working standards provided in national industry contracts and employ legally registered workers.

27.   At the same time, variable pay represents only 4.2 percent of blue-collar workers' pay and 5 percent of white-collar workers' pay. The survey finds that variable pay schemes are mainly in large and medium-sized firms in the north and central regions of Italy (EIRR 1996d: 22).

28.   Drawing from a study of engineering firms, Galeone concludes that "while one may observe a growing [employer] attention to human resource management, this does not involve a strategy of deunionization, does not appear to narrow the scope for union action, and does not come into direct conflict with union interests" (quoted in Ferner and Hyman 1992: 586).

29.   The leaders of the FIOM, the union representing the largest number of employees at Fiat, initially refused to sign the new labor agreement on the basis of their opposition to the participatory approach and their expectation that no performance bonuses would be paid in the near future, given the severe downturn occurring in the Italian car market. Eventually, the FIOM general secretary, reportedly under pressure from the CGIL confederal secretariat, signed the agreement (EIRR 1996e).

30.   Telecom Italia's financial affairs are overseen by STET, a financial holding company in the IRI group of public-sector companies.

# 7

## Summary: Increased Variations within Countries but Similarities across Countries

*[handwritten margin note: employment relations vs. employment systems]*

This book has described the evolution of employment systems in Australia, Germany, Italy, Japan, Sweden, the United Kingdom, and the United States, with a particular focus on the automobile and telecommunications industries. We find increasing variation in employment practices in all the countries and many commonalities in the nature of the variation appearing within the seven countries. The former is producing growing divergences in employment relations within countries, while the latter is leading to a convergence in employment systems across countries. A common set of patterns of workplace practices can be utilized to describe recent employment system changes in the seven countries.

Although the patterns we identify do not precisely define the components of employment systems among which choices are necessarily made, they represent significant analytical commonalities in workplace practices. At the same time, a greater variety of the work practices is being used *within* the various employment patterns (as in the wide variety of team systems of work organization that are being adopted), and variation also is being produced through individualized and contingent work practices, such as contingent compensation. Nonetheless, in all seven countries we observe similar changes in labor-management interactions, including a decentralization of bargaining structures and greater informality in labor-management interactions.

*[handwritten margin note: Implications?]*

The variation in work practices and employment relations has contributed to variation in employment outcomes, including income inequality. Our research finds that countries that have relatively wide variation in employment patterns also exhibit more substantial inequality in their in-

263

*correlation*

come distribution and larger recent increases in income inequality. Although other economic forces are clearly at work, our research suggests a link between the structure of employment systems and labor market outcomes.

Our research also broadens the analysis of growing inequality beyond income by examining the increased variation appearing in a wide range of work practices. Furthermore, diversity in employment systems is altering the roles of unions and management. In this chapter, then, our task is to clarify the problems created for unions and management by growing variation within employment systems.

Alongside the forces producing growing variation, country-specific labor market structures and institutions continue to play a critical role in shaping employment systems. In particular, labor laws, including any codetermination requirements, and other institutions heavily influence the distribution of various workplace practices, such as the extent to which nonunion patterns are spreading. In addition, cross-national differences exist in the exact nature and meaning of these patterns. These differences are apparent where institutions such as works councils, tribunals, or the organization of the shop-steward system vary the relationship between management and labor.

Country-specific institutions also continue to matter much in that the workplace patterns have complemented and not replaced existing institutional arrangements. As a result, to understand how employment relations evolve in any country, it is necessary to understand how new workplace patterns interact with long-standing institutional practices and structures. That is, existing institutions provide different constraints and in different ways shape new workplace practices. Relevant institutional influences include not only the firm-level organization of employee representation and their rights but similarly the structure of unions and employers' associations, and such labor-market structures as training systems.

It is thus, in part, the nature of how national institutions complement and affect the distribution of emerging underlying employment patterns that produces cross-national variation. In this respect, variation consists of a differing distribution among patterns. Furthermore, as the country chapters illustrate, there are also some systemic differences in the precise form and nature of the employment patterns, even given the underlying cross-national commonality in the emerging work-practice patterns.

While these trends in employment systems are especially evident in the key auto and telecommunications industries (which entered the 1980s with relatively high rates of unionization), similar trends prevail in other industries in all seven countries. Factors that have contributed to the growing variation in work practices include an increase in managerial bargaining power;

the pressure for a reorganization of work to improve cost and quality performance but a corresponding uncertainty regarding the economic performance effects of various work practices; the decentralized nature of work restructuring, which has promoted local solutions to production problems; and increasingly flexible and informal bargaining processes through which new work patterns are introduced.

The specific source of economic pressure differs across countries and industries. In some cases, international competitive pressures are most important; in other cases, privatization or deregulation is relatively stronger. Yet, the specific source of economic pressure does not appear to be decisive. Convergent processes and outcomes are apparent in the face of differing specific economic pressures.

An important distinction with this analysis and more usual debates of convergence is that we do not observe firms striving for a single "best practice" model of work organization. Certainly, neither technology nor broader production systems are demonstrably or clearly superior. Economic forces are of substantial importance in motivating economic actors, though uncertainty, experimentation, and differing choices underlie the growth of employment system variation.

Related to this, the role of national-level institutions is more complex and diverse than simply preventing or facilitating the achievement of a "best practice" model. It is not that institutions simply "outweigh" or modify economic forces, nor is it that only other restrictions on market forces prevent convergence to a single model of the organization of production. Rather, national institutional structures affect the distribution of choice among potentially equally viable employment patterns in an uncertain environment, as well as shaping the exact nature of those patterns. Both factors produce national differences in employment patterns.

## The Changing Nature of Employment Systems

A common set of workplace practice patterns can be used to compare the evolving nature of employment systems. In all countries, low-wage, human resource management, Japanese-oriented, and joint team-based patterns of workplace practices are spreading. These patterns (see Figure 1.1) describe clusters of workplace practices that appear across firms in part because the various practices that make up each pattern reinforce one another.

Across workplace practice patterns and across countries, common changes are also appearing in the structure and process of employment relations, including a decentralization in the locus of labor-management in-

*decentralization of wage bargaining =
plant/company level
bargaining.*

teractions. In the United Kingdom, the United States, and Sweden, decentralization has entailed a decline in collective bargaining at the multiemployer level and an increase in company- and plant-level bargaining. Even where formal structures of bargaining have not changed in these countries, the strength of pattern bargaining has weakened as company- (and increasingly plant-) level variation is emerging in pay and working conditions.

In Germany and Japan, in contrast, the formal bargaining structure has not been decentralized because these countries already had relatively decentralized structures for workplace change, while adjustments within existing structures are allowing increased variation in pay and other labor market outcomes. Yet, even in Germany, there has been massive decentralization *inside* existing institutional structures, as works councils have played an increasingly important role in determining basic employment conditions. And in Japan, the enterprise unions, particularly in the auto industry, have increasingly taken on a mediating role between workers on the shop floor and corporate management in facilitating workplace adjustments. In Italy, earlier formal decentralization of collective bargaining structures has been partially reversed in recent years.

Nevertheless, in all countries (including Italy), a downward shift in the locus of employment relations is being driven by a decentralization in corporate structures, work reorganizations, and greater direct participation of employees in production and business decision making.

Another important change in the structure and processes of employment relations across and within the seven countries is an increase in direct communication between employees and management. More direct employer-employee communication has been associated with the more decentralized production methods being adopted at many work sites.

In addition, management at many plants has utilized more direct communication with employees as part of the more informal and more continuous negotiation being adopted as an alternative to traditional arms-length forms of labor-management relations. Enhanced direct communication is also linked to the work restructuring that is occurring including the use of team systems of work organization and other techniques for settling production problems and disputes more quickly on the shop floor. In the process of communicating its case more directly with employees, management has been either circumventing existing union-related negotiation structures or creating alternatives to union representation (such as individual contracts). The latter is particularly evident at work sites with human resource management work practices.

Management has favored most of the changes occurring in employment relations processes and structures, although management has not always gained as much as they had hoped through these changes. For example, management has promoted more decentralized collective bargaining, both as a mechanism to whipsaw unions where the contract is not held by the central union and because decentralized collective bargaining fits with recent decentralizations in corporate structures and strategies, including objectives for changing the structure of work organization.

Nevertheless, more decentralized collective bargaining has not always proven to be advantageous to management, particularly in environments where subsequent bargaining power shifts have strengthened labor's hand.

## TYPES OF EMPLOYMENT SYSTEM VARIATION

### Cross-Country Variation

While there are many commonalities in the work practices that make up the key employment patterns spreading across countries, the relative proportion of the different workplace patterns and the extent to which these patterns operate on a nonunion basis, vary greatly. In the United States and the United Kingdom, and to a lesser degree in some of the other countries, the low-wage, human resource management, and Japanese-oriented workplace practice patterns operate in a nonunion context. In this way, growing employment system variation is linked to declines in the fraction of the workforce represented by unions.

Country-specific institutions also influence the mix of workplace practice patterns and the degree of unionization. For example, German regulations that can extend the terms of negotiated-framework collective bargaining agreements to firms that are not members of the relevant employers' association have helped limit the growth in low-wage and nonunion employment patterns. Furthermore, the legal rights of German works councils have contributed to the relatively high degree of standardization in complaint resolution procedures and the structure of employee representation. As a result, for example, the sort of variation found across U.S. auto transplants in grievance procedures, or the different bargaining roles played by company councils at Nissan and Toyota in the United Kingdom, are not issues in Germany. Likewise, in Germany the rights of works councils means less variation in the information employee representatives receive at either the plant or company level. In Australia, the political strength of the labor movement and the continuing importance of a national wage tribunal system similarly has served to limit the growth of low-wage employment.

Although it is not always obvious how labor market or regulatory institutions exert their influence, the outcomes are rather striking. For example, in the United States, substantial inroads have been made by nonunion Japanese transplants in the auto assembly sector, whereas in Australia all auto assembly transplants remain unionized. In Italy and Sweden, even though the work practices that fit the human resource management pattern are spreading, these practices are complementing collective procedures because of existing institutions and the continuing strength of the labor movement, and they are not associated with the spread of nonunion employment relationships. While it remains to be seen if institutions continue to constrain to such a high degree the spread of nonunion employment relationships in Italy, Sweden, and Germany, to date these institutions have clearly strengthened unions in the latter countries, especially in contrast to developments in the English-speaking countries.

The patterns of workplace practices outlined in Figure 1.1 typically complement pay, work organization, bargaining structure, and many other employment policies and practices that affect employment relations and labor-market outcomes in each country. This is one of the ways that existing country-specific labor market structures and institutions critically affect employment systems. For example, the joint team-based pattern of work practices operates very differently and has very different consequences for labor and management in Germany versus other countries because of the important role exerted by the German dual system of employee representation.

There is less variation in the degree to which employees are integrated into plant-level decision making and the extent of business information received by workers in Germany as compared to the other countries in our study. At the same time, in the 1990s in Germany, the ability of unions and works councils to constrain management strategies on team working and other workplace issues declined in the face of greater use of plant-level agreements on working time, the reorganization of work, job security, and pay. Increased variation in the extent of plant-by-plant and within-plant variation in work practices has followed in Germany in a manner similar to developments in other countries.

Another example of the role played by existing institutions as a factor influencing variation in employment systems comes from Australia, where enterprise agreements have played a key role in shifting the locus of collective bargaining downward. Although enterprise agreements have brought major changes to employee-employer relations, these agreements are complementing, not replacing, the wage tribunal system.

It is also noteworthy that when Australian managers have tried to emulate the aggressive tactics exhibited by their American and British counterparts to dislodge or weaken unions, the Australian Industrial Relations Commission has constrained these managerial efforts. At the least, interventions to date by the commission have maintained a role for employee votes over the course of employment relations and for continued national review of employment standards (through application of a no-disadvantage test). In the end, Australia has experienced much more limited growth of low-wage workplace practices as compared to the United States and the United Kingdom.

### *Within-Country Variation*

A key source of variation within each country are differences in the detailed policies that implement particular work-practice patterns. For example, our analysis of the evolution of auto employment relations reveals wide variation in the systems being adopted as part of the joint team-based pattern. Among other things, differences appear across plants and even within plants in the methods used to select team leaders and in the roles and responsibilities of team leaders and team members. The roles of team leaders, for example, vary much across auto plants in the United States, Germany, and Italy. Another example of within-pattern work-practice variation are the differences in the particular policies being adopted to promote individualized career development as part of the human resource management pattern.

Variation within countries also is growing from work practices that vary increasingly across individuals; pay outcome variation is also being spurred by the spread of contingent pay procedures. There is much interaction across these various practices, illustrated in the way that individualized rewards are often linked to the expansion of contingent compensation payment methods. In the British and Australian telecommunications industries, for example, individualization of employment relations has been promoted in the ranks of senior managers through individual contracts that replace traditional collectively negotiated contracts. This practice is expanding to include all managers and even some sections of the nonmanagerial workforce, as the use of contingent pay grows. The trend is likewise evident in Germany.

Contingent compensation is spreading in all seven countries, although there is wide variation in the form and extent. Contingent pay is particularly evident in the auto industries of all countries, as the share of worker compensation that is set through annual bonuses, pay for knowledge, or payments linked to individual assessments has risen in recent years. In Japan, for example, variation in the annual bonuses received by auto workers at the primary auto assemblers has increased sizably in recent years. In the United States, across the Big Three auto assemblers, where hourly pay had long been standardized, from the mid-1980s on, annual pay has varied substantially as a result of variation in company profit-sharing payouts and also varied within companies through variation in pay for knowledge plans. In Sweden, where auto worker unions had long resisted performance-based compensation schemes, there is a recent expansion in the use of contingent (and more individualized) pay procedures, as in Italy. The trend is similar in Germany, where, in particular, emerging differences in pay among companies are a result of concession bargaining as firms' performance levels vary, and as works councils negotiate company-level employment security clauses.

### Institutional Influences on the Degree of Variation within Countries

Institutionally, at least three broad factors influence the extent of variation in work practices appearing within countries. The first concerns the direct, centralized determination of outcomes, for example, by national unions and employers' associations. This has traditionally included either the use of central contracts (as in Sweden) or strong pattern bargaining (as in Japan's spring offensive) to prescribe a common set of employment conditions and to establish narrow framework agreements within which firm-level variation could occur. Australia's award system has long provided a distinctive form of centralized wage determination. Whatever its form, by directly determining outcomes (including taking wages out of competition), centralization thus had a direct impact on employment system variation.

A second institutional influence concerns the similarity of process (and power) that, on a decentralized level, is used to establish the pattern of employment practices within plants. The greater the similarity in labor-management interaction at the plant level and the narrower the range of power differences among plants, the greater the commonality of outcomes. Although similar forms of a decentralized process of labor-management interaction can be set in collective bargaining at a centralized level, the determination of the decentralized process can equally be established through other means, such as in Germany, where legislation plays a key role. In Italy, to cite another example, the interrelationship between industrial-level and local-level collective bargaining has been guided by a tripartite accord. Thus, the centralized determination of outcomes and the decentralized commonality of processes are distinct though frequently interrelated elements.

The degree of effective coordination among decentralized bargaining structures, and among strategies adopted at the local level, provide a third limitation on variation. This limitation is particularly applicable where, for example, structures of employee representation and union organization facilitate coordination and integration of local actors into broader (national) policy choices. In general terms, such intraplant coordination is relatively high in German and Japan but relatively low in the United States and the United Kingdom.

Thus, a combination of centralization, the commonality of decentralized processes and power, and the active coordination of local actors can constrain the extent of variation. The role of national institutions differs not simply in the extent to which they produce centralized outcomes but also in the extent to which they limit variation in the process and power of labor-management interaction and how they facilitate coordination, especially where bargaining occurs increasingly on a decentralized basis.

Other significant changes in employment relations across all seven countries are the decline in the central determination of outcomes and also a growing flexibility, decentralized variation, and informality in the process of labor-management interaction. For interrelated reasons, decentralization of collective bargaining in the countries analyzed has consisted of a decline in the role of multiemployer bargaining (as illustrated by developments in the United Kingdom), the increased use of more broadly constituted framework agreements (as in Italy, Sweden, and Germany), and also more flexible and less formal processes of labor-management relations at the plant level (in all countries). Yet, despite the common trend in this direction, national institutional structures play an important role not only in the extent of decentralization but also in the range of decentralized processes of bargaining and the ability of unions and employee representatives to coordinate across these decentralized structures. These institutional differences help account for the differences in the degree of variation in the employment patterns across the countries analyzed.

The range of employment system variation apparent in Germany, for example, is narrower not simply because the unions have been more successful in retaining centralized bargaining structures and limiting the scope of framework agreements. Of comparable significance are the legally specified structures, such as works councils, that prevent a wide diversity in the labor-management interaction, even on a decentralized basis. The strength and rights of employee representatives means that even nonunion patterns cannot carry the same implications in Germany as in either the United States or United Kingdom, for example. Works councils protect a degree of independent employee representation even without unions and thus limit the possible range of outcomes. Furthermore, both the inclusive structure of German unions and their close relations with works councils, help produce more tightly coordinated strategies. The role of employers' associations in diffusing "best-practice" work models and coordinating the policies of employers similarly helps retain common outcomes.

The United Kingdom and the United States provide stronger contrasts. The voluntaristic nature of employment relations in the United Kingdom means that the decline of multiemployer bargaining both removed a centralized force on outcomes and also facilitated a greater range of decentralized bargaining processes. The fragmented and largely decentralized structure of unions further inhibited the possibility of coordinating strategies among firms. Again, in contrast to Germany, in the United Kingdom, where unions are not present, the absence of mandated forms of employee representation compounds the extent of variation. Unions in the United States have similarly had difficulty coordinating across union locals, let alone across national unions themselves. Yet even where unions play a strong role at the local level, the processes of labor-management interaction vary greatly, and coordination is frequently weak.

### Factors Contributing to Within-Country Employment Variation

In part, the growing variation in employment systems within countries has resulted from a shift in bargaining power in management's favor, at the same time as management has been under pressure to reorganize work practices. These factors combined have led management to push for changes in labor-management relations and for workplace restructuring. The shift in relative power is also illustrated in the key patterns of workplace practices outlined in Figure 1.1, which frequently operate on a nonunion basis. The continuing growth in nonunion work sites is clearly associated with a decline in union power.

Although nonunion growth is most extreme in the United States and the United Kingdom, sizable nonunion growth also is occurring in Japan and Australia. In the auto and telecommunications industries, nonunion operations have been growing most significantly in the parts or supplier segments of those industries. Yet, even in the core segments of those two industries (respectively, auto assembly and network services), in most of the countries we analyze new nonunion firms now challenge the large unionized firms that traditionally dominated.

Within the unionized sector, one of the key ways bargaining power has been affecting the variation in employment systems is through management-led whipsawing of plants (and local unions). Management bargaining leverage is greater where there are alternative production sites and the production process allows a separation of the various aspects of production. For example, management has gained concessions from auto workers where it can outsource the production of a part or operation, particularly where a low-wage, nonunion supplier is available. This sort of outsourcing has proven to be more difficult although increasingly available in the telecommunications services sector, where management-led whipsawing is constrained by the need to coordinate service provision along the basic telephone network. As this book describes, where management is gaining whipsaw leverage, a wide variety of concessions are emerging, and the ensuing variation in work practices is often linked to work restructuring proceeding at the plant level.

Although unions and workers are often disadvantaged by concessionary whipsawing, work restructuring is providing advantages to the workforce in the form of enhanced shop-floor involvement or changes in work organization, such as team working, that at least some of the workforce prefer to traditional work methods. Work restructuring may well have intensified even if management power had not increased. But because increases in managerial power are so closely interconnected with the spread of work restructuring in all seven countries, it may be futile to try to distinguish the independent influence of each as a cause of the growing variation in employment practices.

Even though management has acquired more power, there is also pervasive confusion and uncertainty among managers concerning the performance effects of various work methods or work practices. As a result, although managers have more power and influence on the course of employment relations, they are not sure what to do with it. Very little concrete evidence is available in any of the seven countries concerning whether one or another workplace practice produces improvements in either productivity or product quality, and even more confusion appears in management's ranks regarding the long-term organizational effects of the various changes in work practices that are being adopted. One illustration of this confusion is provided by the British and Australian telecommunications firms that in recent years have vacillated over whether or not to decentralize their corporate structure.

Another illustration appears at the shop-floor level across industries where management remains uncertain whether to adopt team systems of work organization. One reason that unions in some countries also remain so undecided about teams is that unions (like management) are not sure whether teams produce economic benefits, or whether they will simply compound the changing balance of power between unions and management. This confusion helps explain why there is so much variation in the way team leaders are being chosen and team responsibilities are being defined. In U.S. auto plants, for example, some team leaders are chosen by seniority, while others are selected through elections, joint labor-management appraisal, or rotation. While companies have typically sought to retain significant influence on team leaders through selection, especially where team leaders replace roles previously played by supervisors, unions have been far less confident of whether to try to integrate team leaders' roles into existing representational structures.

In Britain, such strategic uncertainty has meant that unions have found it particularly difficult to form a coherent response to such concepts as human resource management, being uncertain whether to engage employee participation as a positive benefit or reject it as a management tool to circumvent and weaken unions. It has only been as a response to the continued expansion of such management practices that unions have been forced to engage the issue in a more positive manner. Yet such uncertainties, also common in the United States, have led not only to interunion differences but to equally localized intraunion variation in strategies and outcomes.

In Germany, the security of existing representational structures, with stronger legal rights, has lessened (though not eliminated) such concerns for works councils and unions. Many practices associated with human resource management were already more widespread in Germany, since arms-length labor management relationships did not prevail and employee representatives had rights to information and consultation. Also of importance in Germany is that many human resource practices do not challenge existing institutional structures but typically complement them, a difference resulting from the stronger plant-level rights of employee representatives. In Italy, while the representatives of confederal unions have been challenged by autonomous unions and independent worker movements, spreading human resource management practices have complemented rather than supplanted collective forms of worker representation.

Variation is also being produced at workplaces in the seven countries analyzed in this volume as a natural consequence of the decentralization of corporate structures. The shift to business units in the telecommunications industry and the spread of area management concepts in the auto industry illustrate this trend.

Another closely related key source of variation in employment systems is the decentralization of managerial authority and the associated increases occurring in worker involvement in production and business decision making. A central purpose of this decentralization and the associated increases in participation is to allow individuals on the shop floor to more directly solve problems and develop solutions that meet their own needs while also satisfying corporate objectives. The resulting changes in the process of labor-management relations and the "local solutions" on the shop floor are spurring variation in work practices. This is evident in the wide differences apparent in the programmatic operation of the various work-practice patterns (such as the wide variety of joint team-based approaches). In all countries, such decentralization of management structures adds further to variation, as employee representatives are uncertain about what level of management to bargain with and frequently have inappropriate structures themselves.

## UNIONS AND INCREASED WITHIN-COUNTRY VARIATION

To the extent that increased variation in employment relations has come about through the expansion of nonunion operations, unions have experienced a clear challenge to their role and influence. There has already been much discussion of the threat that nonunion operations pose to American unions given the depth of the decline in the share of the American workforce represented by unions and the persistence of declining union representation, even in the face of the unions' efforts to restimulate union organizing. Britain, Japan, and Australia also have experienced sizable declines in the share of the workforce represented by unions. The role played by managerial opposition to unionization varies much across countries, however. While with a few exceptions, unions in Japan and Australia have generally not confronted the aggressive managerial resistance to union representation of the sort common to the American scene, in Britain union derecognition and forms of aggressive union avoidance have become more common.

Unions typically have had great difficulty clearly defining their role where management has installed the extensive communication policies and strong corporate culture common to the human resource management pattern. This is true in America and equally in Britain where, until the mid-1990s, unions generally rejected practices associated with human resource management because of uncertainty over whether they inevitably undermined unions and led to an individualized employment relationship or could lead to more positive forms of joint team-based work practices. The issue has become critical for unions in Sweden, despite their extensive and relatively secure position that country. Union fears include concerns about the decentralization of responsibilities to work groups and the potential erosion of worker and union solidarity in the face of expanded direct employee participation.

In all countries in recent years, management has more frequently been able to use the existence of overcapacity and the threat of outsourcing to increase their bargaining leverage. As bargaining structures have become more decentralized, unions in many countries have found themselves on the defensive against managerial whipsawing and demands for local concessions. Again, the United States serves as an extreme case, yet in other countries cases of local concessions bear strong similarities to U.S. developments, including in Germany, a relatively strong case. In Britain, the pattern of concessions has generally not included wages, instead more broadly incorporating increasingly flexible working practices and a reassertion of managerial prerogative.

Another challenge unions confront is adjusting their internal structures to the demands of decentralized collective bargaining. This compounds the shift in bargaining leverage and is particularly troubling for unions because of the difficulty they encounter in coordinating local bargaining and preventing plant-by-plant competition. Unions generally lack the organizational structures or procedures to facilitate coordinated bargaining across plants and local unions. Even in Germany, where the unions are strongest in this regard, they have found it increasingly difficult to coordinate works council responses to the variety of (often decentralized) managerial teamwork proposals in the 1990s. This has been particularly true where plants themselves have been under concessionary pressure to secure new investment. Elements of "plant syndicalism" are even stronger in the United Kingdom, where union structures are particularly decentralized and national unions relatively weaker.

In most countries, unions entered the 1980s relying on central unions to bargain over wages and fringe benefits through the negotiation of multiemployer master (or framework) agreements. As bargaining has decentralized, however, more of the focus within collective bargaining has shifted to the plant level, even where multiemployer agreements persist. This shift is well illustrated by the spread of enterprise bargaining in Australia.

Furthermore, while wage and fringe-benefit bargaining still matters, the importance of centralized bargaining over these issues has declined, given the ramifications that bargaining over work organization and work conditions has for employment. Detailed work organization issues can only be determined at the local level, to take account of local conditions and the preferences of workers and shop-floor managers. This is particularly true given significant work restructuring, experimentation, and uncertainty. Nevertheless, where national union guidance to local bargainers has been weak, and national unions have found it difficult to effectively coordinate local bargaining over work organization, local unions have been regularly outmaneuvered by managers who have taken advantage of corporate resources and corporate-directed whipsawing threats.

Unions differ in the extent and ways in which their traditional internal organizational structure promotes coordination between national and local
bargaining. German unions, for example, have been able to make use of the
dual structure of employee representation to maintain a relatively high degree of input into plant-level managerial decisions. Yet, it is telling that even
in Germany, unions have had a difficult time in recent years coordinating
the terms of team working and other workplace changes across plants, and
especially in firms. And in Japan, while enterprise unions have drawn on
skills and relationships developed over the years in various joint committees, the coordination and mediation of workplace adjustments often put
these unions in uncomfortable positions with workers who seek to protect
sectional interests (Hiwatari forthcoming).

The various joint steering committees and other joint labor-management
committees that have been developed in all countries commonly across
work sites, especially in those using the joint team-based approach, represent attempts to create coordinated representational structures. Yet, re-
aligning administrative duties and the relative power of central versus local
officials is proving to be a troubling matter for unions.

The telecommunications unions illustrate how difficult it is for unions to
make corresponding internal realignments. These unions are witnessing
massive changes in the structures and strategies of their bargaining counterparts, particularly among the former monopoly service providers. But
the unions have only sluggishly shifted their internal structures away from
the geographic organization that traditionally governed industrial relations
in all the countries. In the United States, United Kingdom, and Australia,
for example, as the former monopoly telecommunication firms shifted to a
business-unit structure, the telecommunications unions were slow to modify their internal administrative structures to fit business-unit lines. This
problem came to the surface very clearly at AT&T, when the CWA had a
hard time identifying which union representatives were to meet with operating managers as part of "Workplace of the Future" committee meetings.
The difficulty for the unions at BT was compounded by continual corporate
reorganizations, such that the unions were (rightly) uncertain of the future
stability of any new corporate structure.

Union mergers have increased in several countries analyzed in our research. These mergers may help promote plant-level bargaining by lessening interunion factionalism. Enterprise agreements in Australia and employee agreements in Sweden, for example, are easier to negotiate where a
single party represents employees at the plant level. It is possible, however,
that union mergers will produce increased union bureaucratization and

centralization that will work against any elevation in the authority of local union officials made necessary by intensified local bargaining.

## MANAGEMENT AND INCREASED WITHIN-COUNTRY VARIATION

Management has promoted many of the changes in employment relations that have led to increased variation, and it has generally benefited from greater variation. The growth in nonunion systems and the shift to more decentralized and more informal problem resolution in unionized settings are two key channels through which variation in employment relations has increased. Both trends clearly give management greater discretion, increased flexibility, and heightened local responsiveness in the conduct of employment relations. Decentralization in employment relations, including greater involvement of operating managers in employment relations matters, also serves management's interests by bringing the structure of employment relations into alignment with the decentralizations occurring in corporate structures. Furthermore, management has clearly favored the weakening of unionism that has facilitated the expansion of low-wage employment patterns and the diffusion of contingent and more individualized pay procedures that produce greater inequality in earnings across workers and plants.

Even though increased employment relations variation provides advantages to management, our research suggests that management has not always benefited from increased variation. The continuing oscillation in the organizational structure of telecommunications companies around the globe, for example, is a telling reminder of the ambiguity that management has come to see in corporate decentralization.

Both BT and Australia's Telstra, for example, in the early 1990s took several steps to recentralize their corporate structure. Both firms had found it difficult to maintain administrative coordination and perceived difficulties in the conduct of employment relations under decentralized corporate structures. BT confronted problems of ensuring appropriately coordinated employment relations and operational policies across the company, while Telstra confronted painful leapfrogging across the multitude of bargaining sites created in the decentralized regime. In effect, these telecommunications companies discovered either that they lacked the requisite structures to coordinate their own requirements and address the diverse and decentralized demands of the unions, or that inexperienced local managers could be outsmarted by the still-centralized unions when the latter were asked to take on new employee relations responsibilities.

In the United States, as in other countries, management generally has benefited from the concessionary contract gains negotiated with the help of managerial whipsaw tactics that played plants off against one another, but whipsawing can be a two-way street. General Motors management in the United States from the mid-1990s on, for example, saw that whipsawing can be reversed when the economic environment shifts bargaining leverage. Union-led local strikes at GM provide an American illustration of the very problem Italian management were trying to avoid through the reimposition of a national incomes policy and other steps that recentralized Italian bargaining in recent years.

The Italian employers' association, Confindustria, in the early 1990s promoted a strengthening of the role of the central unions in order to gain the benefits of coordinated bargaining across various bargaining levels (see Locke and Bacarro 1996; and our discussion of these events in Chapter 6). Italian management worried that decentralized bargaining would strengthen the hand of militant autonomous unions and assist unions of all types in inflationary wage leapfrogging. It has been exactly this fear that has also restrained the German employers' associations from moving to a decentralized bargaining system in other than a very controlled, centralized, and cautious fashion.

Given that decentralized bargaining can facilitate integrative problem solving by facilitating the negotiation of innovative work restructuring, a shift in power back to labor will not inexorably lead to the recentralization of collective bargaining. Rather, the examples cited above and others provided in the country chapters in this volume reveal the complex calculus that management and labor face regarding bargaining structure.

Our research reveals many informal changes in the locus of bargaining along with more formal changes in bargaining structure. Yet as the process of bargaining has become more informal as it becomes more decentralized, bargaining outcomes are likely to be more prone to cyclical shifts in relative power between management and labor. The informal changes are also typically associated with direct communication between managers and workers, informal shop-floor problem solving, and participation by workers and unions in business decisions. As these processes expand, operating managers are increasingly becoming involved in matters that were traditionally under the control of employee relations staff specialists. Here, as in other aspects of the trend toward increased collective bargaining decentralization, management has experienced severe adjustment problems. Numerous cases appear across the seven countries of operating managers who were not prepared for the increased responsibilities in employee relations that were being passed to them. While a downsizing of professional employee relations staff has been especially attractive in the midst of corporate re-engineering initiatives, this downsizing frequently leaves local managers scrambling to find the resources and expertise to address pressing employment relations problems.

Increased variation in employment systems is also directly contributing to the rise in income inequality occurring in most countries. The growth occurring in the relatively low-wage nonunion sector, the low earnings found in the low-wage pattern, the individual pay variation produced by individualized compensation, and the earnings variation produced by contingent compensation schemes all are contributing to income inequality. Decentralized collective bargaining has surely contributed to the processes described above and helps explain why recent statistical analyses have established a strong association between the degree of collective bargaining centralization and income inequality across countries (Blau and Kahn 1996; Freeman and Katz 1995). Yet, these analyses may have overemphasized the role played by the degree of centralization in collective bargaining structures and undervalued the influence of employment system variation and the many other labor market structures and institutions that have contributed to income inequality.

Income inequality is not just a product of the labor-market experiences of individuals. Rather, the work practices within firms and the institutions that affect those practices strongly influence labor-market outcomes. Our research suggests the value of a perspective that recognizes the role of labor-market structures and institutions in income determination. Furthermore, the discussion of labor-market outcome variation should be extended to include analysis of the growing variation in work practices and the working conditions affected by those practices.

## SUMMARY: COMMONALITIES AND THE PERSISTENT INFLUENCE OF INSTITUTIONS

The changes underway in employment systems across countries have a number of commonalities. We find much similarity in the various patterns of workplace practices and also much that is common in the processes and structures of labor-management interactions. At the same time, we find little evidence of a simple new international convergence in employment systems. There is no sign that employment relations in any country, let alone across countries, are converging to either Japanese, lean, American, or any single type of employment relations. Thus, in the auto and telecommunications industries as well as in general trends, we do not find evidence of a unidirectional change in the employment system in any of the seven countries analyzed in this volume.

*diff* [Rather than convergence, we find increasing variation in employment systems within countries through the expansion of various patterns of workplace practices. Variation is also spreading through the substantial differences that appear across firms (and often plants) in the nature of work practices within patterns and through the implementation of contingent and individualized work practices.] *expansion of workplace practices*

*diff.* [The seven countries also differ significantly in the nature and extent of the changes in employment systems, particularly in the relative mix of the various workplace practice patterns.] Our research highlights the influence exerted by labor-market structures and institutions on the mix of patterns. One key difference across countries is the extent to which low-wage and human resource management patterns have spread and the degree to which firms adhere to these patterns operate on a nonunion basis. The United States, and to a lesser degree the United Kingdom and Australia, are distinguished by a diverse pattern of diffusion and the degree to which firms operate on a nonunion basis.

That variation in employment systems is growing within countries everywhere and, in similar ways, across countries lends some credence to the idea that countries are becoming less distinct in terms of their employment practices. In that way, our views are consistent with those of Richard Locke (1992, 1995), who has argued that distinct national systems of industrial relations are disappearing. Yet, the persistence of sizable country differences in the relative mix of various employment patterns, and the role that national institutions play in shaping that mix, suggest a continuing influential role for national employment-related institutions.

Furthermore, while union systems are being challenged by the spread of low-wage, human resource, and Japanese-oriented employment patterns, particularly in the English-speaking countries, unions continue to meaningfully influence the nature and evolution of employment relations in all seven countries we analyzed. Union influence is declining in the pattern-leading auto and telecommunications industries, which are traditional union strongholds, yet in those industries unions continue to exercise sizable influence, even in the English-speaking countries. Thus, it does not appear either that unions are now or shortly will be irrelevant or that "institutionalized industrial relations" have effectively disappeared, as claimed by Leo Troy (1990) and John Purcell (1995).

Nevertheless, recent trends pose severe challenges for unions. Unions have struggled in the various countries analyzed in this volume to define their role in the face of expanding human resource and Japanese-oriented employment patterns, as a result of greater direct communication between employees and managers, and as expanded forms of participation have become available to many employees. Unions are also struggling to reorient their internal administrative structures to respond to the reorganizations in the nature of work, corporate structures, and managerial roles. This is particularly so where they have difficulty in maintaining common (decentralized) processes of labor-management interaction.

As we have noted, management has generally benefited from the changes in employment relations and has often directly initiated many of these changes, but managers, too, face strategic challenges from the growing variation in employment systems. Within management, the tendency is to endorse all measures that promote the decentralization of employment relations and the shift to more informal forms of labor-management interaction and, in doing so, reduce the authority of employee relations professionals within management's ranks. Nevertheless, we find evidence that not all decentralizations have worked out as management intended, and in fact, decentralization has at times opened the door to labor-led whipsawing. Thus, both unions and management faced related problems coping with the growing variation in work practices and in the nature of labor-management interactions.

We are struck by the extensive confusion regarding the economic performance effects of various patterns and particular work practices. Clearly, management, labor, and society would benefit from greater efforts to understand the consequences of various employment practices and the growing variation in those practices.

For the research community involved in the analysis of employment relations, our findings suggest that more careful attention should be paid to the often informal changes in bargaining structures and the process of labor-management interaction, both because informality has increased and because the consequences of increasing informality are not always what the parties, or researchers, expect.

The commonalities in employment patterns is striking even given the programmatic differences apparent in workplace practices across countries and plants (and within plants). This suggests that researchers should also analyze more extensively how and why various work practices fit together as patterns of practice. As they focus more attention on employment patterns, researchers will need to shift away from the preoccupation with national differences and look more closely at the distribution of employment practices within countries. It is through their effects on this distribution that national institutions appear to have their most significant influence.

Institutions play a key role in shaping the employment relationship. Institutions, for example, are affecting the degree to which employment patterns operate on a union or nonunion basis. While we have made some progress in identifying the influence of labor-market institutions on the changing mix of employment systems, much work remains to be done on understanding why and how these institutions matter.

And finally, for those concerned with the public policy consequences of either union decline or income inequality, our research suggests the need for an institutional perspective that pays attention to the processes through which employment systems change as well as to employment outcomes. Our research suggests that income variation is only one among many employment conditions that vary more and more across firms and individuals. To identify the causes of growing inequalities requires recognition of how variation is spreading within and across employment systems. Furthermore, this book shows that an understanding of employment system variation requires analysis of the union decline that underlies the growing variation.

NOTES

1.   As discussed in Chapter 4, in light of the spread of individual contracts, union membership declines, and recent legislative changes, it remains to be seen whether the AIRC and other factors continue to constrain low-wage employment in Australia.

# References

Abraham, Katharine, and Susan Houseman. 1995. "Earnings Inequality in Germany." In *Differences and Changes in Wage Structures*. Edited by R. Freeman and L. Katz, 371–403. Chicago: University of Chicago Press.

Abraham, Katharine, and James L. Medoff. 1985. "Length of Service and Promotions in Union and Nonunion Work Groups." *Industrial and Labor Relations Review* 38 (April): 408–20.

ADAM Report. 1993. No. 1 (October). Sydney: ACCIRT.

——. 1994. No. 2 (February). Sydney: ACCIRT.

——. 1995. No. 6 (August). Sydney: ACCIRT.

——. 1996a. No. 10 (October). Sydney: ACCIRT.

——. 1996b. No. 11 (December). Sydney: ACCIRT.

——. 1997a. No. 12 (March). Sydney: ACCIRT.

——. 1997b. No. 14 (September). Sydney: ACCIRT.

——. 1997c. No. 15 (December). Sydney: ACCIRT.

——. 1998. No. 16 (March). Sydney: ACCIRT.

Addison, John T., Claus Schnabel, and Joachim Wagner. 1997. "On the Determinants of Mandatory Works Councils in Germany." *Industrial and Labor Relations Review* 36 (October): 419–45.

Adler, Paul. 1995. "Hybridization of HRM: Two Toyota Transplants Compared." Unpublished paper, School of Business Administration, University of Southern California, November.

Altshuler, Alan, et al. 1984. *The Future of the Automobile*. Cambridge: MIT Press.

Amin, Ash. 1989. "Specialization without Growth: Small Footwear Firms in Naples." In *Small Firms and Industrial Districts in Italy*. Edited by E. Goodman, J. Bamford, and P. Saynor, 239–58. London: Routledge.

Applebaum, Eileen, and Rosemary Batt. 1994. *The New American Workplace: Transforming Work Systems in the United States*. Ithaca: ILR Press.

Arthur, Jeffrey B. 1992. "The Link between Business Strategy and Industrial Relations Systems in American Steel Mini-Mills." *Industrial and Labor Relations Review* 45 (April): 488–506.

Australian Bureau of Statistics. 1990. *Trade Union Statistics*. Cat. No. 6323.0. Canberra: Australian Government Printing Service.

———. 1996. *Trade Union Statistics*. Cat. No. 6323.0. Canberra: Australian Government Printing Service.

Australian Council of Trade Unions and the Trade Development Council. 1987. *Australia Reconstructed*. Report of the ACTU and TDC Mission to Western Europe. Canberra: Australian Government Publishing Service.

*Australian Enterprise Bargaining Manual*. 1993. Sydney: CCH Australia Limited.

Babson, Steve. 1995a. "Whose Team?: Lean Production at Mazda U.S.A." In *Lean Work: Empowerment and Exploitation in the Global Auto Industry*. Edited by S. Babson, 1–40. Detroit: Wayne State University Press.

———. 1995b. "Restructuring the Workplace: Post-Fordism or Return of the Foreman?" In *Autowork*. Edited by R. Asher and R. Edsforth, 227–302. Albany: State University of New York Press.

Bain, George Sayers, and Robert Price. 1983. "Union Growth: Dimensions, Determinants, and Density." In *Industrial Relations in Britain*. Edited by G. S. Bain, 3–34. Oxford: Blackwell.

Baird, Marian, and Russell D. Lansbury. 1996. "Involving Employees at Australia Post." In *Managing Together: Consultation and Participation in the Workplace*. Edited by E. Davis and R. Lansbury, 146–59. Melbourne: Addison Wesley Longman.

Bamber, Greg J., and Russell D. Lansbury. 1994. *International and Comparative Industrial Relations*. 2d ed. London: Routledge.

———. 1997. "Employment Relations in the Australian Automotive Industry: A Question of Survival." In *Changing Employment Relations in Australia*. Edited by J. Kitay and R. Lansbury, 81–101. Melbourne: Oxford University Press.

Bamber, Greg J., Mark Shadur, and David Simmons. 1997. "Australia." In *Telecommunications: Restructuring Work and Employee Relations Worldwide*. Edited by H. Katz, 122–52. Ithaca: ILR Press.

Batstone, Eric, Anthony Ferner, and Terry Michael. 1983. *Unions on the Board*. Oxford: Basil Blackwell.

———. 1984. *Consent and Efficiency: Labour Relations and Management Strategy in the State Enterprise*. Oxford: Basil Blackwell.

Batt, Rosemary. 1995a. "What Are the Effects of Work Restructuring on Employee Well-being and Firm Performance? Evidence From Telecommunications Services." Working paper 95-29, Center for Advanced Human Resource Studies, Cornell University, May.

———. 1995b. "Performance and Welfare Effects of Work Restructuring: Evidence from Telecommunications Services." Ph.D. dissertation, Sloan School of Management, MIT.

Batt, Rosemary, and Jeffrey H. Keefe. 1997. "United States." In *Telecommunications: Restructuring Work and Employee Relations Worldwide*. Edited by H. Katz, 31–88. Ithaca: ILR Press.

Batt, Rosemary, and Michael Strausser. 1998. "Labor Market Outcomes of Deregulation in Telecommunications Services." In *Papers and Proceedings of the Annual Meetings of the IRRA, 1998,* 126–34. Madison: IRRA.

Bayliss, F. 1993. *Does Britain Still Have a Pay Problem?* London: Employment Policy Institute.

Beatson, Mark. 1993. "Trends in Pay Flexibility." *Employment Gazette* (September): 405–14.

Beaumont, Phillip B., and R. I. D. Harris. 1993. "Diverse Changes in Bargaining Levels Revealed." *IRS Employment Trends* 548 (November): 12–16.

———. 1995. "Union Derecognition and Declining Union Density in Britain." *Industrial and Labor Relations Review* 48 (April): 389–402.

Berger, Suzanne, and Ronald Dore. 1996. *National Diversity and Global Capitalism.* Ithaca: Cornell University Press.

Berggren, Christian. 1992. *Alternatives to Lean Production: Work Organization in the Swedish Auto Industry.* Ithaca: ILR Press.

———. 1996. "Sweden: A Fragile, But Still Innovative System." In *Managing Together: Consultation and Participation in the Workplace.* Edited by E. Davis and R. Lansbury, 193–207. Melbourne: Addison Wesley Longman.

Bergmann, Joachim, Erwin Bürckmann, and Harmut Dabrowski. 1998. "Reform des Flächentarifvertrages?: Betriebliche Realitäten, Verhandlungsysteme, gewerschaftliche Politik." In *Supplement der Zeitschrift Sozialismus,* 1–98.

Beynon, Huw. 1973. *Working for Ford.* London: Allen Lane.

Bird, Derek. 1995. "Membership of Trade Unions Based on Information from the Certification Officer." *Employment Gazette* (May): 205–9.

Bispinck, Reinhard. 1995. "Collective Bargaining Policy in a Transition Economy: Taking Stock after Five Years of Collective Bargaining Policy in the New Germany Länder." In *German Industrial Relations under the Impact of Structural Change, Unification, and European Unification.* Edited by R. Hoffmann et al., 62–77. Düsseldorf: Hans-Böchler-Stiftung.

———. 1997. "Deregulierung, Differenzierung und Dezentralisierung des Flächentarifvertrags." *WSI Mitteilungen* 8-1997: 551–61.

Blackburn, McKinley L., David E. Bloom, and Richard B. Freeman. 1990. "The Declining Economic Position of Less-Skilled American Men." In *A Future of Lousy Jobs?: The Changing Structure of U.S. Wages.* Edited by G. Burtless, 31–76. Washington, D.C.: Brookings Institution.

Blanchflower, David G., and Richard B. Freeman. 1992. "Unionism in the United States and Other Advanced OECD Countries." *Industrial Relations* 31 (Winter): 56–79.

Blau, Francine D., and Lawrence M. Kahn. 1996. "International Differences in Male Wage Inequality: Institutions Versus Market Forces." *Journal of Political Economy* 106 (August): 791–837.

Blumenstein, Rebecca, and Nicole M. Christian. 1996. "Parts Dispute to Remain Despite GM-UAW Accord." *Wall Street Journal,* March 25.

Borland, Jeff. 1996. "Union Effects on Earnings Dispersion in Australia, 1986–1994." *British Journal of Industrial Relations* 34 (June): 237–48.

Botany Site Combined Review Team. 1995. "AWU-FIME\AMWU\ETU\ICI Botany Operations, Section 170 Core Agreement." April. Sydney: ICI Australia Operations.

Bradsher, Keith. 1998. "General Motors and U.A.W. Agree on End to Strike." *New York Times,* July 29, pp. A-1, D-6.

Bray, Mark. 1991. "Australian Unions and Economic Restructuring." Unpublished paper, Department of Industrial Relations, University of Sydney.

Brown, Clair, et al. 1997. *Work and Pay in the United States and Japan.* New York: Oxford University Press.

Brown, William. 1993. "The Contraction of Collective Bargaining in Britain." *British Journal of Industrial Relations* 31 (June): 189–200.

Brown, William, Simon Deakin, Maria Hudo, Cliff Pratten, and Paul Ryan. 1998. "The Individualisation of Employment Contracts in Berlin." DTI Research Paper (June). London: Department of Trade and Industry.

Brown, William, Simon Deakin, and Paul Ryan. 1997. "The Effects of British Industrial Relations Legislation 1979–1997." *National Institute Economic Review* 161 (July): 69–83.

Brown, William, Paul Marginson, and Janet Walsh. 1995. "Management: Pay Determination and Collective Bargaining." In *Industrial Relations: Theory and Practice in Britain.* Edited by P. Edwards, 121–50. Oxford: Basil Blackwell.

Brown, William, and Janet Walsh. 1991. "Pay Determination in Britain in the 1980s: The Anatomy of Decentralization." *Oxford Review of Economic Policy* 7 (Spring): 44–59.

Brulin, Goran, and Tommy Nilsson. 1997. "Sweden: The Volvo and Saab Road beyond Lean Production." In *After Lean Production: Evolving Employment Practices in the World Auto Industry.* Edited by T. A. Kochan, R. Lansbury, and J. P. MacDuffie, 191–204. Ithaca: Cornell University Press.

Buchanan, John, et al. 1997. "Wages Policy and Wage Determination in 1996." Unpublished paper, ACCIRT, University of Sydney.

Budd, John W. 1992. "The Determinants and Extent of UAW Pattern Bargaining." *Industrial and Labor Relations Review* 45 (April): 523–39.

Bureau of National Affairs. 1982. "Auto Workers Held Entitled to Neutrality Pact with Dana Corporation." *Daily Labor Report,* June 8, pp. A-3, A-4.

——. 1983. "Autoworkers Accept New Contract at Dana as Parties Sever Link with Auto Pattern." *Daily Labor Report,* December 12, p. A-1.

——. 1994. "As GM, UAW Officials Negotiate Local Pacts Debate Over Jobs, Contracting Out Expected." *Daily Labor Report,* February 25, pp. A-12–A-15.

——. 1995a. "UAW Negotiates New Agreements with Budd Co. and Allied Signal." *Daily Labor Report,* November 8, p. D-12.

——. 1995b. "UAW Rejects Caterpillar Proposal, But Agrees to End 17-Month Strike." *Daily Labor Report,* December 5, p. D-5.

——. 1996a. "UAW Members in Four States Ratify New Contract Agreement with Dana Corp." *Daily Labor Report,* January 17, p. D-11.

——. 1996b. "Job Security at Parts Plants Key Issue in GM-UAW Negotiations." *Daily Labor Report,* February 13, p. D-6.

——. 1996c. "UAW Members Expected to Approve New Three Year Pact with Ford." *Daily Labor Report,* September 23, p. D-3.

——. 1997. "Bonuses Likely for Autoworkers." *Daily Labor Report,* December 10, p. B-1.

——. 1998a. "UAW and Saturn Corporation Resolve Labor Issues." *Daily Labor Report,* September 8, p. A-10.

——. 1998b. "AT&T Agrees to Bonuses, Card Check in Tentative Agreement with CWA, IBEW." *Daily Labor Report,* May 12, pp. A-11–A-12.

Burniaux, Jean-Marc, Thai-Thanh Dang, Douglas Fore, Michael Förster, Marco d'Ercole, Mira Marco, and Howard Oxley. 1998. *Income Distribution and Poverty in Selected OECD Countries.* OECD Economics Department Working Paper No. 189. Paris: OECD.

Burton, John F., and Terry Thomason. 1988. "The Extent of Collective Bargaining in the Public Sector." In *Public Sector Bargaining.* Edited by B. Aaron, J. Najita, and J. Stern, 1–51. 2d ed. Madison: IRRA.

Callus, Ron, et al. 1991. *Industrial Relations at Work: The Australian Workplace Industrial Relations Survey.* Canberra: Australian Government Publishing Service.

Campling, John, et al. 1996. "The Role of Enterprise Agreements in Lightly Unionized and Non-Unionized Workplaces." Report to the Federal Department of Industrial Relations, ACIRRT, University of Sydney.

Camuffo, Arnoldo, and Giuseppe Volpato. 1994. "Labor Relations Heritage and Lean Manufacturing at Fiat." Paper presented at the conference "International Developments in Workplace Innovation," June 15–16, Toronto, Canada.

——. 1997. "Italy: Changing the Workplace in the Auto Industry." In *After Lean Production: Evolving Employment Practices in the World Auto Industry.* Edited by T. A. Kochan, R. Lansbury, and J. P. MacDuffie, 155–76. Ithaca: Cornell University Press.

Cappelli, Peter. 1985. "Competitive Pressures and Labor Relations in the Airline Industry." *Industrial Relations* 24 (Fall): 316–38.

——. 1995. "Rethinking Employment." *British Journal of Industrial Relations* 33 (December): 563–602.

——. 1997. "Introduction," In *Change at Work.* Edited by P. Cappelli et al., 3–14. New York: Oxford University Press.

Carter, C. F. 1977. *Report of the Post Office Review Committee.* Cmnd. 6850. London: HMSO.

Chauvin, Keith W. 1994. "Firm-specific Wage Growth and Changes in the Labor Market for Managers." *Managerial and Decision Economics* 15 (January–February): 21–37.

Claydon, Tim. 1996. "Union Derecognition: A Re-examination." In *Contemporary Industrial Relations: A Critical Analysis.* Edited by I. Beardwell, 151–74. Oxford: Oxford University Press.

Cole, Robert E. 1971. *Japanese Blue Collar.* Berkeley: University of California Press.

Cole, Robert E., and Taizo Yakushiji, eds. 1984. *The American and Japanese Auto Industries in Transition.* Ann Arbor: University of Michigan.

Communications Workers of America. 1995. "1995 Telephone Negotiation Contract Patterns." Unpublished mimeo, Washington, D.C.

Cully, Mark, and Stephen Woodland. 1998. "Trade Union Membership and Recognition 1996–7: An Analysis of Data from the Certification Officer and the LFS." *Labour Market Trends* (July): 353–63.

Cully, Mark, et al. 1998. *The 1998 Workplace Employee Relations Survey: First Findings.* London: Department of Trade and Industry.

Cusumano, Michael A. 1985. *The Japanese Automobile Industry.* Cambridge: Harvard University Press.

Cutcher-Gershenfeld, Joel. 1991. "The Impact on Economic Performance of a Transformation in Workplace Relations." *Industrial and Labor Relations Review* 44 (January): 241–60.

Cutcher-Gershenfeld, Joel, and Patrick P. McHugh. 1994. "Collective Bargaining in the North American Auto Supply Industry." In *Contemporary Collective Bargaining.* Edited by P. Voos, 225–58. Madison: IRRA.

CWU (Communications Workers' Union). 1998. "Making a Good Job of Employment Policy: A CWU Contribution to the Debate on the Flexible Labour Market." Unpublished manuscript. CWU, London.

Dabscheck, Braham, and John Niland. 1981. *Industrial Relations in Australia.* Sydney: George Allen and Unwin.

Darbishire, Owen. 1995. "Switching Systems: Technological Change, Privatisation, and Competition." *Industrielle Beziehungen* Jg. 2 Heft 2: 156–79.

———. 1997. "Germany." In *Telecommunications: Restructuring Work and Employment Relations Worldwide.* Edited by H. Katz, 189–227. Ithaca: ILR Press.

Darlington, Ralph. 1994. "Shop Stewards' Organisation in Ford Halewood: From Beynon to Today." *Industrial Relations Journal* 25 (June): 136–49.

Davies, Paul L., and Mark R. Freedland. 1993. *Labour Legislation and Public Policy: A Contemporary History.* Oxford: Clarendon Press.

Davis, Edward M., and Russell D. Lansbury. 1994. "Industrial Relations in Australia." In *International and Comparative Industrial Relations.* Edited by G. Bamber and R. Lansbury, 100–125. London: Routledge.

———. 1996. *Managing Together: Consultation and Participation in the Workplace.* Melbourne: Addison Wesley Longman.

Department of Industrial Relations. 1995. *Enterprise Bargaining in Australia: 1994 Annual Report.* Canberra: Australian Government Publishing Service.

———. 1996. *Enterprise Bargaining in Australia: 1995 Annual Report.* Canberra: Australian Government Publishing Service.

Deutschman, Christoph. 1995. "Germany after the Unification: Industrial Restructuring and Labour Relations." In *German Industrial Relations Under the Impact of Structural Change, Unification, and European Unification.* Edited by R. Hoffmann et al., 96–106. Düsseldorf: Hans-Böckler-Stiftung.

Doeringer, Peter. 1984. "Internal Labor Markets and Paternalism in Rural Areas," In *Internal Labor Markets.* Edited by P. Osterman, 271–90. Cambridge: MIT Press.

Doeringer, Peter, and Michael Piore. 1971. *Internal Labor Markets and Manpower Analysis.* Lexington: D. C. Heath.

Donovan Commission. 1968. *Report of the Royal Commission on Trade Unions and Employers Associations.* Cmnd. 3623. London: HMSO.

Dore, Ronald. 1973. *British Factory—Japanese Factory: The Origins of National Diversity in Industrial Relations*. Berkeley: University of California Press.

——. 1992. "Japan's Version of Managerial Capitalism." In *Transforming Organizations*. Edited by T. A. Kochan and M. Useem, 17–27. New York: Oxford University Press.

Dunn, Stephen. 1993. "From Donovan to . . . Wherever." *British Journal of Industrial Relations* 31 (June): 169–87.

Dunn, Stephen, and Martin Wright. 1994. "Maintaining the 'Status Quo'?: An Analysis of the Contracts of British Collective Agreements 1979–1990." *British Journal of Industrial Relations* 32 (March): 23–46.

Dustmann, Christian, and Arthur Van Soest. 1997. "Wage Structures in the Private and Public Sectors in West Germany." *Fiscal Studies* 18 (August): 225–47.

Eaton, Adrienne E., and Paula B. Voos. 1992. "Unions and Contemporary Innovations in Work Organizations, Compensation, and Employee Participation." In *Unions and Economic Competitiveness*. Edited by L. Mishel and P. Voos, 173–216. Washington, D.C.: Economic Policy Institute.

Edin, Per-Anders, and Bertil Holmlund. 1995. "The Swedish Wage Structure: The Rise and Fall of Solidarity Wage Policy?" In *Differences and Changes in Wage Structures*. Edited by R. Freeman and L. Katz, 307–44. Chicago: University of Chicago Press.

Edwards, Paul, et al. 1992. "Great Britain: Still Muddling Through." In *Industrial Relations in the New Europe*. Edited by A. Ferner and R. Hyman, 1–68. Oxford: Basil Blackwell.

Edwards, Richard C. 1979. *Contested Terrain*. New York: Basic Books.

Endo, Koshi. 1994. "Satei (Personal Assessment) and Interworker Competition in Japanese Firms." *Industrial Relations* 1 (January): 70–82.

Erickson, Christopher L. 1992. "Wage Rule Formation in the Aerospace Industry." *Industrial and Labor Relations Review* 45 (April): 507–22.

——. 1996. "A Re-Interpretation of Pattern Bargaining." *Industrial and Labor Relations Review* 49 (July): 615–34.

Erickson, Christopher L., and Andrea C. Ichino. 1995. "Wage Differentials in Italy: Market Forces, Institutions and Inflation." In *Differences and Changes in Wage Structures*. Edited by R. Freeman and L. Katz, 265–305. Chicago: University of Chicago Press.

Ettl, Wilfried. 1995. "Arbeitgeberverbände als Transformationsakteure: Organisationsentwicklung und Tarifpolitik im Dilemma von Funktionalität und Repräsentativät." In *Einheit als Interessenpolitik: Studien zur sektoralen Transformation Ostdeutschlands*. Edited by H. Wiesenthal, 70–77. Frankfurt: Campus Verlag.

*European Industrial Relations Review*. 1990. "Fiat and Olivetti Productivity Bonuses." 200 (September): 9.

——. 1992a: "Lufthansa Settlement." 225 (October): 6.

——. 1992b. "Employee Participation at Zanussi." 217 (February): 16–17.

——. 1992c. "Collective Bargaining in 1991." 227 (December): 24.

——. 1993a. "Germany: IBM Goes It Alone." (April): 16–18.

——. 1993b. "Pioneering New Agreements at Teldec." (May): 18–21.

——. 1993c. "Innovative Fiat Greenfield Site Deal." 234 (July): 10.

——. 1993d. "Collective Bargaining in Transition." 234 (July): 16.

——. 1994a. "Industrial Relations and Industrial Location—A Case Study of Mercedes-Benz." 244 (May): 12–15.

——. 1994b. "Worksharing for 500,000 Engineering Employees." 249 (October): 6.

——. 1994c. "Central Agreement on Company-level Representation." 241 (February): 19–22.

——. 1994d. "Minimum Pay Setting." 241 (February): 23–25.

——. 1995a. "Germany: IG Metall Wins Court Case." 252 (January): 6–7.

——. 1995b. "Landmark Deals in the German Car Industry." 261 (October): 12–13.

——. 1995c. "Motor Industry Supplier Recognises Metal-Working Accord." 253 (February): 9.

——. 1995d. "IBM Agreement Leads to Substantial Savings." 258 (July): 7–8.

——. 1995e. "1995 Bargaining Update." 258 (July): 20.

——. 1995f. "Profit-Sharing Deals Are Varied and Widespread." 261 (October): 11.

——. 1995g. "Pay Deal Signed at Volvo." 261 (October): 19.

——. 1996a. "Flexibility Deal at Mercedes-Benz." 267 (April): 6.

——. 1996b. "BMW Introduces Pioneering Personnel Policy." 271 (August): 23–25.

——. 1996c. "Teamworking in Chemicals and Engineering." 274 (November): 21–23.

——. 1996d. "Flexible Pay Examined." 269 (June): 22–23.

——. 1996e. "Fiat Deal Stresses Union Divisions." 267 (April): 24–25.

——. 1996f. "Gainsharing at BP Exploration." 269 (June): 24–28.

——. 1997a. "Metalworkers' Dispute Settled." 278 (March): 9.

——. 1997b. "Zanussi Reinstates Participatory Model." 284 (September): 7.

——. 1998a. "Job Security Deal at Opel." 290 (March): 24–26.

——. 1998b. "Innovative Deal at Zanussi." 288 (January): 9.

——. 1998c. "Three-Year Deals Secured in 1998 Round." 293 (June): 27–32.

——. 1998d. "Company Bargaining Increases." 298 (November): 25.

Ferner, Anthony, and Richard Hyman. 1992. "Italy: Between Political Exchange and Micro-Corporatism." In *Industrial Relations in the New Europe*. Edited by A. Ferner and R. Hyman, 524–600. Oxford: Basil Blackwell.

Ferner, Anthony, and Michael Terry. 1997. "United Kingdom." In *Telecommunications: Restructuring Work and Employment Relations Worldwide*. Edited by H. Katz, 89–121. Ithaca: ILR Press.

Fernie, Sue, and David Metcalf. 1995. "Participation, Contingent Pay, Representation and Workplace Performance: Evidence from Great Britain." *British Journal of Industrial Relations* 33 (September): 379–415.

Fichter, Michael. 1997. "Unions in the New Länder: Evidence for the Urgency of Reform." In *Negotiating the New Germany: Can Social Partnership Survive?* Edited by L. Turner, 87–111. Ithaca: Cornell University Press.

Fisher, John. 1995. "The Trade Union Response to HRM in the UK: The Case of the TGWU." *Human Resource Management Journal* 5 (Spring): 7–23.

Flanagan, Robert J., David W. Soskice, and Lloyd Ulman. 1983. *Unionism, Economic Stabilization, and Incomes Policies: European Experience*. Washington, D.C.: Brookings Institution.

Flanders, Allan, and Hugh Clegg. 1954. *The System of Industrial Relations in Great Britain: Its History, Law, and Institutions*. Oxford: Basil Blackwell.

Ford Australia. 1995. "Enterprise Bargaining Agreement." Unpublished paper. Melbourne. May.

Foulkes, Fred. 1980. *Personnel Policies in Large Non-union Companies*. Englewood Cliffs, N.J.: Prentice-Hall.

Fox, Alan. 1974. *Beyond Contract: Work, Power and Trust Relations*. London: Faber and Faber.

Freeman, Richard B. 1980. "Unionism and the Dispersion of Wages." *Industrial and Labor Relations Review* 34 (October): 3–23.

———. 1982. "Union Wage Practices and Wage Dispersion Within Establishments." *Industrial and Labor Relations Review* 41 (October): 3–21.

Freeman, Richard B., and Lawrence F. Katz. 1995. "Introduction and Summary." In *Differences and Changes in Wage Structures*. Edited by R. Freeman and L. Katz, 1–24. Chicago: University of Chicago Press.

Freeman, Richard B., and James L. Medoff. 1984. *What Do Unions Do?* New York: Basic Books.

Frick, Berndt, and Dieter Sadowski. 1995. "Works Councils, Unions, and Firm Performance." In *Institutional Frameworks and Labour Market Performance*. Edited by F. Buttler, W. Franz, and R. Schettkat, 46–76. New York: Routledge.

Gall, Gregor. 1998. "The Changing Relations of Production: Union Derecognition in the UK Magazine Industry." *Industrial Relations Journal* 29, no. 2: 151–61.

Gall, Gregor, and Sonia McKay. 1994. "Trade Union Derecognition in Britain, 1988–1994." *British Journal of Industrial Relations* 32 (September): 433–48.

Gallie, Duncan, and Michael White. 1993. "Employee Commitment and the Skills Revolution." London: Policy Studies Institute.

Gardner, Margaret. 1995. "Labor Movements and Industrial Restructuring: Australia, New Zealand, and the United States." In *The Comparative Political Economy of Industrial Relations*. Edited by K. Wever and L. Turner, 33–70. Madison: IRRA.

Garrahan, Philip, and Paul Stewart. 1992a. "Work Organisations in Transition: The Human Resource Management Implications of the 'Nissan Way.'" *Human Resource Management Journal* 2: 46–62.

———. 1992b. *The Nissan Enigma: Flexibility at Work in a Local Economy*. London: Mansell.

Geary, John F. 1995. "Work Practices: The Structure of Work." In *Industrial Relations: Theory and Practice in Britain*. Edited by P. Edwards, 368–96. Oxford: Basil Blackwell.

Geroski, P. P. Gregg, and T. Desjonqueres. 1995. "Did the Retreat of UK Trade Unionism Accelerate During the 1990–1993 Recession." *British Journal of Industrial Relations* 33 (March): 35–54.

Gerst, Detlef, Thomas Hardwig, Martin Kuhlmann, and Michael Schumann. 1999. "Group Work in the German Automobile Industry: The Case of Mercedes-

Benz." In *Teamwork in the Automobile Industry: Radical Change or Passing Fashion?* Edited by J-P. Durand, P. Stewart, and J. Castillo, 366–94. London: MacMillan.

Ghilarducci, Teresa. 1991. "Changing Pension Norms: The Case of Japanese Auto Transplants and U.S. Auto Firms." Unpublished paper, Department of Economics, University of Notre Dame.

GM-Holden. 1992. *General Motors-Holden's Automotive Ltd. and the Federation of Vehicle Industry Unions Enterprise Agreement.* Adelaide, South Australia: Monck Printers. August.

———. 1994. "GM-Holden's Engine Company and the Federation of Vehicle Industry Unions Enterprise Agreement II." Unpublished paper. Victoria, Australia. November.

Gosling, Amanda, and Stephen Machin. 1995. "Trade Unions and the Dispersion of Earnings in British Establishments, 1980–1990." *Oxford Bulletin of Economics and Statistics* 57 (May): 167–84.

Gospel, Howard. 1992. *Markets, Firms, and the Management of Labour in Modern Britain.* Cambridge: Cambridge University Press.

Graham, Laurie. 1995. *On the Line at Subaru-Isuzu: The Japanese Model and the American Worker.* Ithaca: ILR Press.

Gregg, P. A., and A. Yates. 1991. "Changes in Wage Setting Arrangements and Trade Union Presence in the 1980s." *British Journal of Industrial Relations* 29 (September): 361–76.

Gregg, P. A., A. Yates, and Stephen Machin. 1992. "Unions, the Demise of the Closed Shop, and Wage Growth in the 1980s." *Oxford Bulletin of Economics and Statistics* 54 (February): 53–72.

Gregory, Robert G., and Francis Vella. 1995. "Real Wages, Employment, and Wage Dispersion in U.S. and Australian Labor Markets." In *Differences and Changes in Wage Structures.* Edited by R. Freeman and L. Katz. Chicago: University of Chicago Press.

Guest, David, and Kim Hoque. 1994. "The Good, The Bad, and the Ugly: Employment in New Non-Union Workplaces." *Human Resource Management Journal* 5 (Autumn): 1–14.

———. 1996. "Human Resource Management and the New Industrial Relations." In *Contemporary Industrial Relations: A Critical Analysis.* Edited by I. Beardwell, 11–36. Oxford: Oxford University Press.

Hammer, Michael, and James Champy. 1993. *Re-engineering the Corporation: A Manifesto for Business Revolution.* New York: HarperBusiness.

Harrison, Bennett, and Barry Bluestone. 1988. *The Great U-Turn: Corporate Restructuring and the Polarizing of America.* New York: Basic Books.

Heery, Edmund. 1997. "Annual Review Article 1996." *British Journal of Industrial Relations* 35 (March): 87–109.

Hibbs, Douglas A. 1990. *Wage Compression Under Solidarity Bargaining in Sweden.* Stockholm: Trade Union Institute for Economic Research.

Hiwatari, Nobuhiro. Forthcoming. "Economic Adjustment and Japanese Unions," In *The Shifting Boundaries of Labor Politics: New Directions for Comparative Research and Theory.* Edited by R. Locke and K. Thelen. Cambridge: MIT Press.

Höland, Armin. 1995. "Atypical and Precarious Employment in the Unified Germany." In *German Industrial Relations under the Impact of Structural Change, Unification, and European Unification*. Edited by R. Hoffman et al.

Holden-F.V.I.U. 1996. "Work Organization." Unpublished document. Elizabeth, Australia. July.

Howell, Chris. 1995. "Trade Unions and the State: A Critique of British Industrial Relations." *Politics and Society* 23 (June): 149–83.

Howes, Candace. 1993. *Japanese Auto Transplants and the U.S. Automobile Industry*. Washington, D.C.: Economic Policy Institute.

Ichniowski, Casey, Kathryn Shaw, and Giovanni Prennushi. 1997. "The Effect of Human Resource Management Practices on Productivity: A Study of Steel Finishing Lines." *American Economic Review* 87 (June): 291–313.

IG Metall. 1992. "Gruppenarbeit: Gestaltungshinweise und Regelungsvorschläge." IG Metall manuscript, Frankfurt am Main.

Ingram, Peter N. 1991a. "Changes in Working Practices in British Manufacturing Industry in the 1980s: A Study of Employee Concessions Made During Wage Negotiations." *British Journal of Industrial Relations* 29 (March): 1–13.

——. 1991b. "Ten Years of Manufacturing Wage Settlements, 1979–1989." *Oxford Review of Economic Policy* 7 (Spring): 93–106.

Institute for Women's Policy Research. 1995. "Women and Minorities in Telecommunications: An Exception to the Rule." Unpublished mimeo, Washington, D.C.

IPD (Institute of Personnel and Development). 1998. *Performance Pay*. London: IPD.

IRE (Industrial Relations Europe). 1996. "DAG Breaks Ranks." (February): 5.

*IRS Employment Trends*. 1997. "The Changing Nature of the Employment Contract." (July).

——. 1998. "Hyder Maintains Long-Term Partnership." No. 662 (August): 12–16.

Jacobi, Otto. 1995. "Collective Bargaining Autonomy—The Future of Industrial Relations in Germany." In *German Industrial Relations Under the Impact of Structural Change, Unification, and European Unification*. Edited by R. Hoffmann et al, 38–52. Düsseldorf: Hans-Böckler-Stiftung.

Jacobi, Otto, Berndt Keller, and Walther Müller-Jentsch. 1998. "Germany: Facing New Challenges." In *Changing Industrial Relations in Europe*. Edited by A. Ferner and R. Hyman, 218–69. Oxford: Basil Blackwell.

Jacoby, Sanford M. 1985. *Employing Bureaucracies*. New York: Columbia University Press.

——. 1997. *Modern Manors*. Princeton: Princeton University Press.

Japan Institute of Labor. 1995. "Japan Labor Bulletin." May 1, p. 2.

Jürgens, Ulrich. 1995. "Lean Production and Co-Determination: The German Experience." In *Lean Work*. Edited by S. Babson, 292–310. Detroit: Wayne State University.

Jürgens, Ulrich, Thomas Malsch, and Knuth Dohse. 1993. *Breaking from Taylorism: Changing Forms of Work in the Automobile Industry*. Cambridge: Cambridge University Press.

Kahn Freund, Otto. 1959. "Labour Law." In *Law and Opinion in England in the Twentieth Century*. Edited by M. Ginsberg, 215–63. London: Stevens.

Katz, Harry C. 1985. *Shifting Gears: Changing Labor Relations in the U.S. Automobile Industry.* Cambridge: MIT Press.

———. 1987. "Automobiles." In *Collective Bargaining in American Industry.* Edited by D. Lipsky and C. Donn, 13–54. Lexington, Mass.: D. C. Heath.

———. 1993. "The Decentralization of Collective Bargaining: A Literature Review and Comparative Analysis." *Industrial and Labor Relations Review* 47 (October): 3–22.

———. 1997. "Introduction and Comparative Overview." In *Telecommunications: Restructuring Work and Employment Relations Worldwide,* edited by H. Katz, 1–30. Ithaca: ILR Press.

Katz, Harry C., and Jeffrey H. Keefe. 1992. "Collective Bargaining and Industrial Relations Outcomes: The Causes and Consequences of Diversity." In *Research Frontiers in Industrial Relations and Human Resources.* Edited D. Lewin, O. Mitchell, and P. Sherer, 43–76. Madison: Industrial Relations Research Association.

———. 1993. "Training and the Restructuring of Work in Large Unionized Settings." CAHRS Working Paper 93-19, Cornell University, October.

Katz, Harry C., and Thomas A. Kochan. 1992. *An Introduction to Collective Bargaining and Industrial Relations.* New York: McGraw Hill Inc.

Katz, Harry C., Thomas A. Kochan, and Jeffrey H. Keefe. 1987. "Industrial Relations and Productivity in the U.S. Automobile Industry." *Brookings Papers on Economic Activity* 3: 685–728.

Katz, Harry C., and John Paul MacDuffie. 1994. "Collective Bargaining in the U.S. Auto Assembly Sector." In *Contemporary Collective Bargaining in the Private Sector.* Edited by P. Voos, 181–224. Madison: IRRA.

Katz, Harry C., and Noah Meltz. 1991. "Profit Sharing and Auto Workers' Earnings: The United States vs. Canada." *Relations Industrielles* 42 (Summer): 513–30.

Katz, Lawrence, Gary W. Loveman, and David G. Blanchflower. 1995. "A Comparison of Changes in the Structure of Wages in Four OECD Countries." In *Differences and Changes in Wage Structures.* Edited by R. Freeman and L. Katz, 25–66. Chicago: University of Chicago Press.

Katz, Lawrence, and Ana L. Revenga. 1989. "Changes in the Structure of Wages: The United States vs. Japan." *Journal of the Japanese and International Economies* 3 (December): 522–53.

Keefe, Jeffrey, and Karen Boroff. 1994. "Telecommunications Labor-Management Relations: One Decade after Divestiture." In *Contemporary Collective Bargaining in the Private Sector.* Edited by P. Voos, 303–72. Madison: IRRA.

Kelley, Di, and Elsa Underhill. 1997. "Australian Steel: A Corporatist Transformation?" In *Changing Employment Relations in Australia.* Edited by J. Kitay and R. Lansbury, 158–84. Melbourne: Oxford University Press.

Kerr, Clark, John T. Dunlop, Frederick Harbison, and Charles Myers. 1964. *Industrialism and Industrial Man.* New York: Oxford University Press.

Kessler, Ian, and John Purcell. 1995. "Individualism and Collectivism in Theory and Practice: Management Style and the Design of Pay Systems." In *Industrial Relations: Theory and Practice in Britain.* Edited by P. Edwards, 337–96. Oxford: Basil Blackwell.

Kitay, Jim. 1997. "Changing Patterns of Employment Relations: Theoretical and Methodological Framework for Six Australian Industry Studies." In *Changing Employment Relations in Australia*. Edited by J. Kitay and R. Lansbury, 1–43. Melbourne: Oxford University Press.

Kjellberg, Anders. 1992. "Sweden: Can the Model Survive?" In *Industrial Relations in the New Europe*, edited by A. Ferner and R. Hyman, 88–142.

Kochan, Thomas A., Harry C. Katz, and Robert B. McKersie. 1994. *The Transformation of American Industrial Relations*. 2d ed. Ithaca: Cornell University Press.

Kochan, Thomas A., Robert B. McKersie, and John Chalykoff. 1986. "The Effects of Corporate Strategy and Workplace Innovations on Union Representation." *Industrial and Labor Relations Review* 39 (July): 487–501.

Kochan, Thomas A,. and Paul Osterman. 1994. *The Mutual Gains Enterprise*. Boston: Harvard Business School Press.

Kohaut, S., and L. Bellmann. 1997. "Betriebliche Determinanten der Tarifbindung: Eine empirische Analyse auf der Basis des IAB-Betriebspanels 1995." *Industrielle Beziehngen* 4: 317–34.

Koshiro, Kazutoshi. 1990. "Japan." In *The Re-emergence of Small Enterprises*. edited by W. Sengenberger, G. Loveman, and M. Piore, 173–222. Geneva: International Institute for Labour Studies.

Kotthoff, H. 1981. *Betriebsräte und betriebliche Herrschaft: Eine Typologie von Partizipationsmustern im Industriebetrieb*. Frankfurt am Main: Campus.

——. 1994. *Betriebsräte und Bürgerstatus: Wandel und Kontinuität betriebliche Interessenvertretung*. Munich: R. Haupp.

Krugman, Paul. 1996. *Pop Internationalism*. Cambridge: MIT Press.

Kuhlmann, Martin, and Michael Schumann. 1997. "Patterns of Work Organisation in the German Automobile Industry." In *Transforming Automobile Assembly: Experience in Automation and Work Organization*. Edited by K. Shimohawa, T. Fujimoto, and U. Jürgens, 289–304. Berlin: Springer Verlag.

Kuttner, Robert. 1983. "The Declining Middle." *Atlantic* (July): 60–72.

Labit, Anne. 1998. "Group Working at Volkswagen: An Issue for Negotiation between Trade Unions and Management." In *Teamwork in the Automobile Industry: Radical Change or Passing Fashion?* Edited by J-P. Durand, P. Stewart, and J. Castillo, 395–411. London: MacMillan.

Lange, A. 1994. "Arbeitgeberverbandsaustritte—Motive, Abläufe und Konsequenzen." *Industrielle Beziehungen* Jg. 1, Heft 2: 132–54.

Lansbury, Russell D. 1978. "The Return to Arbitration: Recent Trends in Dispute Resolution and Wage Policy in Australia." *International Labour Review* 117 (September–October): 611–24.

Lansbury, Russell D., and Greg J. Bamber. 1997. "Australia: Restructuring for Survival." In *After Lean Production: Evolving Employment Practices in the World Auto Industry*. Edited by T. Kochan, R. Lansbury, and J. P. MacDuffie, 205–30. Ithaca: Cornell University Press.

Lansbury, Russell D., and Duncan MacDonald, eds. 1992. *Workplace Industrial Relations: Australian Case Studies*. Oxford: Oxford University Press.

Lansbury, Russell D., and John Niland. 1995. "Managed Decentralization? Recent Trends in Australian Industrial Relations and Human Resource Policies." In *Employment Relations in a Changing World Economy*. Edited by R. Locke, T. Kochan, and M. Piore, 59–90. Cambridge: MIT Press.

Lawler, John J. 1990. *Unionization and Deunionization*. Columbia, S.C.: University of South Carolina Press.

Lee, Byoung-Hoon. 1996. "Workplace Transformation at Incrementalist Plants: A Cross-National Comparative Study of a Ford and a Hyundai Plant." Unpublished Ph.D. dissertation, Cornell University.

Leslie, Derek, and Yonghao Pu. 1996. "What Caused Rising Earnings Inequality in Britain?: Evidence from Time Series, 1970–1993." *British Journal of Industrial Relations* 34 (March): 111–36.

Lever-Tracy, Constance. 1990. "Fordism Transformed? Employee Involvement and Workplace Industrial Relations at Ford." *Journal of Industrial Relations* 32 (June): 179–94.

Levy, Frank. 1987. *Dollars and Dreams*. New York: Russell Sage Foundation.

Levy, Frank, and Richard J. Murname. 1992. "U.S. Earnings Levels and Earnings Inequality: A Review of Recent Trends and Proposed Explanations." *Journal of Economic Literature* 30 (September): 1333–81.

Lewin, David, and Richard Peterson. 1988. *The Modern Grievance Procedure in the American Economy*. New York: Quorom Books.

Lindena, Bodo, and Helmut Höhmann. 1989. "Allgemeimverbindlichkeit und Publizität von Tarifverträgen." *Der Arbeitgeber* (March): 3–23.

Locke, Richard M. 1992. "The Decline of the National Union in Italy: Lessons for Comparative Industrial Relations Theory." *Industrial and Labor Relations Review* 45 (January): 229–49.

——. 1995. *Remaking the Italian Economy*. Ithaca: Cornell University Press.

Locke, Richard M., and Lucio Bacarro. 1996. "Learning From Past Mistakes? Recent Reform in Italian Industrial Relations." *Industrial Relations Journal* 27 (December): 289–303.

Locke, Richard, Thomas Kochan, and Michael Piore, eds. 1995. *Employment Relations in a Changing World Economy*. Cambridge: MIT Press.

MacDuffie, John Paul. 1995a. "Human Resource Bundles and Manufacturing Performance: Organizational Logic and Flexible Production Systems in the World Auto Industry." *Industrial and Labor Relations Review* 48 (January): 197–221.

——. 1995b. "International Trends in Work Organization in the International Auto Industry: National-Level vs. Company-Level Perspectives." In *The Comparative Political Economy of Industrial Relations*. Edited by K. Wever and L. Turner, 71–114. Madison: IRRA.

——. 1997. "The Road to 'Root Cause': Shop-Floor Problem-Solving at Three Auto Assembly Plants." *Management Science* 43 (April): 479–502.

MacDuffie, John Paul, and Thomas A. Kochan. 1995. "Do U.S. Firms Invest Less in Human Resources?: Training in the World Auto Industry." *Industrial Relations* 2 (April): 147–68.

Machin, Stephen. 1996. "Wage Inequality in Britain." *Oxford Review of Economic Policy* 12 (Spring): 47–64.

Mair, Andrew. 1994. *Honda's Global Local Corporation.* London: St. Martin's Press.

——. 1999. "The Introduction of Teamwork at Rover Group's Stamping Plant." In *Teamwork in the Automobile Industry: Radical Change or Passing Fashion?* Edited by J-P. Durand, P. Stewart, and J. J. Castillo, 254–86. London: MacMillan.

Marginson, Paul, Peter Armstrong, Paul Edwards, and John Purcell. 1993. "The Control of Industrial Relations in Large Companies: An Initial Analysis of the Second Company Level Industrial Relations Survey." Warwick Papers in Industrial Relations No. 45. December.

Marginson, Paul, Paul Edwards, Roderick Martin, John Purcell, and Keith Sisson. 1988. *Beyond the Workplace.* Oxford: Basil Blackwell.

Markovits, Andrei S. 1986. *The Politics of the West German Trade Unions: Strategies of Class and Interest Representation in Growth and Crisis.* Cambridge: Cambridge University Press.

Marsden, David, Timothy Morris, Paul Willman, and Stephen Wood. 1985. *The Car Industry: Labour Relations and Industrial Adjustment.* London: Tavistock Publications.

Marsh, David. 1992. *The New Politics of British Trade Unionism: Union Power and the Thatcher Legacy.* Ithaca: ILR Press.

Martin, Andrew. 1995. "The Swedish Model: Demise or Reconfiguration." In *Employment Relations in a Changing World Economy.* Edited by R. Locke, T. Kochan, and M. Piore, 263–96. Cambridge: MIT Press.

Mathews, John. 1994. *Catching the Wave: Workplace Reform in Australia.* Ithaca: ILR Press.

Matsumura, Fumito. 1995. "Wage Structure Revisions by Japanese Automobile Manufacturers: The Introduction of Ability-based Pay." Working paper, Nagoya City University, presented at the World Congress of the International Industrial Relations Association, May 31–June 4, Washington, D.C.

McLoughlin, Ian, and Stephen Gourlay. 1992: "Enterprise without Unions: The Management of Employee Relations in Non-Union Firms." *Journal of Management Studies* 29 (September): 669–91.

Mealor, Tony. 1996. "From Confrontation to Collaboration at ICI Botany." In *Managing Together: Consultation and Participation in the Workplace.* Edited by E. Davis and R. Lansbury, 130–45.

——. 1997. *ICI Botany: A Decade of Change,* Centre for Corporate Change, Australian Graduate School of Management, University of New South Wales, Sydney, Australia.

Mercedes. 1995. *Rahmenbetriebsvereinbarung Gruppenarbeit in der Mercedes-Benz AG.* Unpublished manuscript, Bremen.

Metcalf, David. 1994. "Transformation of British Industrial Relations? Institutions, Conduct and Outcomes, 1980–1990." In *The UK Labour Market.* Edited by R. Barrell, 126–57. Cambridge: Cambridge University Press.

Milkman, Ruth. 1991. *Japan's California Factories: Labor Relations and Economic Globalization.* Los Angeles: UCLA Institute of Industrial Relations.

———. 1997. *Farewell to the Factory*. Berkeley: University of California Press.

Millward, Neil. 1994. *The New Industrial Relations*. London: Policy Studies Institute.

Millward, Neil, Mark Stevens, David Smart, and R. W. Hawes. 1992. *Workplace Industrial Relations in Transition*. Aldershot: Dartmouth.

Milner, Simon. 1995. "The Coverage of Collective Pay-Setting Institutions in Britain, 1895–1990." *British Journal of Industrial Relations* 33 (March): 69–91.

Ministero del lavoro. 1990. *Report '89: Labour and Employment Policies in Italy*. Rome: IPZS.

Mishina, Kazuhiro. 1995. "What Is the Essence of Toyota's Manufacturing Capability: Self-Management by the Transplant in Kentucky, 1986–1994." In *Communications: Hybridization of Industrial Models*. Edited by GERPISA. Paris: GERPISA.

Mitbestimmung Kommission. 1998. *Mitbestimmung und neue Unternehmenskulturen: Bilanz und Perspektiven Bericht der Kommission Mitbestimmung*. Gütersloh: Verlag Bertelsmann Stiftung.

Mitchell, Daniel J. B. 1980. *Unions, Wages, and Inflation*. Washington, D.C.: Brookings Institution.

Mitsubishi Motors Australia Ltd. 1995. "Mitsubishi Motors Australia Ltd. Enterprise Agreement." Unpublished paper. Victoria, July.

Morehead, A., M. Steele, M. Alexander, K. Stephen, and L. Duffin. 1997. *Changes at Work: The 1995 Australian Workplace Industrial Relations Survey*. Melbourne: Longman.

Mori, Kazuo. 1995. "Shunto, bonasu zyushi senmeini" (Spring offensive raises the importance of annual bonuses). *Nihon Keizai Shimbun*, March 24 (morning edition), 3.

Morishima, Motohiro. 1995. "Embedding HRM in a Social Context." *British Journal of Industrial Relations* 33 (December): 617–40.

Mueller, Frank. 1992a. "Flexible Working Practices in Engine Plants: Evidence from the European Automobile Industry." *Industrial Relations Journal* 23 (Autumn): 191–204.

———. 1992b. "Designing Flexible Teamwork: Comparing German and Japanese Approaches." *Employee Relations*, 14, no. 1: 5–16.

Müller-Jentsch, Walther. 1989. *Basisdaten der industriellen Beziehungen*. Frankfurt: Campus Verlag.

Müller-Jentsch, Walther, and Hans Joachim Sperling. 1995. "Towards a Flexible Triple System? Continuity and Structural Changes in German Industrial Relations." In *German Industrial Relations under the Impact of Structural Change, Unification, and European Unification*. Edited by R. Hoffman et al., 9–30. Düsseldorf: Hans-Böckler-Stiftung.

Murakami, Thomas. 1995a. "Introducing Team Working: A Motor Industry Case Study from Germany." *Industrial Relations Journal* 25: 293–305.

———. 1995b. "Teamwork and the Structure of Representation at Vauxhall Ltd. (UK) and Adam Opel AG (Germany)." Unpublished Ph.D. thesis, University of Warwick.

Nakamura, Keisuke, and Shirio Hiraki. 1997. "Japan." In *Telecommunications: Restructuring Work and Employment Relations Worldwide*, edited by H. Katz, 228–62. Ithaca: Cornell University Press.

Nakamura, Keisuke, and Michio Nitta. 1995. "Developments in Industrial Relations and Human Resource Practices in Japan." In *Employment Relations in a Changing World Economy.* Edited by R. Locke, T. Kochan, and M. Piore, 325–58. Cambridge: MIT Press.

National Center on the Educational Quality of the Workforce. 1994. *First Findings from the EQW National Employer Survey.* Philadelphia: University of Pennsylvania.

NCU (National Communication Workers' Union). 1992. "New Dialogue." Unpublished manuscript. NCU, London.

Negrelli, Serafino. 1997. "Italy." In *Telecommunications: Restructuring Work and Employment Relations Worldwide.* Edited by H. Katz, 295–324. Ithaca: ILR Press.

Newsletter Information Services. 1994. "Toyota." In *Lessons From the First Enterprise Agreements.* Milsons Point, New South Wales: Print n Run: 71–74.

———. 1995a. *Enterprise Flexibility Agreements.* Manly, New South Wales: Print n Run: 3–4, 33–34.

———. 1995b. "Accord Mark VIII at a Glance." In *Workforce Special Report: Accord Mark VIII.* New South Wales: Print n Run, June 30: 2–6.

Nitta, Michio. 1991. "Business Diversification and Human Resource Management Strategy in the Japanese Chemical Textile Industry." Occasional Papers No. 10, University of Tokyo, Institute of Social Science, March.

Ogden, Stuart. 1994. "The Reconstruction of Industrial Relations in the Privatized Water Industry." *British Journal of Industrial Relations* 32 (March): 67–84.

Opel. 1993. "Standortsicherung." Betriebsvereinbarung Nr. 210. Rüsselsheim: Opel and Gesamtbetriebsrat.

———. 1994. "Verbesserung der Wettbewerbsfähigkeit des Werkes 1." Betriebsvereingbarung Nr. 13. Bochum: Opel and Betriebsrat.

Osterman, Paul. 1988. *Employment Futures.* New York: Oxford University Press.

———. 1994. "How Common is Workplace Transformation and Who Adopts It?" *Industrial Relations Review* 47 (January): 173–88.

Parker, Mike, and Jane Slaughter. 1988. *Choosing Sides: Unions and the Team Concept.* Boston: South End Press.

*Pay and Benefits Bulletin.* 1995. "Spectacular Grown in PRP Continues." 373 (April).

———. 1997. "Gainsharing at Owens Corning Building Products." 418 (February): 2–6.

Peetz, David, Alison Preston, and Jim Docherty, eds. 1992. *Workplace Bargaining in the International Context.* Canberra: Paragon Printers.

Pil, Frits K., and John Paul MacDuffie. 1996. "The Adoption of High-Involvement Work Practices." *Industrial Relations* 35 (July): 432–55.

———. 1998. "Transferring Competitive Advantage Across Borders: A Study of Japanese Transplants in North America." In *Remade in America: Transplanting and Transforming Japanese Production Systems.* Edited by J. Liker, M. Fruin, and P. Adler. New York: Oxford University Press.

Pontusson, Jonas. 1997. "Between Neoliberalism and the German Model: Swedish Capitalism in Transition." In *Political Economy of Modern Capitalism.* Edited by C. Crouch and W. Streeck, 55–70. London: Sage.

————. Forthcoming. "Labor Market Institutions and Wage Distribution." In *Unions, Employers and Central Banks.* Edited by T. Iversen, J. Pontusson, and D. Soskice. New York: Cambridge University Press.

Pontusson, Jonas, and Peter Swenson. 1996. "Labor Markets, Production Strategies and Wage-Bargaining Institutions." *Comparative Political Studies* 29 (April): 223–50.

Poole, Michael, and Roger Mansfield. 1993. "Patterns of Continuity and Change in Managerial Attitudes and Behaviour in Industrial Relations, 1980–1990." *British Journal of Industrial Relations* 31 (March): 11–35.

Pragnell, Brad, and Shannon O'Keefe. 1994. "The Optus Enterprise Flexibility Agreement (EFA) 1994." Unpublished paper, ACCIRT, University of Sydney, New South Wales.

Pristin, Terry. 1998. "Bell Atlantic Workers End Strike; Pact Gives Union Job Assurances." *New York Times,* August 12, pp. 1, B4.

Purcell, John. 1991. "The Rediscovery of the Management Prerogative: The Management of Labour Relations in the 1980s." *Oxford Review of Economic Policy* 7 (Spring): 33–43.

————. 1995. "Ideology and the End of Institutional Industrial Relations: Evidence from the UK." In *Organized Industrial Relations in Europe: What Future?* Edited by C. Crouch and F. Traxler, 101–19. Hants, England: Avebury.

Purcell, John, and Bruce Ahlstrand. 1994. *Human Resource Management in the Multi-Divisional Company.* Oxford: Oxford University Press.

Purcell, John, and Keith Sisson. 1983. "Strategies and Practice in the Management of Industrial Relations." In *Industrial Relations in Britain.* Edited by G. Bain, 95–120. Oxford: Basil Blackwell.

Regalia, Ida, and Marino Regini. 1995. "Between Voluntarism and Institutionalization: Industrial Relations and Human Resource Practices in Italy." In *Employment Relations in a Changing World Economy.* Edited by R. Locke, T. Kochan, and M. Piore, 131–64. Cambridge: MIT Press.

Rimmer, Malcolm, and Chrissie Verevis, eds. 1990. *Progress of Award Restructuring: Case Studies.* Monograph 28. Kensington, New South Wales: Industrial Relations Research Centre.

Rose, Robert L. 1995. "UAW to Allow Vote on Caterpillar Offer, Signaling Long Strike May Be Near End." *Wall Street Journal,* November 20.

Rose, Robert L., and Oscar Suris. 1996. "Dana Defeats UAW Drive to Organize." *Wall Street Journal,* September 26, p. A-3.

Ross, Peter K., and Greg J. Bamber. 1998. "Changing Employment Relations in Former Public Monopolies: Comparisons, Contrasts, and Strategic Choices at New Zealand Telecom and Telstra." Unpublished manuscript, Graduate School of Management, Griffith University, Australia.

Roßmann, Witich. 1994. "The Transformation of Industrial Relations in the German Computer Industry: The IG Metall Battles at DEC and IBM." Paper presented to the conference "The Political Economy of the New Germany," School of Industrial and Labor Relations, Cornell University, October 14–15.

Roth, Siegfried. 1995. "Wiederentdeckung der eigenen Stärken? Innovative Producktionskonzepte statt Standortklagen." Unpublished manuscript, November. IG Metall, Frankfurt.

———. 1996a. "Produktionskonzepte in Japan und Deutschland: eine gewerkschaftliche Vergleichsstudie in der Automobilindustrie." In *Vorbild Japan? Stärken und schwächen der Industriestandorte Deutschland und Japan.* Edited by K. Zwickel, 102–74. Frankfurt am Main: Otto Brenner Stiftung.

———. 1996b. "Automobilhersteller und ihre Zulieferer in Deutschland und Japan." In *Vorbild Japan? Stärken und schwächen der Industriestandorte Deutschland und Japan.* Edited by K. Zwickel, 175–205. Frankfurt am Main: Otto Brenner Stiftung.

Rubinstein, Saul, Michael Bennett, and Thomas Kochan. 1993. "The Saturn Partnership: Co-Management and the Reinvention of the Local Union." In *Employee Representation: Alternatives and Future Directions.* Edited by B. Kaufman and M. Kleiner, 339–70. Madison: IRRA.

Sako, Mari. 1997. "Emergent Dualism in the UK Automotive Industry: Should We be Concerned?" Small Business Monograph Series, No. 8, December, Osaka University of Economics.

Scarborough, Harry, and Michael Terry. 1996. "Industrial Relations and the Reorganisation of Production in the UK Motor Industry: A Study of the Rover Group." Warwick Papers in Industrial Relations No. 58. Coventry: IRRU, Warwick Business School.

Schäfer, Claus. 1997. "Verteilungspolitik: Chronik eines angekündigten politischen Selbsmords." *WSI Mitteilungen* 50 (October): 669–89.

Schmidt, John. 1995. "The Changing Structure of Male Earnings in Britain, 1974–1988." In *Differences and Changes in Wage Structures.* Edited by R. Freeman and L. Katz, 177–204. Chicago: University of Chicago Press.

Schnabel, Claus. 1995. "Collective Bargaining in Germany: Recent Trends, Problems and Reform Proposals." In *German Industrial Relations Under the Impact of Structural Change, Unification, and European Unification.* Edited by R. Hoffmann et al., 30–37. Düsseldorf: Hans-Böckler-Stiftung.

Schulten, Thomas. 1998. "Debis AG Agreement a First in Industry-Related Services." *Eironline* (European Foundation on-line service). March.

Schulten, Thorsten. 1999. "Unions Seek Right to Bring Cases against Employers Contravening Agreements." *Eironline* (European Foundation on-line service). January.

Shadur, Mark. 1997. "Employment Relations in the Australian Information Technology Industry." In *Changing Employment Relations in Australia.* Edited by J. Kitay and R. Lansbury, 131–57. Melbourne: Oxford University Press.

Sheldon, Peter, and Louise Thornthwaite. 1993. "Ex Parte Accord: The Business Council of Australia and Industrial Relations Change." *International Journal of Business Studies* 1 (October): 37–55.

Shibata, Hiromichi. 1995. "Japanese and American Workplace Industrial Relations: Skill Formation, Communication, and Conflict Resolution." Unpublished Ph.D. dissertation, Cornell University.

Shire, Karen. 1995. "Bargaining and the Social Reorganization of Production: The Case of General Motors in Austria and Germany." In *Workplace Industrial Relations and the Global Challenge*. Edited by J. Bélanger, P. K. Edwards, and L. Haiven, 137–56. Ithaca: ILR Press.

Silvia, Stephen J. 1993. "'Holding the Shop Together': Old and New Challenges to the German System of Industrial Relations in the mid-1990s." Berliner Arbeitschefe und Berichte zur Sozialwissenschaftlichen Forschung, Freie Universität Berlin, Zentralinstitut für sozialwissenschaftliche Forschung, No. 83, July.

——. 1997. "Political Adaptation to Growing Labor Market Segmentation." In *Negotiating the New Germany: Can Social Partnership Survive?* Edited by L. Turner, 157–76. Ithaca: ILR Press.

Simmons, David E., and Russell D. Lansbury. 1996. "Worker Involvement at Ford Motor Company Australia." In *Managing Together: Consultation and Participation in the Workplace*. Edited by E. Davis and R. Lansbury, 80–100. Melbourne: Addison Wesley Longman.

Sisson, Keith. 1993. "In Search of HRM." *British Journal of Industrial Relations* 31 (March): 201–10.

Sisson, Keith, and William Brown. 1983. "Industrial Relations in the Private Sector: Donovan Revisited." In *Industrial Relations in Britain*. Edited by G. Bain, 137–54. Oxford: Basil Blackwell.

Sisson, Keith, J. Waddington, and C. Whitston. 1992. *The Structure of Capital in the European Community*. Warwick Papers in Industrial Relations, No. 38. February.

Smith, Paul, and Gary Morton. 1993. "Union Exclusion and the Decollectivisation of Industrial Relations in Contemporary Britain." *British Journal of Industrial Relations* 31 (March): 97–114.

Sorge, Arndt, and Wolfgang Streeck. 1988. "Industrial Relations and Technical Change: The Case for an Extended Perspective." In *New Technology and Industrial Relations*. Edited by R. Hyman and W. Streeck, 19–47. Oxford: Basil Blackwell.

Spalter-Roth, Roberta, and Young-Hee Yoon. 1995. "Women and Minorities in Telecommunications: An Exception to the Rule: The Mid-Atlantic Region." Institute for Women's Policy Research, unpublished mimeo, Washington, D.C., September.

Starkey, Ken, and Alan McKinlay. 1989. "Beyond Fordism? Strategic Choice and Labour Relations in Ford UK." *Industrial Relations Journal* 20: 93–100.

Stewart, Paul. 1995. "From 'Welt Work' to Team Work: Tradition and Evolution in the Pursuit of 'Lean Mass Production' at Vauxhall-General Motors UK?" Paper presented to GERPISA conference, "Group Work in the Car Industry: An International Comparison," Paris, June 15–17.

Storey, John. 1992. *Developments in the Management of Human Resources*. Oxford: Basil Blackwell.

Streeck, Wolfgang. 1984. *Industrial Relations in West Germany: A Case Study of the Car Industry*. London: Heinemann.

——. 1996. "Lean Production in the German Automobile Industry: A Test Case for Convergence Theory." In *National Diversity and Global Capitalism*. Edited by S. Berger and R. Dore, 138–70. Ithaca: Cornell University Press.

——. 1997. "German Capitalism: Does It Exists? Can It Survive?" In *Political Economy of Modern Capitalism: Mapping Convergence and Diversity.* Edited by C. Crouch and W. Streeck, 33–54. London: Sage.

Streeck, Wolfgang, and Harry C. Katz. 1984. "Labor Relations and Employment Adjustments." In *The Future of the Automobile.* Edited by A. Altshuler et al., 199–222. Cambridge: MIT Press.

Swenson, Peter. 1989. *Fair Shares: Unions, Pay and Politics in Sweden and West Germany.* Ithaca: Cornell University Press.

Telstra. 1995. "Managing Telstra's New Ear." *Our Future* 128 (July 21): 1–2.

Terry, Michael. 1983. "Shop Steward Development and Managerial Strategies." In *Industrial Relations in Britain.* Edited by G. Bain, 67–91. Oxford: Basil Blackwell.

——. 1995. "Trade Unions: Shop Stewards and the Workplace." In *Industrial Relations: Theory and Practice in Britain.* Edited by P. Edwards, 203–28. Oxford: Basil Blackwell.

Thelen, Kathleen. 1991. *Union of Parts: Labor Politics in Postwar Germany.* Ithaca: Cornell University Press.

Toyota. 1991. "Toyota-AEU Agreement." Unpublished manuscript, October. Toyota, Derby.

Trevor, Malcolm. 1988. *Toshiba's New British Company: Competitiveness through Innovation in Industry.* London: Policy Studies Institute.

Troy, Leo. 1990. "Is the U.S. Unique in the Decline of Private Sector Unionism." *Journal of Labor Research* 11 (Spring): 111–43.

Tsuru, Tsuyoshi. 1992. "Shunto: The Spillover Effect and the Wage-Setting Institution in Japan." International Institute for Labour Studies, discussion paper no. 51, Geneva.

Tsuru, Tsuyoshi, and James B. Rebitzer. 1995. "The Limits of Enterprise Unionism: Prospects for Continuing Union Decline in Japan." *British Journal of Industrial Relations* 33 (September): 459–92.

Turner, Lowell. 1991. *Democracy at Work: Changing World Markets and the Future of Labor Unions.* Ithaca: Cornell University Press.

——. 1997. "Unifying Germany: Crisis, Conflict, and Social Partnership in the East." In *Negotiating the New Germany: Can Social Partnership Survive?* Edited by L. Turner, 113–36. Ithaca: ILR Press.

——. 1998. *Fighting for Partnership: Labor and Politics in Unified Germany.* Ithaca: Cornell University Press.

U.S. Department of Labor. Various years. *Employment and Earnings.* Washington, D.C.: Bureau of Labor Statistics.

Verma, Anil, and Thomas A. Kochan. 1985. "The Growth of the Nonunion Sector within a Firm." In *Challenges and Choices Facing American Labor.* Edited by T. A. Kochan, 89–118. Cambridge: MIT Press.

Walsh, Janet. 1993. "Internalization v. Decentralization: An Analysis of Recent Developments in Pay Bargaining." *British Journal of Industrial Relations* 31 (September): 409–32.

Walton, Richard E., Joel E. Cutcher-Gershenfeld, and Robert B. McKersie. 1994. *Strategic Negotiations.* Boston: Harvard Business School Press.

Watts, Martin J., and William J. Mitchell. 1990. "The Impact of Incomes Policy on the Male Inter-Industry Wage Structure." *Journal of Industrial Relations* 32 (September): 353–69.

Womack, James P., Daniel T. Jones, and Daniel Roos. 1990. *The Machine That Changed The World.* New York: Rawson Associates.

Wright, M. 1993. *Maintaining the 'Status Quo'? An Analysis of British Collective Agreements, 1979–1990.* Working Paper 410, Centre for Economic Policy, London School of Economics.

WSI. 1995. "Baugewerbe mit höchster Zuwachsrate (WSI-Analyse zu Tarifsteigerungen, 1990–1994)." Hans Böckler Stiftung Presse Dienst, May.

Yamagishi, Akira. 1994. Preface to *The Struggle for a Better Living.* Rengo White Paper. Tokyo: JTUC-Rengo.

Zagelmeyer, Stefan. 1997a. "Employment with Temporary Work Agencies in Germany." *Eironline* (European Foundation on-line service). November.

———. 1997b. "The Erosion of Employers' Associations and Industry-Level Bargaining in Eastern Germany." *Eironline* (European Foundation on-line service). August.

———. 1998a. "Company-Level Bargaining Gains Importance." *Eironline* (European Foundation on-line service). March.

———. 1998b. "Membership of DGB-affiliated Unions Falls Again." *Eironline* (European Foundation on-line service). March.

———. 1999. "Private Sector Collective Bargaining Coverage Analysed." *Euronline* (European Foundation on-line service). February.

Zendentsu. 1995. "Memorandum on Employment Policy." In *Zendentsu Described.* Tokyo: Japanese Telecommunications Workers' Union.

Zwickel, Klaus, ed. 1996. *Vorbild Japan? Stärken und schwächen der Industriestandorte Deutschland und Japan.* Frankfurt am Main: Otto Brenner Stiftung and Hans-Böckler-Stiftung.

# About the Authors

**H**arry C. Katz is the Jack Sheinkman Professor of Collective Bargaining and Director of the Institute of Collective Bargaining, NYSSILR, Cornell University. He received the A.B. (1973) and Ph.D. (1977) degrees in economics from the University of California at Berkeley. His previous publications include *The Transformation of American Industrial Relations* (with Thomas Kochan and Robert McKersie), *Shifting Gears: Changing Labor Relations in the U.S. Auto Industry,* and *Telecommunications: Restructuring Work and Employment Relations Worldwide.*

**O**wen Darbishire is the University Lecturer and Fellow, Pembroke College, Oxford University. He received a B.A. (honors) from Balliol College, Oxford University, in 1987 and an M.S. degree from the New York State School of Industrial and Labor Relations, Cornell University in 1993. He is the author of various scholarly articles and books.

# Index

TRW, 46
Tsuru, Tsuyoshi, 231
Turner, Lowell, 169, 187, 188, 189, 192,
    196, 197–98, 206, 207
Two-tier employment structures, 83, 99,
    195

UAW. *See* United Automobile, Aerospace,
    and Agricultural Implement Workers
UBA Development Agreement, 244
Ulman, Lloyd, 243
Underhill, Elsa, 145
Unemployment, 7–8; Germany, 185, 190,
    192; United Kingdom, 73–74, 89–90,
    113–14
Unions: decline, 1, 4, 6, 275; mergers,
    75–76, 140, 225n1, 277–78; power, 6–7,
    9; pressures on, 73–75, 122–23, 180–83,
    196, 224, 281–82; structures, 2, 3,
    14–15, 139–41, 211–14, 241–44, 277;
    union-avoidance techniques, 19, 22, 24,
    58, 82–84, 86–87, 97–98, 129–31, 138;
    variation in work practices, 47–49,
    275–78. *See also* Collective bargaining;
    *individual countries*
Unipart, 95
United Automobile, Aerospace, and Agri-
    cultural Implement Workers (UAW), 11,
    26, 31; automobile parts suppliers and,
    44–46; decentralization and, 47; inter-
    national servicing representatives,
    48–49, 68n39; local unions and, 48–49,
    67n37; national offices, 48; strikes and,
    50–51; wages and, 35–37
United Kingdom, 2, 272; collective bar-
    gaining, 75–82, 96–100; common law,
    71, 74; concession bargaining, 79–82;
    decentralization, 70, 100, 114–16; em-
    ployee involvement, 84–86, 104–5; em-
    ployer resources, 130–31; engineering
    nationwide agreements, 78, 92; govern-
    ment policies, 71–72; human resource
    management, 83, 84–86, 131, 132; in-
    come inequality, 82, 99, 128–29; indus-
    trial relations developments, 71–73; joint
    team-based approach, 86–88, 101–4,
    105, 121–24; low-wage pattern, 83–84,
    121; new work practices, 84–86; single-
    union agreements, 96–97, 110, 131; two-

tier employment structure, 83, 99, 151;
    unemployment, 73–74, 89–90, 113–14;
    variation in work practices, 74–75,
    114–15; wages councils, 76, 77; work or-
    ganization, 70–71. *See also* Shop stewards;
    United Kingdom, automobile industry;
    United Kingdom, telecommunications
    industry; United Kingdom, unions
United Kingdom, automobile industry,
    88–91; auto assemblers, 96–100; auto
    parts suppliers, 94–95, 99–100; con-
    strained partnership, 107–10; decentral-
    ization of employment relations, 91–93;
    employment by plant size, 84, 93–95,
    133–34n13; independent company bar-
    gaining, 91–92; Japanese automobile
    transplants, 89, 94, 95, 96–99, 110–12;
    joint team-based approach, 101–4; piece-
    meal approach, 104–7; production de-
    cline, 88–91; team working and,
    100–101; union decline, 93–96; vertical
    disintegration and, 93–96, 99; wages,
    98–100. *See also* Ford; Rover; Vauxhall
United Kingdom, telecommunications in-
    dustry, 112–13; nonunion sector,
    126–27; telecommunications instruc-
    tions, 114, 118, 135n29. *See also* British
    Telecom
United Kingdom, unions: British Telecom
    and, 122–24; concession bargaining and
    contingent pay, 79–82; decentralized
    bargaining, 78–79; derecognition,
    82–84, 95, 130, 275; managerial prerog-
    ative and, 104–7; mergers, 75–76; pres-
    sure on, 73–75, 122–23; private vs. pub-
    lic sector, 75–76, 78, 133n6;
    union-avoidance techniques, 82–84,
    86–87, 97–98, 129–31; union decline,
    75–79, 93–96, 133n5; Vauxhall and,
    107–10
United Kingdom, wages, 79–82, 108;
    across auto assemblers, 96–100; piece-
    rate pay system, 72, 92, 93
United States, 2, 272; bureaucratic pattern,
    22–23; decentralization, 27–30, 40,
    49–52, 65; employment growth, 7–8;
    general trends in employment relations,
    18–21, 64–65; human resource manage-
    ment, 10–11, 23–24;